Learning in Classrooms

Learning in Classrooms: A Cultural-Historical Approach

Edited by Mariane Hedegaard

ACTA JUTLANDICA LXXV:1

SOCIAL SCIENCE SERIES 23

AARHUS UNIVERSITY PRESS

ISBN 87 7288 841 5
ISSN 0065 1354 (ACTA JUTLANDICA)
ISSN 0106 0937 (SOCIAL SCIENCES)

AARHUS UNIVERSITY PRESS
Langelandsgade 177
DK-8200 Aarhus N
Fax (+ 45) 8942 5380

73 Lime Walk
Headington, Oxford OX3 7AD
United Kingdom
Fax (+ 44) 1865 750 079

Box 511
Oakville, CT 06779
USA
Fax (+ 1) 860 945 9468

www.unipress.dk

Foreword

Education is one of the central points of cultural-historical psychology. Culture and education are interconnected; there is no culture if it is not transmitted and the socialisation of persons will not occur without the appropriation of culture.

The central position of education within the cultural historical tradition was also reflected in the number and diversity of papers presented at the Fourth Congress of the International Society for Activity Theory and Cultural Research (ISCRAT) held in Aarhus, Denmark in June 1998. The chapters in this book with themes related to education and learning in school are revised and extended presentations from this congress. Diversity in the chapters is exemplified not only by the variety of topics connected to school learning, but also by the different countries in the world represented by the research. However, even though education is seen as situated practice within a cultural tradition, the chapters share the conception that social interaction in class activities both between teacher and children and between classmates takes place around material that is personally significant for the participants. Through participation in practice, the knowledge and methods that are developed through the history of school and subject-matter tradition are turned into personal ways of acting and interacting whereby students acquire competence with tools and artefacts that are central in the subject-matter tradition and relevant for the broader community in which the child lives.

This publication is the fourth in a series of books from the ISCRAT congresses. I wish to thank several people at Aarhus University Press for their cooperative support: its former director Tønnes Bekker-Nielsen and present director Claes Hvidbak; a special thanks to Ole Høiris, chairman of the Board, who from the start supported and encouraged the publishing of the ISCRAT series of books; I also want to thank the editors Mary Waters Lund and Pernille Pennington for their help and patience in producing the book.

Mariane Hedegaard
Aarhus, June 2001
President, Fourth ISCRAT Congress

Contents

School Traditions and Learning

Educational Practice that Combines Community Knowledge and Social Science Studies

Classroom Interaction and Discourse

List of Figures and Tables

Contributors

Seth Chaiklin, Institute of Psychology, University of Aarhus, Denmark, seth@psy.au.dk

Angela Creese, Institute of Education, University of London, United Kingdom, AC114@leicester.ac.uk

Ademir Damazio, Faculty of Education, Federal University of Santa Catarina, Brazil, add@unesc.rcf-sc.br

Harry Daniels, School of Education, University of Birmingham, United Kingdom, H.R.J.Daniels@bham.ac.uk

Shaun Fielding, School of Education, University of Birmingham, United Kingdom, Shaun_Fielding@ecotec.co.uk

Maria Teresa de A. Freitas, Faculty of Education, Federal University of Juiz de Fora, Brazil, mtl@artnet.com.br

Paulo R. de Oliveira Frota, Doctoral programme of UFSC, Federal University of Piaui, Brazil, prfrota@ced.ufsc.br

Hartmut Giest, Faculty of Education, University of Potsdam, Germany, giest@rz.uni-potsdam.de

Airi Hautamäki, Swedish School of Social Science, University of Helsinki, Finland, airi.hautamaki@helsinki.fi

Jarkko Hautamäki, Department of Teacher Education, University of Helsinki, Finland, jarkko.hautamaki@helsinki.fi

Mariane Hedegaard, Institute of Psychology, University of Aarhus, Denmark, marianeh@psy.au.dk

Valerie Hey, School of Education, Brunel University, United Kingdom, Valerie.Hey@Brunel.ac.uk

Solange Jobim e Souza, Psychology Department, Catholic Pontifical University of Rio de Janeiro, Brazil, soljobim@ax.apc.org

Olga Kritskaya, Higher, Adult, & Lifelong Education, Michigan State University, USA, kritskay@msu.edu

Peter Kutnick, Education Research Centre, University of Brighton, United Kingdom, p.kutnick@bton.ac.uk

Diana Leonard, Institute of Education, University of London, United Kingdom, D.Leonard@ioe.ac.uk

Carol Linehan, Centre for Applied Psychology, University of Leicester, United Kingdom, cl49@leicester.ac.uk

Maria Cecília Camargo Magalhães, Post-Graduation Program in Applied Linguistics and Language, Catholic Pontifical University of São Paulo, Brazil, cmaga@exatas.pucsp.br

Manuel L. de la Mata, Faculty of Psychology, Laboratory of Human Activity, University of Sevilla, Spain, mluis@cica.es

Kayo Matsushita, Faculty of Education, Gunma University, Japan, kayo-m@edu.gunma-u.ac.jp

John McCarthy, Department of Applied Psychology, University College Cork, Ireland, John.McCarthy@ucc.ie

Pedro Pedraza, Center for Puerto Rican Studies, Hunter College City University of New York, USA, ppedraza@shiva.hunter.cuny.edu

Jrene Rahm, Department of Educational Psychology, University of Northern Colorado, USA, jrahm@bentley.unco.edu

Andrés Santamaría, Faculty of Psychology, Laboratory of Human Activity, University of Sevilla, Spain, santamar@psicoexp.us.es

Marjorie Smith, Institute of Education, University of London, United Kingdom, Marjorie.Smith@newham.gov.uk

Katsuhiro Yamazumi, Department of Social Studies Education, Osaka University of Education, Japan, yamazumi@cc.osaka-kyoiku.ac.jp

Galina Zuckerman, Russian Academy of Education, Russia, emil@agrobio.msk.su

1 Learning through Acting within Societal Traditions: Learning in Classrooms

Mariane Hedegaard

Within the cultural-historical tradition, following Vygotsky, learning is conceptualised as a foundational concept for understanding human life as cultural and societal. Vygotsky conceptualises tool mediation as a core aspect of being human. The capacity to handle tools has to be transferred from one generation to the next. From this perspective learning can be seen as a change in the relation between person and world, through the subject's appropriation of tool use and artefactual knowledge. A child learns to mediate between his needs and the world through the appropriation of the capability to handle tools. Children learn from their interaction with parents and other central persons, and this interaction takes place within social settings. For children, home, school, peer-group and work are the primary settings for learning. These settings are characterised by different traditions for tool use and social interactions, therefore tradition and institutionalisation of tradition have to be taken into consideration when learning is discussed.

The chapters in this book contribute to the discussion of learning primarily within school, an educational institution that has been created historically. Ideally, this institution is an integral part of most peoples' lives from the time of entering as a small non-productive child, until becoming a young adult and productive member of society.

But before we turn to learning in school, some fundamental aspects of learning from a cultural-historical perspective will be brought into the discussion. The first aspect that will be discussed is how learning changes the relations between persons and their environment.

This discussion will be followed by an argument for an extension of the instrumental method of humans' acts, outlined by Vygotsky, to include participation in practice as a key aspect of learning. In the third section, I will discuss the context for learning and argue for a view that relates learning both to situated practice in institutions and to traditions anchored in different cultural fields. In the fourth section I discuss how practice, knowledge traditions and the developmental characteristics of persons contribute to a differentiation between learning in various types of institutions, thereby setting school learning apart from learning in other institutions. The discussion in these first sections leads to the specific focus of the other chapters in this book which cover this special kind of learning found in the context of school practice.

Learning as Change in the Relation Between Person and the World

Vygotsky focused on the changes in human activity, from being a natural process to its development as a cultural activity with the introduction of tools. This process starts from the moment a child is born and is characterised as the instrumental method of acting:

The inclusion of a tool in the behavioural process, first, sets to work a number of new functions connected with the use and control of the given tool; second, abolishes and makes unnecessary a number of natural processes, whose work is [now] done by the tool; third, modifies the course and the various aspects (intensity, duration, order etc.) of all mental processes included in the instrumental act, replacing some functions with others, i.e., recreates, reconstructs the whole structure of behaviour just like a technical tool recreates the entire system of labour operations. Mental processes taken as a whole form a complex structural and functional unity. They are directed toward the solution of a problem posed by the object, and the tool dictates their coordination and course. They form a new whole — the instrumental act. (1997, 87)

These relations can be visualised as shown in Figure 1.1.

In Vygotsky's theory, learning is a social process that takes place between people. He conceptualised learning as internalisation of social interactions in which communication is central. Learning takes place in social interaction in a specific context which becomes internalised by a person. By internalisation, Vygotsky did not mean copying but transforming the external interaction to a new form of interaction that guides the child's actions. Internalisation does not directly mirror the external social relations; it is a transformed

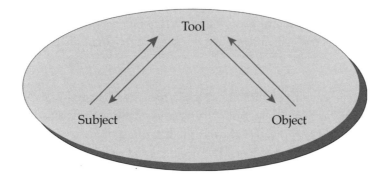

Figure 1.1. The instrumental act: The influence of tool mediation upon the subject himself.

reflection. On the intersubjective plane, it can be understood as an interaction that the person has made into his own; it still is a kind of interaction but now the child takes all the positions in the interaction, i.e., the regulating as well as the action role.

In his experimental work, Luria (1961) has described how this interaction was acquired by the child and how it gradually acquired function as the child's own regulation of his activity. Luria described a series of simple experiments with 3-5 year-old children who learned to react to different colours on two identical figures. The experiments show how adult instruction becomes appropriated by the child, how the child becomes able to inhibit his spontaneous reaction and how he becomes able to control it by using the adult's instructions. In one of the experiments, the children were told that the figures were aeroplanes, and instead of reacting to the colour of the plane the children's attention were brought to the background by the explanation that the plane could only fly when the sky was sunny (yellow), not cloudy (grey). By means of this explanation, half of the three-year-old children and all of the five-year-old children in the experiment learned to control and inhibit their previously learned reaction to different colours of the aeroplane, something they would not have been able to do on their own (Luria 1961).

This experiment demonstrates that learning procedures with artefact (to act with and interpret artefact) are intersubjectively available to begin with, later they become personally appropriated.

Vygotsky also described how the instrumental act with psychological (conceptual) tools turned around and influenced the acting person:

The psychological tool changes nothing in the object. It is a means of influencing one's own mind or behaviour or another's. It is not a means of influencing the object. Therefore, in the instrumental act we see activity towards oneself, and not toward the object. (1997, 87)

The appropriation of psychological tools has mostly been associated with Vygotsky's theoretical work, but if human learning is only discussed as the appropriation of conceptual tools and the handling of the material aspects of tools is neglected, learning loses the dialectic between acting and thinking. It is important to stress both the mental and material aspects of tools as united in the mediation between person and world. A clear distinction between material, technical tools and psychological, conceptual tools is not possible since artefact and tools have a conceptual/symbolic as well as an action aspect. The conceptual/symbolic and material aspects of human learning form a unity within cultural practices whereby humans can both contribute and be influenced. The process of how humans' interact and regulate the object/world as well as their own psychological processes cannot be separated in the understanding of human learning.

Wartofsky points to a third dimension of artefact,[1] the motivational/emotional aspects. He describes artefact as 'objectification of human needs and intentions already invested with cognitive and affective content' (Wartofsky 1979, 204). Wartofsky's explication of artefact as the objectification of human needs and intentions is very important for understanding learning not only as a cognitive phenomenon changing persons' minds and capacities, but also changing the world for the person, cognitively as well as affectively.

The appropriation of learning procedures with artefact results in change in a person's relation to his material and social world. The question dealt with in this book is then: How do we grasp the complexity of appropriation of procedures with tools/artefact that includes the characteristic of situated practice, societal traditions and personal intentions?

Learning as Change in Participation in Practice

Vygotsky's method of instrumental act implies a critique of the behavioural learning tradition of stimulus response and reinforcement. Cognitive theories, but especially social practice theories, have also opposed the

---

1. Wartofsky's concept of artefact can be viewed as a synonym for Vygotsky's tool concept.

behavioural learning traditions which have dominated learning theory and contributed to seeing learning as intentional actions taking place in social interactions and cultural settings.

Piaget's theory focused on action, and he pointed to *imitation and play* (1967) as the type of action that will lead to children's knowledge appropriation. In their theory of scaffolding, Wood, Bruner and Ross (1976) also pointed to action as central for learning but they located action within a social relation of scaffolding so that both the acting (doing) and the social aspect *interaction* are conceptualised as promoting learning. Action and interaction as aspects of learning are important but it is a problem in these two cognitive theories that they primarily focus on the method of learning and acquiring cognition and neglect the content as well as the context of learning in conceptualisation.

Berger and Luckman's social theory and Lave and Wenger's situated learning theory have widened the spectre of learning method and content. These theories view learning as a change in a person's relation to his material and social world through acquiring competence with tools/artefact in situated practice.

In the social theory of Berger and Luckmann (1966), children's learning is conceptualised as socialisation into society by *modelling the actions of emotionally important persons*. The content of socialisation is the child's knowledge of the world and of his/her position in the world — his/her social identity.

In Lave and Wenger's theory of situated learning (1991), social practice as well as production are central. The learning method is conceptualised as participation in practice. By using the concept of peripheral legitimate participation, Lave and Wenger point to change in status as a result of learning, a change from being peripheral to being integrated into the social process of becoming a fully accepted competent participant in a community practice.

In Berger and Luckman's as well as Lave and Wenger's approaches, the situated practice and institutional traditions become concrete aspects of learning, but a focus on how institutional practice is related to both variation in subjects and variation in traditions is still missing and how this variation influences learning, so that learning theory can start to differentiate learning according to the context and the persons participating in the community practice.

Social relations and artefacts/tools are necessary but not sufficient to conceptualise, but learning the concept of context is also necessary. How should we understand the concept of context? Does this mean situated concrete practice as implied by Lave and Wenger's concept of situated learning?

One of Lave's points (Lave 1997) is that learning is never context free, in the meaning that it is always part of a daily practice in a community setting. Learning in school, which mostly is formulated as context-free learning, she argues, also has to be characterised as learning in the special context that school tradition creates.

The questions for further analyses are then: (1) How do we conceptualise variation in context? and (2) What is specific about school as context?

Learning Contexts

Learning takes place in a context and the skill and knowledge of a person is always in interaction with the specific context in which it is realised. If we turn again to Vygotsky, one has to see that the concepts of instrumental and psychological acts both imply activity as a historical process and a concrete practice. The historical aspect of activity is found in the concept of tool/artefact and their procedures. Artefacts are the result of other humans' activity and the history of an artefact is embedded in its traditions for use. Furthermore, the process whereby an artefact/tool comes to play a role in a person's life requires that other persons demonstrate, identify and pass on the procedures for using artefacts/tools and the context in which they are suitable.

Following this argument, context can be conceptualised as practice traditions and one can differentiate between these traditions. Vygotsky's concept of the 'instrumental act' can then be viewed within the practice of an institution and be elaborated to encompass practice in several institutions as shown in Figure 1.2.

Traditions with artefact, not the artefact in itself, are important in conceptualising a theory of learning. Traditions with artefact can both be the activity, as when the person has to learn the practice with a certain kind of artefact, and the surroundings, as when one characterises the conditions that different institutions give for an activity to take place, i.e., learning mathematics in school or learning mathematics through work activity.

Michael Cole (1996) also distinguishes between these two interpretations or types of context; one interpretation is 'that which surrounds' and the other is the practice or activity that a person participates in. He exemplifies context as 'surrounding' with ecological circles, which gives the perspective of a person's 'surrounding' being structured into different levels. Instead of ecological circles I prefer to use Bourdieu's field theory (1984; 1997/org.1994) as the model for the context that surrounds, because this model makes it

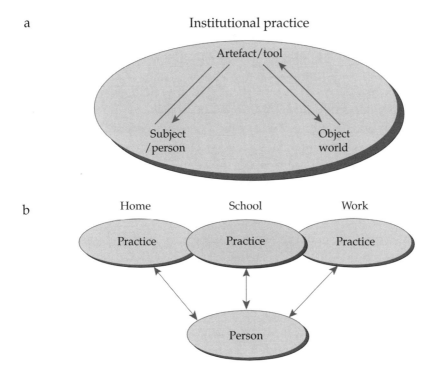

Figure 1.2. Extending Vygotsky's model of the instrumental act into traditions for practice in different institutions.

possible to see the relations between society, institution and person as different levels of cultural fields. With regard to the second type — context as activity — I will refer to the same example as Cole does. He draws on McDermott's model of activity which integrates person with context into a metaphor of a rope that is 'weaved together'.

I will argue that these two interpretations of context can be integrated into a model of learning in institutions as a societal and a person perspective.

Learning Contexts as Cultural Fields

Bourdieu describes how the state/society constitutes a formal structure in which economic, juridical and cultural capital dominate people's interactions. Through the dominance of the different forms of capital, different fields with different social positions are created. Bourdieu especially points to the symbolic/cultural field. Different persons have different positions in the symbolic/cultural field, and according to their position they are more or less influencing and also influenced by the 'field' by being agents and at the same time embodying the knowledge, the values and the ways of acting that characterise the specific field.

Bourdieu's conceptions of cultural and symbolic fields are very helpful in putting into perspective how traditions and structures in society create the conditions of socialisation necessary for a person's embodiment of these traditions and structures, which take place across institutions. One example is time and public space, e.g., differences between Denmark and Spain as to how the day is structured; working time vs. leisure time. In Spain, the siesta creates quite other traditions for time and public space than can be found in the midday lunch break in Denmark. Differences can also be found in the period of time spent at school or work, having dinner, being with friends, etc. There are also differences as to where one can be with family and friends to undertake leisure activities (public space, private space). It is of special interest in this book, how traditions connected to the cultural and symbolic field of gender, ethnicity and special needs influence educational practice.[2]

Bourdieu's theory is about how social structures are handed over from one generation to the next; although it is a theory of practice, this practice is not conceptualised as situated practice in institutions. Bourdieu's conception of cultural fields can contribute to our understanding of learning because this theory introduces the dimension that persons, by having different positions in a cultural field, can also be considered as differing in meaning about the practice in which they participate. This means that persons can be seen attending the same activities in an institution with different ideologies connected to this activity. Different persons participate differently in societal institutions because the meaning of their positions in a cultural field give different meaning to the activities in the concrete institutions; therefore Bourdieu's conceptions of variation in persons' positions in cultural fields are valuable. Different positions in the cultural field lead to difference in the ideologies of how practice should be in the institutions of home, school etc.

Learning Context as Institutional Practice

The second type of context which Cole describes is practice that interweaves a person's environment with his knowledge and skills. Neither the

2. See Daniels, Kritskaya, Kutnick, Hautemäki & Hautemäki, the present book.

mental processes nor the world or context are 'objective', but created through interaction. McDermott (1993) demonstrates this view in his research of how a child's — David's — learning disability is constructed differently in different institutional contexts. McDermott argues that the competence demonstrated by a child, or the lack of competence diagnosed as learning disability, depends on the context the child is entering. In McDermott's observation study, David's reading skills changed and improved, going from a test situation to a class situation and, finally, to an after-school club situation. The point of this story is that a person's competence is interwoven with the context and cannot be viewed as separated. This case points to the importance of recognising learning as being different in different institutional practices. The child learns in the realising of institutional practices in interaction with other persons. Neither the child nor the institutionalised activity/practice in itself create learning or learning problems.

A Model of Learning in Contexts

Bourdieu conceptualises institutions and their practices as constructions (1994, 137). He uses the family as an example of an institution and argues that a family has to be viewed as a construct. Bourdieu's argument is that families are so diverse that this concept has no value as a description of an actual entity but only as an idealised imagined entity, a construct.[3] I find a characteristic of institutions as imagined entities problematic because the situated practice in families and other institutions can be identified, though they vary within the same type of institution, and it is through this situated practice that learning takes place. Even though the situated practice differs within the same type of institutions, core characteristics of the type of practice (the motive of the practice) can be distinguished. Contrary to Bourdieu, I see the state/society with its different cultural fields as constructs. The society exists through its practice in institutions and through the relations they have to each other (see Figure 1.3). In my view, the state/society and its cultural fields/institutional traditions are imagined entities as in Anderson's theory of 'Imagined communities' (1991), kept together by the situated practice of its institutions.

---

3. Bourdieu further argues, that the state/society and its structure with its agents positioned in cultural fields are the real entity and he further argues that persons' positions in different types of fields correspond to structures in persons' meaning systems.

Context in Bourdieu's theory of cultural fields and McDermott's conception of the rope metaphor for the relation between person and environment are two different ways of conceptualising learning environments that can enrich each other. The one type refers to the structure of traditions in society and the other to practice in institutions. Context as field is at the ideological level of meanings and conceptions about societal traditions, while context as activity/practice is at the level of acting within institutional traditions. People anchored in different societal fields can view activity in an institution differently because they relate to different cultural traditions and have different meanings and values connected to an institution.

People can be anchored in cultural fields (different traditions) that create a special ideological relation to the activities in an institution, but learning takes place in situated practice in concrete institutions. One has to take both aspects of context into consideration when discussing learning contexts, e.g., to include both structural conception such as cultural fields and their meaning/value systems, and situated practice in institutions (see Figure 1.3).

From a cultural-historical point of view, learning is an activity situated in institutions where both the participants' motives and the values/meanings associated to traditions contribute to the learning activity. This conception can be visualised in the following model for learning activity where I have integrated both Vygotsky's instrumental method of acting, and Wartofsky's conception that artefact is the objectification of human needs and intentions with Lave & Wenger's theory of situated learning and Bourdieu's theory of a person's meaning systems as reflecting his position in a cultural field (see Figure 1.3). In this model, the institutions are the place for situated practice which is regulated by societal traditions and realised by the person's motivated activities participating in the institutional practices.

Learning Traditions and Motives

It is important to see institutions as well as persons as dynamic and changing entities and not to see the institutions in which children learn as static. The dialectic between institutional traditions and persons' motivation create the situated (actual) institutional practice and learning. In a family, a day-care institution and a school, activity will be marked by the children who take part in these activities as well as by the traditions of these institutions. Both the kind of knowledge and the motives dominating persons' activities differs from home to school, after-school clubs and work. By taking part in the daily practices in an institution, the participants appropriate as

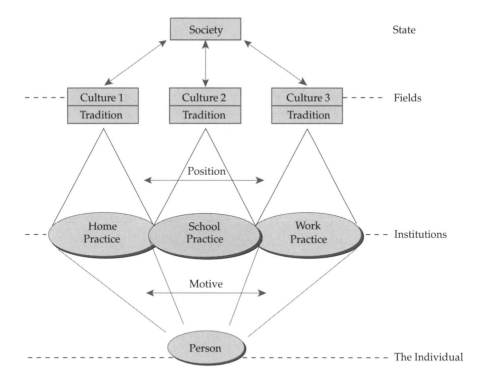

Figure 1.3. Learning through participation in institutionalised practice.

well as contribute to the activities and the development of the practice of the specific institutions.

Learning is qualitatively different in the different types of institutions because practice traditions in the form of knowledge and the persons' motives for participation in the practice are different.

Knowledge Learning: Everyday, Subject-Matter and Professional Knowledge

To be able to nuance how learning takes place for schoolchildren, I will distinguish between everyday knowledge which children carry with them from home/community, subject-matter knowledge which children meet in school and professional knowledge which dominates work activities. One of the differences in knowledge traditions can be found in how methods (procedures) and content of knowledge relate to each other.

Everyday knowledge is connected to practical activities at home, examples are cooking, cleaning, and pleasant 'togetherness'. In everyday activities knowledge procedures and content are melted together, and procedures for 'how to do things' can be characterised as 'silent' knowledge. In school, a distinction between procedure and content of knowledge is introduced, although in many cases this distinction is made explicit by primarily focusing on either the one aspect — the methods/procedures, or the other aspect — the content. In the elementary classes, the focus is primarily on the procedures, i.e., in language learning on: reading and writing; in mathematical learning on: the four basic operations for calculation. When other subjects are introduced in the third grade, i.e., biology, history, geography, the content becomes the primary aspect for learning and the methods that characterise these subject areas are often neglected. In school the methods are very seldom explicitly characterised as special for a certain subject area, though this should be the ideal so that the difference between subject matter areas could be viewed from a methodological perspective as well as from a content perspective. Ideally speaking, children should learn that knowledge is not objective but that the methods of research and exploration contribute to formation of the special kind of knowledge of the different subject areas.

If we take a step further and look at knowledge connected to craftsmanship and professional work, professional knowledge that characterises work places is related to quite different knowledge domains than science and subject matters are. In vocational education content and procedures have developed through work traditions. For the skilled craftsman, knowledge is embodied in procedures and methods as with everyday knowledge, the difference being, however, that professional knowledge can become conscious and reflected upon, and that people working as skilled craftsmen can see the connection between methods and specific problems.

Scribner (1998) is one of the researchers who has shown that different traditions of mathematics dominate at school and at the workplace. She had studied the delivering practices of American milkmen and found that their ways of keeping account of how much milk they had delivered and the payment they had received were done in quite a different way than what one would expect from the basic arithmetical exercises learned in school. Her research showed that mathematical knowledge and skills are not abstract entities but is combined with the institutional tradition of practice.

The aim of school education is that the subject-matter knowledge and skills acquired in school should become the person's own tools for future everyday practice in other institutions, home and workplace. School is an institution that can be seen as preparing children for life in other institutions, i.e., higher education, work, family life etc.

The knowledge a child acquires at home and in day-care institutions is still relevant also in school but the change is that the subject-matter teaching comes to dominate the school teaching and the child's life activity. After entering school, the same type of change can be experienced upon embarking on an apprenticeship. Knowledge of the professional activity then becomes dominant also in relation to subject-matter knowledge and skills. This is what we find at vocational high schools (Basic Vocational Education schools) that are connected to apprenticeship education where subject matter can be integrated into, but subordinated to, teaching an occupational skill, e.g., methods of carpeting. The apprentices have to be able to read and calculate and to have knowledge in several subject matters in order to embark on an occupational education; however, the actual trade will come to dominate both the content and form of the subjects that are integrated in the apprenticeship schools and not the logic of the subject-matter area.

The differences in knowledge traditions between home, school and work also influence instruction so that teaching in the home should follow the child's logic, in the school it should follow the subject-matter logic, and at work it should follow the logic of the professional activity and of the work task.

There is no general agreement in school politics on this matter. The fight is between positions that recommend different educational methods, so what children meet in school is not that teaching should follow the logic of the material and prepare the child for life in other institutions but a mixture of conflicting demands connected to the different positions of parents, teachers, school leaders, politicians, and researchers. So, when the child enters the activities of school s/he meets these in-built conflicts through the educational practice.

Motive Learning and Development

A person's motive is a contributory factor when differentiating between learning practices in different institutions. A person's participation in a practice can be multiply motivated but on the whole one can find a leading/dominating motive that is shared by the participants which makes them understand the activity as a special kind of activity, such as play, learning or work.

A person's personality can be seen in the motive hierarchy that comes to dominate his/her life (Leontiev 1978). Motive development takes place through social interaction in situated practice with shared motivation.

Situations that are experienced or expected to be eventful can be motivating for a child. Eventful situations can be prepared by building up the child's imagination of what is going to happen. Entering school can be an eventful situation if the parents and other central persons contribute to the creation of images of what is going to happen.

The child both contributes to and acquires motivation by entering practices in an institution. Elkonin (1971) relates the main motives that characterise a person to the person's participation in the three dominating institutions in Western industrialised society, namely home, school and work. Then, in an idealised version, the dominant motives are play, work and learning, respectively. A change in a child's dominant motive can be characterised as a developmental change. The development of motives for these three periods are always ahead of the development of cognition in each of the periods. In the early childhood period (the infant and toddler period), children's development of motives is related to their emotional contact with central persons in their family/day-care. This relation results in development of and mastery of the immediate and close everyday world when entering kindergarten. When entering school, the child's learning motive develops and becomes dominating in this middle childhood period. Here, the children's knowledge is characterised by acquisition of methods and competence which in school is seen as central for being able to enter the adult world. In the third period, the late childhood period and youth period, the child's motive development is directed towards engagement in other persons and society. The dominating motive is togetherness with peers — to become socially accepted and at the same time an orientation towards self-worth. The cognitive development of young people can be characterised by their ability to master methods for contributing to society (work).

The child's learning can then be viewed as a life trajectory through different institutions. The picture can be painted with more nuances than in the above version, but the main principle will be the participation in institutional practice that leads to learning of motives and knowledge.

Until now I have outlined characteristic of learning in general but my last argument has pointed to the necessity of analysing learning in the situated practice in specific institutions coloured by the participating persons. This leads to the topic of this book — learning in classrooms which is the content of the different chapters in this book.

Content and Structure of the Book

The theme that binds the articles together in this book is the cultural-historical perspective on schoolchildren's learning and a cultural-historical approach to instruction. This theme has been differentiated into five sub-themes: school traditions, classroom practice and learning activity — educational practice that combines community knowledge and social science studies — everyday knowledge and mathematics learning — diversity in learning — classroom interaction and discourse.

The papers in the first section, *School Traditions and Learning*, discuss how the qualification of persons in the classroom depends on historical and societal conditions outside the classroom. The focus is on the problem area of context as a cultural field, with special focus on national and community traditions and ideologies for school practices. The traditions that are considered relate to (1) conceptions about gender and special needs, (2) educational methods and (3) research traditions.

In the chapter *The Gendering of Social Practices in Special Needs Education,* Harry Daniels, Angela Creese, Shaun Fielding, Valerie Hey, Diana Leonard and Marjorie Smith argue that a focus on interaction on an interpersonal level is too restrictive a view on children's development and learning in school. The social processes through which children become identified as having special needs and receive available provision involve explanation in three areas, the nature of special need, conceptualisation of special need education and analyses of gender inequalities. Daniels et al. point out that the tradition of practice has separated these areas so that each area has its specific focus. Daniels et al.'s study is a first step towards integration of these different disciplines, and the part reported here involves a survey of the relation between allocation of special provision, gender, race and the culture in different schools.

Teaching traditions in different schools in the state of Brandenburg in Germany are studied in Hartmuth Giest's study, *Instruction and Learning in Elementary School*. These traditions are related to differences in the didactics of the schools. Giest compares three didactic strategies, two of these — direct and indirect teaching — dominate school tradition in Brandenburg and in most Western countries. In his research survey, Giest demonstrates that both types of teaching have very little effect on learning that transcends the classroom. Giest advocates a third strategy that is still on the experimental level — 'Developmental Instruction' — which stresses an alternation between self-regulated learning and guided learning within the zone of proximal development.

In his chapter *Expanding the Predominant Interpretation of ZPD in Schooling Contexts: Learning and Mutuality*, Peter Kutnick points to the theory of education behind Vygotsky's concept of the Zone of Proximal Development (ZPD). The concept of ZPD has been interpreted differently over time in ways that correspond to the ideology of the dominating education. Today the educational interpretation emphasises the relation between teacher and student as hierarchical, but from the cultural-historical perspective of Vygotsky, ZPD can be viewed as a collective activity based on teacher and student cooperation. Kutnick argues for reinventing the original conception behind ZPD in favour of children's learning activity.

Both Daniels and Kutnick have researched how gendering of social practice influences students' learning strategies. Kutnick's research demonstrates that girls are more oriented toward cooperation and supporting friends than boys are.

Educational Practice that Combines Community Knowledge and Social Science Studies is the theme for the second section of the book. The four papers in this section all relate teaching to community and forms of practice outside the classroom. Learning is viewed as an activity that takes place within community activity both in a situated and in a historical perspective. Other aspects, also shared in these chapters, are the aim of integrating emotional and intellectual aspects of the thematic subjects studied and to create motives for learning and relating to the community as well as promoting personal development.

Katsuhiro Yamazumi's chapter, *Orchestrating Voices and Crossing Boundaries in Educational Practice: Dialogic Research on Learning about the Kobe Earthquake*, presents a case study of how students and teachers use the event of the Great Kobe Earthquake of 1995 as a theme in social studies in order to cope with the traumatic experiences and to become oriented towards the future. The educational practice was centred on conflicting 'voices' and development of a collective activity to 're-orchestrate these voices'. The theme of the education was 'walking through the stricken city' and the idea was — through various activities — to relate school with community, thereby creating an understanding of this event for the students and thereafter directing their communication towards the victims as well as extending it to other areas. The concept of 'expansive learning' has been used as a theoretical foundation for the educational practice.

The next two articles in this section describe two out-of-school youth projects. These two projects can be an inspiration for classroom activities that connect with thematic issues in the community as well as an inspiration for coordinating classroom activities and youth programmes.

In a study of an After School Programme for Puerto Rican children presented by Hedegaard, Chaiklin and Pedro Pedraza, *Culturally Sensitive Teaching within a Vygotskian Perspective,* the aim was to support children's development of a learning motive and a positive cultural identity. In the planning and the analyses of the educational activities, the concept of 'cultural knowledge' was introduced as a guide to the formulation of culturally sensitive teaching activities. Through participation in the role play of the young scientist club and exploring activities prepared by the teacher, the children gradually acquired subject-matter concepts which they became able to use in analysing the history and cultural and economical characteristics of their community.

Jrene Rham has studied an inner-city gardening youth programme in her chapter *Science Literacy in the Making in an Inner-City Youth Programme: 'They take the Time to Show us how a Plant Grows'*. Underlying the approach of the study is the assumption that science is socially and culturally constructed through participation in community practice. The study focuses on how children became masters of the cultural tools offered in the community garden, including ways of talking, thinking, caring for plants and ways of using knowledge about plant science to market the products of the garden. The project was characterised by a gradual change of roles between teachers and learners into an informal cooperative setting of science learning. Rahm suggests that partnership between youth programme and school teaching in science can be a way of engaging more youth in science because the theoretical concepts of science here connect to a learning environment which is authentic and meaningful for young persons.

In her chapter *Transforming Ethnocultural Tradition in a Modern Environment: Context for Personal Development,* Olga Kritskaya describes an ethnocultural programme that aims at bridging communicative and expressive forms embedded in a folk cultural tradition with the modern environment of school children. The use of a cultural frame should facilitate identity development. In the programme, teaching and learning was based on a metaphor of rite in an ethnocultural space. The structuring elements were rhythm, emotionality and symbol.

The following section, *Everyday Knowledge and Mathematics and Physics*

Learning, contains two chapters that demonstrate the importance of a dialogue about the connections between everyday knowledge and science concepts for students learning and motivation.

In his chapter *Mathematical Cognition in the Classroom: A Cultural-Historical Approach,* Ademir Damazio argues that all knowledge, even abstract mathematical concepts, is socially constructed. Damazio's arguments are based on classroom observation of teaching the concept 'relative whole number'. His observations show that it is possible for the students to appropriate mathematical concepts through a dialogue which moves from everyday events to abstract concepts, and that this type of learning supports the students learning of and motivation for mathematical concepts. He also demonstrates, however, that this is a complete complementary approach to traditional maths teaching and learning, and as it is difficult for the teacher to dare to work with this new teaching practice the risk of falling back into the traditional teaching practice is present.

In the next chapter, *From Monologic to Dialogic Learning: A Case Study of Japanese Mathematics Classrooms,* Kayo Matsushita also demonstrates the importance of dialogue in maths teaching. In his chapter, Matsushita points out that Japanese classrooms are not homogeneous because the students have experience from different forms of teaching. He describes three different forms of mathematic culture: The inquiry maths, the everyday maths and the juke maths. The inquiry maths stresses construction of mathematical meaning and reasoning. The everyday maths uses mathematical ideas embedded in everyday life situations. Juke maths builds on rote memorisation and routine procedures. These three forms of maths can be found in the same classroom, thereby posing difficulties and disturbances as demonstrated by Matsushita in his case study. But, in a later sequence of his study, he also shows how a dialogue could be found so that the classroom came to function as a community of learners, integrating the learners' diverse experience.

The section *Diversity in Learning Modes* contain chapters which research how different aspects of students' life influence their learning activity and create diversity in learning. Diversity between students is studied from the perspective of student strategies, earlier experiences and student/teacher cooperation and gender.

In her chapter *How School Students Become Subjects of Cooperative Learning Activity,* Galina Zuckerman discusses why some students in the classroom engage differently in class activities. To understand a student's activity, she points out, one must determine what the child's activity is directed towards. Different goals determine different students' activities, and only when a child confronted with a problem in class searches for new ways of action, is s/he participating in a learning activity. Zuckerman has researched some of the preconditions for students entering this kind of activity.

How differences in children's precondition can be located in children's experience before entering school is the focus of Frota's chapter *Construction of Distance, Time and Speed Concepts: A Cultural-Historical Approach*. Frota researched how different social living conditions influence school children's experience of distance as a function of time and experience with speed, and how this experience varies at different grade levels.

The influence of student/teacher interactions for students' text comprehension and memory is the object of research in Manuel de la Mata and Andrés Santamaría's chapter *Teacher-Student Interaction, Text Comprehension and Memory: A Semiotic Analysis of Instructional Actions*. In this study, the students were given a text about ancient people's society and culture. The variables researched were educational level, level of interaction: individual versus teacher/student interaction and who of the two were responsible for the interaction.

In their study of *Children's Self-Concept as Gendered and Contextual: Socio-Moral Self-Concepts among 12-year-old Finnish Girls and Boys*, Airi and Jarkko Hautamäki describes how children's scores on a socio-moral self scale indicate that socio-moral selves are both context and gender dependent. They argue that it is important to consider the cultural-historical context in order to understand the differences between the students self-evaluation.

In the following section, *Classroom Interaction and Discourse*, the authors discuss how tradition influences both teachers' and students' strategies and attitudes towards learning activity.

The topic of discussion in Solange Jobim e Souza's chapter, *The Construction of Contemporary Subjectivity: Interactions between Knowledge and School Environment*, is how the content of children's and adults' talk in school uncover the problems of our culture. By means of an interview study, Souza demonstrates that both adults and children, in their everyday settings, often fail to find a common ground of understanding the meaning of studies and school activities. Souza stresses the importance of the dialogue in school between adult and child to create this shared understanding, which presupposes that the adult view the child as a partner in this dialogue.

In their chapter, *A Relational Approach to Understanding Classroom Practice*,

Carol Linehan and John McCarthy discuss the theoretical approach of describing classroom as a community of practice. They point to the danger that such a new approach to describing classroom interaction does not by itself contribute to change in the typical classroom where the teacher controls the activities and the students receive. In their study, Linehan and McCarthy paint a picture of what it means to participate in class as a community of practice which are subjugated to a long tradition of teacher control of students' activities.

The author of the chapter, *Teacher's Experience of School and Knowledge through Childhood Memories*, Maria Teresa de Freitas, describes how one, through interviews, can find the roots of teachers' attitudes to reading and writing in their own experiences from childhood. The teachers' attitudes are based on parents' and grandparents' support to their spontaneous reading and writing activity as children. Freitas demonstrates how children's zest for learning to read is supported by their own imaginative activity also under very restricted conditions. She also argues that children's attitude to reading can be either supported or destroyed by disciplining children's imagination.

How dialogue between teachers and researcher can support teachers' reflections on their activity is the theme of Maria Cecília Camargo Magalhães chapter *Teacher's and Researcher's Interactions in Classroom Discourse: Different Ways of Organising Salient and Problematic Actions*. The problem discussed in this chapter is how teachers can both take part in the process of students' learning to read and write and at the same time be able to reflect on their own contributions to the students' learning activity. Through video recording, the teachers in the study confront themselves with their teaching and thereby appropriate a method to analyse and discuss the process with colleagues and researchers.

Conclusion

By looking into the chapters of this book, one can see that research into students' learning implies a view of the learning person as an active participant in social practice so that the person contributes to the conditions for his/her own learning. Furthermore, problems of learning are located not as those of the students' but as problems associated with the activity in educational institutions. The students are seen as learners participating in the social interaction of a practice tradition where they become involved in a reciprocal process in which their motives and personalities play a part.

References

Anderson, B. (1991). *Imagined communities: Reflections on the origin and spread of nationalism* (rev. ed.). London: Verso.

Berger, P.L. & Luckmann, T. (1966). *The social construction of reality: A treatise in the sociology of knowledge*. New York: Doubleday.

Bourdieu, P. (1984). *Distinction: A social critique of the judgement of taste* (R. Nice, trans.). Cambridge, Mass.: Harvard University Press. (Original work published 1979)

Bourdieu, P. (1997). *Af praktiske grunde* (Original work: *Raison practiques. Sur la théorie de l'action*, Editions du Seul, Paris 1994). Copenhagen: Hans Reitzel.

Elkonin, D.B. (1971). Towards the problem of stages in the mental development of the child. *Soviet Psychology*, 10, 538-653.

Lave, J. (1996). Teaching, as learning in practice. *Mind, culture and activity*, 3, 149-64.

Lave, J. & Wenger, E. (1991). *Situated learning: Legitimate peripheral participation*. Cambridge: Cambridge University Press.

Leontiev, A.N. (1978). *Activity, consciousness, and personality*. Englewood Cliffs, N.J.: Prentice-Hall.

Luria, A.R. (1961). *Speech and the regulation of behaviour*. Oxford: Pergamon Press.

McDermott, R.P. (1993). The acquisition of a child by a learning disability. In S. Chaiklin & J. Lave (eds.), *Understanding practice*. Cambridge: Cambridge University Press.

Piaget, J. (1967). *Play, dreams and imitation in childhood*. London: Kegan Paul.

Scribner, S. (1998). A socio-cultural approach to the study of mind. In G. Greenberg & E. Tobach (eds.), *Theories of the evolution of knowing*. Hillsdale, N.J.: Lawrence Erlbaum.

Vygotsky, L.S. et al. (1982). *Om barnets psykiske udvikling*. [On the child's psychic development] Copenhagen: Nyt Nordisk Forlag.

Vygotsky, L.S. (1985/87). *Ausgewählte Schriften. 1&2*. Cologne: Pahl-Rugenstein.

Vygotsky, L.S. (1997). *Problems of the theory and history of psychology. The collected works of L.S. Vygotsky, Vol 3*. New York: Plenum Press.

Wartofsky, M. (1979). *Models — Representations and the scientific understanding*. Dodrecht and Boston: D. Reidel.

Wood, D.J., Bruner, J.S. & Ross, G. (1976). The role of tutoring in problem solving. *Journal of Child Psychology and Psychiatry*, 17, 89-100.

School Traditions
and Learning

2 The Gendering of Social Practices in Special Needs Education

Harry Daniels, Angela Creese, Shaun Fielding,
Valerie Hey, Diana Leonard and Marjorie Smith

This paper will explore some of the ways in which the perspective of gender casts light on the social processes of identification of need and resource allocation in the 'special educational needs' provision in mainstream schools. It will also raise some initial suggestions for the development of an approach to the study of learning and gender. In doing so, the paper will develop themes derived from post-Vygotskian understandings of the relationship between context and cognition. The ultimate intention is to investigate the relationship between the institutional culture of schools and gendered disparities in educational attainment.

Context and Cognition

Initial studies of developing cognition tended to ignore the context or to provide a very partial view of the relationship between context and cognition. The early cognitivist approach tended to exclude societal and cultural factors from its notion of context. The initial theorising in ecological psychology tended to focus on the description of settings and to ignore the relations between persons acting and those settings.

More recent times have witnessed a rapid growth in the number of approaches which attempt to investigate the development of cognition in context using non-deterministic, non-reductionist theories. Amongst these are cultural historical activity theory (Cole, Engeström and Vasquez 1997), sociocultural approaches (Wertsch 1991; Wertsch, Del Rio and Alvarez 1995), situated learning models (Lave 1996), distributed cognition approaches (Solomon 1993). They all share the view that the theory developed by L.S. Vygotsky provides a valuable tool with which to interrogate and attempt to understand the processes of social formation of mind (see Daniels 1996).

The essence of the developmental model advanced by Vygotsky is a dialectical conception of the relations between personal and social life. Specific social practices may be associated with modes of discourse, and modes of personal thinking. (See Olson and Torrance 1996). The key concept of 'mediation' opens the way to a non-deterministic account in which 'psychological tools' serve as the means by which the individual acts upon and is acted upon by social, cultural and historical factors. Some approaches have tended to focus on a semiotic means of mediation (Wertsch 1991) whereas others have tended to focus more on activity itself (Engeström 1993).

In that the original theory and its subsequent developments seek to combine semiotic and activity based accounts of the effects of the social on the individual, the potential for understanding cultural and social factors as they impact on individual understanding and learning is afforded. However, a good deal of the post-Vygotskian research conducted in the west has focused exclusively on the effects of interaction at the interpersonal level, with insufficient attention paid to the form of collective social activity with specific forms of interpersonal communication interrelations between interpersonal and sociocultural levels.

As a rule, the socio-institutional context of action is treated as a (largely unanalysed) dichotomised independent variable — or left to sociologists. (Cole 1996, 340)

Wells (1993, 1994) has attempted to bring together theories of discourse with activity theory in the analysis of teaching and learning in the classroom. Volosinov (1973, 20-22) emphasised the importance of the relationship between utterance and context in the analysis of meaning: 'the sign may not be divorced from the concrete forms of social intercourse.' The concept of genre as developed in Australia (e.g., Christie 1985, 1993) and North America, may be taken to refer to a set of formally definable text features that certain texts have in common across various contexts. Bazerman (1988, 1994), extends this notion of 'genre' beyond that of textual forms, to 'forms of life, ways of being, frames for social action' in his attempt to theorise environments for learning and teaching. Both Bazerman and Wells provide extensions to the concept of genre as developed in Christie's (1985, 1993) formulation of curriculum genres. These studies contribute to the development of a theory of learning and discourse within the activity of schooling; yet, they still do not provide a verifiable model of socio-institutional effects.

Researchers working from within both the 'situated learning' and 'activity theory' approaches have expressed dissatisfaction with the lack of theo-retical progress in this aspect of the field. Lave has suggested that — 'with-out a theoretical conception of the social world one cannot analyse activity in situ' (Lave 1996, 7). Similarly, Axel has noted limitations within activity theory — 'Leontiev talks about an activity system not about social organis-ations and formations. His combination of social theory and psychology remains too abstract and is only rudimentarily and inconsistently developed' (Axel 1997, 140). These post-Vygotskian developments have, as yet, to real-ise some of the goals sketched in the original thesis.

Although he did not develop an appropriate methodology, Vygotsky attached the greatest importance to the school itself as an institution. His particular interest lay in the structuring of time and space and the related system of social relations (between pupils and teacher, between the pupils themselves, between the school and its surroundings, and so on) (Ivic 1989). In their overview of current thinking that claims a Vygotskian root, Minick, Stone and Forman (1993) argue that the culturally specific nature of schools demands close attention to the way in which they structure interactions between people and artefacts such as books. They also emphasise the need to focus on the ways that actors interact with one another in particular edu-cational contexts.

… educationally significant human interactions do not involve abstract bearers of cognitive structures but real people who develop a variety of interpersonal rela-tionships with one another in the course of their shared activity in a given institu-tional context … modes of thinking evolve as integral systems of motives, goals, values, and beliefs that are closely tied to concrete forms of social practice. (Minick et al. 1993, 6)

In their use of the term 'in a given institutional context', Minick et al. imply that differences between institutional contexts may be of significance. This suggestion seems to be both under-theorised and under-investigated. For example in a discussion of recontextualisation of everyday activities within schooling, Wyndhamn and Säljö (1997) state that:

… institutions of formal learning have established themselves as yet another 'sys-tem of activity' which to a certain extent has developed autonomous rules and tra-ditions for communication and for the definition of phenomena such as learning and competence. (p. 328)

They appear to suggest that schooling is a generic activity as if it were a social institution which is uniform in its psychological effects. However, it is highly likely that within schools and between schools there are differences in the content, structure and function of interpersonal communication. There is a need to articulate the different modalities of pedagogic practice within the activity theory framework and investigate the relation between these modalities and the forms of communicative competence that are regarded as appropriate.

Our suggestion is that particular forms of pedagogic practice may be associated with specific ways of speaking and acting with respect to gender and race. These ways of speaking and acting may be thought of as pedagogic genres. These pedagogic genres constitute the 'tool' within an activity theory framework. The pedagogic genres may be seen to be associated with specific patterns of division of labour, forms of community and social and pedagogic rules within an activity system such as schooling.

Russell argues that activity theory analysis of genre systems may offer a theoretical bridge between the sociology of education and Vygotskian social psychology of classroom interaction, and contribute toward resolving the knotty problem of the relation of macro- and microstructure in literacy research based on various social theories of 'context'. Russell (1997, 1). Alternatively, it may be possible to use the concept of 'genre' as a means of differentiating between activities in analysis. It is this alternative which we pursued in the context of our current study.

School and Gender Effects

For many years we have been told that 'schools make a difference'. But too rarely do we talk about the ways in which schools do make differences and also try to find out rather more about the kinds of differences that schools make. Reynolds and Cuttance (1992) refer to the need to examine data for gender differences in quantitative effectiveness research literature:

Gender differentials should be examined in determining whether a given school or group of schools is effective or becoming more effective. (p. 29)

Scheerens' (1992) book 'Effective schooling' began to reveal controversy, with some studies claiming that 'factors enhancing educational productivity' worked equally well for different sub-groups, while others found evidence for differential school effects with regard to sex and ethnic background. The key implication is that some schools narrowed the gap between boys and girls or between students of high or low attainment on entry, whereas some other schools were found to be widening the gap.

The discussion here will focus on the ways in which the individual schools, in one LEA,[1] made differences to the ways in which special needs resources were allocated. The differences which we studied were those revealed when perspectives of gender and race were brought to bear on special needs allocation practices and outcomes. We would argue that these differences often remain invisible when issues of differentials in effectiveness of schools are brought into question. We would suggest that questions of effectiveness must be linked with principles of equity if we are to bring about major improvements in school performance.

The arguments against 'individualisation' within the 'special educational needs' (SEN) field focus on how practice has been driven by principles of accountability, justification and compliance. There does need to be some account for individuality in the processes of identification and resource allocation. Nevertheless, these events should take place in a context where policies are in place to ensure that pupils are identified appropriately and that resources are distributed equitably and not diverted into ineffective practices. Halpin and Lewis (1996) argue that the tensions between equity, equality and individuality are not resolved through the denial of individuality. They do so in an analysis of how SEN issues were neglected in the development of the National Curriculum in England and Wales. We wish to extend their argument to suggest that this denial of individuality within the population of pupils who are identified as having SEN is all the more serious when the allocation of resources is analysed by gender and race. Gendered processes in education generally have been the focus of an effective and comprehensive feminist critique during a period in which the position of pupils with SEN has received much attention. Nevertheless, as Delamont (1989) pointed out, despite the close relations of race and gender issues in Equal Opportunities legislation initiatives, almost no one looked at gender and SEN in the UK until the late 1980s. The boundaries that exist in the social organisation of academic life are also reflected in the texts that have been produced in our area of research. An initial literature search revealed a dearth of research in

---

1. In England and Wales local government control over education is executed by the Local Education Authority (LEA)

which attempts had been made to bring the perspective of gender to bear on matters of concern within special needs education.

It has long been established that there are gender differences in SEN categorisation processes within systems of special schooling. Most recently the National Longitudinal Transition Study of Special Education Students reported that while girls are underrepresented, those who are so defined have more severe difficulties:

Females in secondary special education represented a different combination of abilities and disabilities than males. As a group, females were more seriously impaired; even among males and females with the same disability category, females had marginally greater functional deficits than males. (Wagner 1992, 33-34)

We also know that there has been marked disparity of provision for boys and girls in access to many special schools in the UK (see for example Cooper, Upton and Smith 1991).

In many ways, it would seem as if the practices of SEN had been insulated from the gaze and voice of equal opportunity initiatives. This may be because the socially driven account of disadvantage and failure which is located in the discourse of equal opportunity is 'switched off' when we turn to the discourse of SEN within which many of the preferred explanations of causation derive from models of individual deficiency.

Here then is a case for asking whether the notion of genre as advanced by Bazerman may be used as a tool to understand the consequences of the categorisation of pupils and the grouping of professionals and academics. Are these social groupings created by — and do they create — dominant ways of being, talking and acting?

A genre is ordinarily best analyzed at the level of operation, a typified use of some tool(s), some mediational means, to carry out a typified, routine action, an action which in turn furthers the motive and acts upon the object of some collective (activity system). (Russell 1997, 6)

Resource Allocation as a Gendered and Raced Social Process

If we focus not only on *who* gets special educational provision, but also on *how and why*, we need to look both at national, local and institutional (school) policies and provision, and at the social processes through which children come to be identified as having special needs, understand themselves to have 'special needs', and receive (or do not receive) available provision — as well as establishing how all such policies and processes are connected to gender and race. However, we are a long way from being able to provide such a full account, largely because explanations in the three areas involved — the nature of special educational provision, the conceptualisation of special educational needs, and analyses of gender and race inequalities — each have their specific foci and are the concern of different academic disciplines (and hence use different language and concepts/discourses); and because these different sorts of explanation have, up to now, been assiduously kept apart.

Empirical Study

The study of special educational needs resource allocation for 7-11 year olds consisted of three phases, two of which will be discussed here. The goal was to understand the impact of race and gender on decision-making processes. The first phase consisted of an audit of provision and was followed by an in-depth study of process in a subset of schools which exemplified particular forms of social practice.

Phase one of our study involved a broad survey of the allocation of the special provision made available in the one Local Education Authority at Key Stage 2. The overall gender ratio data were collected initially for the schools and subsequently for individual pupils within schools.

Twenty-one schools provided access to data on each pupil receiving additional support. Information was gathered on:

— gender
— date of birth
— ethnic background
— first language
— eligibility for free school meals
— home background (parents living with the child, type of accommodation)
— type of SEN registered by the school
— provision allocated by the school

Three hundred and fifty-eight pupil profiles were obtained in this survey. The overall gender ratio of 2.6 is similar to that found in special schools.

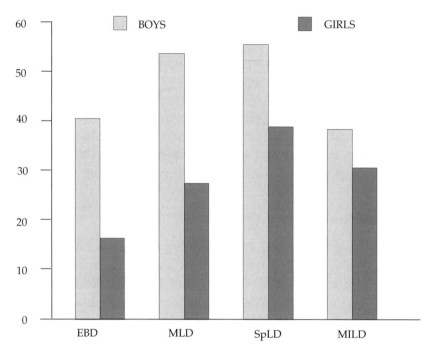

EBD = Emotional and Behavioural Difficulty
MLD = Moderate Learning Difficulty
SpLD = Specific Learning Difficulty
MILD = Mild Learning Difficulty

Figure 2.1. Numbers of boys and girls placed within categories of SEN.

The variation between schools, however, was compelling evidence and suggests that schools as institutions may exert considerable influence over local practice with respect to gender.

To find one school working with twice as many girls as boys and another working with eight times as many boys as girls in situations which appear remarkably similar within one local education authority will most surely raise the eyebrows of those concerned with equity in resource allocation practices. These are significant school differences which appear to stand outside the gaze of current monitoring procedures.

Moreover, within schools gender differences were seen to vary as a function of category of SEN used by teachers to describe pupil difficulties. As can

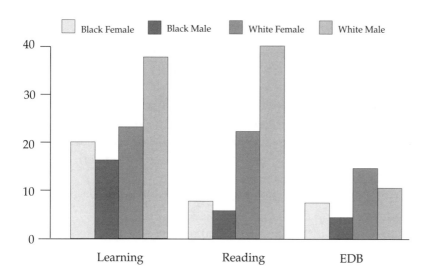

Figure 2.2. Analysis of placement in categories of SEN by gender and race.

be seen in Figure 2.1, the most marked difference was revealed within the category 'emotional and behavioural difficulty', the least in the mild learning difficulty category.

Gender differences also appeared to vary as a function of race as can be seen in Figure 2.2.

In Figure 2.2 the vertical axis reveals the numbers of pupils in each category. The male/female ratio is close to 1.0 in the African Caribbean group and above 2.0 in the white English group. (There were very few Asian children living in the local education authority). When examined by ethnicity *and* gender, patterns of categorisations appear to vary significantly. The categories of ethnicity used here were those adopted by the local education authority. In the chart below the category 'black' is comprised of African Caribbean and 'black other' and the category 'white' is comprised of 'white English' and 'white Irish'. Children who are in the process of acquiring English as a second language have been omitted from this analysis. Again, the categories of SEN cited are those used by the teachers and SEN Teacher Co-ordinators to describe the pupils' difficulties.

Within both black and white groups, gender differences are greatest in the emotional and behaviour difficulty category. The data displayed in the block graph suggest that gender differences are much greater in the white group than the black group. In addition, black children appear to be more likely to be allocated to the category 'general learning difficulty' than 'reading difficulty' when compared with their white peers. This would appear to be a value judgment made on the basis of school performance, and it is clearly biased in favour of white pupils who are more likely to be allocated to a category which is socially more acceptable. If we are concerned about equity for all then we need to understand much more about SEN practices from the perspectives of gender and race. There are causes for concern about the evidence provided by this dataset.

Our data also suggest that not only are significantly more boys than girls allocated additional help in mainstream schools but also they are given more (in time/amount) of this help and that are usually allocated the more prestigious and expensive forms of support.

Our strong impression is that social processes serve to bias and distort the allocation of mainstream support for SEN. In the allocation of scarce and precious resources we need to monitor and evaluate the decision making processes from the perspectives given by these social forces in order to improve the chances of equitable distribution. Thus within the general activity system of schooling there would appear to be a dominant genre within which gender differences emerge in SEN resource allocation practices. Given the variation we observed between schools we were keen to understand the means by which schools established their own position within this general discourse. We were concerned to understand the forms of local school activity and ways of being that produced the differences we had identified.

Schools as Specialised Sites — Local Genres: The First Study

Phase one of the study gave us an overview of the outcomes of differing forms of practice in schools. These results enabled us to select particular forms of outcome of resource allocation practice in order to study the forms of social and pedagogic practice which gave rise to such outcomes. In this second phase of the study, four schools of similar pupil population were identified on the basis of gender ratio, amount of additional educational needs budget per head and level of emphasis on equal opportunities policy and practice. They were examples of particular types and combinations of circumstance (see Table 2.1).

School	Gender ratio[2]	Additional educational needs Allocation per head	Influence of school's equal opportunity policy
a	0.4	high	no mention
b	8.3	high	low visibility
c	1.94	high	high visibility
d	7.37	mid range	low visibility

Table 2.1. Sample of phase two schools.

Table 2.1 gives descriptions of the phase 2 schools against criteria of gender ratio, amount of money allocated for Additional Educational Needs and the visibility of Equal Opportunities policies in the schools.

It is our contention that the differences that these schools made in terms of their SEN practices could be related to the general meaning attached to SEN in management practices, and thence within teachers' practices.

All schools recruited predominantly working class pupils despite the fact that some were in socially mixed areas. We grouped them crudely in two categories moving (or 'learning enriched') and stuck (or 'learning impoverished') (Rosenholz 1989) and linked this to how both 'types' predominantly conceive of their typical pupil as either a learner or as a social casuality. Rosenholz argues, that 'stuck' schools are characterised by a highly individualised culture with a lack of certainty about policy and roles, low morale and, generally, poor academic standards. Teachers in these 'stuck' schools suggest that once they have acquired the skills and techniques necessary to be an effective teacher then life as a teacher becomes relatively unproblematic. Teachers in such schools rarely take any risks and develop quite inflexible patterns of working. In contrast in 'moving' schools one is more likely to find a collaborative culture with respect to planning and the sharing of ideas and resources, and support for problem solving.

If we turn our questions of pedagogy, Resnick and LeGall (1996) suggest that school cultures may act to position learner and teacher beliefs. She believes that schools which are oriented to promoting pupil effort, with a continuous press for strategic learning behaviour, and which embody a belief in

2. Adjusted for overall gender ratio in the school.

each child's ability are those which are more likely to be successful. She further argues that teachers in such schools are more likely to believe that they can successfully teach each child and also to view 'themselves' as learners. That is, they treat teaching as a competency to be continuously increased and a child's failure to learn as a problem to be solved by teaching. These are the characteristics of the 'moving' school. If we reverse the 'polarity' of these statements, we arrive at the outcomes that David Hargreaves (1978) announced in 'What Teaching Does to Teachers' — the 'stuck' teacher in the 'stuck' school.

In the schools we studied in detail, we found examples of both types of school. We found two schools which we felt were most appropriately categorised as 'stuck' and two schools which we felt could be described as 'moving'. The management systems appear to be associated with 'folk' psychology concepts of causality and belief about professional practice and development. It is, perhaps, in this sense that the term genre provides a more sophisticated analytical tool by virtue of the linkage with the notion of activity system.

… genre is an analytical category useful for understanding both individual behavior (psychology) and collective behavior (society or culture). By operationalizing recurring actions into genres, individuals participating over time in an activity system come to recognize and perform actions in typical ways using typical tools, thus appropriating ('picking up' or learning) the tools (including discursive tools) and perhaps the object, motive, and subjectivity (identity) of the collective. Similarly, by operationalizing recurring actions into genres, collectives [re]create and temporarily stabilize their object, motive, tools (including discursive tools), and collective identity. (Russell 1997, 6)

The descriptions of the four schools studied provide what may be seen as a first step in the identification of the genres in place at specific sites.

Genre One: Moving Schools — Learning Pupils

School A

This was a school with a gender distribution which favoured girls. The head teacher specifically rejected the idea that a boy with behavioural problems was necessarily a pupil with SEN. The school had developed positive behaviour rules on the basis of lists constructed by each group for their classroom. These were discussed and developed by staff and parents. After a full period of consultation and adjustment, these rules were displayed and monitored. Bullying, name-calling, social isolation, teasing and verbal abuse were taken seriously as impeding learning. Interventions were designed to facilitate their learning. The school has detailed planning procedures, curriculum review meetings and training linked to identified targets. Consistency of values is seen as a priority by the head.

In responding to behaviour through an effective whole-school policy, this school avoids the need to divert SEN resources from supporting learning. In addition, the school used objective tests as part of the process of identifying pupils who might need additional support. This could be part of an effective approach to ensuring that girls receive the support to which they are entitled. In this school, SEN resources were targeted towards individuals, and were seen as providing learning support for pupils who were currently under performing.

School B

School B was attempting to develop a similar form of practice to that observed in School A. The following story told to one of the team illustrates the extent to which the school regards itself as having developed from a 'low base'.

School B 'Early Days'

The children running in and out of the staffroom and screaming things, going into the head's office without knocking and barging through, no respect for hardly any of the adults that were in here, and my friend came on a visit and she walked through the playground and she asked somebody really nicely 'Would you tell me where Miss X is?' and the boy replied 'How the f*** should I know!'

This new school emerged from an unhappy merger between two other schools and was now 'under new management'. Although explanations of pupils' difficulties could have rested on social disadvantage, the school was attempting to address a difficult situation. It has developed a focus on systems development and raising the standards and aspirations of the children. However, in this chaotic but 'moving' situation there was still some confounding of the needs of the school with the needs of the pupils. Funding which could have been used to support individual pupils was diverted into improving the classroom practice of inexperienced teachers working in difficult situations.

Genre Two: Stuck Schools — Social Casualties

School C

This is a school which the Head considers to be 'a very tough inner city school'.

The allocation of SEN resources reveals a global conceptualisation of need. Problems are defined with reference to social disadvantages. The uniform distribution of resources across classes is rationalised in terms of the global social disadvantages which all the pupils encounter. This is taken as an act in favour of equality of opportunity. This action is often referenced to race.

The school's account of a 'race' effect appears in two contradictory ways. Negatively in the difficult and disruptive behaviour of black boys. Positively with respect to black girls who are said to be doing well and are praised for acting as school playground and even classroom monitors:

So you find you have to make a conscious effort to try to make sure the girls aren't swallowed up by the boys 'cause they're very dominating but right from the start it was a case of there are only eight girls … fortunately we've got … I could say half of them very strong girls so they're (able to look after themselves) … they've actually been used to help settle some of the more unsettled boys and they've been wonderful. I mean its hard work getting him (Keith) to sit down and do anything and Naomi's brilliant we're talking about strong girls like Natalie and Charmian who sit on people like Keith … (!) (Class teacher African Caribbean woman)

The rationale of equal *lack* of opportunities leaves no space for distributing the resources to individual need. And the construction of the situation as being primarily about toughness immediately has conceded the ground to the boys.

School D

This is the second of the 'stuck' schools. Nurture and understanding are the first responses to those children with difficult or 'challenging' behaviour. The teachers talk of getting behaviour right before learning can take place. Pupils with SEN were largely perceived as 'socially damaged', a view which inevitably led to SEN resources being substantially used to provide behaviour support almost exclusively to boys.

These four schools exhibit a high degree of similarity in pupil populations and yet differ markedly in the gender ratios within SEN categories.

School A kept a pedagogic focus throughout. It was organised to learn about itself. School B was starting to 'move', albeit slowly. It was starting to develop systems and practices of institutional learning and development. As a consequence, the perception of pupil difficulty was also in the process of change. Schools C and D were both 'stuck'. These schools all made differences. These differences may be seen as genres within the more general activity system of schooling which take up different positions on both gender and race.

If these genres are regarded as qualitatively different tools within an activity theory framework then historical and empirical analysis of activities within the institutions should reveal different subject positions and outcomes.

Gender and Learning: The Second Study

Our first study gave us evidence that different forms of educational outcome in schools were associated with particular forms of social 'language', forms of social practice informed by specific forms of pedagogic belief and practice. From this base, we then moved to consider gendered differentials in attainment of pupils in relation to particular forms of pedagogic belief.

The discourse of disadvantage has reemerged as a debate about the nature and causation of boys' underachievement. Whilst particular groups of boys have *always* been the subjects of anxiety about their educational underperformance, the recent debate has inferred that the ways in which primary learning is structured (especially reading) renders it less productive for boys' learning compared to girls. It is thus of particular interest to empirically investigate to what extent learning *is* a gendered activity as well as identify those schools which seem capable of 'repositioning' all their pupils (both boys and girls) to become successful learners.

A preliminary hypothesis which guides our work is that boys experience a contradiction between cultural messages and practices associated with hegemonic masculinity and those teaching practices conducive to optimal learning within primary schooling. A masculine orientation to learning may be invested in autonomy (authority, aggression and technical competence) whereas the discourses and practices of learning within primary schooling are centred around group and teamwork. Such collaborative practices presume co-dependency. In order to shed light on these interactive practices, it is essential to re-engage with girls' experience of learning in order to cast more light on why boys appear to be adopting less effective strategies.

Specifically we suggest that males are encultured into a view that they should learn alone or under the guidance of the teacher. This is contrast to females who we suggest are more likely to seek and offer help to each other in learning. We argue that this aspect of emergent masculinity in schools gives rise to the higher level of bidding for teacher attention from males. Given the limited amount of teacher time available for individual support, males must either become self-sufficient learners or seek other means of bidding for attention, and these means are often disruptive. This is in contradistinction to girls who are more likely to engage with peers in learning related dialogue. Whilst we accept that much of this dialogue may not take place between a learner and a 'more capable peer', we suggest that given the economics of classroom time, girls are more likely than boys to be in receipt of appropriate 'scaffolds' for their learning. Our current research seeks to investigate the beliefs that teachers and learners hold about classroom dialogue and about learning. It will seek to establish whether such beliefs are connected to gender and race. It will further seek to establish whether such beliefs condition classroom practice.

Dweck and Leggett (1988) suggest that the beliefs of teachers and learners about the relation between attainment, effort and ability are gendered. More recently Resnick, and Nelson LeGall, (1996) have argued that just as some national or regional cultures seem to socialise individuals into particular learning goals, so school cultures may act to position learner and teacher beliefs. They believe that schools which are oriented to promoting pupil effort with a continuous press for strategic learning behaviour and which embody a belief in each child's ability, are those which are more likely to be associated with success. In our research, schools which differ in the extent to which attainment is gendered will be selected for study. This sampling will extend across state and private sectors and will involve those institutions with high and low levels of mean attainment. The intention is to pursue an analysis of institutional culture in relation to beliefs, behaviours and outcomes associated with gender and race. We will seek to theorise the gendered construction of individual belief and learning practice within specific educational activities. We would echo Russell's statement of the political value of such work:

Helping teachers, students, educational institutions, and professions understand the ways their various written genres are (re)negotiated within and beyond classrooms may help them appropriate and (re)construct genres to make those systems of human activity more inclusive and just. (Russell 1997)

We suggest that we are developing an evidence base which demonstrates how these context specific means of mediation are associated with specific forms of outcome at the level of institutional resource allocation and also individual attainment. Taken together these findings support the fundamental tenets of an activity theory approach to the study of education. More important perhaps is the suggestion that the concept of genre could itself be used as a tool in the development of activity theory. Certainly the concept itself requires further development if it is to be of substantial analytical power. Specifically the concept of boundary between genres remains unclear and underdeveloped. Empirical work requires the theoretical basis for classifying and distinguishing between genres if outcomes are to be attributed to genre difference.

Despite the underdeveloped nature of a concept of genre that is truly compatible and useful within activity theory, it does go some way towards meeting the concern raised by Bernstein:

From the point of view of Vygotsky the 'tool' is not subject to analysis although the articulation of the zone of proximal development may well be. Once attention is given to the regulation of the structure of pedagogic discourse, the social relations of its production and the various modes of its recontextualising as a practice, then perhaps we may be a little nearer to understanding the Vygotskian 'tool' as a social and historical construction. (Bernstein 1993, xix-xx)

It may be that the existing concept of genre provides a starting point for the development of the concept of tool within activity theory. The connection between tool and community, rules and division of labour within the activity system would seem to be crucial if we are to understand the regulation of the structure of the tool that is pedagogic discourse.

References

Axel, E. (1997). One developmental line in European activity theories. In M. Cole, Y. Engeström & O. Vasquez (eds.), *Mind, culture and activity: Seminal papers from the Laboratory of Comparative Human Cognition.* Cambridge: Cambridge University Press.

Bazerman, C. (1988). *Shaping written knowledge: The genre and activity of the experimental article in science.* Madison: University of Wisconsin Press.

Bazerman, C. (1994). Systems of genres and the enactment of social intentions. In A. Freedman & P. Medway (eds.), *Genre and the new rhetoric.* London: Taylor & Francis.

Bernstein, B. (1993) Foreword. In H. Daniels (ed.), *Charting the agenda: Educational activity after Vygotsky.* London: Routledge.

Christie, F. (1985). *Language education.* Geelong, Australia: Deakin University Press.

Christie, F. (1993). Curriculum Genres: Planning for effective teaching. In B. Cope & M. Kalantzis (eds.), *The powers of literacy: A genre approach to teaching writing.* London: Falmer Press.

Cole, M. (1996). *Cultural psychology: A once and future discipline.* Cambridge, Mass.: The Belknap Press of Harvard University.

Cole, M., Engeström, Y. & Vasquez, O. (1997). Introduction. In M. Cole, Y. Engeström & O. Vasquez (eds.), *Mind, culture and activity: Seminal papers from the Laboratory of Comparative Human Cognition.* Cambridge: Cambridge University Press.

Cole, M., Engeström, Y. & Vasquez, O. (eds.) (1997). *Mind, culture and activity: Seminal papers from the Laboratory of Comparative Human Cognition.* Cambridge: Cambridge University Press.

Cooper, P., Upton, G. & Smith, C. (1991). Ethnic minority and gender distribution among staff and pupils in facilities for pupils with emotional and behavioural difficulties in England and Wales. *British Journal of Sociology of Education,* 12(1), 77-94.

Daniels, H. (ed.) (1996). *An Introduction to Vygotsky.* London: Routledge.

Delamont, S. (1989). Both sexes lose out: Low achievers and gender. In A. Ramasut (ed.), *Whole school approaches to special needs.* London: Falmer.

Department of Education (1994). *Code of practice on the identification and assessment of special educational needs.* London: DFE.

Dweck, C.S. & Leggett, E.L. (1988). A social cognitive approach to motivation and personality. *Psychological Review,* 95(2), 256-73.

Engeström, Y. (1993). Developmental studies of work as a testbench of activity theory: The case of primary care medical practice. In S. Chaiklin & J. Lave,

Understanding practice: Perspectives on activity and practice. Cambridge: Cambridge University Press.

Halpin, D. & Lewis A. (1996). The impact of the National Curriculum on twelve special schools in England. *European Journal of Special Needs Education*, 11(1), 95-105.

Hargreaves, D. (1978). What teaching does to teachers. *New Society*, 9, 1978, 540-42.

Ivic, I. (1989). Profiles of educators: Lev S. Vygotsky (1896-1934). *Prospects* XIX (3), 427-36.

Lave, J. (1996). The practice of learning. In S. Chaiklin & J. Lave, *Understanding practice: Perspectives on activity and practice*. Cambridge: Cambridge University Press.

Minick, N., Stone, C.A. & Forman, E.A. (1993). Introduction: Integration of individual, social and institutional processes in accounts of children's learning and development. In E.A. Forman, N. Minick & C.A. Stone (eds.), *Contexts for learning: Sociocultural dynamics in children's development*. Oxford: Oxford University Press.

Olson, D.R. & Torrance, N. (eds.) (1996). *Modes of thought: Explorations in culture and cognition*. Cambridge: Cambridge University Press.

Resnick, L.B. & Nelson LeGall, S. (1996). Socializing intelligence. Paper presented at the 1996 Annual Conference of The British Psychological Society: The Piaget-Vygotsky Centenary Conference, 11-14 April at the Brighton Centre.

Reynolds, D. & Cuttance, P. (1992). *School effectiveness: Research, theory and practice*. London: Cassell.

Rosenholtz, S. (1989). *Teacher's workplace: The social organisation of schools*. New York: Longman.

Russell, D. (1997). Rethinking genre in school and society: An activity theory analysis. Iowa State University.
http://www.public.iastate.edu/~drrussel/at%26genre/at%26genre.html

Scheerens, J. (1992). *Effective schooling: Research, policy and practice*. London: Cassell.

Solomon, G. (1993). *Distributed cognitions: Psychological and educational considerations*. Cambridge: Cambridge University Press.

Volosinov, V.N. (1973). *Marxism and the philosophy of language* (L. Matejka & I.R. Titunik, trans.). New York: Seminar Press. (Original work published 1929)

Wagner, M. (1992). Being female — A secondary disability? Gender differences in the transition experiences of young people with disabilities. Paper presented at the Annual Meeting of the American Educational Research Association, San Francisco.

Wells, G. (1993). Re-evaluating the IRF sequence: A proposal for the articulation of theories of activity and discourse for the analysis of teaching and learning in the classroom. *Linguistics and Education*, 5, 1-37.

Wells, G. (1994). The complementary contributions of Halliday and Vygotsky to a 'language-based theory of learning'. *Linguistics and Education*, 6, 41-90.

Wertsch, J.V. (1991). *Voices of the mind: A sociocultural approach to mediated action*. Cambridge, Mass.: Harvard University Press.

Wertsch, J.V., Del Rio, P. & Alvarez, A. (eds.) (1995). *Sociocultural studies of mind*. Cambridge: Cambridge University Press.

Wyndhamn, J. & Säljö, R. (1997). Word problems and mathematical reasoning: A study of children's mastery of reference and meaning in textual realities. *Learning and Instruction*, 7, 361-82.

3 Instruction and Learning in Elementary School

Hartmut Giest

Introduction

The progress of mankind is characterised by a cumulative process of knowledge development gathered from a history of expertise within different subject matters. This knowledge is passed on from one generation to the next and increases steadily. The elder generation in this process takes over the part of teaching (in the sense of passing on their experience and knowledge) and the younger generation the part of learning (the appropriation of knowledge).

In more developed cultures the school takes over the main part of the process of transferring knowledge between generations. In this process teaching becomes a profession and learning a socially sanctioned task. Instruction therefore is the centre of school life.

The aim of our research has been to contribute to an increase in the quality of classroom activity in the sense of improving its efficiency with regard to the development of the children. Having this aim in mind we focused our research on interaction between teaching and learning in the classroom.

In this paper I shall compare two existing types of classroom teaching strategies that today are used in different schools, and their effects on the outcome of learning, with a third strategy which is still at the experimental level and which I shall call 'developmental instruction'. Notably, it is shown that the strategy of developmental instruction has stronger effects on children's learning and development than the two others.

Instructional Strategies in Classroom

Instruction in school can be characterised by a special kind of pedagogical interaction between learner and teacher or, in other words, by a special interrelation between learning and teaching. Particularities of the interrelation between actions of the teacher and the learners are character-ised as *instructional strategies*. Learning and teaching are two poles, which can be marked in different ways depending on instructional strategy. Dif-ferent instructional strategies are positioned on a spectrum between the two poles.

Direct Instruction

The following features are characteristic of this instructional strategy that characterises traditional classroom teaching:

— instruction is seen as being ahead of the development of the child
— often it is based on exogenetic theories of development
— the activity of the teacher is characterised by a high degree of pedagog-ical optimism (that means the teacher's trust in developmental effects as results of his own pedagogical activity or the belief in influencing the child's development by means of his own activity) and a relatively low trust in self-regulated activity of the children
— the teacher takes over the leading part in the classroom.

Helmke & Weinert (1997), Weinert (1996) call this instructional strategy 'direct instruction'.

Indirect Instruction

The alternative position is to stress domination of learning in class-room. This teaching strategy is called 'indirect instruction' and is character-ised by the following features:

— instruction follows development
— the instructional strategy is often based on endogenetic (or mentalistic) theories of development
— there is a low degree of pedagogical optimism and instead supporters of this position trust in (self-regulated) activity of the child
— the teacher increasingly takes the part of a moderator of the child's learn-ing, he accompanies the learning process more than he guides it.

The teaching strategy of direct instruction in one way or another represents the ideal of classroom in the former German Democratic Republic (GDR). Its effects are relatively well investigated.

The teaching strategy of indirect instruction ideally corresponds to the 'open instruction' but there is little evidence that it is put into a broader practice. Brügelmann (1996) reports that about 5-10 percent of the teachers in one and 20-30 percent in another investigation tried seriously to open their classroom in the sense of indirect instruction. This tendency, we expect, is also correct for the teachers in the state of Brandenburg at present.

Both strategies are in competition. The results of research on the controversy between advantages or disadvantages of more opened or closed strategies of instruction, direct or indirect instruction in the classroom are not very clear (Brügelmann 1996, 1998; Weinert 1996, 1997; Weinert & Helmke 1997; Einsiedler 1997).

To sum up one could say that now, as ever, all questions put in this regard have not yet been satisfactorily answered.

Developmental Instruction

If we at this point look at the present discussion of the background of the approaches of 'guided participation' or 'cognitive apprenticeship' (Newman, Griffin & Cole 1998; Rogoff 1990; Rojas-Drummond, Hernandez, Velez & Villagran 1998) it becomes evident that it is necessary to overcome the controversy between the two above mentioned strategies. It is our opinion that this can be done based on the conception of 'the formation of learning activity' (Lompscher 1999; Giest 1998b). This conception enables unity between learning and instruction in the classroom, self-regulated and systematic learning under the guidance of a teacher, project learning and course of instruction, learning and teaching activity in the sense of interaction, cooperation, and shared activity between student and teacher. I shall call this teaching strategy 'developmental instruction'.

Development is characterised by changes over time. These changes can be seen from a more quantitative perspective (application of existing knowledge and abilities) or qualitative perspective (formation or change in understanding concepts, cognitive structures, new psychic entities).

More than anything else, human development is a result of culture and its development throughout the history of mankind. Therefore instruction (directed on appropriation of culture leading to new psychic qualities) could not follow development but must be ahead of it. However, instruction is not independent of development. Development can only be influenced by instruction, if it is orientated to the zone of proximal development of the children.

If we pay attention to the special quality of the two zones of development it is possible to integrate moments of 'indirect instruction' (if the learning proceeds in the zone of current performance) and moments of 'direct instruction' (if the learning requests are in the zone of proximal development) into the teaching strategy 'developmental instruction'.

We can distinguish three stages or steps in developmental instruction.

In the *first step* the teacher allows a high degree of self-regulated learning and discovery learning in the zone of current development of the children. S/he tries to stimulate the emergence of problem situations in the classroom. The problems for their part in this phase of instruction correspond to main tasks, aims and contents of education.[1] In such problem situations learning goals emerge, when the learners' efforts are not only directed toward solving but also towards reflection on their own prerequisites in relation to the demands of the situation in order to find out what is not known or cannot be performed, and what — and why — something can be done well. These (conscious) learning goals are prerequisites and the motivational basis for the powerful learning effects of the direct instruction contained in the strategy of developmental instruction.

The *second step* is more characterised by direct instruction and systematic learning. The teacher's task is to help pupils to reach their own learning goals by stimulating their learning activity. The central point is to help children to acquire what is necessary to know and what must be performed in order to solve the problems and to reach the learning goals. Among other things this can be done by modelling the learning requests and stimulating the acquisition of learning actions.[2]

1. Because it is not arbitrary what children have to learn, one necessary step and starting point of the teacher's activity in the developmental instruction is the analysis of the subject of instruction (objective demands of learning, which are necessary for the children to acquire a learning subject) in connection with the children's prerequisites of learning — zone of current performance. On the basis of this analysis he or she has to build up a (here still abstract and hypothetical) process of development in learning activity (course of instruction). This course of instruction will again and again be modified in the real process of learning and instruction in classroom. A precise pre-planning for a single lesson is not possible but arises from the progress of the learning process and the process of the children's immediate development in classroom.
2. Stepwise formation of mental actions (see Galperin 1992).

In the *third step* of developmental instruction the children solve the problems by themselves and work out projects. The new zone of development allows self-regulated learning, discovery learning and a new phase of indirect instruction starts — but on a higher level of learning and instruction.

Arrangement of Investigations

The changes in school and classroom which were connected with the political change in the former GDR gave us the chance for comparative investigations on cognitive development on the background of different classroom praxis.

We focused our investigation on the effects of the above-mentioned instructional strategies concerning the cognitive development of children.

For that purpose we conducted several studies in an elementary science classroom which were focused on observation in the classroom and on analyses of the learning results. We completed these studies with interviews of teachers, university students and children in an effort to gain insight into their opinions about school and classroom.

Observation studies were carried out from 1984-87 in the GDR (dominated by direct instruction in classroom — see Giest 1991, 1997c) and from 1994-95 in the state of Brandenburg (tendencies towards indirect instruction — see Giest 1997a). In order to get a real picture of these tendencies a long-term study was started at the same time which included the observation of 80-100 teachers in classroom each year. These interview-studies were carried out from 1994-95 (Giest 1999b).

Learning-result studies were conducted from 1984-87 in the GDR (Giest 1991, 1995), and in the state of Brandenburg from 1992-96 (Giest 1994, 1996, 1998a, 1999).

In the GDR in 1988 a longitudinal study was started which continued to 1991 in order to investigate the particularities of the cognitive development of first-fourth grade children (concept formation and conceptual thinking), which was repeated in the state of Brandenburg in 1996.

In 1991 a formation experiment (FE) in classroom (4th graders — two experimental and three control-classes) was carried out (Giest 1994, 1996, 1997b). The approach used here (the teaching strategy of 'developmental instruction') aimed at development of scientific thinking in the primary school classroom.

A short overview of the investigations is given in Table 3.1.

OC-studies and I-studies

Subject	Kind of investigation	Random sample
Activity-orientation in classroom	Observation in lesson – GDR (1984-87)	200 teachers
	Observation in lesson/ registration of data via questionnaire (1994/95)	67 teachers
	Long-term study – started in 1994	80-100 teachers per year
Teachers' opinions of school and school lessons	Questionnaire	43 teachers
	Questionnaire	39 university students
Children's opinions	Interview	60 children

LR-studies

Subject	Kind of investigation	N	1	2	3	4	5	6	7	8
						Grades				
Knowledge acquisition in elementary science lessons	Tests (1984-87 – GDR)	1800		800	600	400				
	Test (1996 – state of Brandenburg)	964			204	216	277	267		
Problem-solving	Structured interviews 1992 – Berlin	237				118		119		
	Structured interviews 1994 – Brandenburg	234				72		88		74
Particularities of concept formation and conceptual thinking	Structured interviews (longitudinal study 1988-91 – GDR)	138	30	36	40	32				
	Structured interviews 1996 – Brandenburg	197	47	42	61	47				
	Structured interviews (longitudinal study) 1996 started in Brandenburg	240	60	60	60	60				

FE – study

Subject	Kind of investigation	N	1	2	3	4	5	6	7	8
Development of components of scientific thinking	Formation-experiment 1991					26				
	Control-classes					60				

Table 3.1. Overview of investigations of teaching strategies.

Comparing Different Instructional Strategies of Teachers' Activity and Learning Results

Direct Instruction: GDR Primary Science

Teachers' activity is central for direct instruction. However, the effect of classroom instruction on the cognitive development of children depends on children's learning activity. Teachers' activity must maintain children's own learning activity.

In connection with investigations which had the aim to evaluate the curriculum and central instructional material used in elementary science classrooms in the GDR, we observed teachers' activity. These classroom observations showed:

— that above all, the teachers concentrated their activity in the classroom on implementing the topics of the curriculum
— the textbook held a central role in the classroom
— teachers had great problems concerning time-management in the classroom, i.e., being able to complete the topics on the curriculum within the available time
— much emphasis was placed on curriculum topics and not enough on the activity of the learners; the observers noticed only poor cognitive activity of the children
— the instructional design was minimally oriented towards individual development of the children because of its orientation towards an abstract average child.

The analyses of children's knowledge with reference to the demands of the curriculum showed:

— good knowledge of facts (about 60-80%)
— increasing verbalism towards grade 4 (poor understanding of abstract concepts)
— poor performance regarding the understanding of connections between facts and problem solving
— poor development of components of scientific thinking
— poor competence regarding co-operative learning.

In sum, the analyses showed that the children were only to a lesser extent subjects of their own learning. Even the teachers themselves had only little chance of taking over the role of being subjects of their own activity, because the curriculum and central instructional material was created to determine their teaching activity as well as the learning activity of the children. Therefore, the results of the investigations were not very surprising for us. They showed some of the basic limitations of direct instruction and represented the central point of our criticism of this instructional strategy in classroom praxis. Because of these limitations we created an alternative approach to learning and instruction in classroom.

Tendencies of Indirect Instruction: Primary Science in the State of Brandenburg

Along with the political change which took place in 1998-90 in the former GDR, the school and classroom practice changed. Teachers were engaged in searching for new teaching strategies and tried to open up their classroom in the sense of indirect instruction.

With the help of a questionnaire we asked 43 teachers for their opinion about the basic concepts of primary school-planning, execution and evaluation of school lessons.

The teachers' opinions revealed that:

— the teacher and the children together discuss the aims and contents of the lessons and that they share decisions are much more important than the curriculum. (The teachers, however, rejected an opening of the classroom in the direction of parents, community or general public.)
— a good lesson is characterised by a variety of instructional methods and self-directed learning of the children.
— regarding the execution and evaluation of lessons, the teacher has to concentrate on the activity of the children.
— the planning of the lessons is mostly influenced by available teaching material and the questions and problems of the children.

Forty-nine percent of the teachers think that their lessons are good, whilst 47 percent think they are only partially good. The teachers' opinion is that their own qualifications have a positive effect on the quality of lessons, whilst a lack of time has a negative effect on good lessons.

In summary most of the teachers prefer open instruction as the basic concept of good lessons.

Having the findings of Brügelmann (1996, 1998) in mind we asked if the teachers really could put their opinions into practice. To answer this question we observed the same teachers, who took part in the first study in the classroom.

A main characteristic of indirect instruction is the orientation on the activity of the learners. Therefore we focused this research on the interaction between the activity of teachers and pupils in classroom. We were interested especially in the interaction between teaching and learning actions. Therefore we systematically observed components of action-regulation in children's learning activity (formation of action-goals, planning, executing and judging actions by the children) and how the personal characteristics of the teachers influenced these components.

The data emanating from the systematic observations showed that teachers do have some problems putting their good intentions into practice. We observed 70 lessons and found:

— The formation of learning goals was not a function of the children's activity but of the teacher's activity. In most cases the teacher told the children the aim of the lesson. Or it was developed by the teacher in conversation with the children.
— Self-regulated planning of the action by the children was almost missing.
— The execution of an action was either characterised by trial-and-error learning, or the teacher demonstrated the action and the children imitated it afterwards.
— Real co-operation between the teacher and the children seldom took place.
— Control and assessment of action in the lesson seldom took place. When it was observed, it took place with a view to the actual results of the action and not the aim and procedure of learning. And it was the teacher who guided control.

It seems to be a very difficult task to put good instruction in the classroom into practice. Open instruction seldom took place although the teachers preferred this conception.

In the interview-study we asked 60 children for their opinion about good lessons. These children were present at the observed lessons.

They answered that they often had to do what the teacher said. It was seldom that they could decide together with the teacher about the aims and content of lessons. They told us, however, that they enjoyed lessons if they could do something on their own and could participate in determining what would be done in the lesson. Notably, most of the children liked school. Only 10% said that they did not like to go to school.

The findings of the above research do not allow us to draw conclusions about the influence of the classroom on children's cognitive development. They merely show some of the expected conditions on which cognitive development depends.

In order to be able to generate hypotheses about trends in students' cognitive development in the classroom, we presented 4th, 6th and 8th graders with a complex problem task.

Some 234 students from two urban and two rural schools in the state of Brandenburg (122 girls, 112 boys, 72 4th graders; 88 6th graders, 74 8th graders) had to solve a problem task with ecological content. The task was presented in text form, supplemented with a pictorial representation.

The problem included in the text consisted of having to explain why (not as expected on the basis of mono-causal reasoning) the herds of cattle belonging to the nomads living in the Savannah areas of Africa had become smaller despite the construction of deep wells (a measure of developmental aid). The problem was solved in the context of one-to-one sessions which were recorded on videotapes. Where help was required for solving the problem, students were given information about underlying concepts and relationships by way of index cards in verbal or pictorial form.

Table 3.2 shows, in summary, how well the problem was solved by the entire sample, by grade level, by gender, as well as by performance level.[3]

The presented means correspond to the average of all forms of utilised help which contributed to the solution of the problem and were assessed on an interval scale ranging from 1 to 6. The value for the quality of problem solving has to be interpreted according to the grade scale in school ranging from 1 = best, to 6 = poorest academic performance.

---

3. General Academic Performance (GAP) represents the average of reports in major subjects.

	Mean	Std. dev.	Cases
Altogether	2.77	1.67	234
Boys	2.66	1.76	112
Girls	2.87	1.59	122
4th graders	2.90	1.78	72
6th graders	2.88	1.49	88
8th graders	2.50	1.76	74
Academic performance:			
Group I	2.62	1.70	78
Group II	2.90	1.61	78
Group III	2.78	1.72	78

Table 3.2. Children's performance level differentiated by gender, grade and problem-solving.

As a trend, we found differences between classes, between gender and academic performance (boys solved the problem better than girls, students in 8th grade performed better than those in 4th and 6th grade, students with high academic performance outperformed those with poor academic performance).[4] These differences are not statistically significant, however. This is rather surprising, because, after all, there were four school years of instruction between 4th and 8th graders. An analysis of variance[5] (quality of problem solving by type of school, position of school — rural or urban, mean grades, grade level, and gender) yielded a significant main effect ($p \leq .03$). However, this is mainly accounted for by academic performance ($p \leq .012$). There is some evidence though that the task used was untypical for the common lesson. At this age boys normally show weaker academic performance than girls, but here they solved the problem better than girls.

4. The slightly better results of group III (poor academic performance) in comparison with group II can be explained by the interaction between academic performance and gender: Two thirds of the boys are represented in group III, however, they generally solved the problem task better than girls.
5. 5 between subjects analyses of variance (ANOVA).

It can be concluded, that four years of classroom instruction did not have considerable influence on the development of the ability to solve problems adequately. This is a clear indicator in support of my thesis about the rather small effect of today's instruction on the development of cognitive abilities (at least for the specific ones within the examined domain).

In another study the extent, content and quality of children's knowledge was analysed. In special investigations (Giest 1999a) we found that children of the examined age had great problems dealing with concepts about subjects connected to social life — e.g., 'work' (even on a very low or elementary level of scientific thinking) but not so with concepts connected to nature and science. Therefore, in order to investigate the development of scientific thinking (concept formation and conceptual thinking) we examined their knowledge about some plant-species. This subject is a prototype for science study in primary school.

Contrary to the problem-solving task the analysis of selected knowledge supports a hypothesis of development. But it is not clear if this is an effect of instruction and learning in classroom. In everyday-life, as well as in the classroom, children are confronted with many species of plants. We have to pay special attention to specific features of knowledge (e.g., structure, differentiation, hierarchical organisation). These features correspond to scientific thinking in a higher degree than to everyday thinking. They are higher forms of cognitive functions and depend on explicit learning, whereas primary cognitive functions (e.g., mechanical memory) depend much more on implicit or unconscious learning (Geary 1995). Our findings were that the extent of knowledge was increasing. (As an example the 6th graders reproduced more different tree species than 4th graders. However, the structure of the knowledge was less developed. On average the children reproduced eight tree species. We could have expected 12 common tree species — the fruit-tree species like apple, cherry, plum, pear; the species linden, oak, chestnut, birch as well as pine, spruce, fir and larch, which can be easily named.) The children's knowledge was rather abstract and poorly concrete. Only 16 percent were able to describe in detail the tree species of their own choice, so that the species could be identified by the given features. Fourth and 6th graders outperformed 3rd and 5th graders.

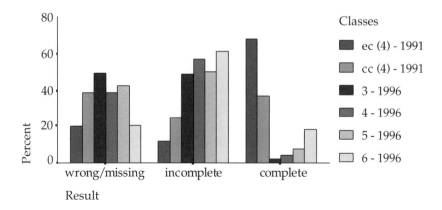

Figure 3.1. Children's results of solving the Conceptual-Pyramid-Task (1991 and 1996).

Comparing the Effects of Different Instructional Strategies: Aspects of Children's Development of Concept Formation and Conceptual Thinking

Which of our investigated teaching strategies has the best effect on children's cognitive development? First, to get an answer to this question we compared findings from the learning result-studies 1988-91 (direct instruction) and 1996 (tendencies of indirect instruction) and from our formation experiment-study 1991(experimental classes — developmental instruction; control classes — direct instruction).

In order to prove the generality and integration of the concepts in a conceptual system, we asked the children to generate a conceptual hierarchy (class inclusion) for the generic term 'plant'. As can be seen clearly in Figure 3.1, the solving of the task currently creates the greatest problems — the teaching strategy which we find in today's classrooms has apparently little influence on this aspect of children's cognitive development. But *both* control and experimental classes in our formation experiment-study of 1991 clearly got better results in comparison with the classes examined in 1996. Only the 6th graders had similar results. In 1991, 68 percent of the children of our experimental classes and 37 percent of the children of the control classes (both 4th grade) accomplished the task. In 1996, only 18 percent of the pupils of 6th grade were able to do so. We interpreted such a low hier-

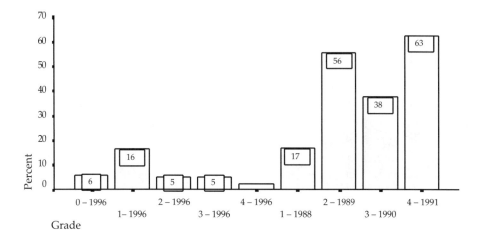

Figure 3.2. Systematic explanation of identified concepts in 1-4th grades (1996 and 1988-91).[6]

archical organisation of available concepts as a lack in the formation of scientific concepts and conceptual thinking. It has to be pointed out here that this task was not explicitly practiced in our experimental lessons but we made a point of forming the learning activity of the children while they at the same time were given freedom for autonomous learning acts. Nevertheless, this strategy showed the greatest influence on the development of cognitive performance assessed in this study.

Another investigation was focused on the concept formation and concept identification of plants.

Structured interviews were used to analyse the learning results comparing the studies of 1988-91 and 1996. The results showed that with the identification of pictorially presented plants the children succeeded as well in 1996 as in 1988-91. There were no significant differences between the two random samples. Explanation of the conceptual identification: Sensorical features are dominant in comparison to categorical ones.

6. In 1996 we also examined children in the eldest kindergarten-group — grade 0) The unexpected difference between grade 2 (1989) and grade 3 (1990) cannot be explained satisfactorily. It looks like a regression (not significant). Possibly the reason is, that in grade 2 the curriculum was explicitly oriented on the morphological features of plants but this was not the case in grade 3.

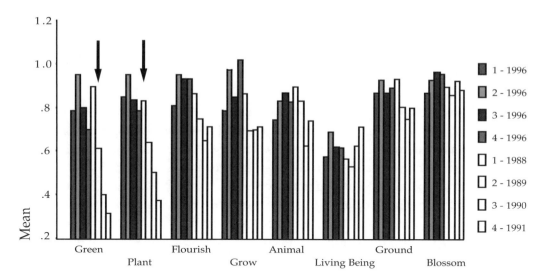

Figure 3.3. Rating of verbally-given features for flowers being plants in 1-4th grades (1996 and 1988-91).

We analysed the explanations of the defining features of the identified concepts (e.g., the plant is characterised by the feature-set — fruits, leafs, stem and root) and found significant differences between 1991 and 1996. The reason for this finding can be found in the curriculum, which in 1988-91 included the above mentioned feature-set of plants but not in 1996.

The same results were found when we asked the children to explain systematically their decision, whether pictorially presented objects are plants or not (see Figure 3.2). We assumed that children having appropriated components of scientific concepts and thinking must use a relatively constant feature-set in their explanations (whether this or that pictorial presented object is a plant or not).

Finally we asked the children to rate verbally-given features for flowers to be plants. They had to decide whether in 10 given sentences it was correctly explained why flowers are plants: 'Flowers are plants because they are green/ planted/ they flourish/ grow/ are not animals/ living beings/ grow out of the ground/ have the features — fruit/ blossoms, leaves, stems and roots'. Less irrelevant features were interpreted as an indicator of components of scientific concepts and scientific thinking. In 1988-91 the children marked significantly less irrelevant features (see Figure 3.3).

In sum the results show that in 1996 the children failed the cognitive demands which correspond to scientific thinking. But there were no differences between 1996 and 1988-91 in children's mechanical memorising (reproduction of single facts, free recall — low levelled or primary cognitive demands).

The effects of the classroom with reference to the cognitive development of children seem to have decreased since the 1988-91 study. Higher levelled cognitive demands (e.g., learning of scientific concepts) depend on explicit learning. Explicit learning is a complex competence which demands a systematic formation of learning activity in the classroom. Neither direct nor indirect instruction includes this task, so both strategies were not able to show classroom-effects on cognitive development. Only 'developmental instruction' (formation of learning activity) showed an effect in the desired direction.

Conclusions

Our investigations have shown that traditional classroom instruction in the form of direct teaching has little influence on children's cognitive development: the dominant orientation on teaching only restrains children's learning (without consideration of the interaction with the children's learning activity).

In today's schools (at least in those investigated in the state of Brandenburg and Berlin) teachers do try to pay more attention to opening up their instruction for children's activity. But relying only on the self-regulated learning of children without guiding them into good learning activities will not lead to better results. On the contrary, their cognitive development will be less.

Our investigations have shown, however, a possible approach that could improve classroom instruction so that it affects the development of children's concept formation and conceptual thinking. This can be done by paying more attention to the unity of learning and teaching in the classroom (see also Vermunt & Verloop 1999). We must strongly stress, though, the importance of interaction between children's and teacher's concrete activity in the classroom. This is the deeper sense of developmental instruction (and of an action-orientated classroom and is often to be found in demand in current discussions in primary schools). The main components in this approach are: formation of learning-goals, planning of learning-actions, regulation of action-execution and action-control. If we further take into account that development is characterised by a dynamic relationship between the zone of current development and the zone of proximal development, then we can create a constructive synthesis between direct and indirect instruction in the classroom with regard to developmental tasks: Instruction in the classroom has to stress self-regulated learning and indirect instruction if the learning requests are related to the zone of current performance of the children, but if the learning requests are related to the zone of proximal development, stress must be placed on guided learning and direct instruction.

References

Brügelmann, H. (1996). Noch einmal: Was heißt 'Öffnung des Unterrichts' — und welche Strukturen setzt sie voraus? Projekt OASE, Bericht 4, Siegen. Primarstufe, FB 2 der Universität-Gesamthochschule.

Brügelmann, H. (1998). Öffnung des Unterrichts, Befunde und Probleme der empirischen Forschung. In H. Brügelmann, M. Fölling-Albers & S. Richter (eds.), *Jahrbuch Grundschule: Fragen der Praxis — Befunde der Forschung*. Seelze/ Velber: Friedrich.

Einsiedler, W. (1997). Unterrichtsqualität und Leistungsentwicklung: Literaturüberblick. In F.E. Weinert & A. Helmke (eds.), *Entwicklung im Grundschulalter*. Weinheim: Beltz.

Galperin, P.Y. (1992). Stage-by-stage formation as a method of psychological investigation. *Journal of Russian and East European Psychology*, 30(4), 60-80.

Geary, D.C. (1995). Reflections of evolution and culture in child's cognition. *American Psychologist*, 50, 24-36.

Giest, H. (1991). Psychologische Aspekte der Aneignung fachspezifischen Wissens im Rahmen sachbezogenen Lernens. *Empirische Pädagogik*, 5(3), 229-43.

Giest, H. (1994). Rinderherdenaufgabe — ein Beispiel für Problemlöseanforderungen in der Grundschule. *Lern- und Lehrforschung, Berichte*, 9. Potsdam: Universität Potsdam, 59-113.

Giest, H. (1995). Zum Problem der Begriffsbildung in der Grundschule. *Lern- und Lehrforschung, Berichte*, 10. Potsdam: Universität Potsdam, 35-79.

Giest, H. (1996). Besonderheiten des Problemlösens bei Schülern 4., 6. und 8. Klassen. *Empirische Pädagogik*, 10(3), 307-42.

Giest, H. (1997a). Wie handlungsorientiert ist der Sachunterricht? In B. Marquardt-Mau et al. (eds.), *Forschung zum Sachunterricht*. (Probleme und Perspektiven des Sachunterrichts, Bd. 7). Bad Heilbrunn: Klinkhardt.

Giest, H. (1997b). Zur kausalgenetischen Methode in der Unterrichtsforschung. In E. Glumpler & S. Luchtenberg (eds.), *Jahrbuch Grundschulforschung*, Bd. 1. Weinheim: Deutscher Studienverlag.

Giest, H. (1997c). Voraussetzungen und Bedingungen des Sachunterrichts in den

Neuen Bundesländern. In H. Giest (ed.), *Sachunterricht — Fragen, Probleme, Standpunkte zur Entwicklung des Sachunterrichts aus der Sicht der Neuen Bundesländer.* Potsdam: Universität Potsdam.

Giest, H. (1998a). Grundlegende Bildung und Kognition im Sachunterricht. In B. Marquardt-Mau & H. Schreier, *Grundlegende Bildung im Sachunterricht.* (Probleme und Perspektiven des Sachunterrichts, Bd. 8). Bad Heilbrunn: Klinkhardt.

Giest, H. (1998b). Von den Tücken der empirischen Unterrichtsforschung. In H. Brügelmann, M. Fölling-Albers & S. Richter (eds.), *Jahrbuch Grundschule: Fragen der Praxis — Befunde der Forschung.* Seelze: Friedrich.

Giest, H. (1998c). Unterrichtsstrategien und Lernergebnisse. *Lern- und Lehrforschung, Berichte,* 18. Potsdam: Universität Potsdam, 125-46.

Giest, H. (1999a). Kann man das Lernen lehren oder nur lernen — Unterrichtsstrategien zwischen Lernen und Belehren. In H. Giest & G. Scheerer-Neumann (eds.), *Jahrbuch Grundschulforschung,* Bd. 2. Weinheim, Beltz: Deutscher Studien Verlag.

Giest, H. (1999b). *Lernen und Lehren in der Grundschule — Empirische Erhebungen im Sachunterricht an Brandenburger Schulen.* Potsdam: Universität Potsdam.

Lompscher, J. (1999). Learning activity and its formation: Ascending from the abstract to the concrete. In M. Hedegaard & J. Lompscher (eds.), *Learning activity and development.* Aarhus: Aarhus University Press.

Newman, D., Griffin, P. & Cole, M. (1998). *The construction zone: Working for cognitive change in school.* Cambridge: Cambridge University Press.

Rogoff, B. (1990). *Apprenticeship in thinking: Cognitive development in social context.* Oxford: Oxford University Press.

Rojas-Drummond, S., Hernandez, G., Velez, M. & Villagran, G. (1998). Cooperative learning and the appropriation of procedural knowledge by primary school children. *Learning and Instruction,* 8(1), 137-63.

Vermunt, J.D. & Verloop, N. (1999). Congruence and friction between learning and teaching. *Learning and Instruction,* 9(3), 257-81.

Weinert, F.E. (1996). Für und Wider die 'neuen Lerntheorien' als Grundlage pädagogisch-psychologischer Forschung. In E. Witruk & G. Friedrich (eds.), *Pädagogische Psychologie im Streit um ein neues Selbstverständnis. Bericht über die 5. Tagung der Fachgruppe 'Pädagogische Psychologie' in der Deutschen Gesellschaft für Psychologie e.V. in Leipzig 1995.* (Psychologie, Bd. 12). Landau: Verlag Empirische Pädagogik.

Weinert, F.E. & Helmke, A. (1997). Theoretischer Ertrag und praktischer Nutzen der SCHOLASTIK-Studie zur Entwicklung im Grundschulalter. In F.E. Weinert & A. Helmke (eds.), *Entwicklung im Grundschulalter.* Weinheim: Beltz.

4 Expanding the Predominant Interpretation of ZPD in Schooling Contexts: Learning and Mutuality

Peter Kutnick

Introduction

It is not the intention of this paper to fully criticise the theoretical basis of Vygotsky's theory of the development of mental processes and the social support underlying the theory. Rather, it is the naive application of Vygotsky's work to the educational and instructional field that illustrates problems created for the theory by those who consider their work as Vygotskian.

There are two levels of critique pursued in this paper, that of historical background of the theory and that of applications in the real world of relationships and educational contexts. The historical background concerns the origin of Vygotsky's theory as taking place in a culture, but a culture that was undergoing radical change. Vygotsky's study of the socialisation of rural and communal village life into state dominated collectives holds much interest for the understanding of development from anthropological as well as anthromorphic/ontogenetic views; both are discussed by Vygotsky (1966) under the title of 'Genesis of Higher Mental Functions'. This research leads to practical critiques concerning the Zone of Proximal Development as it has been interpreted and used in the West and its real usage in (formal and informal) teaching and learning situations.

As will be shown, students' and pupils' own development has a strong reliance on their social relationships which are mutual (as opposed to hierarchical) even as they take place within a culturally mediated situation. Examples from three different studies are provided. The studies show support for learning in real classroom situations among teachers training for work in primary schools, among pupils in classrooms, and by competent teachers in secondary schools who 'plan' peer tutoring to support the learning processes within their classrooms. These studies challenge 'conventional' statements attributed to Vygotsky concerning the ZPD, especially the relationship of ZPD to educational and learning processes that may take place within schools. Fundamentally, the studies show that a mutual/sharing among equal partners form a basis for learning; this should not be seen to seriously challenge Vygotsky's view of ZPD, but offers a different view of ZPD from writers who consider themselves 'Vygotskian'. Thus, this paper will endeavour to show the historic origin of ZPD and how it has been interpreted as based on a hierarchical (expert/novice) social relationship. Further, the paper will extend the interpretation of ZPD to show the importance of mutuality in allowing the alternate conditions for learning to take place.

Historical/Theoretical Critiques

For the convenience of this paper, the history of Vygotsky's theory can be sub-divided into three sections: the history of Vygotsky and the time that he worked within the Soviet Union; the theory itself (here limited to the Zone of Proximal Development); and immediate educational implications.

History behind Vygotsky's Theory

Exploration of the history behind the theory will not delve into Vygotsky's life, aside from noting that many dramatic political changes occurred during his lifetime and are represented in his theory (Davydov 1994). Bruner (1985) applauds Vygotsky's integration of psychology and sociology into a developmental theory that was used to solve the very practical problem of overcoming illiteracy and innumeracy in a country dominated by peasant societies, within the framework of historical materialism. The historical view of the theory, thus, has both political and practical aspects: Politically, Vygotsky's analysis of the role of historical materialism shaping people's consciousness was amply demonstrated in the early comparisons of pre-literate and pre-numerate peasant society to workers on the newly collectivised state farms. Vygotsky's research has been interpreted by Bruner (1984) as showing the impact of collectivism on peasant thought; giving rise to Vygotsky's stages and an 'anthropomorphization' of cognitive development.

Let me now return to the main theme — the hidden agenda in Vygotsky's idea of the zone of proximal development. I believe that the idea is a fusion of the idea of collectivism and of the role of consciousness. Indeed, as I see it, the ZPD is a direct expression of the way in which the division of labour expresses itself in a collectivist society. It involves the sharing not only of knowledge but also of consciousness, albeit an historically shaped consciousness. Those who 'know' more, those who have 'higher' consciousness share it with those who know less, who are less developed in consciousness and intellectual control. Each in his or her own time comes to have a mind shaped by the history and economic circumstances of the period ... In the case of the Uzbek peasant collective worker, it is brought by the direct participation in the more advanced technical life of the kolkhoz, in whose day-to-day process of production and planning he participates ... it is a matter of somebody with knowledge and awareness of scaffolding a task for somebody without knowledge and awareness until the latter becomes capable of reaching higher ground. (Bruner 1984, 94-95)

This embodies an interesting contradiction between the potential of the theory and its historical/material use by a number of its interpreters. The theory v. interpretation argument is framed by Wertsch (1985) in consideration of the enhancement of change in society. Citing Marx's Theses on Feuerbach (1845/1994), in which the infamous quotation of 'philosophers have sought to interpret the world, what matters is to change it' is made, we see Vygotsky trying to advance an illiterate peasant society to a technical/collective one. Here we must consider the fundamental point of socialisation and cultural transmission: Does Vygotsky present a picture of psychological theory helping to 'break the mould' or simply a theory of social instruction? The literature is ambiguous, Vygotskians such as Davydov (1994) have written of change as mould breaking (with strong political overtones) and even Bruner saw this potential in his early comments on Vygotsky. On the other hand, forces of cultural socialisation, perhaps exemplified in work by Cole (1976), Bruner (1985, when referring to scaffolding), Cole & Wertsch (1996), only describe the process of instruction (but not a dynamic of change). Daniels (1993) refers to this focusing on instruction as a 'de-politicizing' of Vygotsky's theory. Smith's (1996), and also Duveen's (1994), comparison of Vygotsky and Piaget provides greater focus for these interpretations, noting Vygotskians as presenting a 'transmission' argument while Piaget establishes a theory which allows for social change. In an applied situation such as schooling, transmission has been aligned with 'passivism' (Beveridge 1997) — a real contradiction within the interpreted sup-position that Vygotsky presented a theory of 'change'. The political analysis appears to be well made; that historical-materialist analysis provides a tell-ing picture of society including its means of production and the social rela-tionships that exist to support it. With regard to change, Vygotsky may have been on less certain ground. He tells us that within the inception of the Soviet state the social relationships of the collective (demonstrating mutuality) changed from the hierarchy of peasant life (landowners v. serfs) and this change in material circumstances was associated with change in cognitive circumstances.

Theory of ZPD

Vygotsky's equation of anthropological/cultural development with ontogenetic development was most forcefully made in Luria's book (1976), *Cognitive Development*, with qualifications therein by Michael Cole; this was also supported in the statement by Bruner (1984): 'Luria most certainly dis-cusses the pre-collective peasant as if he were a child in need of induction into the grown-up world of the collective farm' (p. 94). Vygotsky, in fact, stated:

The very essence of cultural development is in the collision between mature cul-tural forms of behaviour with the primitive forms that characterize the child's be-haviour. (Vygotsky 1966/1991, 34)

What evidence we have of the transition is supplied by examples of col-lective life (provided by Vygotsky and Luria) — which raises a contradiction as to the material conditions which allowed the transition to take place, and reflecting upon the earlier question of cultural transmission (with its ZPD agent) versus cultural change. In commenting on the material conditions of transition, we are given examples of movement in thought when 'peasant' labour became 'collective' labour. We are also introduced to the term ZPD as an explanatory devise.

The distance between actual developmental level as determined by independent problem solving and the level of potential development as determined through problem solving under adult guidance or in collaboration with more capable peers. (Vygotsky 1978)

The historical/use of theory question I wish to pose is whether the ZPD def-inition in this presently accepted guise is adequate as a sole explanation (or the valued explanation) for the peasant/collectivist transition. Theoretically, we must consider other aspects of Vygotsky's writing, and the basis of ZPD in social and emotional relationships:

... it is interesting to note that the genetic role of the collective changes in the de-velopment of the child's behaviour, that the higher functions of the child's think-ing first manifest themselves in the collective life of children and only then lead to the development of reflection in the child's own behaviour. Piaget has found that precisely the sudden transition from preschool age to school age leads to a change in the forms of collective activity and that on this basis the child's own thinking also changes. (Vygotsky 1966/1991, 36)

Consideration that movement from peasant to collectivised society and the definition of ZPD (above) hardly appears an adequate explanation of the transfer. This interesting section in 'Genesis of Higher Mental Functions' (1966) concerns types of social relationships that facilitate the transition: Vygotsky drew upon Piaget's social research, the *Moral Judge-ment of the Child* (1932), to describe the social relationships of the collective as having a non-hierarchical, co-operative orientation to problem solving and cognitive development. This collective alternative to peasant hierar-chies is neglected in most discussions of Vygotsky and development, and one wonders why.

The neglect of the potential for development generated between mutual-ly co-operating peers is emphasised in the culturally bound interpretations presented by Bruner, Cole, Wood and Wertsch. Political and methodological arguments may be drawn upon which help to explain the asymmetrical focus of these ZPD interpretations. Politically, Vygotsky's post-revolution and collective support for mass literacy was paralleled in American move-ments towards 'collective education' that was building up through the 1920s; but, as Pepitone (1980) emphasises, once American capital under-stood this implication, funding for peer-based research and teaching was cut dramatically circa 1930.

Wertsch (1985) clearly states that Vygotsky's account 'reduces develop-ment to learning in instruction' (p. 73) while identifying that ZPD incor-porates a situational definition, inter-subjectivity and semiotic mediation to reinforce the existence of the asymmetrical relationship. This ZPD definition explains an asymmetrical teacher-pupil dynamic that characterises the control of knowledge in society (and classrooms) but excludes alternative, co-operative relationships that may also promote learning and development. This exclusion is difficult to attribute solely to Vygotsky (who actually realised the alternative power of the collective in 'Genesis of Higher Mental Functions' (1966)). And, it is unlikely that Vygotsky's interpreters were unaware of the mutual relational alternative for cognitive enhancement researched in the field of socio-cognitive development (for further discussion see Smith 1989; Bearison 1982; Doise & Mugny 1984; Perret-Clermont 1980).

Educational/Developmental Implications

In the interpreters' favour, the existence of the relational dynamics and knowledge asymmetry characterised in their interpretation of ZPD is a good working hypothesis (or explanation) for the development of language in early childhood cited by Bruner (1983, 1985) and in scaffolding and contingencies used to promote teaching and learning described by Wood (1991; originally considered in Wood, Bruner & Ross 1976). We can also identify that the methodology drawn upon in these studies made the asymmetry both an easy and logical explanation.[1] A tension between asymmetrical transmission and symmetrical mutuality is exemplified in Bruner's (1983, 1984) interpretation of language development in the asymmetrical child-parent relationship. Bruner attempted to show how child conversations and words are 'scaffolded' and 'appropriated' (for an explanation of these terms, see Mercer 1991) by parents into sequences of culturally approved language. Bruner (1983) uses the description of mother as an 'agent of the culture' (p. 94) and later states:

The mother restricts the task to the degrees of freedom that she believes that the child can handle, and once he shows signs of doing better than that, she raises the level both of her expectations and of her demands on the child … For the aim of her fine-tuning is certainly not refinement for its own sake. It is the achievement of functional appropriateness that she is after. (p. 124)

---

1. This point was confirmed in conversation with J. Bruner, Aarhus, June, 1998.

In focusing solely on the child-parent relationship we are, perhaps, seduced into believing that language must be culturally approved. Writers (as Bruner 1984) who cite language as an example of ZPD often underplay the importance of a relational basis to language development; that is, social interactions take place in the security of the mother-child dyad. Curiously, Bruner does not discuss effects of that dyadic relationship in any but cognitive terms and this descriptive approach is similar to that described in Wood's view of 'scaffolding'. Both researchers neglect the possibility of an alternative development in co-operation. Drawing upon Wood & Middleton (1975) as a further example, we are all probably aware of the impact of this 'classic' study for our current concepts of scaffolding and contingency. While acknowledging that human development is 'essentially social and interactional' (p. 181), they set-up a fascinating experiment that is discussed in purely cognitive/social terms. The critical point to be made is not of the quality of the study, but within its method. The authors only drew upon mother-child (asymmetrical) dyads as subjects. 'Subjects: Twelve children aged between 3.2 and 4.2 and their mothers' (p. 183). They cite that 'It is possible that mothers "know" on the basis of their general knowledge or understanding of the child the best level to intervene' (p. 182), but do not consider that the quality of the relationship will affect the problem solving outcome. Wood, Bruner & Ross (1976) used a tutor in this further experiment and stated that the tutor (Gail Ross) 'brought to the task a gentle appreciative approach to the children' (p. 92) yet the discussion did not mention the tutor in a relational sense — only in terms of contingency and scaffolding. These 'classic' studies and experiments were intent on establishing a Vygotskian view of the asymmetrical ZPD, and the studies did so! In neglecting to question the closeness of mother-child, the sensitive tutor relationships and the affect of 'closeness' the researchers were led to an uncritical assessment of asymmetrical ZPD as well as limiting ZPD to 'enculturation' — disallowing the relational dynamic that may promote 'change'.

While language and scaffolding are good examples of asymmetric semiotic and cultural mediation, we must be aware and open to the multiple other forms of semiotic actions that can take place between people; perhaps, some encouraging change. The apparent contradiction between development through social/cultural relations and the possibility of change are characterised in Bearison's (1982) discussion:

... whereas for dialogical theories (as in Vygotsky) it is language, as a shared social symbol system, that embodies the social origins of thought, for Piaget it is from the co-ordination of actions that thought arises. (p. 206)

Studies of co-ordination of action have the 'potential to reveal more about the process of cognitive change than the verbal products of childrens' solitary reflections' (Bearison 1982, 206).

In this discussion of current interpretations of ZPD and aligned processes, I have tried to identify that there is more insight to be gained than simply stating that the mother-child dyad is a potent learning (ZPD) force. Embodied within the dyad is a social relationship that expresses an emotional security and facilitates learning and instruction between an expert and a novice. Cooperative or symmetrical relationships are often overlooked as a site for ZPD precisely because peers do not often show the emotional security that will allow them to 'learn together' as found in UK-based studies (Galton 1990). Only in the specific situation where peers maintain a secure and supportive relationship are they likely to co-act towards common resolutions of problems (Kutnick 1994) and allow a symmetric ZPD.

Let me digress here to make two summary points before moving the discussion forward:

1. The asymmetric social relationship which often describes effective instances of ZPD has an underlying element of emotional security; and
2. Vygotsky, himself, was aware of the relational basis of ZPD, but was also aware that this quality of relationship could take place among peers as well as expert/novice. As van der Veer and Valsiner (1991) identify:

In the investigation of the cognitive development of the child it is usual to think that indicative of the child's intellect in only that which that child can do himself ... It is usual to think that indicative of the degree of development of the child's intellect is the independent, unassisted solving of the task by the child. If we would ask him leading questions or demonstrated to him how to solve the task and the child solved the task after the demonstration, or if the teacher started to solve the task and the child finished it or solved it in cooperation with other children, in short, if the child diverged however so much from the independent solving of the task, then such a solution would already not be indicative of the development of his intellect. (Vygotsky 1933/1935, 41)

The political and methodological criticism of asymmetric interpretations in the ZPD should not challenge the benefits of the didactic relationship as seen in Bruner's discussion of language development. It does, however, point to a substantive shortcoming of this as a 'sole' interpretation of the theory. Minimally, as many teachers will confirm, pupils are capable of creative work, and much of this work is undertaken amongst mutually (naive) classroom peers. If Piaget's theory of moral development appears to creep back into the picture, the paper would not be adverse to equating Vygotsky's work to a heteronomous morality; thus asking us to extend ZPD to include the role and use of co-operation (leading to a relational theory of autonomy, see Kutnick 1990). An alternative theoretical development by researchers as Rogoff (1990), characterised as neo-Vygotskian, has moved to include mutual peer relations that can support cognitive development into the ZPD; in this development the asymmetrical and mutual relations are equated to focused and open-ended tasks as two types of cognitive development respectively.

Studies of Mutuality, a Critique of ZPD

The foregoing discussion does not preclude us from acknowledging (as Cole & Wertsch 1996) that both the child and the environment are active contributors to development. This discussion questions how much 'control' cultural heritage is attributed within cognitive activity. It is comparatively easy to show that the prominent interpretation of ZPD can be used in small intimate situations (ex. mother-child dyads) but difficult to apply in a classroom of 25-35 children (see Bennett et al. 1984; Munn 1992; Bliss et al. 1996). Yet, there are a number of practical examples in real classrooms and teaching/learning situations where principles of ZPD have been found to take place. Within these examples readers will notice that the relational basis of ZPD has expanded to include symmetry or mutuality and these provide a number of insights into current social issues.

The Studies

While not denying the important role of asymmetrical relationships in ZPD, three brief studies will be drawn upon to show the parallel importance of symmetry and mutual relationships. The studies are concerned with teaching and training of teachers for the classroom as well as achievement within the classroom. The studies are diverse in focus and should involve a degree of self-explanation.

The background of the first two studies is in initial teacher training in the UK. Over the last two decades, there has been a double-faceted move towards school-based (reflective-apprenticeship) training with a strong degree of external accountability (as in the early work of Vygotsky, there is little opportunity to understand this research without acknowledging that there is also a political explanation for its current state). More practically, these moves have meant that programmes for training have moved towards:

1. Partnerships between schools and universities, where a reflective 'reproduction of practical knowledge' is gained to provide explanation of
   classroom experience (Edwards 1995), and
2. 'Competence' driven assessment of student achievement by classroom
   outcomes reigns, a form of 'performativity' (Ball 1994).

These moves have lead to a tension in perspective of teacher training between those who see the potential of a Vygotskian pedagogic process of 'induction of novices by experts into culturally based understandings and skills' (Edwards 1995, 598) and those who see this training as a simple list-ing of professional competencies to be assessed in the course of training. Within this frame, a small-scale study (Kutnick 1997) was undertaken with-in one of the most advanced school-based post-graduate training courses in the UK (which has been in existence for over twenty-five years). Students finishing their course were asked to complete an open-ended questionnaire (adapted from a previous study by Lacey 1977); reflecting upon and de-scribing the most rewarding aspects of the course. Of the 55 students who completed training to become teachers in primary schools, 47 (88.6%) of the students completed the questionnaires. Seventy-one percent of those who answered this question wrote of student-peer 'companionship' as the most rewarding and learning facilitative aspect of the university course. Com-ments included:

— meeting so many people of the course and sharing ideas
— people and discussion
— meeting other students — advise and encouragement
— support gained from student groups — being able to discuss problems
  and successes together

— meeting everybody and talking through school experience
— ideas for teaching — from other students
— interaction with other students
— friendship and support/ideas from fellow students

Thus, while these training teachers were able to demonstrate classroom competencies and performed well within the culturally defined asymmetric situation with their mentors and tutors, it was the mutuality and support of their peers that helped them achieve this success.

Diverting the flow of discussion into the realm of classrooms, I now cite case studies of classrooms within the West Indies where observations and interviews were made concerning pupils who were successful and unsuccessful in classroom achievement (Kutnick, Layne & Jules 1997). The study was grounded in previous research which showed that girls generally achieved better test results than boys and the concern that too many males were withdrawing from school (Jules & Kutnick 1990). In the study, naturalistic observations in nine classrooms (including four secondary school classrooms and five primary school classrooms) were undertaken by two research observers who observed over a full school year. From analysis of field notes and interviews we found: classroom teaching was highly didactic, at both primary and secondary school levels; classroom activity showed that participation rates were higher for girls than for boys (this was not surprising as didactic teachers tended to select those deemed capable of answering questions in preference to those who did not volunteer or those who were deemed low achievers); in its extreme form (often found in these classrooms) the didactic nature of teaching discouraged student participation. A research observer reported:

A teacher, in School B — Form One, was noted by the students as using a didactic teaching style, and the one-way communication confused them.
Ms G has distributed workbooks and the students are correcting the work previously completed by other students in the class. They are very confused by what the teacher is trying to explain to them and so the exercise is not proceeding very well.

An alternate, more inclusive way of teaching involved the mutual cooperation of the children, which can be demonstrated by another English teacher:

The teacher then gave the students an exercise to do in pairs. Hansa and Tricia were the first pair of students to finish.

T: Excellent, continue with the other questions.

When all the students completed the exercise she corrected the questions orally and every student had the correct answers. The teacher is very patient with the students of Form One L. She praises her students and they enjoy her class thoroughly.

Students, especially girls, showed a mutual way of 'coping' with the predominantly didactic teaching. They formed cliques or groups for both intellectual and social support. Girls did not undertake schoolwork and studying on their own. In each of the classes observed, groups of girls often came together for social support as well as academic sharing of schoolwork. The best described of these groups took place in School B — Form One. The researcher stated:

During this 15-minute period I went to check on the female students. The Home Economics teacher was not present because she was attending a staff meeting. The female students are in their form classroom. The students of East Indian descent are all doing school assignments together. Dana and Suzette are doing English homework. Melanie is alone reading. The other students are conversing about the group which they formed; SAS — Single Average Sisters. They are discussing the rules under which all members must conform:

— Everything discussed must remain within the group.
— If any member has a problem they must first seek help within the group.
— No member must bad-mouth another member of the group.

The SAS's solidarity provided social support and the girls shared information for schoolwork as well. This group had to be 'officially' dismantled because other members of the class thought it may have been based on racial lines (there were rumours that SAS meant Single African Sisters). When it was dismantled, its members told the researcher:

Toni explained that 'Average' was used because the members did not want to be vain and label themselves as brilliant. On the other hand they know that they are not dull. Krystal explained that the dismantling of the group was a disadvantage to her because the group was basically a study group and that the members were support systems when needed. She also said that the group members ensured that homework was done on time, something she was not able to accomplish on her own. The SAS group members are very disappointed because they feel that they were not given an opportunity to voice their opinion.

And, finally, one aspect of mutual cooperation that further helped girls in their achievement was the non-verbal ways in which they supported each other in the 'individualistic' question and answer sessions that dominated most of their classroom time: The predominant teaching style of question and answer engaged the child as an individual. Boys and girls worked separately in the classroom. There were few opportunities in which they were asked to work together. Working as an individual left the child 'alone' when he or she could not answer a question for the teacher. Boys rarely attempted to help each other when they could not answer a question. The researcher described boys standing at their desks and looking down rather than at the teacher. When girls were unable to answer a question, they often looked around the classroom and received a non-verbal (eye-to-eye) contact that supported an attempt to answer.

The example of girls helping each other was found in all classes, during class time and during 'teacher-less time' (when teachers were not present in the classroom). Girls spoke to the researcher about their learning activities and showed more interest than boys in the class. They were concerned about other girls in the class. During teacher-less time, girls shared answers with one another and read together. Some of the girls would telephone others to discuss homework. Girls rarely teased one another. During recess and play-time, girls were often found walking around the periphery of the playground and talking among themselves. In teacher-directed question and answer sessions, when girls gave a correct answer they often smiled at friends. If a girl was unable or unsure of providing an answer, she tended to look around and often received supportive contact which encouraged the attempt to answer. Girls' solidarity was shown in sharing food and drink and offering sympathy and support for one another. The sharing of experience and information was especially evident among top attaining girls.

As an interesting third example of the role of cooperation in school-based training and learning, it appears that the more 'competent' a training teacher becomes, (especially in her/his area of curriculum specialty), then the more likely the student will arrange for pupils to have mutual engagement in classroom learning time. In a study of training teachers, Edwards et al. (1997) focused on differences in teaching approach between confident curriculum specialists who were able to draw upon pedagogic approaches rather than didactics (from Tochan & Munby 1993). Interviews were undertaken with students completing postgraduate training for teaching in secondary schools. Students were asked to reflect and review their actual classroom practices. A number of students who struggled with their course of teaching practice described classroom practice in terms of teachers providing and supporting information for pupils; yet one confident student went beyond this narrow focus and noted:

R: When you were introducing the task you had Nicola, Jenny and Mark (pupils) come up to the board and write examples on the board, what were your aims?
L: I wanted them to actually get practice in writing co-ordinates. It showed me whether they understood what they were doing and it would show others how to do it as well. I think I could have just written it down on the board but they might not have taken quite as much attention as if their friends were writing on the board.
...
R: Where do you think you got that idea from, actually get one child to demonstrate to another:
L: I've been using that quite a lot ... I don't think that I should always have to count things out because that children get bored. So, It's better if they have their friends do it. So, I think that's where that's come from really.

These three studies show in separate ways that peer mutuality helps individuals 'learn'; an example of the mutuality of real ZPDs. Note also, that the students and pupils do not simply refer to their peers, but to companions and friends. Thus, as well as identifying that ZPD interpretations should include asymmetrical and symmetrical relationships, this paper also poses that ZPDs will be more effective if they take place within a zone of close relationships.

Conclusion

This paper should remind psychologists, teachers and others involved that there are shortcomings in our perceptions of Vygotsky's work. His work should not be placed uncritically upon a pedestal, nor should it be thrown out when criticisms are brought to bear. We should be aware of the power and limitations of the current interpretation of ZPD, so that it may be understood in a more eclectic, but problem-oriented manner which will have greater relevance to the fuller teaching and learning processes. Minimally, we should be aware that Vygotsky used an expanded ZPD (involving both hierarchical and mutual interpersonal relationships) which coincides with the critical integration of socio-cognitive studies concerning mutual peers. The three studies cited above show that mutual cooperation is commonly found among peers (both school-aged and teacher-aged) and used to support their learning and development. Like Vygotsky, and opposed to many well-meaning interpretations of Vygotsky, we draw upon both hierarchical and mutual relationships to support learning within the ZPD.

There are a range of alternatives posed with regard to interpretation of the concept of ZPD that have been constrained by relational and cultural dynamics. Interpreters of Vygotsky's work should be aware of, but untainted by, political and cultural orientations. As shown in this chapter, interpretation of ZPD as 'mutual learning' has been used by Vygotsky and colleagues although this type of interpretation has not been made evident in the dominant writings on Vygotsky. Further, a number of international studies have found that interpretation of learning as mutual can be used at all levels of education to support learning and development, by children as well as teachers. In this chapter we have only focused on one aspect of the Vygotskian literature, but our suggestion is that we need to explore the literature in greater depth (going beyond the main interpreters) and expand this critical approach to concepts other than the ZPD.

References

Ball, S. (1994). *Education reform*. Buckingham: Open University Press.

Bearison, D. (1982). New directions in studies of social interaction and cognitive growth. In F.C. Serafica (ed.), *Social-cognitive development in context*. New York: Guildford Press.

Bennett, N., Desforges, C., Cockburn, A. & Wilkinson, B. (1984). *The quality of pupil learning experiences*. London: Lawrence Erlbaum Associates.

Beveridge, M. (1997). Educational implementation and teaching: 'school knowledge' and psychological theory. In L. Smith, J. Dockerill & P. Tomlinson (eds.). *Piaget, Vygotsky and beyond*. London: Routledge.

Bliss, J. Askew, A. & Macrae, S. (1996). Effective teaching and learning: scaffolding revisited. *Oxford Review of Education*, 22(1), 37-61.

Bruner, J. (1983). *Children's talk: learning to use language*. Oxford: Oxford University Press.

Bruner, J. (1984). Vygotsky's zone of proximal development: the hidden agenda. In B. Rogoff & J. Wertsch (eds.), *Children's learning in the 'zone of proximal development'*. San Fransisco: Jossey-Bass.

Bruner, J. (1985). Vygotsky: a historical and conceptual perspective. In J. Wertsch (ed.), *Culture, communication and cognition: Vygotskian perspectives*. Cambridge: Cambridge University Press.

Cole, M. (1976). Foreword. In A.R. Luria, *Cognitive development; its cultural and social foundations*. Cambridge, Mass.: Harvard University Press.

Cole, M. & Wertsch, J. (1996). Beyond the individual-social antinomy in discussions of Piaget and Vygotsky. *Human Development*, 39, 250-56.

Daniels, H. (1993). *Charting the agenda; educational activity after Vygotsky*. London: Routledge.

Davydov, V. (1994). The influence of L.S. Vygotsky on education theory, research and practice. *Educational Researcher*, 24(3), 12-21.

Doise, W. & Mugny, G. (1984). *The social development of the intellect*. Oxford: Pergamon Press.

Duveen, G. (1994). Children as social actors. In P. Guarreschi & S. Jorchelovitch (eds.), *Testos sobre representagoes sociais*. Rio de Janeiro: Vozes.

Edwards, A. (1995). Teacher education: partnerships in pedagogy? *Teaching and Teacher Education*, 11(6), 595-610.

Edwards, A., Twiselton, S. & Ogden, L. (1997). Pedagogy: the missing ingredient in initial teacher training for primary school teaching? Paper presented to the European Association for Research in Learning and Instruction conference, Athens.

Edwards, D. & Mercer, N. (1987). *Common knowledge: the development of understanding in the classroom*. London: Methuen.

Galton, M. (1990). Groupwork. In C. Rogers & P. Kutnick (eds.), *The social psychology of the primary school*. London: Routledge.

Jukes, V. & Kutnick, P. (1990). Determinants of academic success within classrooms in Trinidad and Tobago: some personal and systemic variables. *Educational Studies*, 16(3), 217-35.

Kutnick, P. (1990). Social development of the child and the promotion of autonomy in the classroom. In C. Rogers & P. Kutnick (eds.), *The social psychology of the primary school*. London: Routledge.

Kutnick, P. (1994). Use and effectiveness of groups in classrooms: towards a pedagogy. In P. Kutnick & C. Rogers (eds.), *Groups in schools*. London: Cassell.

Kutnick, P. (1997). Perceptions of preparation for teaching competence by PGCE students. *Journal of Further and Higher Education*, 21, 219-28.

Kutnick, P., Layne, A. & Jules, V. (1997). *Gender and school achievement in the Caribbean. Education research paper 21*. London: Department for International Development.

Lacey, C. (1977). *The Socialisation of Teachers*. London: Methuen.

Luria, A.R. (1976). *Cognitive development: its cultural and social foundations*. Cambridge, Mass.: Harvard University Press.

Marx, K. (1994). Theses on Feuerbach. In J. O'Malley (ed. and trans., with R.A. Davis), *Marx: Early political writings*. Cambridge: Cambridge University Press. (Original work published 1845)

Mercer, N. (1991). Accounting for what goes on in classrooms: what have neo-Vygotskians got to offer? *British Psychological Society, Education Section Review*, 15(2), 61-67.

Munn, P. (1992). Teaching strategies in nursery settings. Paper presented at the British Psychological Society Education Section Conference, Easthampstead Park, Berkshire.

Pepitone, E. (1980). *Children in cooperation and competition*. Lexington, Mass.: Lexington Books.

Perret-Clermont, A-N. (1980). *Social interaction and cognitive development in children*. London: Academic Press.

Piaget, J. (1932). *Moral judgement of the child*. New York: Free Press.

Rogoff, B. (1990). *Apprenticeship in thinking: cognitive development in social context*. New York: Oxford University Press.

Smith, L. (1989). Changing perspectives in developmental psychology. In C.W. Desforges (ed.), *Early childhood education* (British Journal of Educational Psychology Monographs, Series 4). Edinburgh: Scottish Academic Press.

Smith, L. (1996). With knowledge in mind: novel transformation of the learner or transformation of novel knowledge. *Human Development*, 39, 257-63.

Tochan, F. & Munby, M. (1993). Novice and expert teachers' time epistemologies; a wave function from didactics to pedagogy. *Teachering and Teacher Education*, 9(2), 205-18.

van der Veer, R. & Valsiner, J. (1991). *Understanding Vygotsky. The quest for synthesis*. Oxford: Blackwell.

Vygotsky, L. (1933/1935). Dinamika umstvennogo razvitija shkol'nika v svjazi s obucheniem. In L. Vygotsky, *Umstvennoe razvitie detej v processe obuchenija*. Moscow-Leningrad: Uchpedgiz.

Vygotsky, L. (1966/1991). Genesis of higher mental functions. In A. Leontiev & A. Luria (eds.), *Psychological research in the USSR: Vol 1*. Moscow: Progress Publishers. Re-printed in P. Light, S. Sheldon & M. Woodhead (eds.), *Learning to think*. London: Routledge.

Vygotsky, L. (1978). *Mind and society: the development of higher mental processes*. Cambridge, Mass.: Harvard University Press.

Wertsch, J. (1985). *Vygotsky and the social function of mind*. Cambridge, Mass.: Harvard University Press.

Wood, D. (1991). Aspects of teaching and learning. In P. Light, S. Sheldon & M. Woodhead (eds.), *Learning to think*. London: Routledge.

Wood, D., Bruner, J. & Ross, G. (1976). The role of tutoring in problem solving. *Journal of Child Psychology and Psychiatry*, 17, 89-100.

Wood, D. & Middleton, D. (1975). A study of assisted problem solving. *British Journal of Psychology*, 66, 181-91.

Educational Practice that Combines Community Knowledge and Social Science Studies

5 Orchestrating Voices and Crossing Boundaries in Educational Practice: Dialogic Research on Learning about the Kobe Earthquake

Katsuhiro Yamazumi

Introduction

Educational practice as an activity system develops from the multiple perspectives and the various voices of those participating in it. From the standpoint of social practice, teaching and learning in schools can be defined as 'work for others', in which the radical issue of events we call 'education' is 'interchange' among participants in a sociocultural setting, that is, the classroom.

Educational teaching-learning practice involves 'work for others' which is practiced by teachers and children interactively. Such works are characterised by the positions from which different people attempt to coexist by mutual learning and the unclosing of themselves to other people. Classroom discourse aims to expand the participants' positions toward such coexistence from the classroom to actual society. The work involves recognising actual social problems in the relationship with other people, not only at present but also in the past and in the future.

The purpose of this chapter is to show how an integrated curriculum could be constructed as a re-orchestration of multiple voices, of the different viewpoints and positions of the various participants in comprehensive learning in a Japanese high school. As a matter of fact, central to school and curriculum reform today in Japanese public schools is the development of a unique school-based integrated curriculum in elementary, junior high, and high schools, respectively. In order to develop such curriculum across traditional subjects, teachers, children, parents, educational researchers, and various professions and citizens build multiple teams for school change and try to transform school curriculum and educational practice together.

Integrated curriculum in comprehensive school is concerned with social problems in modern informational and global society — as, for example, world peace, environmental disruption, information technology, human rights, and social welfare — and a more complex approach to students' motives for school learning and school-going than traditional subjects. Integrated curriculum may start with local social problems and then expand to recognise global social problems. The work of recognising social problems consists of criticising existing rationality and articulating social problems by communication. This work may be defined as 'learning by expanding' (Engeström 1987) in that it attempts to generate the context of learning critically about the social problems.

In searching for coexisting contexts, individuals expand the meaning of their lived experiences in their own history and culture to construct new social viewpoints. It is important for such work to criticise the existing rationality and to articulate these meanings by way of a historically 'new voice' and formulate them while listening to and appreciating the different voices of others. Therefore, integrated curriculum must include a variety of different viewpoints or voices in it. In this context, children can think in contextualised speech events, and the classroom becomes a practical community of speech and action if the unique voices of the children are involved in it.

In this chapter, I will report on a dialogic research programme concerning an integrated curriculum in comprehensive learning in a Japanese high school. This curriculum and the teaching-learning activity faced a traumatic intensity in my hometown, that is, 'the Great Kobe (Hanshin-Awaji) Earthquake Disaster' occurred on January 17, 1995, which was the worst earthquake catastrophe to hit a Japanese city and resulted in over 6,000 dead or missing people. After the disastrous earthquake, educational practices in the stricken area have primarily been dealt (a) in terms of learning to make the best use of the experiences arising out of this disastrous earthquake, and (b) in terms of mental health.

The teachers and students in a Kobe high school created the programme 'Walking in the Stricken City' as an integrated curriculum with an educational practice that I will examine in the following. Acknowledging the concept of 'expansive learning' and its collective educational project for applying cultural-historical activity theory, I will analyse an attempt by the participants in the school to create an expansive collective educational project transforming the victims' voices of the terrible and disastrous memories into an expansive learning project.

In this regard, at the beginning of the following sections, I will discuss Vygotsky's (1929/1989) methodology of a '[r]enewed division into two of what had been fused in one' (p. 58) and Bakhtin's (1981, 1986) ideas on heteroglossia and dialogicality in order to open up a dialogic understanding of the middle-level phenomena of classroom culture. I will then present an educational practice concerning the integrated curriculum and learning about the Kobe Earthquake that demonstrates the educational challenges of the concepts of expansive learning, orchestrating voices, and crossing boundaries. Finally, I will conclude by discussing how an integrated curriculum and collective educational project might be conceptualised as an expansive and boundary-crossing learning activity.

Dramatising the Classroom and Renewing Folk Pedagogy

In his idea of 'concrete human psychology', Vygotsky (1929/1989) tries to relate the genesis and development of higher mental functions to 'real relations between people':

Any higher psychological function was external; this means that it was social; before becoming a function, it was the social relation between two people. The means of acting upon oneself is first a means of acting on others and the action of others on one's personality. (p. 56)

Posing the principal problems of collective psychology (child psychology) on this basis: everything is inverse of what is now done. (p. 61)

Vygotsky considers the problems of concrete human psychology from the viewpoint of 'drama': 'the dynamic of the personality is drama' (p. 67). His view rests on the fundamental idea that the genesis of concrete personality is dramatised. Since any higher mental function — as for example thinking — is genetically linked to social relations among people, it can be seen that mental functions are able to emerge from the dynamic between persons in terms of drama. Vygotsky states, 'It is not thought that thinks: a person thinks' (p. 65). Vygotsky uses the term 'homo duplex' to show that '[g]enetically social relations, real relations between people, underlie all higher functions and their relationships' (p. 58). Not inner essence but 'social role' — as, for example, judge or physician Vygotsky argues — generates thinking functions as higher mental functions in the personality. In the dynamic of personality, that is, a drama, mental functions relate to and clash with one another.

The issue is: *Who thinks, what* role, function does thinking fulfill in the personality? ... Social role (judge, physician) determines a hierarchy of functions: *i.e., functions change the hierarchy in different spheres of social life. Their conflict = drama.* (p. 69)

Mental functions become an interdependent system according to a social role; a hierarchy of them involved in a sphere of social life. 'Drama', as Vygotsky argues, means a zone of clash and conflict between such systems (hierarchies) of mental functions where a sphere of social life comes in contact with another. In order to make a research problem of drama, Vygotsky shows the principal method is the renewed division into two of that which had been fused into one in the experimental unfolding of a higher mental process. The small drama of the classroom combines spheres of social life that build on the intersubjectivity of teachers and children, including the thinking process that takes place between them. As to the social relations, it is necessary to look to 'folk psychology' about other minds that is linked to interaction (teaching and learning) with one another in the setting of school.

The schoolroom, as Bruner (1996, 44) put it, is a living context, where education is concerned, in a broader culture. In that living context, individuals try to understand and interpret other minds — what other minds are like. In other words, they are steered in ordinary interaction by their notions of what other minds are like. Bruner calls such meaning making about other minds 'folk psychology'.

Folk psychologies reflect certain "wired-in" human tendencies ..., but they also reflect some deeply ingrained cultural beliefs about "the mind". ... Just as we are steered in ordinary interaction by our folk psychology, so we are steered in the activity of helping children learn about the world by notions of *folk pedagog.* (p. 46)

Folk pedagogy reflects teachers' notions of 'what children's minds are like and how to help them learn'. In short, it reflects beliefs and assumptions about the children. The other side of this coin, a child's learning, is affected by his or her notion of the teacher's mind-set. From the viewpoint of folk pedagogy, explaining what children *do* is not enough, but 'the new agenda is to determine what they *think* they are doing and what their reasons are for doing it' (p. 49).

Bruner shows that there are four dominant models of learner's minds that have held sway in our times:

Different approaches to learning and different forms of instruction — from imitation, to instruction, to discovery, to collaboration — reflect differing beliefs and assumptions about the learner — from actor, to knower, to private experiencer, to collaborative thinker. (p. 50)

For a cultural approach to folk pedagogy, the most important part of this argument is that '[t]hese models are not only conceptions of mind that determine how we teach and "educate", but are also conceptions about the relations between minds and cultures' (p. 53).

Participation in a 'drama' as an educational practice is mediated by multiple and various performances and sense makings of participants based on folk beliefs about education. In other words, participants practice some folk pedagogies in the time and sequence of actions. Folk pedagogy is a means to operate the realm of meaning in the classroom. Therefore, 'an innovation in teaching will necessarily involve changing the folk psychological and folk pedagogical theories of teachers — and, to a surprising extent, of pupils as well' (p. 46).

Folk pedagogy, which is provided by both the classroom's micro-culture and the broader macro-culture surrounding the classroom, is organised by such dramatic and narrative forms as how people are, how and why they act, and how they cope with trouble. In other words, these actions of folk pedagogies are organised by means of dramatic and narrative forms that are historically accumulated in the community of the classroom. Individuals in the classroom can survive in a world of meaning by making up and interpreting the form of dramatised and narrativised folk pedagogy about interweaving experiences. The point here is that participants can interpret and evaluate meanings of their own actions, the actions of others, and teaching and learning only in the context of dramatised and narrativised folk pedagogy.

Through the recreation of folk pedagogy, there is a possibility for renewal of pupils' roles, in order to collectively transform educational practice as 'work for others' in the community. Through this practice a historical and mutual new positioning of participants is possible.

Furthermore, it is worth noting whether educational research is able to turn the discourse of school learning and teaching 'from an instrumentalist belief in controlling and manipulating variables — an orientation based upon the suppression of subjectivity — to a dialogic discourse' (Britzman 1991, 1) in understanding such folk pedagogy as mediational means to transform and innovate the sense-making, identity formation, and motivation among students and teachers. To borrow an argument from Bakhtin (1974/1986), a matter of importance here is that understanding can only be dialogic.

Understanding as correlation with other texts and reinterpretation, in a new context (in my own context, in a contemporary context, and in a future one). ... The text lives only by coming into contact with another text (with context). Only at the point of this contact between texts does a light flash, illuminating both the posterior and anterior, joining a given text to a dialogue. (pp. 161-62)

As Bakhtin emphasises over and over again, it is important to note the impossibility of a single consciousness or a single voice and the possibility of dialogic understanding in the practice of teaching and learning. Such understanding as dialogue between teachers, students and researchers can only become boundary crossing as follows:

It never gravitates toward a single consciousness or a single voice. The life of the word is contained in its transfer from one mouth to another, from one context to another context, from one social collective to another, from one generation to another generation. (Bakhtin 1963/1984, 202)

In the following sections, I would like to listen to the voices of teachers and students, understand dialogically their presence, and consider how they come to create the form of teaching and learning in cycles of expansive transformation with communities of practice, especially focusing attention on the sense- and identity-building features and motivational sphere in participating a drama of teaching-learning practice. In other words, this concern is with how educational research becomes a dialogue with practitioners. Educational research needs to understand that teaching-learning is always 'the process of becoming: a time of formation and transformation, of scrutiny into what one is doing and what one can become' (Britzman 1991, 8). Such research concerned with 'the process of becoming' is a methodology for following, facilitating, and analysing 'the present, in its all openendedness', which Bakhtin (1941/1981) argues as follows:

It is precisely the zone of contact with an inconclusive present (and consequently with the future) that creates the necessity of this incongruity of a man with himself. There always remain in him unrealised potential and unrealised demands. The future exists, and this future ineluctably touches upon the individual, has its roots in him.

An individual cannot be completely incarnated into the flesh of existing socio-historical categories. … There always remains an unrealised surplus of humanness; there always remains a need for the future, and a place for this future must be found. All existing clothes are always too tight, and thus comical, on a man. (p. 37)

'Walking in the Stricken City' as Expansive Happenings

The case of educational practice that I am now moving on to concerns the teaching-learning process for a school year carried out by second year classes and the teacher team at the Suma Senior High School in Kobe City and based on the experience of the 1995 Kobe Earthquake. This practice was named 'Walking in the Stricken City'. It was during the 1997 school year that the practice was accomplished; two years had passed since the earthquake struck the city.

The recent curriculum in Japanese normal high schools consists of nine school subjects — Japanese, geography and history, civics, mathematics, science, physical education, art, foreign languages, and home economics — and each subject has its respective teacher. Rather, it is possible to say that students' daily classroom practices are compartmentalised by subject teaching. In an effort to solve this problem, in the forthcoming reformation of the high school curriculum in 2003 it is planned to introduce integrated curriculum across subject-matter areas, apart from the compartmentalised subjects, based on the national educational policy.

The practice in Suma High School, 'Walking in the Stricken City', was one of the collaborative educational projects created by students, classroom teachers, and subject teachers, together as a team, crossing over the boundaries which usually divide the work of subject teachers and classroom teachers. Teachers, and students also, were crossing boundaries of compartmentalised subjects and classrooms by putting their energy together. This educational project, 'Walking in the Stricken City', attempts to unite a collective learning activity, which becomes possible by sharing a somewhat expanded object of activity, which differed somewhat from the divided tasks of the individual subject matter.

Let me introduce an outline of the practical journey 'Walking in the Stricken City' which took place over the course of a year. The project began with a field trip to the most damaged area in their school in May 1997. The school district contained both enormously damaged areas and comparatively undamaged areas. This meant the extent of damage to be witnessed was different for each student. Some 320 second year students were divided into groups of six or seven members who walked around the stricken city, visiting, for example, a shopping mall which had collapsed and burnt down, churches, the 'Wall of Kobe' which was the wall that had escaped the fire and was known to people in this district as a monument of the disaster, and so forth. For many students it was the first time to walk around this area after the quake. They listened to what the people living in the temporary houses and stores, as well as volunteer church workers, had to say. Right after that, each group started to write wall-newsletters and the collaborative work lasted until October.

In June, they started to script a play entitled 'Never Forget the Day' about the disaster, completing it in July. The story was an original work of fiction and was about high school students who began to notice the significance of volunteer activity. In the story, the characters at first hesitate to join the activity but then the death of a girl who was doing her volunteer service in temporary houses makes them consider the significance of volunteer service. Some 36 students voluntarily joined this play activity, and one teacher, though not knowledgeable about the play at all, also joined as a director. A teacher team and the students scripted the play themselves, and rehearsed over and over again during the summer vacation and after school. They also created the set design. In October, 'Never Forget the Day' was performed at their school festival before an audience comprising people associated with the school as well as local people from this district, including those who took temporary refuge in the school building immediately following the earthquake. A musical suite, 'Wall of Kobe' was composed for the school festival by a music teacher from the school and sung by a mixed choir — consisting of members of a chorus club and some voluntary teachers. They invited a soprano singer, who sometimes came to the music class to teach, to be the soloist with the choir. This suite consisted of some pieces of poetry written by an unknown writer — found under the 'Wall of Kobe' and read by a volunteer of the wall monument preservation movement, as well as stories of remembrance told by the people living in this district. At the festival, students had the opportunity to exhibit in the wall-newsletters accounts of what they had experienced and learned from visiting the stricken city in May. They held a bazaar in the shopping mall which had been so badly hit by the quake. Here they sold croquettes and all profits were contributed to the mall.

On the third anniversary of the disaster, January 17, 1998, the students and teachers got together in front of the 'Wall of Kobe' and exhibited their wall-newsletters together with some works of art in memory of the disaster. They also performed the suite 'Wall of Kobe'. This memorial event was planned to let the people in this district know about the students' actions. In addition, members of the broadcasting club collaborated with the local FM station which offered an information service programme. At a contest between municipal high schools in Kobe, some of the Suma Senior High School students made a speech in English about their actions. Then the teacher team and students published a report entitled 'Walking in the Stricken City' which covered all of the July 1998 activities.

The one year journey through this educational practice created new forms of collective activity and new collective tools and concepts: i.e., re-mediating and re-instrumentalising the pre-existing teaching-learning actions of high school, like searching outside school, investigating/ observing/ interviewing, reporting, school festival, play, club activities, choir, and a speech contest in English. In other words, 'Walking in the Stricken City' became a new integrated curriculum and team- and network-based teaching organisation in which a new 'instrumentality' (Engeström et al. 1996, 14) including multiple cognitive artefacts and semiotic means was created.

I attach special importance to 'walking' as tools and concepts in this case. This integrated curriculum started with the actual walking actions of students' in the stricken area, thus enabling individual actions to be gradually transformed and developed into a collective activity. The chief teacher of the second year classes commented in the report of educational practice, 'Walking in the Stricken City' (Suma High School 1998); 'the aim of walking in the stricken area was to face the Kobe City after two years had passed since the earthquake' (p. 1). Preparing them for their field trip, the teacher who constructed this curriculum told students at the meeting:

I want you to see the traces of the quake again anyway, and somehow think about it as a student of our school. Our school is located at the center of the stricken area. As of now, some buildings have already been re-built and you cannot see the ruins of a fire. Although a lot of people were living here around two years ago, kids were playing, and dogs were running, most of them have not come back yet. Many are still suffering severely from the quake and are forced to live here ... I am not sure what we can do. But I want you to feel something ... I guess most of you live in Kobe. I wonder if there are some possibilities of changing this awful experience into something meaningful through our activities, for the sake of the people who left this world. (pp. 121-22)

When we recollect the earthquake in Kobe, our memories are mediated by a unified, fixed orderly story or collective representation, for instance a typical speech genre of the news media. This means that each individual's unique and singular traumatic experience is generalised and ordered in some way. Such generalisation/ordering seems to be based on what Benjamin (1940/1968) indicated, 'the concept of its [historical] progression through a homogeneous, empty time' (p. 261). A kind of historical narrative concerning events or experiences of the Kobe Earthquake can be seen as 'a homogenizing approach to the past, an attempt to write it into a master narrative continuous with the dominant ideological constructions of the present' (Fiske 1991, 183-84). On the other hand, according to the idea of the cultural consumer's 'tactics of consumption', that is the concept of 'the procedures of everyday creativity', which is pointed out by de Certeau (1984; see also Wertsch 1998), 'walking' as a kind of people's everyday urban practice or spatial practice 'carries away and displaces the analytical, coherent proper meanings of urbanism' (de Certeau 1984, 102). He illustrates 'another production', called consumption as resisting the urbanistic project, that is, 'the technological system of a coherent and totalizing space', as follows:

The networks of these moving [the practices organizing a bustling city], intersecting writings compose a manifold story that has neither author nor spectator, shaped out of fragments of trajectories and alterations of spaces: in relation to representations, it remains daily and indefinitely other. (p. 93)

Stories diversity, rumors totalize. If there is still a certain oscillation between them, it seems that today there is rather a stratification: stories are becoming private and sink into the secluded places in neighborhoods, families, or individuals, while the rumors propagated by the media cover everything and, gathered under the figure of the City, the masterword of an anonymous law, the substitute for all proper names, they wipe out or combat any superstitions guilty of still resisting the figure. (pp. 107-8)

Japanese high school education or learning at present is still keeping 'a series of more or less disconnected though systematically repeated learning actions' (Engeström 1987, 104). As Engeström (1987) figures, the features of the activity of school-going are determined by the primary contradiction of capitalistic socio-economic formation, the double nature of commodity as a unity of exchange value and use value, thus, the object 'text' of school learning has a twofold meaning:

First of all, it is a dead object to be reproduced for the purpose of gaining grades or other 'success markers' which cumulatively determine the future value of the pupil himself in the labor market. On the other hand, text tendentially also appears as a living instrument of mastering one's own relation to society outside the school. In this respect, the school text possesses potential use value. As the object of activity is also its true motive, the inherently dual nature of the motive of school-going is now visible. (p. 102)

We can see the enormous influence of industrial-capitalism and the consumer society on learning in the Japanese high school education of today. Between such high school learning and the students who are strongly affected by the market and grow up in it, a tension of fundamental contradictions is increasing and now 'school-going may well be approaching a crisis of new qualitative dimensions' (p. 104). From these points of view, we can make sense of the integrated curriculum in the Suma High School. It is a challenge for learning activity, whereby learners can question the relevance of existing school education and seek a context of broader life activity.

This high school's integrated curriculum is becoming a new educational practice to innovate the existing practice, by expanding the different subjects to the reality outside the school and by trying to bring new forms of communication and collaboration to construct the expanded learning activity. I expect that the ethical principles of the teachers who were involved played an important role in starting this educational practice. For instance, the teacher, who usually carried out this curriculum, narrated that the motive of that practice for him emanated from his memory of a student's 'face', the unforgettable face of a student in his class at the time the earthquake occurred. On being interviewed, he told the following (quoted from an article in the *Asahi newspaper*, 19 November 1998):

There is a face of a student that I cannot wipe out. I had not heard from her for one month. At long last when we met, she said to me, 'I will show you something nice.' It was a picture of this girl standing by her house ruined by a fire. The face I cannot forget is the face of her when she showed me the picture — with a complicated smile. She said to me that she was wearing the uniform of Suma High School which she had just gotten before her house burned down.

The need for this teacher was as I quoted before; 'I am not sure what we can do. But I want you to feel something. ... I guess most of you live in Kobe. I wonder if there are some possibilities to make this awful experience into something meaningful through our activities, for the sake of the people who left this world.' According to the points of view of cultural-historical activity theory (see Leontiev 1978), if a human need comes in contact with an entity of the outside world, an object of activity is constructed and sharing the object within a collective activity system becomes the participants' motive for activity. 'The object determines the horizon of possible individual actions within the collective activity' (Engeström 1998). Take the educational activity in Kobe's public schools as an example, the cultural-historical content and evolution of the object/motive may be gained through such questioning as 'what' we can do for the disaster experience of teachers and students in traumatic intensity and 'why' we can do that. Teachers and students as the subject of collective activity in the Suma High School were re-constructing and re-defining the object of learning activity — 'what' we can do from the individual experiences of disaster — through specific situated actions and their responsible ethics in relation to the otherness of others, including the victims of the quake.

As a further discussion in the next section, the educational practice 'Walking in the Stricken City' creates the expansive learning activity which transforms the survivors' terrible voices of memories into expansive happenings. The object of activity, as Engeström, Engeström and Vähäaho (1999) supposes, is expanded through the expansive learning. After the practice 'Walking in the Stricken City', the teacher I mentioned before has wrestled since May 1998 with an educational practice to expand further the object of learning activity. He narrated (quoted from an interview of *Asahi newspaper*, 19 November 1998):

The theme of our education in this school year is 'Kind Heartedness for All Over the World'. We will have a drive to gather money for charity for the kids in the Mongolian People's Republic, who suffer from poverty and are living even in a manhole because of poverty. The theme, whose central concept is for thinking about the importance of life which cannot be replaced by anything, has the same basic idea as the theme we looked at before — 'Walk in the Stricken City.' All of the themes are so heavy and difficult ones. But people living in Kobe should not forget that. How the students grasp this and develop their ideas, that is what I want to follow up. I want to give a certain hope for living through our activities.

Toward Boundary-Crossing Learning from Memories We Cannot Forget

We have attempted to regard the learning activity based on the experience of the 1995 Kobe Earthquake as expansive learning (Yamazumi and Yamazumi, in preparation). In our research project, we follow the possibility of expanding the individual child's storytelling action of the disastrous experience to the creation of historically new voices and sociality for a better world. Based on Engeström's (1987) theory of *expansive learning*, we pursue the teaching-learning activity by expanding the object, the disastrous experience, takes the form of working in cycles of transformation with community of practice and the processes of expansive learning generate new relations between schooling and other cooperative activity systems and new patterns of communication and collaboration.

Nakai (1997), who is a psychiatrist, describes that the experience of the Kobe Earthquake has transformed and re-outlined the existing post-War image of earthquake disaster in modern Japanese cities into an object which we have to cope with as follows.

The nightmare of the Cold War was full-scale nuclear war. Another nightmare in Japan during this same period was an earthquake disaster. The Great Kobe Earthquake changed our concept of earthquake from a nightmare to a reality which had to be coped with. Although earthquake procedures in the Tokai and Kanto areas were as if groping in the dark, specific procedures are now being established because of experiences with the Great Kobe Earthquake. In other words, perhaps people have gotten rid of their image of earthquake: a disaster of a monster destroying major cities. They renewed their idea of earthquake that it is a severe reality that people must cope with. (p. 91)

What is important here is the expansive learning processes which start from struggling with real experiences in various practical communities, questioning, negating, and envisioning a springboard and design for a new model, implementing it, and then generating a new type of communication and collaboration through sharing the expanded object of activity. To understand what Nakai points out implies a breakthrough of the individualistic treatment of suffering by creating a collective activity system which orchestrates the voices of the survivors of the disaster.

In our civil society, the conventional attitude (against disasters) was that damage is only suffered by individuals, and that such survivors should suffer in silence, stand mourning, anger, and estrangement. As time passed following the Great Kobe Earthquake, however, this conventional attitude has changed dramatically. The feelings of survivors must be recognized and respected. Thus, survivors' voices should sound and be heard. I believe that at such times, psychiatrists will hopefully be ready to play a vital role. (p. 176)

Such an activity system is not like one monologic formation. Also, it should not be seen as establishing the authority of a totalising voice. Rather, as Engeström (1991b) mentions, an activity system is 'by definition a multivoiced formation' (p. 15).

An activity system contains a variety of different viewpoints or 'voices', as well as layers of historically accumulated artifacts, rules, and patterns of division of labor. This multivoiced and multilayered nature of activity systems is both a resource for collective achievement and a source of compartmentalization and conflict. (Engeström 1998, 78)

The socio-linguistic site of an activity system has a heteroglossic nature emerging from historical struggles and conflicts. Bakhtin (1934-35/1981) sees into 'heteroglossia' clearly:

... at any given moment of its historical existence, language is heteroglot from top to bottom: it represents the co-existence of socio-ideological contradictions between the present and the past, between differing epochs of the past, between different socio-ideological groups in the present, between tendencies, schools, circles and so forth, all given a bodily form. These 'languages' of heteroglossia intersect each other in a variety of ways, forming new socially typifying 'languages'. (p. 291)

In the case of the city of Kobe, suffering from the earthquake, the disaster was concentrated along the borders of the historically accumulated parts of the city because the city was a fragmented patchwork resulting from city planning made at the different times (see Okazaki 1999). The disaster was, therefore, concentrated in the area of the old inner city. Moreover, most of the old buildings that escaped World War II damage collapsed in this earthquake. Such different conditions of suffering had been compartmentalised and accumulated not naturally but historically (see Hirayama 1999). On the temporal dimension, there are borders of gaps and conflicts between the standardised, ordered time after a disaster in which individual experiences of events in detail are immediately named and hastily absorbed into a unified representation, and the multi-negotiated time individual survivors would try to recover from their awful experiences, that is, multiplicity of time experiencing the disaster (see Hosomi 1999). Those conflicts, which are emerging from the spatial and temporal boundaries, become one of the main contradictions in the disaster experiences.

At the same time, in the context of teaching and learning in the experience of disaster, it is needed to create the horizontal movement crossing over multiple boundaries. It differs from such teaching and learning activity as stepping through a pre-determined, programmed chronotope. Rather, it can be characterised by boundary crossing learning from the disaster experience. Here, I will pick up the report of educational practice, 'Walking in the Stricken City', written by the teachers and students of Suma High School in Kobe City, especially students' writings about their learning experiences from the quake. In this case, I will argue that students' learning is not mastery within the tacitly closed boundaries of given tasks or problem contexts, but crossing various boundaries of social worlds and becoming the creation of a new chronotope in which boundary-crossing learning is able to emerge.

The first point we can see is that the expansive cycle of learning starts from gaps between the teachers' and the students' motives, or rather from their confrontation in the first phase. That is, the starting point of learning activity is 'individually manifested doubt, hesitation and disturbance' (Engeström 1987, 322). The following writing of a student seems to reflect her (and maybe also other students) puzzled state at the beginning of a learning activity.

Frankly speaking, it was not much fun for me to go on a field trip to the stricken area. I have lost nothing in the earthquake — like my family, friends, and house … But I thought it was hard for the people who have lost something. Visiting the destroyed area — I did not want to go, if possible. For I had to think of that. But I was ashamed of myself when the people in this town said, 'welcome' to me. 'Please take time to look around.' Although they suffered much from the quake, they welcomed me. Then I was very ashamed of my thinking that I do not want to visit here. (Suma High School 1998, 29)

Students' sense making and conception of walking in the stricken city as 'not much fun' is different from the teachers', although the teachers themselves, when they suggested a plan for a field trip to their students, presupposed that the students would not be satisfied with planning this kind of activity outside the school, since students expected something interesting. Actually, they complained about the plan with remarks like, 'Why should we go there? Who decided it? It is not so far from my house. Boring. I want to go to the amusement park. I cannot tell my friends from other schools about our excursion, it's shameful.'

Ritva Engeström (1999) looks more closely at sense making of actors in the organisation, that is, teachers, students, parents and researchers, in a local Finnish middle school. She also studies these actors in the teachers' 'change laboratory'. The present concern, as she makes clear, is that sense making for students tends to be that 'instruction is boring' and for the teachers tends to be that 'students are apathetic'. Therefore, the teacher team has to make 'war against apathy', a steppingstone to designing a new practice. In order to do that, the teacher team needs to negotiate what should be learned, that is, what object of learning activity should be taken, with students. Teachers and students have to do the decision-making concerning their learning organisation and then attempt to share the object of learning activity in an expansive way. In this site, it is needed to cross over the boundary arising out of the estrangement between 'boring' and 'apathy.'

As I have mentioned in the former section, the practice called 'Walking in the Stricken city' is created as an integrated curriculum in which teachers and students cross the boundaries of compartmentalised subjects in high school by making and exhibiting wall-newsletters, reporting, having a school festival, play, club activities, choir, English speech contest and so forth on the basis of learning outside school. Although it is really difficult for high school students, living themselves in Kobe, to define their own object of work as 'what can we do from our experiences of the earthquake disaster', they could push forward to shaping a new object and motive and designing a new model of work, by creating integrated curriculum as new collective tools and concepts. The new instrumentality, integrated curriculum across subjects in schooling can mediate what Engeström (1987) describes as 'expansive learning activity', that is, 'to expand the discrete, internally contradictory learning actions occurring within the activity. ... expanding the tasks into objectively novel activity systems' (p. 135). We can see the process of 'mastery of expansion from actions to a new activity' (p. 125) by participating in integrated curriculum in the following writing of a student:

Because of the earthquake, we decided to perform a play in an original fiction. Through this experience, we could get some opportunities to join some events which were related to the local restoring.
I sang a song in front of the 'Wall of Kobe'. Although it was not a big success, I think we tried hard. The audience would know our passion. I was surprised that there was a video camera from the TV station. (Suma High School 1998, 68)

Let me say here that what makes it possible that joint co-operative actions can push 'a historically new form of activity' into emergence is 'knotworking' (see Engeström, Engeström & Vähäaho 1999, for detailed arguments of the concept 'knotworking'). The high school students' learning activity is knotworking with other related local restoring activities from the disaster in the city, and makes it possible to push new relationships, new ways of communication and collaboration into emergence. In this educational practice, through constructing the object and its sense-making over the 'Wall of Kobe' which is known as a monument of the disaster, the learning activity in school and the local restoring activities in the city can build communication and collaboration with each other. Namely, such object construction and its sense-making may make the process of the students' learning boundary crossing.

We can also look at more expansive learning processes in 'borderland', which Giroux (1992) characterises in his concept 'border pedagogy', as a rich educational chronotope. Giroux argues 'borderland' from the view of student identities and subjectivities construction as follows:

... [T]he concept of border pedagogy suggests more than simply opening diverse cultural histories and spaces to students. It also means understanding how fragile identity is as it moves into borderlands crisscrossed within a variety of languages, experiences, and voices. There are no unified subjects here, only students whose multilayered and often contradictory voices and experiences intermingle with the weight of particular histories that will not fit easily into master narrative of a monolithic culture. Such borderlands should be seen as sites for both critical analysis and as a potential source of experimentation, creativity, and possibility. (p. 34)

It generates students as subjects of learning, and border-crossers, to open up their activities and identities so that they are not restricted by the boundaries of the given tasks of schooling but instead have the possibility of finding answers, of having experiences, and of confronting voices within different areas. Such activities and identities can be appropriate for the witness and participant in historical events. Thus, boundary-crossing learning makes it possible for students to enter the broader contexts of life activity outside of the classroom — as Engeström points out, 'learning by expanding' is 'constructing an expanded context of the context' — and to create their own new tasks and problems. The following note shows a life activity in a living context:

The saddest thing is about solitary death after the earthquake. My grandmother, she died last year, was surrounded by the families at that moment. I have never thought of solitary death before. I came to notice that dying alone is a really sad thing. Now I am not reminded of the earthquake only by watching TV or talking about it. I am beginning to forget that we used significantly less water then or that we were kind to others. I think it is good if we can make it into daily practice what we learned from the earthquake. (Suma High School 1998, 64)

As I already mentioned, the educational practice which intends to intervene the historical proceeding of the earthquake disaster comes across the compartmentalisation, conflict, crash and struggle, that is, the historical struggles and conflicts of differences and asymmetry among various voices. We can see a lot of borders, for instance, between apathy and ethics, different city planning, differently negotiated times and rhythms, between reduction to an urgently unified representation and each experience or memory unique to the individual, between our possible narration and deep silence, and so forth — of course, we can see some more differences in time and space. The following student's writing shows that crossing over such compartmentalisation and boundaries is needed for educational practice.

My house was not so damaged as totally collapsed or half, since I lived in Tarumi Ward. As I went to the most damaged area, the collapsed buildings were already swept away; I did not feel actuality when I watched the fire on TV as it was happening in the next ward. Although I was crushed under the bookshelf then, so in a sense I can say I am a kind of sufferer, I never know how more seriously damaged sufferers feel. ...

It is almost impossible to get to know how the sufferers feel but I think we can help them with sympathy. (pp. 64-65)

The high school educational practice called 'Walking in the Stricken City' attempts to introduce the various conflicting sufferers' voices into a contact zone to develop a collective activity system to re-orchestrate these voices. Thus, by pushing such a cultural-historically new activity system through — including new objects, new tools, and so on — it seems that we can attempt to open up the possibilities of resonating, orchestrating, and sharing the events, experiences, and memories, and to re-write and re-inscribe new histories and identities for students:

Conclusion: Educational Practice as Sociohistorical Poetics

One of the students who joined the suite, 'The Wall of Kobe', made a speech about his own experience at the Municipal Senior High Schools' English Speech Contest, as follows:

... [O]ur music teacher ... visited the Wall of Kobe and was moved by it. He composed a chorus suite 'Wall of Kobe'. He adapted the poem hung on the wall as the first movement. He planned to perform the suite at the school festival on October fourth and began collecting members. At first only three members joined the chorus, including me. During summer vacation, we practiced every day, and the members gradually increased. When we were practicing, I remembered some of the painful experiences of the disaster. I nearly forgot the memories which I must not forget. I have returned to the same daily routine as before the earthquake and tend to forget the fact that many people have not gotten over the disaster. We tried to sing with feeling, not nervous about tune. One of the members said, 'When I sing this chorus, I feel myself released from stress'. (Suma High School 1998, 99)

The student who played the host named 'Kaori' in the play at the school festival, 'Never Forget the Day', the theme of which was volunteer activity, wrote of her own experience as follows:

In November, I had already memorized all the lines, so I was so keen on the play. The play meant a lot to me and had a different impact then. Now I wonder how I could stand such a hard practice. But I think they were most satisfying days and I enjoyed them so much, even though they were hard days and I was complaining all the time. On the one hand, I was satisfied with the play being completed by us, but I also felt much uneasiness on the other. The biggest anxiety was that I would lose my voice. Even when I went beyond myself, I could hold on because of the friends. Through working on this play, I realized an important thing, the warm heartedness of my friends. I am thankful to all of my friends. Conversely, one week before the school festival, I became calm. The play was a part of myself and 'Kaori' was also the other side of me. I felt that this one-week was such a short term. (pp. 93-94)

Here we can see learning by qualitative expansion and transformation, as Vygotsky (1925/1971, 243) describes, '[i]nitially, an emotion is individual, and only by means of a work of art does it *become* social or generalized'. This learning by qualitative expansion and transformation means that students' own experiences, memories and identities are under construction in a new, different, historical, and social activity. The expansive and trans-formational learning which will go beyond the given reality makes use of 'the language of the "not yet"' (Giroux 1992, 78) as an instrument. That is, socio-historical poetics — which expansively re-orchestrate various and multiple voices of criticising the unified and fixed dominant culture, re-imagine those voices in different ways, and mobilise and transform them to their hope for the future — becomes the sociality of developmental and ex-pansive instructional activity.

In relation to the conception of 'student voice', Lensmire (1998) views it as conflict generated among students, between teacher and students, and within individual students. 'The cultural politics perspective ... on voice as-sumes conflict across and within the border lines of social groups in society, assumes struggle over identity, meaning, authority' (p. 272). Further, he grasps that 'student voice' is in the process of becoming a time of transform-ation, and of who one can become in the critical collective project of voices.

We need a revised, alternative conception of student voice — one that affirms workshop and critical pedagogy commitments to student expression and partici-pation, but also helps us see the student voice as in-process and embedded, for bet-ter and worse, within the immediate social context of the classroom. (p. 279)

This perspective of the 'student voice as in-process and embedded' could be connected with Emerson's (1996) conception of the 'novelistic gap' based on Bakhtin's identification that the nature of the novel differed from the epic as the form of literary consciousness. On this point, we can apply this idea 'novelistic gap' to catch sight of orchestrating voices in educational practice. According to the idea, the very gap between inner and outer, self and other, individual and societal structure, action and activity, hero and environment, and the present and the future may generate actor's dialog, temporal development and consciousness. On the one hand, his/her struggling over the barriers between inner and outer and the breakthrough of them, critical testing, and learning by boundary-crossing may be a dangerous speculation, but they can also be a great possibility to change and transform one's own sense-making, identities, histories, existences, and practices through mobilising their speculations. Emerson mentions:

The eternal and inevitable inadequacy of all names permits new meanings to happen and new messages to be created. This permission — or intermission — is Bakhtin's novelistic gap, which not even the author can (nor should wish to) bridge. And it is the lack, the absence at the center, that keeps the outer word and our inner speech in permanent dialogue, out of that danger Bakhtin saw of collapse into single consciousness, which would be non-existence. Inside that gap, it is always worthwhile to try naming again. (p. 138)

As Engeström (1987) argues, related to 'the ontogenetic emergence of learning activity', expansive learning activity is emerging 'when the subject faces historically and individually pressing inner contradictions within his or her leading activity — be it work, school-going, science or art' (p. 137). The disastrous earthquake was an event that occurred suddenly from the outer world and struck us. From a view of cultural-historical activity theory, an approach to social-educational practices by people after the earthquake should be taking concrete shape by pursuing collective and artefact-mediated activity systems intending to construct what is 'disaster' as an 'object' and constantly undergoing developmental transformations. In this chapter, I reported how the teaching-learning activity from the memories of the earthquake that we cannot forget, was becoming in a high school in Kobe City an expansive happening, which is to say the expansive naming and re-naming, sense-making of the experiences facing inner contradictions on the borderlines between the outer and inner world of the disaster, under the vision of expansive learning activity.

The theoretical implication can be summarised in the following ways. It will be possible to expand and construct the object of activity in the context of object-oriented, collective and artefact-mediated activity systems, through horizontal movement crossing over multiple boundaries, communication and collaboration between different activity systems, and boundary-crossing learning. Constructing an expanded context of the context, expansive learning activity is connected to and transforms a temporal development. That is to say 'novelness', as Bakhtin argues in 'Epic and Novel', in which we can face the indetermination to maximally open on the future. This indetermination must be nothing but the guarantee of freedom to create new meanings and messages. In concluding, I should note that the free space which ought to be grasped as the notion of indetermination must be an expansive chronotope of developmental teaching, learning, and educational activity as novelistic chronotope, in which educational practitioners face historically and individually pressing gaps emerging from the re-orchestration of multiple voices based on the 'social relations' as Vygotsky (1929/1989) mentions. We can be fairly certain that we as researchers together with practitioners, doing a cultural-historical activity theory research on expansive educational practices, continuously answer and/or intervene in such a free chronotope characterised by its indetermination in dialogic ways (see Hosaka 1999, for argument on a participatory action research with a elementary school teacher team and its attempt to discover and understand a new chronotope in educational practice developing integrated curriculums and their practices, which are the central agendas of today's Japanese school reform movements). Oriented to such object of activity theory research, we must be connected to 'a piece of the history of the future' (Engeström 1987, 335) at least.

References

Asahi newspaper. Osaka: Asahi Shinbunsha (in Japanese).

Bakhtin, M.M. (1934-35/1981). Discourse in the novel. In *The dialogic imagination: Four essays by M.M. Bakhtin* (M. Holquist, ed.; C. Emerson & M. Holquist, trans.). Austin: University of Texas Press.

Bakhtin, M.M. (1941/1981). Epic and novel: Toward a methodology for the study of the novel. In *The dialogic imagination: Four essays by M.M. Bakhtin* (M. Holquist, ed.; C. Emerson & M. Holquist, trans.). Austin: University of Texas Press.

Bakhtin, M.M. (1963/1984). *Problems of Dostoevsky's poetic* (C. Emerson, ed. and trans.). Minneapolis: University of Minnesota Press.

Bakhtin, M.M. (1974/1986). Toward a methodology for the human sciences. In *Speech genres and other late essays* (C. Emerson & M. Holquist, eds.; V.W. McGee, trans.). Austin: University of Texas Press.

Benjamin, W. (1940/1968). Theses on the philosophy of history. In *Illuminations: Essays and reflections* (H. Arendt, ed.; H. Zohn, trans.). New York: Schocken Books.

Britzman, D.P. (1991). *Practice makes practice: A critical study of learning to teach.* Albany: State University of New York Press.

Bruner, J. (1996). *The culture of education.* Cambridge, Mass.: Harvard University Press.

Certeau, M. de (1984). *The practice of everyday life* (S.F. Rendall, trans.). Berkeley: University of California Press.

Emerson, C. (1996). The outer word and inner speech: Bakhtin, Vygotsky, and the internalisation of language. In H. Daniels (ed.), *An introduction to Vygotsky.* London and New York: Routledge.

Engeström, R. (1999). Expanding the construction of 'students': Scenes for a change laboratory in a Finnish middle school. Paper presented at the 1999 Kyoto/Kobe Symposium on cultural-historical Activity Theory, Kyoto, Japan, August.

Engeström, Y. (1987). *Learning by expanding: An activity-theoretical approach to developmental research.* Helsinki: Orienta-Konsultit.

Engeström, Y. (1991a). Non scolae sed vitae discimus: Toward overcoming the encapsulation of school learning. *Learning and Instruction,* 1, 243-59.

Engeström, Y. (1991b). Activity theory and individual and social transformation. *Multidisciplinary Newsletter for Activity Theory,* 7/8, 6-15.

Engeström, Y. (1998). Reorganizing the motivational sphere of classroom culture: An activity-theoretical analysis of planning in a teacher team. In F. Seeger, J. Voigt & U. Waschescio (eds.), *The culture of the mathematics classroom.* Cambridge: Cambridge University Press.

Engeström, Y. (2001). Making expansive decisions: An activity-theoretical study of practitioners building collaborative medical care for children. In C.M. Allwood & M. Selart (eds.), *Decision making: Social and creative dimensions.* Dordrecht: Kluwer Academic Publishers.

Engeström, Y., Engeström, R. & Vähäaho, T. (1999). When the center does not hold: The importance of knotworking. In S. Chaiklin, M. Hedegaard & U.J. Jensen (eds.), *Activity theory and social practice: Cultural-historical approaches.* Aarhus: Aarhus University Press.

Engeström, Y., Virkkunen, J., Helle, M., Pihlaja, J. & Poikela, R. (1996). Change laboratory as a tool for transforming work. *Lifelong Learning in Europe,* 1(2), 10-17.

Fiske, J. (1991). *Reading the popular.* New York and London: Routledge.

Giroux, H.A. (1992). *Border crossings: Cultural workers and the politics of education.* New York and London: Routledge.

Hirayama, Y. (1999). Earthquake disaster, city, and space: From the field of housing and community reconstruction. Paper presented at the 1999 Kyoto/Kobe Symposium on Cultural-historical Activity Theory, Kobe, Japan, August.

Hosaka, Y. (1999). Collective configuration of expansive narrative and identities: Create the borderland together in a Japanese public school. Paper presented at the 1999 Kyoto/Kobe Symposium on Cultural-historical Activity Theory, Kyoto, Japan, August.

Hosomi, K. (1999). The earthquake disaster and *SHOAH*: Recalling scenes of common remembrance. Paper presented at the 1999 Kyoto/Kobe Symposium on Cultural-historical Activity Theory, Kobe, Japan, August.

Lensmire, T.J. (1998). Rewriting student voice. *Journal of Curriculum Studies*, 30(3), 261-91.

Leontiev, A.N. (1978). *Activity, consciousness, and personality.* Englewood Cliffs: Prentice-Hall.

Nakai, H. (1997). *The third collection of essays.* Tokyo: Misuzu (in Japanese).

Okazaki, K. (1999). Responsibility. In A. Isozaki & A. Asada (eds.), *Anywise.* Tokyo: NTT (in Japanese).

Suma High School (1998). *Walking in the stricken city.* Kobe: Kobe Municipal Suma Senior High School (in Japanese).

Vygotsky, L.S. (1925/1971). *The psychology of art.* Cambridge, Mass.: MIT Press.

Vygotsky, L.S. (1929/1989). Concrete human psychology. *Soviet Psychology*, 27(2), 53-77.

Wertsch, J.V. (1998). *Mind as action.* New York: Oxford University Press.

Yamazumi, K. & Yamazumi, K. (in preparation). Continuing the dialogue with the catastrophic event: A mourning work and expansive learning project of the Kobe Earthquake.

6 Culturally Sensitive Teaching within a Vygotskian Perspective

Mariane Hedegaard, Seth Chaiklin and Pedro Pedraza

Introduction

We believe that education can help children comprehend some of the contradictions and conflicts that they have or are likely to encounter in their community as part of living in a multicultural society. Research within the Vygotskian teaching and developmental learning tradition (Aidarova 1982; Davydov 1988; Lompscher 1984; Hedegaard & Lompscher 1999) has focused on forms of knowledge and subject matter content. There has not been much attention paid to the concrete cultural-historical conditions of the pupils. This chapter will present a developmental learning approach to subject matter teaching that explicitly takes the pupils cultural-historical background into account and gives some insight into how it is possible to work with a Vygotskian approach that is sensitive to the cultural-historical conditions of the pupils.

To accomplish this we have conducted a project with culturally sensitive teaching in an after-school project with Puerto Rican children in New York City.

In this approach the children's active engagement and feeling of self worth are very important both to orient themselves in the themes of the teaching and appropriate relevant methods and concepts. Therefore our main goals were to motivate the children for school activity and help them to develop their cultural identity through the teaching activities. The general content and methods of the teaching were social science activities that addressed issues in their everyday life as well as literacy activities supported by computer use. The meeting between the children's everyday life and the content of formal education provides the opportunity to simultaneously address intellectual development and motivational development.

A school child's motive and cognitive development are connected through the activities in which the child participates together with other people: in everyday family routines and activities, leisure time activities, as well as study activities connected to school life. To become developmental these activities have to take place inside the zone of proximal development. The zone of proximal development can be understood as an evaluation system that not only refers to a single child, but also can be used for the activities taking place among a group of schoolchildren with the same background. The upper level of this zone can be understood as subject-matter knowledge which the children are going to learn, and the lower level can be related to the experience and everyday knowledge that children share both from their community life and from their school life.

Culturally Sensitive Teaching Relates Everyday Knowledge and Subject-Matter Knowledge

Culturally sensitive teaching can be seen as an extension of teaching within the ZPD. Culturally sensitive teaching is aimed at helping children to use subject matter knowledge to understand the relations encountered in daily life between their community culture and other cultures (mainstream culture, school culture, culture of other communities).

Vygotsky (1982) argues that the acquisition of subject-matter knowledge extends the meaning of everyday knowledge, while subject-matter knowledge can only be understood and become functional for the child if they build on the child's everyday knowledge. If teaching succeeds in creating this relation the child will be able to use the learned subject-matter knowledge as a tool for analysing and reflecting about his everyday activities. The subject-matter knowledge thereby becomes integrated with the child's everyday knowledge and can develop into functional concepts for the child where content and form define each other.

One of the important aspects of concept formation that Vygotsky formulated is that the concepts both symbolise abstract and concrete aspects of the subject area conceptualised. He characterises a child's cognitive development as an increase in complexity of the relations between the concrete and abstract aspects of the conceptualised area (Vygotsky 1998).

The children must have specific knowledge about their community if they are going to have the possibility of understanding their culture in relation to a dominant culture; factual knowledge alone is not sufficient. The children need some way to make sense of facts. One way to make sense is to use theoretical modelling as a tool to analyse concrete phenomena (Davydov 1982; Hedegaard 1990, 1995; Lompscher 1985). However, this tool is worthless if the children have no interest in formulating questions, that would require the use of this tool, hence the importance of motivation. Once the children (supported by the teacher) have formulated questions, they need to know specific procedures for seeking answers. If we can realise these objectives in the teaching, then the children have acquired tools for analysing their societal conditions so that they can explicitly relate their own cultural traditions and history with the more dominant one within which they live. In particular, the children have also acquired knowledge that contributes to the development of their cultural identity.

Motivation and Interest

Motivation has either been characterised as external, i.e., punishment or reward, or as internal. Both views centre upon the individual child, but motivation does not lie with the child only. Motivation is developed from the child as well as from collective activity in which the child takes part. The child's motivation can never be characterised independently of the activities in which the child participates but is also always determined by the individual interest.

Interest is anchored in stable motivational structures that are formed through the child's development. They result from those activities that the child has participated in at different developmental periods, and how these activities turned out for the child. Interest can be regarded as a result of activities but also as incentives for the child's future activities.

In our opinion, the work with children's motivation for and interest in the content of subject matter content and skills demands teaching which allow children to be active and explorative. However children's activity must neither result in a blind trial-and-error method nor in activity around that which they already know. Therefore the teacher must plan the activity to a certain degree. The teacher's task is to guide the course of the activity and exploration in the class. However, we must emphasise that it is the direction that must be guided and not the actual elaboration of activities toward certain solutions.

Before describing the teaching, the setting in which the teaching took place will be characterised.

The Puerto Rican After-School Project

An experiment with culturally sensitive teaching was conducted in an after-school teaching programme in East Harlem, two afternoons a week. Most of the children in the teaching project were born in New York City, but their parents were likely to have been born or lived for some period in Puerto Rico.

Societal Conditions for Puerto Rican Children Living in New York City

East Harlem is one of the largest and oldest Puerto Rican settlements in New York City (History Task Force 1979). The political influence, economic resources, and educational opportunities in this community are considerably less than what can be found in most other communities, and the statistical indicators of the quality of life (e.g., unemployment, crime, inadequate housing, teenage pregnancy, school drop-out rates) are among the worst in the United States (Kolata 1989; Nieto 2000). The children in this community live in a society that discriminates against Hispanics. Their daily life includes many cultural activities and practices that are rejected, minimised or ignored, both in the activities they encounter in school and in mass media.

One consequence of these conditions is that children in the community experience conflicts that affect their cultural identity. For example, the children in our teaching experiment resist using Spanish, tend to downplay the value of their neighbourhood and tend not to recognise any value in the cultural traditions in their community.

The Aim of the Teaching Experiment

Puerto Ricans are the second largest minority group in New York City, comprising about one million of the city's eight million inhabitants. The social worlds created in the school curriculum have not enabled Puerto Rican children to learn about their own history and culture, or to understand their culture in relation to the societal values and images they encounter in school. Consequently, in trying to build the cultural identity of Puerto Rican children, we wanted to help them develop a means to understand their culture in relation to a dominant culture.[1]

---

1. Puerto Rico is legally a Commonwealth of the United States; in practical terms it is an American colony. People born in Puerto Rico are American citizens and issued

The objectives of the experiment were on several levels. On a formal level the aim was to support children's acquisition of literacy skills facilitated by computer use, because the after-school programme were given a donation of 20 computers. The development of computer literacy skills became at the project level embedded into a process of learning social science skills (Chaiklin, Hedegaard, Navarro & Pedraza 1990). The dominating objective was to help children learn to value their culture, while still functioning in a society with a different, dominant culture. At the project level the aim was to create motivation and self-respect by having the student exploring their own history and acquiring knowledge of the positive aspects and potentials of their own community.

Culturally Sensitive Teaching Strategies

Culturally sensitive teaching is accomplished through a *double move approach* to teaching (Hedegaard 1990, 1995). This teaching approach should lead to *developmental learning* and builds on Vygotsky's concept of the zone of proximal development transformed into classroom teaching and learning.

The four main principles that this approach builds upon are:

1. use of a core model to guide instruction;
2. use of research strategies to structure the students learning activity in ways that are analogical to the researchers way of exploring and formulating knowledge within a subject area;
3. creating phases in the teaching process based on the qualitative change in the child's learning process;
4. formation of motivation in the class activity through facilitating communication and cooperation between students.

We wanted the students to understand that neither their own community nor families in general always look the same, but that they have changed, are changing and will continue to change in the future, and that these changes should be understood in relation to resources and work in society.

American passports, but those who live there do not pay Federal taxes and do not have voting representation in the United States Congress. American corporations, with the support of the United States government and collaboration of the Puerto Rican government, have developed and maintained an economic policy that has left Puerto Rico without adequate employment levels nor means of self-sufficiency. Therefore, many people have migrated to the United States seeking better opportunities.

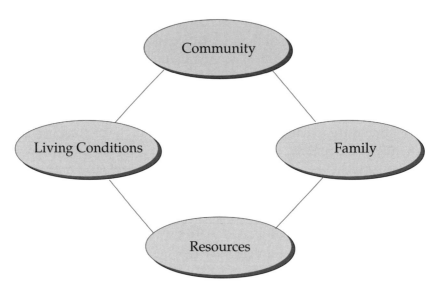

Figure 6.1. The core model.

The Problem Area Investigated

The domain of social history used in the after-school teaching project was formulated into a research area with the following questions: What are our roots? What are the characteristics of the society we live in today? How do we relate to this society as a member of a Puerto Rican community? These questions focus on the living conditions in the community and how these conditions are formed in relation to the larger society of New York City of which the Puerto Rican community in East Harlem is a part.

We created tasks for the children to explore these problems by examining Puerto Rican traditions for family life and the resources found in their community for a good life. Family life, resources, living conditions and community were chosen as the basic conceptual relations for the core model guiding the teaching (see Figure 6.1).

In selecting content for our teaching programme, we chose topics that would help children develop skills to understand their community culture in relation to the city where they currently live.

The concrete problems investigated as part of developing and using this model are:

— The children's location in the world and their ancestor's location (by using maps).

— Puerto Rico at the turn of the century before large-scale immigration to the U.S.

— New York at the beginning of the 20th Century when Puerto Ricans started to immigrate.

— East Harlem community today, its location and characteristics in relation to New York City.

The relations in the model were the starting points for guiding the creation of learning tasks that explored the conditions of the children's community. In exploring these conditions, the activities were structured around the concepts of the core model (e.g., the characteristics of family life, living conditions, work, and resources in different historical periods and at different places). The teacher's model was not presented directly to the children. We had to conduct many teaching activities to help children form their own model.

Research Procedures

The children's exploration was facilitated through learning to use a general research procedure (see Figure 6.2) as well as specific procedures (interviews, computer drawings, and graphs). The general procedure was used with the aim (a) that children should learn to conduct a joint investigation of a problem area, and (b) that the daily class activities gradually could be self-guided.

The general research procedures were based on the six questions shown in Figure 6.2.

The teaching reflected this research procedure by the teacher organising each session: (a) starting with a resume of the activities which the previous session formed as a dialogue around the questions in the research procedure, and by (b) the structure of the sessions where the children and the teacher in cooperation formulated the goal for today's session activities, conducted the activity, and reviewed what was accomplished in the resume for the following session. The teacher initially took more responsibility for organising and managing the educational activities, but the children gradually took over as they learned the procedures and the particular relations of the core model.

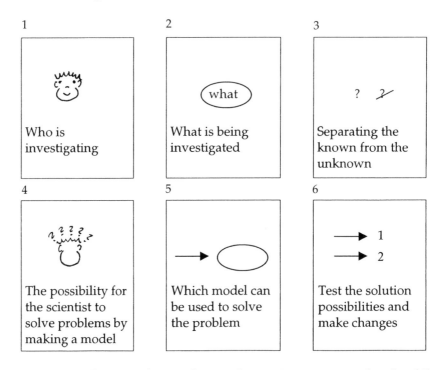

Figure 6.2. The general research procedure as it was presented to the children.

Planning and Evaluating Teaching Sessions

Each teaching session was recorded by writing a protocol by a participant-observer. Also each week the research group, including the teacher, met to plan the upcoming teaching sessions. The group used the observation protocols as well as the general model in Figure 6.1 as a tool for evaluating the activities as well as planning specific activities for the next teaching session.

Teaching Phases

At a macro-level the school year was divided into three main phases: first 'problem formation', second 'formulation of core relations based on research and analyses', third 'use of the core relations to explore and understand their own community'. Each phase was accomplished through giving the children learning tasks that changed qualitatively from the first to the last phase.

The problem formulation was the first phase in the process of teaching and learning, but this activity did not end when the second and third phase started — the formulation of core relation and research. In these later phases problem formulation was no longer the dominating activity, it was subordinated and became part of other activities but was still part of the process and the main problems were reformulated and differentiated throughout the whole teaching/learning process.

Each theme in the teaching activities was related to the general problem that organised the teaching plan for the year: The historical development of the Puerto Rican community in New York City, with a particular focus on the change in living conditions and family life from Puerto Rico at the start of the century to the present-day East Harlem community.

Motivation

The first step in solving the motivation problem in our teaching experiment was to work out tasks for the children. These tasks were related to the overall conception of the content. But then the problem arose as to how the children's interest and commitment in the task was ensured. We tried to solve this problem in different ways. First we planned the instruction on the assumption that children at middle school age are starting to be conscious of: Who they are. What were their origins. How other children in their neighbourhood /community live. How children in different places live, and how they lived in different times.

The next step was to make the children work actively with these problems which we approached through formulating the after-school programme as 'The young scientist club' where they had to formulate and explore problems, and then taught them procedure so they could become capable of exploring problems. Besides these general initiatives to create motivation we also considered some specific approaches.

Specific ways of creating motivation in the course of instruction:

— Creating tasks that contained, opposition, contrast and conflicts.
— Setting tasks that make the children's explorative activity genuine and not a pseudo activity where the teacher had the correct solution 'up his sleeve'.
— Using cooperation among children in pairs or small groups.
— Using class dialogue so that children's solutions, suggestion or com-

ments could be confronted with other solutions, suggestions and comments.

Teaching and Learning in the Programme

The analyses of the protocols are presented in the following for each of the three teaching phases: (1) problem formation, (2) formulation of core relations and research (3) use of core relations to explore their own community. The teaching and learning were evaluated from the aspects seen in Figure 6.3.

Problem Formation

Themes, tasks and children's concept formation. The research question structuring this period was: (1) Where do we come from? How did people live in Puerto Rico in the old days? (2) The young scientist club, which involved working as a researcher and using a computer.

The first theme the children worked with was living conditions in Puerto Rico at the beginning of the 20th century. This theme introduced the children to some aspects of their culture and history that would be unknown to them. This historical contrast highlights the specific aspects of the first relation we worked with — family life and its relation to living conditions. We organised a variety of activities to develop the children's understanding of this relation as well as introduce them to some basic methods of social science research — analysis of photographs, films, and maps.

The photographs were selected to show family and living conditions. One set showed living conditions in Puerto Rico at the beginning of the 20th century. The children were asked to compare the living conditions seen in the pictures with their living conditions in New York City. The children also analysed a film about life in Puerto Rico at the beginning of the 20th century. They located Puerto Rico in relation to New York City on the world map and located places where relatives in Puerto Rico lived.

'The Young Scientist Club': To formulate questions as part of doing research became part of the children's activity already in the first session, because the second topic of the class discussion was: what are we going to research. The teacher extended the children's naive conception of doing research in the second session by focusing on three steps: (a) who is doing the research, (b) what to research and (c) how to get information.

Teaching themes and tasks — children's concept formation.
–   Which conceptual relations, themes, tasks and procedures are introduced and how?
–   Did the children work with the task?
–   Did they respond to and become able to use the conceptual relations and work with the procedures?
–   What are the products of the class activity?

Children's motivation and problems.
–   What are the sources of the children's motivation?
–   Did the children's motivation develop?
–   What kind of problems came up during a teaching session?
–   Way of participating in the class dialogue.

Figure 6.3. Categories for analysing the observation protocols.

When computers were introduced in the fourth session the children were allowed to explore and familiarise themselves with the computer, assisted by the adults participating in the programme. In the fifth session the teacher gave a short lecture about the different menus and drawing functions in the software programme. At the sixth session the children all got the same task — to draw their family household — and from now on the computer was accepted as a tool and not only something to play with. The computer activity had started to become related to the content of the activities connected to the research area.

Motivation and problems. We hoped these topics of Puerto Rico 'in the old days' would interest the children because of the contrast between their own living conditions and the living conditions of their parents or grandparents as children. Our expectation was supported. The children liked to participate in the class dialogue and all contributed, but in the first session and also in the third session they got restless talking about doing research. But later in the third session, when they had to ask the adults about their relatives in Puerto Rico they became eager and the interest continued when they were given the task of describing the three pictures of children in the old days in Puerto Rico. They were also interested when they had to make a list about what a researcher can explore. At this early period of the teaching the children were motivated when they were engaged in activities but they did not want to talk too long afterwards about the activities. The children were eager about using the computers and they approached this activity full of energy and excitement.

Formulation of Core Relations and Research

Themes, tasks and concept formation. The themes domination this period were: (1) formulating and drawing the core relations into a model, (2) acquiring interview as a research method.

The first core relation was living conditions-family life. The goal was to help the children acquire a basic understanding of the interdependence of these two aspects of life, so that they could analyse that a change in the one aspect will influence the other. In particular, the children should understand that social and material conditions influence size, relations and traditions of the family, and the size and structure of the family also influences the social and material conditions.

'Interview training': The children were trained and got skilled in doing interviews, an activity which the teacher gradually extended through demonstrations and small tasks until they became so skilled that they were able to cooperate in a long interview with an elderly male citizen (see Figure 6.4). The skill of interviewing was something that was not just accomplished but gradually was built through several small tasks.

The information that the children got from doing these interviews was conceptualised into charts about living conditions and family life in the old days in Puerto Rico (see Figure 6.5). This conceptualisation brought other activities into the teaching. The children took turns writing the characteristics on the chart. They helped each other by spelling in chorus. They drew characteristics of living conditions and family life on the computer and glued the pictures on the charts. And they spontaneously counted residents in the apartment buildings where they lived to figure out the number of people in a community.

Through viewing two films — one about a Puerto Rican boy in New York City in the late 20th century, the second about a Puerto Rican family at the beginning of the 20th century in Puerto Rico — the children were able to

CARLOS QUESTIONS

1 – Were you born when the black could not be with the white?

2 – How were school in old the time?

3 – Did you like the old times?

4 – Was you in wars?

5 – Did you work hard?

6 – Did you have friends?

7 – Was life nice in those days?

8 – Did thins cost alot in those days?

9 – Did you work hard?

10 – Did you have a job?

11 – Did people have clothes like now?

12 – Did you like the thins in those times?

13 – Did you live in a big house?

Figure 6.4. A child's interview guide about living conditions and family life.

compare the Puerto Rican way of life in the old days with the modern life for Puerto Rican's in New York City today. This activity also brought the distinction up between being poor or rich.

When they analysed the two films, the children were capable of using the concepts from their chart of living conditions and family life. They talked about and confronted being poor and rich under both conditions — Modern New York City and Puerto Rico in the old days — and they also discussed how they imagined it would be for a poor family from the Puerto Rico of 'the old days' to come to New York City today, something which none of the children could imagine these people would be capable of managing.

Other relations in the model — resources and community — came up spontaneously in the children's investigations of living conditions and family life. This second relation, resources and community, was then openly introduced by the teachers through a new theme for activities with new tasks. This second theme focused on life in New York City at the beginning of the 20th

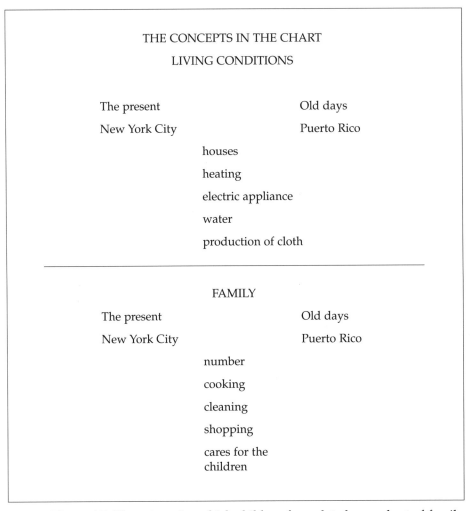

THE CONCEPTS IN THE CHART

LIVING CONDITIONS

| The present | Old days |
| New York City | Puerto Rico |

houses

heating

electric appliance

water

production of cloth

FAMILY

| The present | Old days |
| New York City | Puerto Rico |

number

cooking

cleaning

shopping

cares for the
children

Figure 6.5. The categories which children formulated on a chart of family and living conditions.

century. The children were taken on a trip to the Museum of the City of New York to learn about the kinds of institutions that existed and the type of work people did at the beginning of the 20th century in New York City. They also conducted a second interview with the 90-year old man to find out what kind of work there was and what life was like in New York when he first arrived in 1925. The information they gathered was again contrasted with their knowledge of work today and the consequences of work for living conditions.

Motivation and problems. The children gradually came to master interviewing. It was an activity they were ignorant about in the beginning and did not pay attention to the task. By small interview tasks and having the activity worked through in class, they became eager to go into teamwork, interviewing each other. The interview activity with the elderly citizen seemed to be highly motivated for the children because they concentrated for more than an hour on interviewing, even though the interviewed person spoke Spanish and the children spoke English, so everything had to be translated. They all waited patiently for the translations and for each other to ask their questions.

The children got excited and were eager to contribute when they conceptualised the interview questions into the charts about family life and living conditions. They all contributed to the discussion and made pictures of the different characteristics of these categories and controlled that each written characteristic had a corresponding picture.

The children introduced the concepts poor and rich and they discussed this opposition enthusiastically with both emotional and ethical reactions to the fairness of the differences. During the 19th session (the last before Christmas) the children got tired of summarising living conditions and family life and it was obvious that the teaching had to proceed to the next theme.

Using the Core Relations to Research one's own Community

Themes, tasks and concept formation. The third phase focused on life in the immediate community. First, the children worked with locating their community by a series of tasks involving maps of New York City and of East Harlem. The second theme in this phase was to get the children to formulate topics that they would like to investigate about life in their community, in terms of the basic relations — family-life, living conditions and work. Third the theme was to draw models of what they knew about their community.

If the children could not model the relationship between community, family life and/or living conditions then they were asked to make a list characterising the life in their community. Based on this list the teacher asked the children about the relationship between these different items as a step for building models (see Figures 6.6 and 6.7).

THE FAMILY

He pay by working in the sorty he pay 45 dollier

The mother stay home and kind the house and cook

The mother go to work and come home to cook

Figure 6.6. A child's model of living conditions and family relation.

Following the model drawing, a new theme was brought up that the children should get inspiration from what is around them in their community. Then the task was introduced that they should formulate ideas of a good life in a community. As a result of the class dialogue, the teacher made a chart of what was important in a community for a good life (see Figure 6.8) and introduced a discussion of how the children empirically could test their ideas.

The activity decided upon was to find out what resources were present in their community. They divided into three groups that each took responsibility for going to different streets and counting the kinds of buildings, stores and institutions that were on the streets. They recorded their findings and back in the class the teacher helped them produce bar graphs of their data — first by hand and then with a computer spreadsheet. The different

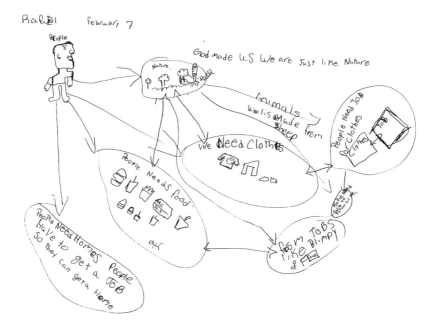

Figure 6.7. A child's model of a good life.

groups compared their results and then the children compared their combined results with similar data for New York City as a whole. This helped the children get a concrete image of the institutions that make up their community, as well as learn about the procedure of collecting, processing, and interpreting quantitative data.

The children discussed how to survive in the community without having paid work, which is a problem for some families in their community. Through their discussions the children also showed that they could make an abstract analysis of problems in the community. The plan was to use the model as a way of localising and understanding special problems (e.g., homelessness). We started this activity, but ran out of time for further exploration with the children.

Motivation and problems. The expectation was that after the children started to work on building their models, certain issues, questions, and topics would arise that they would like to know about, and that would be the basis for forming questions that they would want to investigate. However the

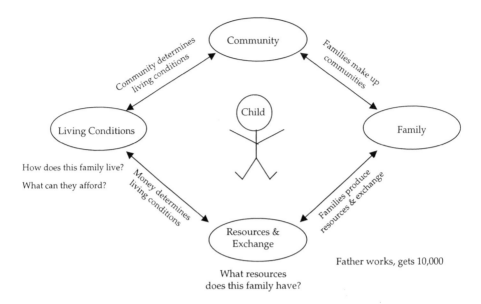

Figure 6.8. The model of a good life.

students' community model-making did not go so well, because the model activity was not planned and outlined sufficiently. The children did not know if they should make models of the buildings and how this relates to the core relation of living conditions and family life they had worked with.

The confusion that characterised both the teacher's and the children's conceptions and modelling was reflected in the low motivation during January. However, the children's engagement in the research activities by going out to record the different types of resources that were in the community changed this picture. The disintegration, which resulted from the January sessions, disappeared when the children began these activities. However some new activities and experiences were needed so that the children could develop an understanding of the historical change of their local community.

Discussion

We have presented an approach to working with minority children in a culturally-sensitive educational programme. Learning was seen both as a process of building motivation as well as of formation of concepts about the children's surroundings. The children enjoyed very much that they could help each other, that they worked in pairs most of the time and that they had a discussion in the classroom of the implication of their research activities. The atmosphere was warm and the children engaged themselves in the different tasks. The content of the activities was engaging in relation to their community and family life and could be seen as supporting their development of cultural identity. But the content and methods were also central for their learning from a subject matter perspective. The children learned to:

— use historical and social science concepts to investigate the regional history and relate it to present-day life in their community.
    move between abstract concepts and concrete events
— use social science methods: Comparative analysis of pictures and films, preparing and conducting interviews and write the results down, to prepare and produce graphs, and draw simple models; in this process the children used pencil and paper as well as computers.

An after-school setting is not the same as a school class; some important elements make a difference. There is no sanction if the student does not turn up. There is no test that counts for the students' future academic carrier. These are the aspects that give both students and teacher freedom. The students do not need to feel afraid about not passing an exam, or being stigmatised because s/he is not doing well enough. The teacher can experiment with subject matter themes and concepts. At the same time, however, after-school teaching is a setting for learning. Both the parent and the student expect that they will learn something valuable and the teaching has to be meaningful for the student otherwise they 'vote with their feet'. Experiments with content and methods in after-school programmes therefore give possibility for innovation in teaching.

We shall argue that some of the ideas in this after-school project can be of value in school teaching.

The specific project — The Young Scientist Club — inspired a teaching project with immigrant children in Denmark. A new type of school for school dropouts was made, drawing on the experience from the school experiment in East Harlem (Hedegaard 2000). In New York City, Pedro Pedraza, as a member of the Puerto Rican Study Center at Hunter College, continued the after-school project 'The Young Scientists Club' in another after-school in East Harlem (Pedraza & Ayala 1996), and this project gave inspiration to the El Puente Academy for Peace and Justice (Rivera & Pedraza 2000). But the general ideas advanced in this project are possible to transfer to the classroom. The project supports Paradise's (1998) advice that school teaching should take inspiration from what is learnt in community and family, where there are no failures and dropouts. The anxiety and fear that children can experience when taking tests in school can be a serious problem for their learning. McDermott (1993) illustrates this problem very well in his case description of a boy, Adam, in the different settings of test activities, school class activities and after-school activities. The case shows that Adam's reading competence change within these different settings. A way to overcome this is formulated by students in the Torres-Guzman & Thorne (2000) research. In this study the students point to the importance of cooperation between children and the caring attitude of the teacher for their engagement and learning.

We shall also argue that this cooperative and caring atmosphere has to be combined with both concepts and methods that are important from a societal perspective as being a source that influences students' learning and motivation.

Several projects with an interest in making the content of school instruction more relevant to children's background and experience have focused on studying the immediate community in which children find themselves. For example the Foxfire project which originated in Georgia in 1967 is one example in which students have been motivated to engage in literacy activities through the investigation of their Appalachian community and culture (Puckett 1989).

Hime (1977) conducted science projects, in collaboration with community organisations with Navajo Students in 1966. The projects were initiated from student-formulated interests, with an explicit requirement to use community-based knowledge sources and topics rooted in Navajo traditions.

Diaz, Moll and Mehan (1986) describe an example in which students, organised by their teacher, conducted a community survey about attitudes toward bilingualism as a foundation for writing a report on this subject.

In Puerto Rico, Quentero (1989) initiated a project that aimed at improving the quality and success of schooling in an unsuccessful school district in San Juan, Puerto Rico, in which children displayed an interest in their community after they were allowed to make some theatrical presentations about problems there.

In New York City, there have been other projects focussing on students with a Puerto Rican background.

Torres-Gusmán (1991) describes an example of teaching in a New York City high school in which students became engaged in investigating industrial pollution in their own neighbourhood.

Mercado (1992) introduced research activity into normal classroom teaching. The children chose topics to investigate focusing on questions that directly affected their community (e.g., teenage pregnancy, drugs). Her work showed that children in high school are capable of taking responsibility for doing intellectual work with greater sophistication and complexity than might be expected for this educational level and from the societal position of the school.

The diversity of settings in which these examples occurred suggest that many groups of children may be interested in investigating their communities, especially when they are given some choices about what to investigate and are supported in producing genuine, high-quality products as a result of their work. But it is important to point out that the mere presence of culturally relevant materials is not in itself sufficient for children to understand the significance of this material in relation to the subject matter traditions or in relation to the implications for their own lives. In other words, it is not community studies alone that are critical, but also their potential to develop a closer connection between content of schooling, the interests and motives of the students and their social development.

The kind of teaching that we have advocated is teaching that combines subject matter knowledge and methods with socialisation and identity formation, a process that is very important in school age as an explicit process (Berger and Luckmann 1966). This project supports the idea that cultural identity is not as a core but as relation between person and context. Cultural identity is situated and context dependent (Barth 1969; Eriksen & Sørheim 1994). This conception supports a view of the child as developing through participating in different institutions with different cultural history, in the concrete example through participating in the Puerto Rican family, and that this need not be in opposition to also developing through participating in a the rural school system of New York city if the Puerto Rican child can feel at home both places.

References

Aidarova, L. (1982). *Child development and education* (L. Lezhneva, trans.). Moscow: Progress.

Barth, F. (1969). Introduction. In F. Barth (ed.), *Ethnic groups and boundaries. The social organization of culture differences*. Bergen, Norway: University Press.

Berger, P.L. & Luckmann, T. (1966). *The social construction of reality: A treatise in the sociology of knowledge*. New York: Doubleday.

Chaiklin, S., Hedegaard, M., Navarro, K. & Pedraza, P. (1990). The horse before the cart: A theory-based approach to the use of computers in education. *Theory into Practice, 29*, 270-75.

Davydov, V.V. (1982). Ausbildung der Lerntätigkeit. In V.V. Davydov, J. Lompscher & A.K. Markova (eds.), *Ausbildung der Lerntätigkeit bei Schülern*. Berlin: Volk und Wissen.

Davydov, V.V. (1988-1989). Problems of development teaching. *Soviet Education, 30*, No. 8-9-10.

Diaz, S., Moll, L.C. & Mehan, H. (1986). Sociocultural resources in instruction: A context specific approach. In *Beyond language. Social and cultural factors in schooling language of minority students*. Boston: South End Press.

Eriksen, T.H. & Sørheim, T.A. (1994). *Kulturforskelle i praksis. Perspektiver på det flerkulturelle Norge*. Olso, Norway: Gyldendal.

Hedegaard, M. (1990). The zone of proximal development as basis for instruction. In L.C. Moll (ed.), *Vygotsky and education: Instructional implications and applications of sociohistorical psychology*. Cambridge: Cambridge University Press.

Hedegaard, M. (1995). The qualitative analyses of the development of a child's theorethical knowledge and thinking. In L. Martin, K. Nelson & E. Toback (eds.), *Sociocultural psychology. Theory and practice of doing and knowing*. Cambridge: Cambridge University Press.

Hedegaard, M. (2000). Cultural knowledge, identity and learning. Paper presented at The III conference for Sociocultural Research, Campinas July 16th-20th, 2000.

Hedegaard, M. & Lompscher, J. (eds.) (1999). *Learning activity and development*. Aarhus, Denmark: Aarhus University Press.

Hime, C. (1977). Ethnoscience: An educational concept. In V.L. Melnick & F.D. Hamilton (eds.), *Minorities in science: The challenge for change in biomedicine*. New York: Plenum.

Kolata, G. (1989). Grim seeds of park rampage found in East Harlem streets. *The New York Times*, May 2, C1, C13.

Lompscher, J. (1984). Problems and results of experimental research on the formation of theoretical thinking through instruction. In M. Hedegaard, P. Hakkarainen & Y. Engeström (eds.), *Learning and teaching on a scientific basis*. Aarhus: Aarhus University, Institute of Psychology.

Lompscher, J. (1985). *Persönlichkeitsentwicklung in der Lerntätigkeit* [The development of personality in learning activity]. Berlin: Volk und Wissen.

McDermott, R.P. (1993). The acquisition of a child by a learning disability. In S. Chaiklin & J. Lave (eds.), *Understanding practice*. Cambridge: Cambridge University Press.

Mercado, C. (1992). Researching research: A student, teacher collaborative project. In A.N. Ambert & M.D. Alvarez (eds.), *Puerto Rican children on the mainland*. New York: Garland.

Nieto, S. (2000). Puerto Rican students in US schools: A brief History. In S. Nieto (ed.), *Puerto Rican students in US schools*. Mahwah, N.J.: Lawrence Erlbaum.

Paradise, R. (1998). What's different about learning in schools as compared to family and community settings? *Human Development*, 41, 270-78.

Pedraza, P. & Ayala, J. (1996). Motivation as an emergent issue in an after-school program in El Barrio. In L. Schauble & R. Glaser (eds.), *Innovations in learning. New environments for education*. Mahwah, N.J.: Lawrence Erlbaum.

Puckett, J.L. (1989). *Foxfire reconsidered: A twenty-year experiment in progressive education*. Urbana: University of Illinois Press.

Quentero, A.H. (1989). The University of Puerto Rico's partnership project with schools. A case study for the analysis of school improvement. *Harvard Educational Review*, 59, 347-452.

Rivera, M. & Pedraza, P. (2000). The spirit of transformation: An education reform movement in New York City Latino/a community. In S. Nieto (ed.), *Puerto Rican students in US schools*. Mahwah, N.J.: Lawrence Erlbaum.

The History Task Force, Center for Puerto Rican Studies (1979). Labor migration under capitalism: The Puerto Rican experience. *Monthly Review Press*.

Torres-Guzmán, M.E. (1991). Stories of hope in the midst of despair: Culturally responsive education for Latino students in an alternative high school in New York City. In M. Sarvia Shore & S. Alvizu (eds.), *Cross cultural literacy: Ethnographies of communication in multiethnic classrooms*. New York: Garland.

Torres-Guzmán, M.E. & Thorne, Y.M. (2000). Puerto Rican/Latino student voices: Stand and deliver. In S. Nieto (ed.), *Puerto Rican Students in U.S. Schools*. Mahwah, N.J.: Lawrence Earlbaum.

Vygotsky, L.S. (1982). *Om barnets psykiske udvikling*. Copenhagen: Nyt Nordisk Forlag.

Vygotsky, L.S. (1998). *The collected works of L.S. Vygotsky, vol. 5. Child Psychology*. New York: Plenum Press.

7 Science Literacy in the Making in an Inner-City Youth Programme: 'They Take the Time to Show us how a Plant Grows'

Jrene Rahm

The educational value of youth programmes that exist alongside schools is not yet widely recognised. Instead, most studies have addressed children's learning in school settings or in academic domains such as mathematics, science or reading (Schauble, Beane, Coates, Martin & Sterling 1996). Given changes in our society, such as less family support for children's learning and development, increasing levels of poverty, and higher demands in a fast changing technological society, many youths are no longer well equipped to cope with the challenges adulthood poses (Carnegie Council on Adolescent Development 1992). It is also recognised that schools can no longer bear the burden of education alone (Heath & McLaughlin 1994b, 1994c; Resnick 1990). It is for this reason that youth organisations have become important sites for researchers to study since they do provide children with 'educative contexts that can supply overlapping and reinforcing opportunities for learning, practicing, and applying skills and knowledge in supportive and positive surrounds' (Schauble et al. 1996, 6).

Studies of out-of-school learning have focused on craft practices and workplace environments (e.g., Chaiklin & Lave 1993; Engeström & Middleton 1996), on everyday mathematics practices (Lave 1988; Nunes, Schliemann & Carraher 1993; Saxe 1991), and on everyday science practices in museums and after-school programmes (Hofstein & Rosenfeld 1996; Ramey-Gassert 1997). Yet, only recently have researchers taken up the task of describing the learning opportunities youth programmes provide at the neighbourhood and community level. For instance, work by Heath and McLaughlin (1994a, 1994b, 1994c; see also McLaughlin, Irby & Langman 1994) has examined resources and programmes that are available to youth in diverse urban settings and identified characteristics of organisations that youth found supportive and relevant. In addition, the Carnegie Council on Adolescent Development (1992) conducted a study of youth organisations, and their goals and role in youth development. The task force concluded that 'community-based youth development organizations represent a valuable national resource with considerable untapped potential' (p. 11). Recently, work in Brazil has demonstrated the value of 'Education in the Open Environment', a pedagogical framework developed by street social workers that offers educational activities in open spaces where street youth 'hang out' (deOliveira & Montecinos 1997, 3). For instance, a system of several circuits was developed, providing youth with learning opportunities to prepare for life. These studies all point to the important developmental role youth programmes can and do play. Yet, little is known about the kinds of learning opportunities such informal settings provide for youth.

Clearly, learning in informal settings differs significantly from learning in institutions such as schools. For instance, learning is not the primary goal in informal settings but instead collaboration and active participation is valued as something that leads to the production of some tangible result (Schauble et al. 1996; Heath & McLaughlin 1994b). Participation is also voluntary and hence youth programmes strive to be fun, engaging places that provide youth with multiple authentic and meaningful activities (Schauble et al. 1996). Informal settings also tend to be more responsive than schools to needs, interests and talents of individual children (Carnegie Council on Adolescent Development 1992). Typically youth, rather than the curriculum, are at the centre. This allows for youth agency rather than the mere consumption of a curriculum as is the case in school (Heath & McLaughlin 1994b). Evaluation functions to improve the work, rather than rank individuals (Schauble et al. 1996). Hence, youth programmes provide contexts for learning very different from schools, and further studies are needed that address the kinds of literacies such practices support.

This study makes an attempt to fill this gap by examining the ways children talk and think about science in an inner-city youth gardening programme I shall call 'City Farmers'. In the City Farmers programme youth were in charge of growing, harvesting, and marketing herbs, flowers, and some vegetables. Participants received an hourly stipend for their work which also lends itself to the teaching of work ethics and life skills. The goal of the City Farmers programme was three-fold as summarised by the programme director: 'The main goal was to establish a way for kids to learn plant science; the other was to have them use their discretionary time in a positive way; and a third goal was to have them earn and learn some pre-job skills.' In this paper, I shall focus on the kinds of learning opportunities the programme offered in plant science. Contrary to most summer programmes, the City Farmers programme was not driven by the intention to improve youths' school performance in science and hence provided truly alternative occasions for science literacy practices (Resnick 1990). What those occasions were and how they became enacted in practice through action and talk is addressed in this paper.

Conceptual Framework

The study was driven by my interest in how the meaning of science could, through the medium of speech, be made and conveyed in this setting. Underlying my approach to the study was the assumption that science is socially and culturally constructed through participation in communities of practice. Learning entails becoming fluent in the discourse, beliefs and values about science shared within a community of practice (Gee 1990; Latour 1987). That is to say, scientific knowledge is socially constructed through introduction into a symbolic world (Vygotsky & Luria 1994). Accordingly, this study is informed by the dialogic model of communication that emphasises the active and social nature of learning and conceives of talk as a medium through which meaning is conveyed and made (Maybin 1994; Wells 1992).

Inherent to the notion of science as a form of cultural knowledge is also the recognition that the meaning of science and being a scientist is constituted by practice (Eisenhart 1996; Eisenhart & Finkel 1998). Accordingly, through a focus on the activities and discourse in the garden, I hoped to derive the meaning of science and being a scientist in the City Farmers programme. Since science 'got done' in the garden by doing, I anticipated the forms of science practices in the City Farmers community to differ significantly from conventional school science practices. In the City Farmers programme, doing science entailed becoming a master of the cultural tools offered in the community garden, including ways of talking and thinking about plants, ways of caring for plants and ensuring their growth, ways of processing the crops for the market, and using knowledge about plant science to market the products of the garden. In contrast, in a conventional classroom, science is typically perceived as an activity whereby 'scientific theories are derived in some rigorous way from the facts of experience acquired by observation and experimentation' (Chalmers 1982, 1). Hence, the forms of science practices that the City Farmers programme supported were particular to this setting, and provided occasions for the development of science literacy that was different in character and scope from what we typically take to represent school science literacy.

Despite differences in the forms of science practices, I used my understanding of the kind of activities in plant science that schools support as an interpretive template. For instance, in school, children learn about what plants need in order to grow (water, light, soil), about how plants feed, and about the function of plant parts such as roots or leaves (Wood-Robinson 1991). Hence, I expected City Farmers to learn something about how to ensure growth of plants, and interpreted this as science. Plant identification and classification is also an essential component of the school science curriculum, and I anticipated that City Farmers needed some plant identification skills in order to weed, harvest, process and package crops. This suggests some overlap in content between the City Farmers programme and the conventional science classroom. However, since science 'got done' in the garden by doing, I anticipated the forms of science practices to look different in this setting.

Science discourse studies in classrooms also informed my definition of science talk (Lemke 1990; Snow & Kurland 1996). Science talk or talk about science, two terms I use interchangeably, was defined as any talk in which plant science terms were invoked (e.g., names of plants, names of tools, planting terminology). In addition, talk pertaining to the subject matter of plant science (the planting of seeds, plant identification, tool use, watering, weeding, harvesting, plant processing and plant packaging), was considered as science talk.

In this paper, I address two issues: First, I describe the forms of science practices the City Farmers programme supported, and second, I examine ways of talking about science and its contribution to the meaning of science in the programme. In particular, I focus on participants' questions and show in what ways they led to learning opportunities in science not intended but supported by the programme structure. Thereby I demonstrate in what ways questioning became a tool for meaning-making in this context.

Setting, Participants and Procedures

The City Farmers programme is an eight-week summer programme that meets in a community garden, three half-days for three-and-a-half hours each day. The garden plot hosting the City Farmers programme is set in an ethnically diverse neighbourhood in a low-income inner-city area in the Mid-West. The eight weeks in the garden are structured around four activity settings among which teams rotate in a two week cycle: (1) nurturing,

(2) harvesting, (3) marketing and (4) special projects. In nurturing, participants prepare the soil, plant different vegetable seeds, transplant seedlings of herbs and ensure proper growth by watering and weeding. Participants learn about the use of different gardening tools, the needs of different plants and how to identify plants. In harvesting, crops are harvested and processed for the marketing team. Participants learn to identify marketable crops, to harvest crops correctly and to prepare them for the market. In marketing, the produce is sold to neighbourhood businesses and at local markets. Participants contact businesses by phone or through visits, fill out order and delivery sheets and develop marketing skills as they sell produce at local markets. To beautify the garden through art work (i.e., mural), the planting of trees, and the setting of sandstone paths are activities central to special projects. The group is also in charge of community outreach and provides tours of the garden for visitors. Prior to the gardening work, a three-week training session introduced the participants to the kind of plant science, work and life skills central to the programme. In this paper, I shall only focus on activities that took place in nurturing and harvesting.

Twenty-three youths (twenty-one African-American, two European American; eight female and fifteen male), ranging in age from eleven to fourteen years, participated in the City Farmers programme when I conducted the study. Four adult team leaders (two African-American; two European American), two master gardeners (both European American), and the programme director (African-American) provided the guidance needed for the successful growth of marketable crops.

I completed a qualitative case study of the gardening programme. An ethnographically informed discourse analysis guided the design of the case study allowing for the simultaneous examination of the science activities of gardening and the discourse embedded in those activities. Ethnographic methods provided the means to understand the meanings, social structures and organisation of the programme from the insider's perspective, and the discourse data provided a window into issues salient to members of the community (Hymes 1974; Spencer 1994). By combining and integrating the two approaches, what it meant to do science in the gardening programme could be determined. In order to cover all aspects of the programme, I followed one team of six youths with a video camera every day. My recordings were supplemented by field notes, artefacts, and interviews of the team members at the beginning and end of the programme, and interviews of additional programme members and the adults at the end of the programme.

Verbatim transcriptions of discourse segments pertaining to gardening were integrated with my field notes. In order to infer what it meant to do science in the City Farmers community, I conducted a domain analysis of these extended field notes and developed taxonomies of the kinds of activities the programme supported (Spradley 1980). I also used my understanding of the kinds of activities in plant science that schools support as an interpretive template. Discourse analysis entailed the identification of different participation structures of the City Farmers community and the kinds of discursive devices (e.g., questions, analogies) adults and youths used to convey and make meaning of science concepts particular to this setting (Lemke 1990). From these analyses, I constructed vignettes illustrating forms of science practices particular to this setting (VanMaanen 1988). I also selected excerpts that portray the way meaning was made of science, and conveyed through talk, and some quotes from interviews to make the case for the value of the programme.

What it Meant to Do Science in the City Farmers Community

Tamara is about to plant Swiss chard in a small pot that is filled with potting soil and calls out, 'I need a ruler.' Buddy is busy potting his seeds and asks, 'why do you need a ruler?' Tamara responds quickly, 'because it said half-thirteen millimeter … that's a lot deep!' Tarr who just finished potting his seeds has some advice, 'just stick your finger in there and see!' Tamara wondered, 'my finger? The first one? Not including my finger nail?'

It is our first day in the garden and Marc, one of the Master Gardeners explains: 'Here in the raised beds area we grow most of the herbs the market wants. And some of the herbs are annuals and some of them are perennials. Behind us are most of the annual types like dill and cilantro, and right in front of you are most of the perennial types like chive and tarragon.' Marc asks Coretta to rub her finger against an oregano leaf. He wanted to know what it smelled like and whether it reminded her of anything. 'Maybe tea' Coretta offered? 'Close, I think of a nice pork pot roast. Lot's of herbs and stuff! One of the things we need to do here is, we need to learn how to identify plants.' He brakes off a couple of stems from the huge chive plant and asks Marti, 'what does it smell like to you?' 'Onions' Tamara interjected. Marc confirmed, 'onions is right, chives are related to onions. It is kind of like a mild onion.'

Tarr was asked to harvest green salad leaves. After some thought, Estelle advised him to 'actually pull out the Valeria lettuce.' That lettuce was approaching the end of its harvesting season. Will was about to do the same with the Simpson lettuce, but Estelle stopped him just in time, 'I don't want you to pull them out. What you have to do is going down (to the root) and then pick out the leaves. I know it is kind of tedious.' Estelle demonstrated what she meant and added, 'remember how I told you to pick the whole leaf?' That was important in order for the product to be marketable. Marti was done with the spinach and was now asked to harvest some collard leaves, 'let's do about ten leaves.' Tarr was wondering about the looks of a salad leaf. Estelle reminded him, 'you don't want it jagged. You want it like ...' she picked one and held it up so Tarr could see. Estelle explained, 'you see this one is nice and round all over. You want that rather than this.' She picked up another leaf, a bad model, and held them both in the air side by side.

Will is busy washing cilantro, 'a long dragging process'. Nannie is washing salad leaves and just found a bug. Estelle, the team leader, reminds everybody to do 'quality control.' Estelle gives some paper towels to Will so he can spread out the wet cilantro. 'I thought we would use the drier?' 'Well, yeah, but Tarr is using it so why don't we just go with the towels' Estelle suggests. 'So I am gonna put it on the paper towel, and then bag it and then weigh it?' Will asked. Estelle corrects, 'how about you first weigh it', Marti is about to weigh the basil and verifies with Estelle, 'one ounce?' Estelle confirms, 'yeah, you guys know how to measure one ounce, right?' Marti mumbles 'yeah, OK, one ounce' as he is about to load the scale with basil leaves.

These four vignettes depict the forms of science practices particular to the City Farmers community. Opportunities to plant seeds, as illustrated in the first vignette, emerged in training and nurturing. After having had numerous opportunities to plant seeds, City Farmers could provide advice to each other about ways it could be done. Tamara thought of using a ruler to determine planting depth. Tarr reminded her, however, that using her finger is precise enough, a form of science practice this programme supported and valued. Previously, City Farmers had practiced how to plant without a ruler by using their fingers as measurement tools. At the same time they were reminded that if seeds were planted to deep, they would have a hard time to make it to the surface and rot instead. Hence, exact science as is typically emphasised in conventional science classrooms was not of value here (e.g., use of ruler for planting). Instead, one had to be precise enough in a practical sense. To be successful at planting seeds, City Farmers needed to know the names of plants they were to grow from seeds, how far apart, and how deep seeds were to be planted — all of which I took as examples of factual science knowledge. In addition, City Farmers needed to know how seeds were to be planted and how spacing and depth for planting were to be determined; these were examples of what I took to entail practical science knowledge.

Another important form of science practice entailed the identification of plants in the garden, as the second vignette illustrates. Contrary to science classrooms, however, plant identification was not done by careful examination of the leaf structures of plants, but instead, the use of the senses was emphasised. City Farmers were encouraged to taste and smell plants in order to identify them. When physical features were noted, the focus remained on a plant's general structure. For instance, dill was considered to look somewhat 'bushy' and maybe like 'a cactus'. Hence, City Farmers had to know the names of plants (factual science knowledge) and be able to make use of their senses to identify and differentiate plants (practical science knowledge), a very different form of plant identification practice if compared with a conventional science classroom (Jantzen & Michel 1989).

Plant identification also figured in harvesting activities as the third vignette indicates. Here, Estelle, the team leader, taught City Farmers different harvesting techniques — practical science knowledge. Almost every kind of crop entailed another method depending on the kind of crop it was (plant identification) and the time of year. City Farmers were also reminded to only harvest crop that was marketable and looked nice. Note also that much of the teaching by the adults was done through demonstration and little talk. Knowing how to harvest the different crops was taken as representative of practical science knowledge.

The fourth vignette illustrates the processing and packaging procedures a City Farmer had to master. As with harvesting, such methods varied depending on the product and entailed the pursuit of a number of steps (washing, drying, weighing, packaging). Accordingly, much practical science knowledge had to be acquired by observing experts such as Estelle and by doing it under her guidance.

The four vignettes portray how the factual and practical science knowledge particular to this programme were embedded in the work that got done in nurturing and harvesting. Figure 7.1 provides a summary of how factual and practical science knowledge figured within the learning opportunities that I identified as doing science in the City Farmers community.

Accordingly, to do science in the City Farmers community entailed the knowing and doing of planting and the harvesting and processing of crops. The programme director (Kyle) summarised the way plant science figured in the four activity settings of the garden as follows:

Learning Opportunities in Science	Factual Science Knowledge	Practical Science Knowledge
Planting of Seeds:		
•Name of plants	X	
•Planting Instructions	X	
•Planting		X
Plant identification:		
•Name of plants	X	
•Knowing how to identify & differentiate plants (use smell, taste)		X
Tool Use:		
•Name of tools	X	
•Knowing when to use a certain tool	X	
•Knowing how to use tool effectively		X
Watering:		
•Knowing how to water		X
•Knowing why to water in a certain way	X	
Weeding:		
•Names of plants (Plant Identification)	X	
•Differences between plants and weeds	X	X
•Knowing how to weed effectively		X
Harvesting:		
•Names of plants (Plant Identification)	X	
•Knowing how to harvest different plants		X
Plant Processing:		
•Names of plants (Plant Identification)	X	
•Knowing how to process plants (wash, weigh, quality control)		X
Plant Packaging:		
•Names of plants (Plant Identification)	X	
•Packaging Skills (Labelling, Presentation, Holes in Bags)		X

Figure 7.1. How science figured in nurturing and harvesting activities.

Excerpt 1

KYLE: ... in terms of nurturing, they have to know what plants are, identify plants, [know] how plants work, why they need water ... and in harvesting, just little techniques like how, how to cut a plant, how to prune leaves, those are things they need to learn ... which ones will need to be pulled from underground ... why you cover plants ... what kinds of temperatures plants need ... and the marketing they start to discover how long things last, stay fresh ... they get to see how things are used in the market ... in special projects it's plant science in terms of, oh, like if you're going to build an arbour, why do you use grape plants or sandstones in terms of setting up a walkway ... and it's not necessarily plant science ... in some ways they're learning a little bit about construction.

Kyle listed the kinds of activities that he identified as doing science and that I took to represent doing science, as summarised in Figure 7.1. At the same time, when talking about marketing and special projects, Kyle also hinted at the role of business or work skills. In fact, Kyle's talk suggests that science, business and work skills were not always distinguishable but instead 'interwoven with each other' (Cole 1996, 120). Put another way, factual and practical science knowledge were constitutive of doing science in the City Farmers community. This contrasts with the conventional science classroom, that tends to emphasise factual science knowledge. While there is some overlap in the kind of factual knowledge the City Farmers programme emphasised, how science got done set it apart from school science. City Farmers did not engage in experimentations with plants, the kind of practical science knowledge some conventional classrooms might stress. Rather, City Farmers had to become masters of much factual and practical science knowledge that ensured the growth of plants and led to marketable crops. As noted by Kyle, such factual and practical science knowledge was acquired as participants mastered 'little techniques' by doing, 'discover[ing]', and 'see[ing] how things are'.

Ways of Talking About Science

To illustrate the way in which talk about science contributed to the emergent meaning of science in this setting, I provide an illustration from a planting project (planting of squash seeds) that took place over a couple of days in nurturing. In doing so, I focus on the questions City Farmers posed as they were engaged in that project. A total of 114 youth initiated questions were identified in the whole data set — a startling number since youth initiated questions are typically rare in the classroom given the assumption that questions are 'the teacher's stock in trade' (Wells 1992, 295). However, it was not only the frequency of youth initiated questions that made it an interesting construct to examine, but also the characteristics of the questions. Of particular interest to me were the ways children's questions led to learning opportunities in science not intended by the programme structure or the adults in charge, but supported by the setting. Any response (at least one sentence long) to a question pertaining to plant science was taken as illustrative of a learning opportunity in science. The planting project I am about to discuss also makes apparent the ways youths' questions were occasioned by the environment.

The planting of squash seeds was an important and elaborate project. First, the soil had to be prepared. This entailed the construction of an elaborate trench watering system around piles of dirt or mounds, on top of which squash seeds were to be planted. Such a construction prevents potentially deadly mildew from developing on the leaves of squash plants. Much work had already been done, and the team was busy planting the squash seeds on top of their mounds. In the following Excerpt, Marie, the Master Gardener, demonstrated how seeds were to be planted:

Excerpt 2
MARIE: OK. We put about two seeds in each hole. And, uhm … I'll show you once again so we don't get uhm … get them covered, uhm, too deeply because sometimes you do not get growth from … uhm, each one.
Will: [hard to understand something like: What would happen if we would get growth from each one.]
MARIE: It's fine, the strongest plant wins.
Will: So it's like survival of the fittest here.
BILL: Right.
MARIE: Yeah.
Will: Ah, that's neat.
MARIE: And then you cover it over … and … pat it down.
Buddy: Let's go.

Marie's demonstration led to Will's question about what would happen if growth from each seed would ensue. Marie explained competition between seeds in simple everyday terms whereas Will invoked a scientific expression (survival of the fittest) to make meaning of that situation. This brief exchange is illustrative of a learning opportunity in science that emerged due to Will's questioning. Marie simply intended to teach participants 'how' the seeds were to be planted (e.g., how deep, how many in one hole — practical science knowledge). Marie focused on getting the work done and did not intend to provide a reason for planting more than one seed other than, typically, growth does not always result from each seed. Only through Will's questioning did that become an issue for further discussion.

Afterwards, seeds were distributed, leading to the following exchange:

Excerpt 3
MARIE: We got yellow here.
Will: Got blue?
MARIE: Ah, that's the acorn squash and then …
Will: I want that one.
Tarr: I want that one.
MARIE: Mmmh, one, two …
Buddy: Do squashes grow [underground]?
MARIE: Uhm, no, there's plenty of seeds if for … mmh … I'm counting here to … I am sorry, do they what?
Buddy: Do squashes grow underground?
MARIE: Underground? No, no, no, they come on vines. That's why the vine comes down. That's why it is built up on the mound.

It is unclear why Will asked for 'blue'. This might refer to the colour of the seed package and not the colour of squash. That question remained unchallenged by Marie since she was busy trying to count and distribute the seeds that were available. Buddy posed a question somewhat unrelated to the seeding activity, yet illustrative of his active meaning making. Since City Farmers were instructed to plant seeds knuckle-deep in the mounds, Buddy was confused about how the seeds actually grow, leading him to wonder if 'squashes grow underground.' Marie not only provided an explanation in words but also illustrated the ways 'vines come down' with a movement of her arms. Marie reiterated her earlier instructions about why the construction of mounds was needed, 'and the reason for this is because squash gets big huge leaves and vines. But if you water it on top, it gets mildew and a fungus and it just collapses and dies. And this is why we do trench watering with squash'. By posing a question, Buddy could gather the information Marie attempted to teach previously.

Since various kinds of squash seeds were available, a question about mixing different types of seeds emerged:

Excerpt 4

Buddy: [something about wanting to start planting seeds]
Will: Yeah, give me a couple of seeds guy.
Marti: Give me some seeds, actually man … like I'm gonna try to make some grow [mumbles on] [other mumbling going on]
Will: Hey dude, do you want some seeds?
Marti: I sure do.
Will: We can't mix green with yellow? [mumbles on]
MARIE: No.
Will: We cannot put like green over here and yellow over there?
MARIE: No.
Will: Why not?
MARIE: Because what you can get is a cross-hybrid …
Marti: Can I just have some extra seeds?
             [mumbling and talk about seeds; unclear]
MARIE: Yeah, but that's why they have seeds in these packages, and, then, some-times it happens anyway. That's why I put the zucchinis down here be-cause I have seen the zucchini cross with the long straight yellow squash and you get a white squash.
Will: Ah, that's sweet. Did it taste good?
MARIE: Yeah, it tastes just like squash.

This instance is illustrative of a learning opportunity not intended by the programme structure yet supported by the context within which it emerged. A discussion about cross-hybrids was not essential to the successful comple-tion of the project, given Marie's monitoring and supervision. By organising the planting of zucchini seeds (green) at one side of the plot and squash seeds (yellow) at the other end, Marie ensured that growth would not result in cross-hybrids. Yet, participants were not oblivious to Marie's actions, which led Will to inquire about the organisation of the planting. Note also how Marie never explained the meaning of 'a cross-hybrid.' Instead, Marie noted what kind of crop such a process would lead to (i.e., white squash), that might taste fine but would be difficult to market. In that sense, Marie missed a 'teachable' moment. At the same time, this example indicates that the programme emphasised the growth of marketable crops and not the teaching of concepts such as 'a cross-hybrid', a genetic concept central to agriculture.

As is apparent in my discussion, the participants' questioning served as a testing ground for the factual and practical science knowledge they were in the process of constructing. In many instances, youths' observations of intriguing matters in the garden led to questioning and hence, also to additional learning opportunities in science not explicitly intended but not precluded and thus implicitly supported by the programme. Given the support for participants' questioning, the view of science as something that is worked on and made meaning of together was conveyed.

These excerpts further underline that science in the City Farmers community is best described as a form of practice constituted of factual and practical science knowledge that is made by doing and talking. By digging holes and putting seeds in and talking about why more than one seed is needed in each hole, City Farmers became part of this community of practice, and appropriated its ways of doing and talking. This is apparent in a dialogue that emerged towards the end of the programme as I revisited the mounds with Tarr and Will. The squash plants were now sizable. The following dialogue arose:

Excerpt 5

Tarr: This one is Tamara's and this one is mine! [he points them out to me]

JRENE: Wow, they are BIG!

Will: Buddy's didn't grow and Marti's didn't grow.

JRENE: Why do you think it didn't grow?

Tarr: I put like four seeds in each one!
        [Will adds that he also put four seeds in each one.]

Will: And Buddy stole some of mine that's why they didn't come up.

Tarr: I am not sure I don't think they put enough seeds in there.

JRENE: OK. So not enough of them germinated?

Tarr: No!

JRENE; Do you see any blossoms on there? Are they making any fruits yet like squash?

Tarr: They are starting to, I can see little *buds*.
        [he unfolds the leaves to see underneath]
        Oh, there is one of the seeds … one of the seeds …

JRENE: It came back out or what happened?

Tarr: Mmh, one of the seeds that didn't *thrive*.

JRENE: Oh, that didn't grow.

Tarr: [still looking]

         Yeah there are a lot of blossoms here ... but they didn't *sprout* ...

JRENE: Great! So we got four out of six? Is that what we got?

Will: That's a good lot.

Tarr: Ugh ... these are full of dirt [shows seeds in the air — then throws them away]

JRENE: Do you think that's a good outcome, four out of six?

Tarr: They said put two in each, but I did put at least four ...

JRENE: So you think that you put four or even six into one hole [that] was a good idea?

Will: Yeah, they have more of a chance to grow because if they all start *sprouting* then if they fight whoever wins is the biggest. So you are definitely gonna get some growth.

Note how the issue of putting more than one seed in each hole immediately surfaced. Participants could now see the result of not putting enough seeds. Tarr claimed that by putting four seeds in each hole some growth was ensured. When I asked Will whether putting more seeds into each hole was a good idea, Will commented, 'yeah, they have more of a chance to grow because if they all start sprouting then if they fight whoever wins is the biggest. So you are definitely gonna get some growth.' Here, Will integrated Marie's comment about 'the strongest plant wins' (see Excerpt 2) with his own notions about 'survival of the fittest' by referring to the plant that wins the 'fight' as the 'biggest' plant.

Note also the scientific terms Tarr invoked as he described his plant (in italics in Excerpt 5). Tarr had appropriated ways of talking particular to this setting, as is apparent in his use of terms such as 'buds' or by referring to seeds that did not make it as 'seeds that didn't thrive' and 'didn't sprout.' The ease with which Tarr incorporated these words into his description of the mound project suggests that he appropriated not only the linguistic code, but also the underlying meaning of each term. Accordingly, action and talk facilitated City Farmers appropriation of factual and practical science knowledge in addition to the science genre inherent in this community of practice. Furthermore, the frequency of youth initiated questions indicates that the meaning of science in the garden was something to be constructed together rather than simply conveyed and made by the adults.

Differences	Conventional science classroom	City Farmers programme
Meaning of Science	Science is an activity in which evidence is gathered through observation and experimentation to explain and predict natural phenomena. (Chalmers 1982)	Science is a form of practice constituted of factual and practical science knowledge that is made by doing and talking.
Source of Science Knowledge	• Teacher • Textbook • Classroom Discussions • Experimentation in Laboratory	• Talk with Master Gardeners, Team Leaders & Peers • Environment • Action
Method	• 5 standard steps of scientific method • Memorising • Lectures & laboratory activities	• Doing work • Invoking analogies • Asking questions
Goal	To prepare students to 'view the world through the eyes of science and to develop scientific habits of mind.' (Ahlgren & Rutherford 1993, 20)	To teach enough factual and practical plant science knowledge to get work done and to grow marketable crops.
Role of Science	Science as an end.	Science as a means to an end.

Figure 7.2. Science in the conventional classroom and the City Farmers programme.

Figure 7.2 summarises some of the differences that set the City Farmers programme apart from a conventional science classroom.

As noted in Figure 7.2, participants could gather a sense of science particular to this setting through their interactions with the environment (e.g., observing different kinds of plants), through their actions (e.g., harvesting salad leaves) and through talk (e.g., wanting a ruler, questioning). This set the programme apart from a conventional science classroom, where the teacher and the textbook are typically the primary two sources of science knowledge. As the vignettes and excerpts illustrate, participants made use of questions when in doubt about the kind of factual and practical science knowledge the programme valued (e.g., wanting a ruler to determine planting depth). In addition, my discourse analysis showed that analogies were frequently invoked by both adults and participants to make meaning of new science concepts. This contrasts with most conventional science classrooms, where language is perceived as a resource to provide information, rather than to socially construct new meanings in the manner observed in this setting (Wells 1992). Furthermore, the posing of questions by City Farmers attests to their active involvement and the youth-centred nature of the programme. This contrasts with the school setting which is curriculum driven and tends to be supportive of questions posed primarily by teachers (Wells 1992).

Such differences are attributable to the goal of each setting and the role science plays in each. The City Farmers programme intended to teach its participants enough factual and practical science to grow marketable crops, the primary goal. Accordingly, the kind of science knowledge City Farmers developed served as a means to achieve that goal. In contrast, in the classroom science tends to be an end in itself. That is to say, schools attempt to prepare students to 'view the world through the eyes of science and to develop scientific habits of mind' (Ahlgren & Rutherford 1993, 20). Hence, the forms of science practices supported by the City Farmers programme differed in character and scope from school science practices and were driven by a different goal.

Implication of Findings: What Is the Educational Value of a Youth Programme?

As noted by Heath and McLaughlin (1994b), youth spend 40% of their waking hours outside of school. While much of that time may be wasted, programmes such as the one discussed here provide a means to use that time constructively. As one youth stated, '[it is] just a good opportunity for you to do something instead of watching TV or doing nothing in the summer ... you could come to this programme and get something out of it.' Another noted, 'other summers were just long ... I usually stay at the house or go swimming all the time or go to movies or something … but this was fun. I actually got to have a job this summer. Wasn't like any other summer.' Finally, Buddy had to say, 'it's fun, it gives you some extra money at the end of the programme and it gives you a good experience with gardening and it can help you in the future … maybe you want to be an entrepreneur in the future'. As is obvious from these quotes, participation in the garden programme provided the young people with something they considered valuable and, further, their comments underlined that few opportunities existed for them to spend their summer time in constructive ways. Yet, what kind of occasions for science literacy practices did the City Farmers programme provide?

When I asked the young people to describe the forms of science practices the programme offered in comparison to school, all could immediately refer to differences. Tamara noted, 'here they put you through it and at school they just put it on paper'. Later, she added, in school 'they just teach us they don't show us'. Similarly, Benita noted, 'here you get to do the whole package.' Tarr and others said, 'out in the garden [we are] like doing it ourselves and then like in school … we just talk about it'. Stephen added, 'I think I learn more in this programme than I'll ever learn in school.' Stephen then described how they dissected plants in school. Buddy added, 'here they take the time to show us how a plant grows' whereas in school they typically talk about parts of a plant or the needs of plants. In fact, to be able to see a plant grow from a seed was something that was new to most City Farmers and something they highly valued. It was for this reason that Tarr with great pride showed me the size of his squash plant on the mound he had constructed.

Given the programme's emphasis on doing science by planting and harvesting crops, City Farmers could gather much factual and practical science knowledge particular to this setting although perhaps of little use beyond the programme. Participation offered them a means to experience and gather an understanding of plants that is typically only available to youth growing up in rural areas. The understanding of plant science as reached by City Farmers is reminiscent of a statement made by Dewey in 1946, 'understanding has to be in terms of how things work and how to do things. Understanding, by its very nature, is related to action; just as information, by its very nature, is isolated from action' (p. 49). Hence, in consideration of the study's implication for education, three points can be made.

First, a combination of educational models is apparent in the programme and may be related to its educational success. For instance, the structure of the programme resembles many facets of experiential education in that participation in the programme was voluntary while the programme itself had a clear purpose that was reflective of youths' needs. Furthermore, emphasis rested more on participation, whereby youth could also gain ownership of the programme (Druian, Owens & Owen 1986). In terms of the activities, they are best thought of as authentic since they emerged from, and were embedded in the gardening work (Brown, Collins & Duguid 1989). Learning itself happened through interaction with the environment, through demonstration and guidance by adults, and by discussion, characteristics illustrative of an apprenticeship model (Brown et al. 1989). And as proponents of the model of situated learning and historical apprenticeship have stressed, the setting and social relations were important in defining the kind of knowledge and kind of actors the City Farmers programme produced (Lave & Wenger 1991). It suggests the value of combining different facets of diverse learning models — such as experiential education, cognitive and historical apprenticeship — in current educational practices.

Second, even though the study of the City Farmers programme suggests ways in which current educational practices may become more youth-centred, the study also makes clear that the programme can in its own right be thought of as providing an important environment for the development of inner-city youth. Hence, the goal of the study should not be seen as primarily informing and challenging current school practices. Instead, the study should be thought of as highlighting the need to find ways for schools to 'work with community agencies to construct a unified system of youth development, a joint enterprise that recognises the common goals of schools and community agencies while respecting their inherent differences and strengths' (Carnegie Council on Adolescent Development 1992, 114). Such an approach is reflective of Vygotsky's note that everyday learning contributes significantly to classroom learning and lifelong patterns of learning. It also acknowledges the fact that many differences exist between the kind of science literacy the programme and conventional science classrooms promote, while recognising that both settings serve different functions and are important for youths' development.

Third, by studying youth programmes, we as researchers and educators might be challenged and forced to think of academic domains in broader terms. For instance, the kind of science that got done in the City Farmers programme differed significantly from conventional school science. Some people might even argue that little 'real science' got done in the City Farmers community. Maybe so. The City Farmers programme does not produce laboratory scientists as schools might, but rather workers who can invoke factual and practical science knowledge in order to grow marketable crops. An ability to use science to act upon one's environment can also be thought of as an important facet of science literacy, however. Hence, the study seems to suggest the need for a re-evaluation of current science practices in schools and the facets of science which they currently stress and ignore.

What really differentiates the City Farmers programme from traditional educational settings is its emphasis on the education of the whole person. That is, even though science was an important component of the programme, work and life skills were taught as well, and opportunities for participants to contest issues of interest were provided. In that sense, the programme was youth-centred rather than simply curriculum driven. Whether schools are in charge of educating the whole person, or simply provide instruction in specific subject domains is open for debate (Lave & Wenger 1991). Yet, to create more youth-centred learning environments may be a more realistic and valuable goal for which to strive. The value of such broader educational goals is apparent in Adrian's, Zig's, and Benita's statements about what they learned in the programme and with which I conclude:

Excerpt 6

Adrian: I learned a few things. One, how to harvest, package and wash different herbs. Two, how to plant different seeds, care for them and nurture them and to see if they would grow right, or if they wouldn't. And I just like to say that this programme is excellent and I would recommend it to any of my friends because it gives them a little something to do in the summer or gives them a little extra change throughout the summer.

Zig: The thing that I have learned the most is the value of money. Before I got into this programme, the only money I got was from allowance and I didn't have to work for it, but now that I got into this programme I had to work for money.

Benita: The thing that I think I learned from this programme was how you have to nurture a plant, you have to take very good care of it and you cannot just forget about it because it won't grow right or anything.

References

Ahlgren, A. & Rutherford, J.F. (1993). Where is project 2061 today? *Educational Leadership*, 50(8), 19-22.

Brown, J.S., Collins, A. & Duguid, P. (1989). Situated cognition and the culture of learning. *Educational Researcher*, 18(1), 32-42.

Carnegie Council on Adolescent Development (1992). *A matter of time: Risk and opportunity in the nonschool hours*. New York: The Carnegie Corporation of New York.

Chaiklin, S. & Lave, J. (eds.). (1993). *Understanding practice: Perspectives on activity and context*. Cambridge: Cambridge University.

Chalmers, A. (1982). *What is the thing called science?* Indianapolis: Hackett Publishing.

Cole, M. (1996). *Cultural psychology: A once and future discipline*. Cambridge, Mass.: The Bellknap Press of Harvard University.

deOliveira, W. & Montecinos, C. (1997). Education in the open environment: Conceptualization and practice. *Humanics*, 6(2), 3-6.

Dewey, J. (1946). The challenge of democracy to education. In *Problems of man*. New York: Philosophical Library.

Druian, G., Owens, T. & Owen, S. (1986). Experiential education: A search for common roots. In R.J. Kraft (ed.), *Experiential education and the schools*. Boulder, Colo.: Association for Experiential Education.

Eisenhart, M. (1996). The production of biologists at school and work: Making scientists, conservationists, or flowery bone-heads? In B.A. Levinson, D.E. Foley & D.C. Holland (eds.), *The cultural production of the educated person*. Albany, N.Y.: State University of New York Press.

Eisenhart, M. & Finkel, E. (1998). *Women's science: Learning and succeeding from the margins*. Chicago: University of Chicago Press.

Engeström, Y. & Middleton, D. (eds.) (1996). *Cognition and communication at work*. Cambridge: Cambridge University Press.

Gee, J.P. (1990). *Social linguistics and literacies: Ideology in discourses*. New York: The Falmer Press.

Heath, S.B. & McLaughlin, M.W. (eds.) (1994a). *Identity and inner-city youth: Beyond ethnicity and gender*. New York: Teachers College Press.

Heath, S.B. & McLaughlin, M.W. (1994b). Learning for anything everyday. *Journal of Curriculum Studies*, 26(5), 471-89.

Heath, S.B. & McLaughlin, M.W. (1994c). The best of both worlds: Connecting schools and community youth organizations for all-day, all-year learning. *Educational Administration Quarterly*, 30(3), 278-300.

Hofstein, A. & Rosenfeld, S. (1996). Bridging the gap between formal and informal science learning. *Studies in Science Education*, 28, 87-112.

Hymes, D. (1974). Toward ethnographies of communication. In D. Hymes (ed.),

Foundations in sociolinguistics: An ethnographic approach. Philadelphia: University of Pennsylvania Press.

Jantzen, P.G. & Michel, J.L. (1989). *Macmillan Life Science*. New York: Macmillan.

Latour, B. (1987). *Science in action*. Cambridge, Mass.: Harvard University Press.

Lave, J. (1988). *Cognition in practice*. Cambridge: Cambridge University Press.

Lave, J. & Wenger, E. (1991). *Situated learning: Legitimate peripheral participation*. Cambridge, Mass.: Cambridge University Press.

Lemke, J.L. (1990). *Talking science: Language, learning and values*. Norwood, N.J.: Ablex.

Maybin, J. (1994). Children's voices: Talk, knowledge and identity. In D. Graddol, J. Maybin & B. Stierer (eds.), *Researching language and literacy in social context*. Philadelphia: The Open University.

McLaughlin, M.W., Irby, M.A. & Langman, J. (1994). *Urban sanctuaries*. San Francisco: Jossey-Bass.

Nunes, T., Schliemann, A.D. & Carraher, D.W. (1993). *Street mathematics and school mathematics*. Cambridge: Cambridge University Press.

Ramey-Gassert, L. (1997). Learning science beyond the classroom. *The Elementary School Journal*, 97(4), 433-50.

Resnick, L.B. (1990). Literacy in school and out. *Daedalus*, 119, 169-85.

Saxe, G.B. (1991). *Culture and cognitive development: Studies in mathematical understanding*. Hillsdale, N.J.: Lawrence Erlbaum Associates.

Schauble, L., Beane, D.A.B., Coates, G.D., Martin, L.M.W. & Sterling, P.V. (1996). Outside the classroom walls: Learning in informal environments. In L. Schauble & R. Glaser (eds.), *Innovations in learning: New environments for education*. Mahwah, N.J.: Lawrence Erlbaum Associates.

Snow, C.E. & Kurland, B.F. (1996). Sticking to the point: Talk about magnets as a context for engaging in scientific discourse. In D. Hicks (ed.), *Discourse, learning, and schooling*. Cambridge: Cambridge University Press.

Spencer, J.W. (1994). Mutual relevance of ethnography and discourse. *Journal of Contemporary Ethnography*, 23(3), 267-79.

Spradley, J.P. (1980). *Participant observation*. New York: Harcourt Brace Jovanovich College.

VanMaanen, J. (1988). *Tales of the field*. Chicago: University of Chicago Press.

Vygotsky, L.S. & Luria, A. (1994). Tool and symbol in child development. In R. van der Veer & J. Valsiner (eds., trans.), *The Vygotsky reader*. Cambridge, Mass.: Blackwell.

Wells, G. (1992). The centrality of talk in education. In K. Norman (ed.), *Thinking voices: The work of the National Oracy Project*. London: Hodder & Stoughton.

Wood-Robinson, C. (1991). Young people's ideas about plants. *Studies in Science Education*, 19, 119-35.

8 Transforming Ethnocultural Tradition in a Modern Environment: Context for Personal Development

Olga V. Kritskaya

Introduction

In a world that is changing rapidly in so many ways, educators are concerned with how people make and maintain their individual and collective identities. What seems to be a critical need we are going to face in the 21st century is *intercultural competence* — people from every part of the world need to become cognitively and interpersonally creative to live with other cultures and within other cultures. In connection with this, the questions that the educators are seeking to explore are:

— How do educators organise and orchestrate the educational process?
— How do educators connect the instructional strategies, individual actors of the educational process, and the knowledge areas in order to bridge the many components of learning and identity development?

In other words, the educators need to look at the 'systems' that serve to bridge these components of learning. One such system is offered by a complex phenomenon — culture: helping people think about this complex idea, both youngsters and adults, becomes an important part of education in today's diverse world.

This paper is organised around three main ideas:

1. The use of a cultural frame as a means to foster identity development.
2. The vision of teaching and learning based on a metaphor of a rite.
3. Ethnocultural space and its features as the unit of analysis: Rhythm, Emotionality, Symbol.

The use of the cultural frame is approached by describing the educational programme at the Ethnocultural School Paraskeva in St. Petersburg, Russia, in an attempt to think of this programme as a model for creating learning environments for children and adults. The programme is borrowing forms of communication and expression from the Slavic cultural tradition and is transforming those in a contemporary cultural context. This is done under the assumption that the dynamics and characteristics of processes embedded in a traditional culture are quite applicable to certain forms of communication within educational processes. The paper focuses on developing a conceptual understanding of the features of the programme, which come to occupy special positions of influence in an educational setting and relate particularly to personal development and modern identity transformation. Given the rapid changes in Russia, these issues become particularly important for an educator as he or she is trying to help people become cognitively and interpersonally creative in order to cope with the multiple constraints of the societal turmoil.

Our understanding of the phenomenon of personal development and identity transformation is grounded in sociocultural perspectives. Using the concepts originated by Vygotsky, it is the intention of this analysis to contribute to a better understanding of the influence of culture on personal emotional and intellectual development.

The Use of a Cultural Frame as a Means to Foster Identity Development

Arif Dirlik (1987) argues that we need culture as one, if not the primary, source for radical inquiry; for culture shapes our ways of seeing things and it is those we must question first, if we are to make changes in action at either micro- or macro-levels. I would use the term 'culture' understood both as a characteristic of the knowledge and practices people share within social groups and/or their ethnic and linguistic origins, and also as a process of diffusion of ideas among people in contact and their nurturing of growth and development in social groups (Wax 1993; Florio-Ruane 1997).

One means for helping people to think of culture is through engaging them in an experience within the rich contextual material which is offered by the traditional folk culture. This becomes possible due to a repertoire of possible interlocutors — communicative and expressive means embedded in the cultural heritage. Education rarely provides students of any age with opportunities to experience directly such learning that is dialogic in nature and aimed at framing and solving complex problems. Experience of communicative situations and forms of self-expression encapsulated within a folk cultural tradition may expand the horizons of one's thinking. In other words, an educator is challenged to find ways to help people understand culture, as well as the means through which culture shapes the ways people live their lives and develop a sense of their identity.

This paper examines this possibility by exploring the following questions:

1) What are the ways of the creative use of traditional communicative forms, their temporal and spatial characteristics that provide conditions to reveal emotionality attached to deeply seated issues of the participants?
2) How can cultural artefacts, objects and symbols, become energisers and tools within the system of educational activity?

To address this challenge, the author has designed, taught and reflected on a programme which was implemented specifically for multi-age groups of children at the Ethnocultural School Paraskeva. It is important to note here that, from the very beginning, these groups came to involve adults as equal participants of each educational session. First invited to join were the children's parents. As the programme evolved, the adult population of the classroom extended to include the prospective teachers enrolled at the time at the Hertzen State Pedagogical University of Russia (St. Petersburg) and the St. Petersburg Conservatory. Other adult students enrolled in educational and cultural programmes conducted by the School specifically for adults also joined. The importance of having adults as active and equal participants for each and every session will be addressed later in the paper.

In the educational programme named above (further referred to as 'the programme'), the teacher crafts communicative situations by using multiple kinds of literary forms, music, myth and drama. The latter are borrowed particularly from folk culture. We would argue that the programme could be exemplary of the ways in which the cultural language of mankind — its archetypal meanings embedded in the integrity of the folk culture — can be used for pedagogical purposes. The verbal, musical, and dance folklore; the specific properties of the crafts; the symbolism of the rites — all these 'texts' of the traditional culture, in their symbolic and functional integrity, provide a way for a learner to enjoy not only the acquiring of new skills and linguistic competencies, but also adopting new perspectives of the world and a new social identity. This approach presents a view on the potential bridging of the communicative and expressive forms embedded in a folk cultural tradition, on the one hand, and a person in a modern environment, on the other. The following sections will address the use of such bridging as a means to enhance integrated learning and to facilitate personal identity development. In other words, we will address the use of a cultural frame in pedagogy as a potential basis for fostering participants' self-inquiry and co-construction of 'self' and 'other' — a way for identity development.

I will first provide a brief overview of the current practices of the School, which was chosen as an example to support our conceptual understanding of some of the critical features of the educational process.

Ethnocultural School Paraskeva

As mentioned above, all programmes offered at the School are borrowing the forms of interpersonal communication and expression from the Slavic cultural tradition to transform them in a contemporary cultural context. The general educational orientation of the School can be characterised as 'A Man in the Ethnocultural Environment'. It is designed to serve both children, elementary through high school, as well as adults, and aims to accustom participants to the world of language, music, movement and arts in their integrity. The curriculum design is based on thematic units, which are united by identification with the history, ethnography and ethnology of the Slavs, on the one hand, and the nature of the universe on the other.

I would like to emphasise that the School's reproduction of rituality, characteristic of the traditional folk culture, is not its prime educational goal but rather a means. By having the participants 'live through' a situation, which can be reenacted through communicative and expressive patterns of a rite (or its metaphoric simulation), a teacher aims to provide an impact on the participants' understandings of 'self' and 'others', in their interconnectedness. We are talking here about the use of the rite as a metaphor for communicative media, which has a potential to foster the participant's identity development.

Programmes at the Ethocultural School of Paraskeva: Dimensions

1. Educational programmes in integrated arts, ethnography, history and ecology. The school offers these programmes to:
   a) multi-age groups of children together with their parents (vocational)
   b) youth (as part of the regular middle and high school curriculum)
   c) adults (folk culture clubs organised around specific crafts and/or aspects of traditional culture).

2. Joint projects with the Ethnographic Museum of Russia, St. Petersburg:
   a) Studies in traditional slavic culture based on the Ethnographic Museum collections and expeditions (this includes Eastern and Western Slavs, as well as Scandinavian countries).
   b) Scientifically based reconstruction of traditional crafts (equipment, materials, techniques) and creating the environment for their preservation.
   c) Joint performing in museums and cultural centres around Russia, which aim to explore the ways of transforming the traditional Slavic cultural artefacts in a contemporary cultural context (artefacts include crafts, rituals, verbal and musical folklore, in their interconnectedness).
   d) International forums on cultural and ecological issues.

The example of the last dimension of the programme would be the International Forum on Preservation of the Area of Poles'je, its ethnology and ecology. Located at the centre of the interface between the Eastern and Western Slavic world, the territory of Poles'je includes the contemporary territories of Russia, Belarus and Ukraine and occupies a very specific position in the total ecological and cultural context of Europe. It is the geographical ancestor of the Eastern Slavic culture, which has been preserved in this region until the present. Taking the above into consideration, the effort of the Forum was to demonstrate the peculiarities of this unique ethnocultural region of the Slavic world in its integrity, commonalty of cultural systems, and genetic significance. This issue was of special importance in conjunction with the ecological catastrophe in Chernobyl that almost destroyed this unique treasury of Slavic culture.

This example with the Forum on Chernobyl sought to demonstrate the need for a pedagogy which would help bring new generations to an appreciation of the world's cultural and ecological treasures, as well as under-standing personal responsibility for the preservation and further develop-ment of those treasures. This concern challenges an educator to seek ways in which one can enhance learning of 'self' and 'others' in a global context. In other words, an educator is challenged to find the ways to help people understand culture and the means through which culture shapes the ways people live their lives and develop a sense of their identity.

Having this idea in mind, how do we orchestrate the educational pro-cess? We believe, the key issue here is the interactive (relational) view of meaning making which can be constructed within a learning setting. The advocates of the social theories of mind recognise that our individuality emerges from our social being. Philosophically, this argument is reminiscent of the perspective of A.A. Bogdanov, the Russian sociologist, that

objective, physical reality is shared-meaning. It is similar to the general concept that our understanding of the physical world is a function of social agreement, that it is socially harmonious and socially organized experience. (Bogdanov in Vygot-sky 1987, 157)

Holquist (1983) treats meaning not as something 'owned', but rather as something 'rented' by individuals. A large body of contemporary literature refers to Vygotskian perspectives and his socially based theory of mind. Ac-cording to Vygotsky (1987), construction of meaning of a situation occurs through intersubjective interactions between people and does not occur in their absence. What will be taken up by a learner, will depend on the particu-lar intersubjective patterns of communication between the learner and the more knowledgeable person that will drive the process of social learning. Using Dewey's (1930) metaphor of a seed, what 'the seed' becomes is critic-ally dependent on the nature of social interactions.

Specific mechanisms for social interactions can be found in the forms of traditional folk culture which offers an educator an endless world of objects and language, allowing the enhancement of 'a socially harmonious and socially organised experience' for all participants of the educational process. The intention to borrow from the traditional cultural forms of communica-tion and expression is grounded in our beliefs about the process of teaching and learning. Let me emphasise some aspects of the educational process, which, in my view, are crucial for integrated learning in childhood and iden-tity transformation in adulthood.

Perspective on Teaching and Learning

Our perspective on the process of teaching and learning can be described in the following terms:

— An educational process can be viewed as essentially a process of communication.
— An educational process can be viewed as an act. Historically, the unity between conscience and activity, and the mediating of such phenomenon through the personality, constitutes the peculiar feature of Russian psychology.
— Education is socially embedded, that is, carried out through social relations. It implies a certain group dynamic that involves actions that build a sense of community.
— The process of teaching and learning is holistic, i.e., it is not divided into separate subject majors, but rather integrates those within each session organised in an environment, which is authentic to the context.
— It is a drama, or a theatricalised action, which implies a potential to enhance one's creative self-expression.
— It is a rhythm-bounded process, where rhythm serves as an element responsible for mutual understanding between communicating people.
— It is a process that includes both teachers and students as co-learners. Team teaching and a serious parent involvement are anticipated and considered to be the crucial ingredients of an educational programme.

The advantage of such a view of learning and teaching is, in my understanding, that when the instructional design borrows from the contexts and communicative processes embedded in a traditional culture, it allows for co-construction by the participants of a learning experience, which is associated with the specific meaning of a particular context. Due to the integrity of the instructional 'material' — the interconnected themes of the traditional culture — such co-construction of the meaning happens without being infected by the illness of today — 'the schizophrenic dismembrance' (Levi 1981), which shows itself in a divided consciousness in all aspects of life.

Referring to the above, to enhance the identity formation, a beneficial approach to the teaching strategy seems to focus on creating a situation image, a 'story', by use of multiple expressive means: the word, music, movement, art have, in their integrity, a potential to unlock the participants' imagination, which, in turn, provokes one's inquiry into the self. Direct verbal explanation or instruction may have a 'blinding' effect on what is actually happening. Mostly we understand not the meaning of the words, but the situation, and this is the key to context. Whatever story we imagine to be the 'situation' — a story told verbally, or demonstrated in motions, or vocally, or, better still, presented by a synthesis of all of these means — it is right, if it unlocks one's imagination. The Russian dramatist and producer Stanislavsky used to say: 'Always build the circumstances in which actions are performed'.

To sum, the creating of a situation image on a basis of any cultural 'text' that has a potential to provoke one's imagination appears to be a core-teaching objective when focusing on identity formation. For children, the image of a 'story' — a situation — created by multiple expressive means can be considered as an intellectual scaffold, in Bruner's terms (1977), i.e., can enhance their ability to monitor their understanding unassisted. For adult participants, imagination — born by some kind of surprise — provokes self-inquiry into 'Who I am', 'Who I am amongst others', into the relationship between 'Self' and 'otherness'.

The Image of the Ethnocultural Environment as an Instructional Tool

In an attempt to find mechanisms for creating an educational process described above, an educator can find the pedagogical tool for such creation in the cultural language of traditional cultures, which is common in its archetypal meanings around the globe. I refer here to a pedagogical tool, which is encapsulated in a syncretism of cultural artefacts: tonality and rhythm of music, movement, art, and drama that are present in any traditional ceremony, in the very way of life, and come into play in compliance with the natural cycles of seasons. In the programme that borrows this syncretism from the traditional culture, each session builds an ethnocultural environment — 'ethnocultural space' — which provides a contextual basis for building mutuality of understandings among the participants, thus allowing for the beginning of inquiry into the Self. All elements of the ethnocultural environment serve a mediatory function through a system of interactions between the participants of the learning experience. We believe that the phenomenon of identity development can become manifest within the context of the ethnocultural environment.

This belief is grounded in three main propositions:

1) All elements of the ethnocultural environment are combined into rhythmic patterns of the human life cycle and that of nature. This union of the physical and mental (symbolic) provides a medium for learning for both children and adults.
2) One of the fundamental characteristics of the ethnocultural environment is the ability of its image 'to crystallize and call forth the unconscious emotions and concerns of the participants'.
3) The concerns people have and the mechanisms of participants' interactions within a communicative setting manifested through expression in cultural artefacts, both material and symbolic, which are the cross-sections of the personality and the culture.

Modelling educative situations by use of a metaphor of an archaic folk ritual — with its syncretism of word, gesture, mask, motion, rhythm — allows the kinaesthetic, auditory, and visual senses of the participants of educational experience to be used, thus opening new avenues of communication and self-expression to them.

I would like to specifically highlight further the three features that, in my view, are critical for creating the ethnocultural environment and make it a special space for cultural education and identity development. I am referring particularly to rhythm, emotion and the mediating power of a symbol. To be able to do so, let me introduce an example, which describes one of the ancient Slavic rituals reenacted annually at the School, by its whole community, i.e., the 'Dressing of the Image of Paraskeva'. This reenactment of the ritual does not appear as a special unit in the curriculum for any of the programmes run by the School, but rather should be seen as an event which brings the whole School community together, bridging the curricular themes across the various programmes and student ages. It relates to other School activities and curricular themes in a way in which any event in a traditional folk culture relates to others: the traditional rites, being performed at certain times of the folk calendar are all interrelated through the functional and symbolic meanings of the procedures, expressive means, and the purposes that bring people into play and connect them to the rhythmical flow of the seasons. In my view, the 'Dressing of the Image of Paraskeva' manifests the spirit and the essence of all the School's activities.

The Dressing of the Image of Paraskeva

A cross is an authentic representation of the human being. One of the rituals of ancient Slavs was devoted to the decoration of a sacred cross with hand-made artefacts. This cross would then be associated with the name of Saint Paraskeva. St. Paraskeva is the Saint whose image was adopted by the Christian culture from the ancient prototype of the goddess — 'The Great Goddess', Makosh — to be known as a Christian Martyr in later times. She was believed to come out of the holy waters of the Earth to patronise the most important instances of human life: fertility, the harvest, handicraft making, and trade. She would often be called 'Paraskeva Pyatnitza' (Paraskeva Friday), because important trade events — markets — would occur most often on Fridays. One can find a similar symbolism in the images of German Freitag, English Friday and French Venus.

At the School, which bears the name of the Saint, the ritual devoted to her is creatively simulated every year, early in November, by way of creating an image of an object — a cross. The date on the folk calendar devoted to St. Paraskeva is deeply rooted in seasonal traditions and is associated with the end of the reaping season and the beginning of spinning and looming. It is also associated with the crossing of the boundary between the past and the forthcoming harvest seasons. Although the modern urban environment of St. Petersburg does not bear the features of these traditions, the meaning of the event has great significance for the participants in the School programme.

The entire school community participates in this act. The wooden cross is set up in the biggest room in the school — a common space for the school community gatherings. A group of women — primarily school faculty and club members — dressed in traditional Slavic costumes, moving solemnly and singing an old, timeless, wedding song, start the ritual of the 'Dressing'. Piece by piece, handmade artefacts of traditional life and meanings — woven belts, loomed tapestries, embroidered towels — would be brought to the cross and arranged around it so that an image of the one who is to be perceived as St. Paraskeva over the next year emerges in front of an amused audience. In a traditional ritual, the 'audience' would be the community members — the citizens of the village, extended family members. At the School of Paraskeva, the audience includes its faculty, club members, students — both children and adults as well as the family members of those and the guests of the School. After the 'Dressing' is over, the

'Giving' starts. Everyone present comes up to Paraskeva — the decorated image that has emerged right in front of them — giving her something of particular personal importance. All artefacts donated as gifts at this moment, i.e., attached somehow to the dressed cross, are handmade. The adults, for instance, might give their personal hand-woven belts and children might bring dolls they have made themselves, pieces woven from straw or made of threads and flax, etc. Everyone approaches Paraskeva with his or her own wishes, which are addressed to her, and with very specific meanings of what should emerge in this given space and time as the ritual proceeds. The following year new artefacts will be given to Paraskeva and the gifts of the previous year become the basis for the construction of a new image of the Saint.

The described event invites an educator to explore what Shotter would call 'a special kind of knowledge ...' — 'joint action' and 'knowing from within' (Shotter 1993, 3). In light of an interactive view of meaning making, emphasised earlier in the paper, it directs the educator to think of joint practices, the things people do together, and the ways in which these things are beneficial and effective in reaching the 'creative and adaptive potentials' of the people (Giddens in Eisenberg 1990, 143). The discussion in the following section investigates such 'ways', focusing on the three critical features noted earlier as important for creating the ethnocultural environment — a special space for enhancing identity formation. I will provide our conceptual understanding of these features, which, in turn, will help me further relate those features to some specific implications for the current curriculum for children.

Symbol, Rhythm and Emotion: Features of the Ethnocultural Space

Sign, Symbol, Object

The ritual of the dressing of Paraskeva is an example of how the physical universe is buffered by a symbolic universe of people's own creation — objects, which reflect their being human. A belt, brought to the image of Paraskeva as a gift, can be seen as a cross-section of the personality and the culture, the opportunity to reveal the internal spiritual values and attitudes in the real modern environment. The act of giving comes to signify a reflection of individuals' souls on the multidimensional essence of

Paraskeva's image. Thus, a mythology of an object — a cultural sign — is constructed, in which the structure of the object is dissolved in symbols, or meanings attributed by the people. It is a sacred process of materialising the world. A sign, or a symbol, therefore, appears to be one of the critical features noted. This reenactment of the ritual reveals the power of mythology of a sign, or an object, as a resource for constructing the meaning of a social action, participation in which enables the participants to embrace higher, collective values. The mytho-poetic meaning of objects (both material and symbolic) in a traditional culture, along with its energising function allow or force the participants, individually and as a group, to see their selves in new ways and work with their souls.

Rhythm

Reenactment of a rite is, in a way, the telling of a story. An essential element of creating 'a story' is the element of breath, i.e., of physiological response to rhythmic repetition of the elements within a rite: the solemn motions of the women, the slow steps of the dressing, the rhymes of the timeless song, the acts of donation that are repeated again and again, weaving into the stem of the ritual. The symbolism of the ritual comes back to the participants every year, charging old memories with associations of the new day. So every session of the curriculum can be viewed as stemming from a little ritual, building upon its element of breath — the rhythmic repetition of that which the students have grasped. It is this element that is essentially responsible for the mutuality of understanding in a group of communicating people. The following examples help us see in which ways the element of breath, in other words, the physiological sensorimotor of the natural rhythm of breathing, responding to an 'external' rhythm (for instance, the rhythm of sounds or a melodic structure) can significantly enhance the learning of students of any age.

Nina Berger, professor of the St. Petersburg Conservatory, Russia, describes how she suggests that her students (both young and adult) in the introductory rhythmical course use syllable 'TA' while taking a deep breath (inhalation) and pronounce 'TE' upon expiration at the time when they chant durations (beats): 'TE' is the sound for strong beats, while 'TA' — for weak ones (Berger 1993). Edwin Gordon, in his music education programme for young children, uses rhythm syllables such as 'DU' and 'DE', though chanted for different durations in a rhythm pattern (Gordon 1990). Both professors consider it necessary for a student to learn to coordinate naturally her/his breathing with her/his movement. This approach is echoing the educational philosophy of Rudolf Steiner and Karl Orff.

Emotionality

Participation in a game, a rite, or in a special performing act in the museum, all represent examples of a collective action within the ethnocultural environment. They all involve intensively human emotions. Engaging in collective singing and movement lifts your feelings up high. The collective act of giving brings you a sense of belonging. To give your personal belt means to trust. I believe these emotional statements are characteristic of all programmes at the School. Emotionality, being initially individual, becomes social in the course of and by means of a rite — its actual reproduction or a simulation of its communicative modes, which a regular session of an educational programme can use as an instructional device. The syncretism of a word, gesture, rhythm, mask, motion, along with the dramatic conflict of a ritual, organises social feeling and collective action within a rite, as well as within any traditional game that you can probe with a group. The image of such an environment is built in compliance with the dynamics of: 1) group participation in the act; 2) mass emotional display with the situation (its plot); 3) emotionally living through the situation — in the same way as it happens in a rite, according to the law of a game. That is why the scenic composition of every curricular unit seems to benefit if approached as a programme for emotional rallying, as a programme for personal socialisation and for building collective emotions and relationships.

The theoretical propositions above are important to the author to clarify which particular features of communicative and expressive means, encapsulated in a cultural tradition, can help create what we called earlier an ethnocultural environment or *ethnocultural space*. The latter becomes a metaphor for a particular approach to instructional design. The above described 'Dressing of Paraskeva' — an event, which, although independent of the curriculum bridges its themes across programmes and student ages, was intended to provide the reader with a feeling of how a syncretic educational session can be. The metaphor of a rite (or a game) is viewed by the author as a frame for curricular design and describes the communicative dynamics that builds each and every session.

I would like to emphasise further that the instructional design is not defined ultimately by the developmental age of the participants — young or adult. The teacher seeks opportunities to present the topic at multiple levels of its intellectual intensity, so that both kids and adult participants would find their 'own language' to work around the topic. However, it is the creating of the image of a topic-bound situation, which relies on the syncretic nature of the ethnocultural space that becomes the major building block for the design of each session.

In the following section I shall briefly describe one session, designed by the author within the programme for multi-age groups of children and their parents. This vocational programme is intended for a three-year enrolment in the School, but allows for the same cohort of participants to continue educational experiences within this programme over a longer period. The curriculum assumes meetings with students in session durations of two and a half and five hours, dependent on the number of years the students and families have been attending the programme (the beginners would start with shorter sessions). The example below relates to a version of the programme for the first-year students, with one session per week, September through May. Its curriculum is organised thematically around the folk seasonal calendar.

In general, each session would incorporate the following domains: a conversation around, for instance, a topic on ethnography or the cultural history of Slavs; pieces of verbal, musical, and dance folklore; folk arts or crafts; folk theatre; traditional games; traditional food. Each session in this programme is supported by a scenario plan. Such 'scenarios', as well as their domains, are thematically connected according to the logic of the folk calendar and are very flexible in incorporating, at any moment, varying materials from the instructional repertoire as well as the ideas of the participants themselves, both children and adults. Each session would start with gathering in a circle, often with finger-games to greet each other and to learn how everybody is today. Then the conversation would start. Here is the example.

'The Mistress of the World': A Game — in its Form, a Myth —
in its Content

The session 'The Mistress of the World' (Khozyaika Mira) is offered on or close to the calendar date devoted to St. Paraskeva. 'Paraskeva is walking around the world … People draw her image with paints, inlaid with threads …' — the teacher begins telling a story (this might be a regular talk, or a ballad, or a song). Varying displays of Paraskeva's images that the folk memory stores in multiple forms would support the 'story'. A tow, a thread, an item of clothes comes along as an artefact of special significance in the image of this character. '... People throw the tow into the streaming water ...' — the story goes on. Paraskeva has always been respected as a patron of those who care: 'On that day, one vows to fulfil a particular task or a job for the sake of someone's recovery ...'

The Saint has also been known as a patron of crafts and trade. Traditional games, or pieces of verbal folklore, associated with one feature or another of the Paraskeva's folk image, would be started in a circle. They would start with the least amount of introductory instruction, but mostly modelling and encouraging the participants to follow by using gestures and the very patterns of a game or a rhyme. The teacher might include games with objects, bearing those particular features that would bring the participants' attention again and again to the traditional image of Paraskeva, such as a tow, a flax thread, belts, balls of wool, a spindle, a traditionally modelled doll, a distaff, etc. Gradually, these games would include more and more movement, which would often be rhythmised, and accompanied by singing, as many folk games or dances are. In fact, most of the traditional games are at the same time songs and dances, and even theatricalised pieces, telling a story and involving alternating roles and various expressive means.

During these games, the interactive aspect of communication among the participants comes particularly into play. Each game involves participants in a dialogue, contexts of approval and disapproval, agreement and disagreement which are both aspects of one process of the individual's identity development. In these situations, participants learn to understand other persons in terms of their intentions and beliefs. Participants of a game will:

— take the roles of one another
— change the roles of leaders and followers
— engage in joint attention with the other
— try 'mind reading of the other', attribute 'mental states of the other' (Tomasello et al. 1993)

Interestingly, during these sessions, parents experience roles that are different from those in their families, and their relationship with their children gain here new, unpredicted characteristics. I will return to the children-adults relationship later. First let me briefly return to the session.

The atmosphere of a game, often rhythmised, as mentioned earlier, serves a particular educational objective — to provoke the active engagement of students in response to the expressive means upon which such atmosphere has been built. The latter relies on the natural, physiological mechanisms of human response to external stimuli such as sounds. The author introduces every new rhyme to the children through motions that follow the rhythm encapsulated in the rhyme, highlighting the strong beats within each metrical duration. She is, thus, modelling one of the possible ways to reflect on that rhythm kinaesthetically. Some kids, however, after staying with the programme for a while (for approximately half a year), are able (and are free, of course) to try out their own ways of responding. The same rhyme would then be tried out in other ways. For example: through different tonality while singing; through a set of steps and shifts in space that children and participating adults would do in pairs or in groups. What the participants, especially young, exercise here can be compared to a preparatory audition, both tonally and rhythmically, described by Gordon:

Tonally, the emphasis is on vocal fold movement (covert movement) in conjunction with breathing. Rhythmically, the emphasis is on torso, arm, hand, foot and leg movement (overt movement). … in rhythm, movement is initiated by and is an outgrowth of breathing; in singing, breathing is initiated by and is an outgrowth of movement. (Gordon 1990, 88)

The session gradually moves further into its next domain — traditional arts and crafts, by using a particular point in time — for instance, a certain twist in the scenario of one of the games — as an 'excuse for interruption'. If the spontaneity of the playful situation permits, the 'turning point' of a game which leads to the next domain of the session, is perceived by the participants as an integral part of the whole scenario. Decorative pieces for the Dressing of Paraskeva; modelling and dressing dolls, which would introduce the symbolism of traditional women's costume; a virtual tour to the treasures of the Kiev-Pechersky Lavra Monastery as a rich resource of symbols embedded in the applied traditional arts — any of these might be options for turning the energy of the participants into creating their own cultural artefacts. These students' own creations would be used in later sessions, serving as special 'gripping devices' (Perkins & Salomon 1989) to recall the special meanings that would be associated with this particular session. The student creations would also help ignite a new playful activity, which although organised around a different topic or a theme is, as any event or artefact in a cultural tradition, inherently connected to the earlier one both functionally and symbolically.

Based on tradition, but allowing for students' creativity, the author would often initially model possible ways of manipulating with materials. Whether it be thread, straw, wood or paint, — the modelled ways of 'playing' with these materials would be reminiscent of the rhythm embedded in a recent movement that has been experienced by the participants earlier in the session within a game, or a song, or a rhyme. This rhythm might be reproduced in a woven pattern, for instance, and even in the very process of weaving, or through trying certain colours on paper or wood. In a different session, the playful activity that organises its major rhythm can emerge out of a piece of music, or a piece of painting, or an architectural ensemble (for 'more experienced' participants). Such activity can also be well developed based on the simulation of a traditional game within a contemporary context. Of importance is that whatever 'subject' we use; it gives birth to a scenic plot of a session while its rhythm, signs, symbols and emotionality, together, rule the dynamics of the communicative exchange.

All the domains of the session's activity — the story told or sung, the gestures used, the rhythm of the rhymes and motion, the patterns encapsulated in students' pieces of art — contribute in unique ways to the building of its special image, organising the social feeling of a group. As the activity evolves, the participants acquire a sense of belonging to this situation — its space, time and drama. The created image of the playful situation bears all the attributes of a traditional ethnocultural space and is owned by the group, where children appear to be equal contributors with adult participants. This space becomes the ground for the emotional rallying of a group, the individual participants' socialisation, and the building of new relationships.

As educators, we are dealing here with a complex of instructional modes which a teacher can use to communicate to students certain aspects of a cultural, historical or ecological phenomenon. Such modes aim to provoke the game-type (playful) activity and students' imagination. This is a very difficult task for a teacher to accomplish — in the right place, during the real time of 'the game', 'within' the process of the classroom activity. The educational process would, therefore, be considered to be a theatricalised synthesis, putting it in terms of the metaphor of a rite: a thought-out system of expressive means that provoke and stimulate the collective emotional 'infection' and appeal to the participants' faculty of thinking and willing. The session described above exemplifies the ways, in which teachers could incorporate in their practice valuable mechanisms for the active involvement of learners in a powerful communicative exchange. These mechanisms are offered by the folk cultural tradition, with its way of life, its way of perceiving the world, treating people, and, particularly, with its quintessence — the rite, or game, and its integration of multiple means of self-expression.

I would like to elaborate further on another important feature of the programme: the active involvement of adult participants in the sessions.

What Do Children and Adults Learn From Each Other?

As mentioned earlier in the paper, the programme for multi-age groups of children included adults: parents, teachers, students of the Pedagogical University and Conservatory. How the children interact with adults during the sessions, especially with their own parents, as well as how the parents react to their children's creativity is important, particularly for understanding the specific tool-like role of signs, emotions, and repetitive refrains that, in their integrity, build the image of the situation within which all participants come together. While emerging seminally in a process of child-adult interaction (as a medium for this interaction and as a tool guided by the partner's behaviour), these signs, emotions and repetitive refrains are transformed during internalisation within the medium provided by the playful situation or thinking activity medium. As Bruner puts it, the adults have here 'a monopoly on foresight' (in Wertsch 1985, 29). The children are induced to try to engage in communicative exchanges. Long before children have actually produced their first 'word', or before any conscious thought has emerged out of the thinking activity medium provided by adults (and more experienced kids), they are treated as if they do in fact have something 'to say'. As the participants learn, the more experienced continue to consider and treat the youngest to be expressing a communicative intention. In an educational process, modelled in compliance with a metaphor of a rite, this assumption of communicative intention surely becomes a crucial part of what the more experienced do for the less experienced.

The analysis of the responses of adult participants involved in the programme shows that such involvement was very meaningful for them. Particularly, the programme helped them to:

— 'shake up' their self-image and their own thoughts
— make connections between personal values and engagement in social action
— strengthen their spiritual base to the extent applicable to them personally.

I would attribute these responses to the advantages provided by the particular features of the programme as discussed earlier in this paper.

Movement into the spiritual realm, beyond the ego, as a result of social action participation, is a significant learning through experience. Wishes, whispered to the image of Paraskeva, mobilise passions. Those wishes 'will not (and should not) all be acted on, but they are vitally important in unleashing potential' (Kao 1996, 167). As an educator, I would especially emphasise that participation in a collective act like the one with the dressing of Paraskeva has a potential to become a transcendent resource in people's lives. It can help them learn to be adept in making social change and, thereby, incorporate powerful self-images.

Conclusion

This paper aimed to illustrate how the metaphor of a traditional rite, implied by a teaching strategy, can serve the educational goal of fostering identity development. It emphasised that the nature of the ethnocultural space, which manifests through its syncretism of word, gesture, mask, movement, and symbol, offers an educator a valuable means to provoke one's imagination and creativity. The unleashed creativity, in turn, has the potential to trigger one's questioning of assumptions which underlie the seeing of 'self' and 'others', as well as the very need for self-expression in a creative way. The experience of being part of a rite, or a simulated analogue situation, is yielded in the collective meanings of those situations, which, as Bakhtin would have put it, lie 'on the borderline between oneself and the other' (Bakhtin 1981, 293). The participants in such experience, both young and adult, 'acquire the skills and conventions of those around them' (Tomasello et al. 1993), train self-regulation of emotions, and learn about who they are.

The following conclusion seems to be of particular interest for an educator:

If the social rallying embedded in communicative situations of a traditional folk game or a rite is connected contextually, within the same session, to other cultural artefacts — such as music, movement, word, and material artefacts like handicrafts, including the very process of crafts making, — then a teacher gains a tool to facilitate social interaction between the participants in such a situation in ways which allow for both transmission of knowledge (through the co-constructed meaning of the situational context) and the creation of new cultural products. The latter will manifest the emergence of new processes of social learning.

The author would like to share an example from her experience in teaching multi-age groups of children and their parents, which is thought to illustrate the last statement.

At one session (around the middle of an academic year), the author had introduced a group of 5-7 year-old children to several new rhymes, having 'turned' the participants into birds or other imagery figures. The children and participating adults — parents and teachers — while occupying the 'branches of the trees', recited the rhymes in a roll-call. They competed with a partner, experimenting with the sounds, reproducing the energy and rhythm that were encapsulated in the rhyme. They would switch their roles, shift their locations, skilfully manipulating with their arms, legs and bodies. Children enjoyed that exercise very much. The rest of the session included games, dances and songs that were related in their genre and represented the life of birds in one way or another. It was concluded with 'baking' the birds (or the 'bird-looking' figurines) and decorating the table with them at teatime.

Three weeks later, the whole group of children and their parents was hosted by one of the families in their country cabin. The group gathered for the celebration of one of the Russian holidays. After a long walk, a festive gathering around a fire in the woods, and having enjoyed the traditional food and the hospitality of our hosts, we witnessed a scene on our way back in the train that fascinated the author. Two second-year students, while sitting on a bench near the adults, and paying no attention to them, started playing with words. They recited to each other one of the rhymes from our class in the same manner as they did in class, but soon, rather spontaneously, both girls took a great interest in manipulating with the familiar rhyme. They changed the words, divided them and selected the 'outcomes' in their own way, competing vividly in creativity. Yet, they were still committed to keeping the rhythm of the rhyme. Each contributed in her own pace, but both enjoyed the process greatly. The author observed her young students as they were revealing their associations with the previous enjoyable, whole-body experience, which was actualised by the meaningful social environment, created earlier that same day. Now, while on the train, this association worked as a 'general gripping device' (Perkins & Salomon 1989, 141) for retrieving the meaning of the classroom situation and constructing their own modes of response. Having internalised the classroom experience by virtue of creative interactions with the newly acquired concept, the students acquired the ability to 'improve' and transform it intentionally.

This episode is also an exemplar of transforming the cultural artefact in a contemporary context: the girls picked up on a way of acting — one of the tools for reflection that the cultural tradition of poetry stores. Then they made a step toward further use of this tool by ritualising it and taking a conscious thought. We believe that, by borrowing from the communicative and expressive means embedded in a cultural tradition, a teacher can arrive within an educational setting at the crucial match, which Bruner refers to as a 'match between a support system in the social environment and an acquisition process of the learner' (in Wertsch 1985, 28).

For an internationally oriented educator, an important implication of such an approach would be allowing the forms of communication and self-expression, embedded in different cultures, to convene cross-cultural issues. This would be a significant contribution to the education of what Vygotsky (1987) called 'the social techniques of feelings' — a source for surviving, for living.

References

Bakhtin, M. (1981). *The dialogue of imagination: Four essays.* Austin: University of Texas Press.

Berger, N.A. (1993). *Music for all.* St. Petersburg, Russia: St. Petersburg Conservatory.

Bigner, J.J. (1994). *Individual and family development.* New Jersey: Prentice-Hall.

Bruner, J. (1977). Early social interaction and language acquisition. In H.R. Schaffer (ed.), *Studies in Mother-Infant Interaction.* London: Academic Press.

Clift, R.T., Veal, M.L., Holland, P., Johnson, M. & McCarthy, J. (1995). *Collaborative leadership and shared decision making. Teachers, principals, and university professors,* 5. New York: Teachers College Press.

Dewey, J. (1930). From absolutism to empiricism. In George P. Adams and William

P. Montague (eds.), *Contemporary American Philosophy*, 11. New York: Macmillan Company.

Dirlik, A. (1987). Culturalism as hegemonic ideology and liberating practice. *Cultural Critique*, 6, 6-27.

Eisenberg, E.M. (1990). Jamming: Transcendence through organizing. *Communication Research*, 17(2), 139-64.

Elkonin, D.B. (1967). The problem of instruction and development in the works of L.S. Vygotsky. *Soviet Psychology*, 5, 34-41.

Florio-Ruane, S. (1997). To tell a new story: Reinventing narratives of culture, identity, and education. *Anthropology and Education Quarterly*, 28(2), 152-62.

Gabert, E. (1978). *Verzeichnis der Ausserungen Rudolf Steiners Über den Fremdsprachenunterricht*. Stuttgart: German Steiner School Fellowship.

Gergen, K. (1985). The social constructionist movement in modern psychology. *American Psychologist*, 40, 266-75.

Giddens, A. (1981). *A contemporary critique of historical materialism*. Berkeley: University of California Press.

Golod, V.I. & Knox, J.E. (1993). *Studies of the history of behavior: Ape, primitive, and Child*. Hillsdale, N.J.: Lawrence Erlbaum.

Gordon, E.E. (1990). *A music learning theory for newborn and young children*. Chicago: G.I.A. Publications.

Holquist, M. (1983). The politics of representation. *The Qualitative Newsletter of the Laboratory of Comparative Human Cognition*, 5, 2-9.

Kao, J. (1996). Jamming. In *The art and discipline of business creativity*. New York, N.Y.: HarperCollins.

Levi, V.L. (1991). *The art to be yourself*. Moscow: Znanie.

Perkins, D.N. & Salomon, G. (1989). Are cognitive skills context-bound? *Educational Researcher*, 18(1), 16-25.

Reid, L.A. (1969). *Meaning in the arts*. London: Allen & Unwin.

Shotter, J. (1993). *Cultural politics of everyday life: Social constructionism, rhetoric and knowing of the third kind*. Buckingham, UK: Open University Press.

Tomasello, M., Kruger, A. & Ratner, H. (1993). *Cultural learning. Behavioral and Brain Sciences*, 16, 495-552.

Vygotsky, L.S. (1971). *The Psychology of Art*. Cambridge, Mass.: The M.I.T. Press.

Vygotsky, L.S. (1987). Thinking and speech. In R.W. Rieber & A.S. Carton (eds.), *The collected works of L.S. Vygotsky: Vol.1 Problems of general psychology*. New York: Plenum Press. (Original Russian version 1934)

Wartofsky, M.W. (1983). From genetic epistemology to historical epistemology: Kant, Marx, and Piaget. In L.S. Liben (ed.), *Piaget and the foundations of knowledge*. Hillsdale, N.J.: Lawrence Erlbaum.

Wax, M. (1993). How culture misdirects multiculturalism. *Anthropology and Education Quarterly*, 24(2), 99-115.

Wertsch, J. (ed.) (1985). *Culture, communication and cognition: Vygotskian perspectives*. Cambridge: Cambridge University Press.

Williams, M. (1989). Vygotsky's Social Theory of Mind. *Harvard Educational Review*, 59(1), 108-26.

Everyday Knowledge and Mathematics and Physics Learning

9 Mathematical Cognition in the Classroom: A Cultural-Historical Approach

Ademir Damazio

Introduction

The present article analyses the teacher/learner/mathematical knowledge interactions which take place during a mathematics class. It focuses mainly on the mathematical discourse concerning the study of 'relative whole numbers' in elementary education. This analysis considers categories taken from the theoretical background of the cultural-historical approach to education.

The interactions which involve learner, teacher and mathematical knowledge have been an important subject in mathematical education research. Within this concern lies the search for the understanding of an educational process which aims at the qualitative transformation of mathematics teaching and the learning process.

In the present study, we will report an investigation of mathematical cognition in the classroom. At the same time, we seek to contribute to the debate on the relationship between theory and action in the pedagogical process, specifically in the mathematics class. There are different ways of conceiving and observing the process of teaching and learning mathematics. In the construction of concepts and points of view, the teacher many times unconsciously absorbs elements from several theoretical-philosophical tendencies that concern the process of teaching mathematics. Our intention, in this study, is to uncover and describe classroom situations that might help maths teachers to reflect on the difficulties and also advantages that are inherent in the different concepts and views of the act of teaching, and, therefore, in the act of learning.

The Cultural-Historical Approach to Learning/
Teaching Characteristics

When analysing the mathematics teaching-related academic productions in the last two decades, one will notice two quite evident aspects: a critical view of the teaching based on conservative pedagogy (traditional) and the rise of new experiences based on new premises as an attempt to break with the old tendencies.

The experience of a new pedagogical practice in the teaching of mathematics appears and is driven either by new theories acquired during preparatory courses or by the teacher's personal will, after frustrated results and expectations.

This new attitude has made teachers and researchers question themselves about the different ways of teaching and the different ways students learn. This new outlook on the classroom and on pedagogical action has driven teachers towards a dialogue with the conceptions of the cultural-historical perspective in mathematics teaching. This perspective understands mathematics, as well as all fields of knowledge, as historical knowledge in permanent construction, a product of social relations and, therefore, possessing its own concepts and its own language. 'This language has become precise, formal and strict, to the point of hiding the processes which took mathematics to such a high level of abstraction and formalization' (Fiorentini 1995, 32).

The understanding of mathematics as the process of acquisition of a particular language and a form of thought implies the understanding of a unit constituted by knowledge, learning and development.

Mathematical knowledge is human creations; it evolves and changes constantly in consonance with the historical motion of each society. According to Vygotsky, human knowledge and thought are themselves basically cultural and their distinctive properties are an outcome of social activity, of language, discourse and other cultural phenomena. This knowledge is acquired by the subject, in social interaction, in the search to understand oneself, the other and the surrounding world.

The broader sense of the word 'social', according to Vygotsky (1995, 151), 'means that all that is cultural is social. Culture is the product of social life and human social activity'.

Learning and Development

Vygotsky, when analysing the relationship between development and learning in the social formation of the mind, defines the concept of the 'Zone of Proximal Development' (ZPD) as a means to explain the difference which exists between individual and social angles in problem and cognitive task resolution.

In other words, the zone of proximal development is the difference between the level of tasks that can be achieved with the help of adults and the level of tasks that can be solved with independent activity. Thus, the ZPD emerges as a moving region created in interactions and in dialogue, having as mediators the knowledge employed by participants in distinct levels of development.

The learning process takes place precisely in the ZPD. In a first stage, the learner is capable of doing and knowing only with the help of an adult. With new functions and new learning, the child becomes apt to do and know things without help. For Vygotsky, the concomitance of development and learning creates the area of potential development.

The teacher's understanding of the ZPD becomes very useful in the process of teaching and learning, according to Vygotsky. Teaching and learning within the zone of proximal development makes it possible to awaken 'the child's activity, putting in motion an entire series of developmental processes' (1973, 37). Vygotsky emphasises that this is only possible when the child interacts with the people who surround him and cooperates with his classmates.

This understanding has important implications in the everyday school life since it recognises the value of the teacher's role in the classroom, the importance of collective work, the heterogeneous classes and the dialogue as a means of acquisition and elaboration of knowledge.

Learning and development are therefore part of educational practice and are only accomplished through social interaction. The acquisition of knowledge happens in a process of interchange among subjects with different experiences.

The presence of students with distinct possibilities in the classroom becomes a fundamental factor in the creation of an adequate environment for social interaction, which will be the mediating element for learning and development. From a historical-cultural viewpoint of learning and development, the heterogeneity, a common trait in any human group, is seen as an essential element for classroom interaction.

Through social interaction, the student learns to regulate the cognitive processes, by following mainly the teacher's indications and directions. With this, an internalisation process is created in which all that the student can learn at first with help from the teacher (inter-psychological regulation) and then it becomes progressively something that can be done by oneself (intra-psychological regulation).

It is fundamental to employ pedagogical intervention in the teaching and learning process, with the aim of providing the necessary interactions for knowledge elaboration and interchange. This elaboration emerges from diversity, as a collective process of 'meanings and significations' that are produced, questioned, rebuilt and refused in the course of the intercourse generated in the classroom.

Language, Speech and Mathematical Concepts

The social interactions in the learning and development process depend to a large extent on the forms of mediation. According to Vygotsky, mediation is processed through the use of psychological tools. Vygotsky considers as psychological tools and their complex systems: language, various systems of counting, mnemonic techniques, a system of algebraic symbols, works of art, written material, schemes, maps, mechanical blueprints, every kind of conventional symbol.

In this process of interaction-mediation, language has a decisive role, according to Vygotsky. It is the instrument that regulates action and thought. It acquires communicative function when used as a means of execution of differentiated forms of behaviour. Moreover, language acts as a regulator of cognitive processes, since, in social interaction, the intercourse of verbal formulations aimed at communication demands that speakers reconsider and reanalyse what they intend to communicate. When confronted with other's language the process of interiorisation shifts from external, social, inter-psychological regulation of cognitive processes to interiorised, individual, intra-psychological regulation.

Among the many modes of language, speech is an instrument which should be widely used in the classroom. Specifically, according to Souza et al.:

The mathematical speech is identified by juxtaposition of three determinations: historical affiliation (diacronism), present consensus (synchronism) and enunciation function. In the first determination, the speech is considered mathematical because of its historical affiliation to mathematics scientific practice. In the second determination, the speech is considered mathematical because they emit the opinions of social subjects, i.e., the mathematicians. And in the third determination the speech is said to be mathematical because its function is to keep the object in the chain of significant, i.e., mathematical rigor. (1995, 10)

When considering the learning of mathematics as a discursive process that presupposes mutual actions, teacher-student interaction by means of words becomes a priority. In the daily life of the school the interactions must overcome the mere contact between people, replacing it with meaningful action conducted by engaged subjects, questioning certainties, negotiating viewpoints, uncovering contradictions, distinguishing constant from variable, and other things.

For that reason, these interactions are mediated by a mathematical speech that is indispensable in the course of mathematical concept elaboration. According to Vygotsky (1989), in the concept elaboration process, the student must maintain a dialogue with the concepts, articulating it with the voices, findings and experiences of his and others' social groups.

Vygotsky distinguishes two kinds of concepts — scientific and everyday. The first kind is acquired in educational activities carried on in the school; the second is apprehended in any other place within the social and cultural context in which the student lives. Scientific concepts are seldom connected to everyday experience and are based in a specific class of the semiotic activity, like, for instance, definitions. For him, the most important distinction between both concepts is the absence of a system in everyday concepts. In everyday concepts, the child's attention is directed to the object which is represented and not to the act of thought which grasps it.

On the other hand, scientific concepts, which have a very different relationship with the object, are mediated by other concepts due to its internal hierarchic system of interrelations. (1989, 93)

Vygotsky said that scientific concepts have a key function in the evolution of higher psychological processes since they are formed consciously, and, therefore, under voluntary control. He said:

The power of the scientific concepts is evident in the sphere that generally defines the ultimate domain of concepts: conscious achievement and voluntary action. At the same time, in this same sphere we can observe the pleasure of the child's concept, concepts that are powerful in the sphere of concrete application, situation specific, spontaneous, in the sphere of experience and empiricism. (1993, 254)

In a mathematical concept-learning context, one of the teacher's duties is to be prepared for what Vygotsky calls everyday and scientific concepts' descent and ascent movements. The school has the obligation to enhance the student's scientific knowledge acquisition. The scientific knowledge enables the learner to comprehend everyday concepts, and, consequently, to see their limitation in relation to the variety of meanings that the scientific knowledge offers.

Another characteristic that is inherent in scientific concepts is the fact that they are displayed in the absence of a contextualised situation, that is, they derive from decontextualised situations.

This attribute is an important input for the daily mathematics teaching practice. In the learning process of a certain concept, the starting point is the relationships with contextualised situations. However, these relationships need to be gradually overcome by mental relationships demanded by scientific concepts. Hence, the final stage of the elaboration of a mathematical concept is reached when the student thinks in a decontextualised way, that is, abstractly. The term decontextualised does not mean that it is disassociated from reality, but rather in the sense of a higher form of elaboration and abstraction, with no need to relate it to the concrete reality. Taking as an example the concept of relative whole numbers, the decontextualisation is connected to the rise of a numerical system, through which it is possible to represent a certain quantity without a perceptive context.

In this sense, when reassuring his belief in the role of language in the formation of superior psychological processes, Vygotsky says it has an implicit decontextualisation potential. For that reason we may use language to refer to a certain quantity as 'minus three' without specifying what. For him, it is via formal school education that the student is introduced into the correspondences among signs, and produces and understands scientific concepts and abstract definitions.

Since mathematics deals primarily with generalising and abstract object properties and its relationships, there are two components that may influence thought formation: the visual imaginative components and logical verbal components. Krutetsky, based in B.B. Korrov's studies, claims that one of the requisites for mathematical ability is the importance of the logical verbal aspect instead of the visual imaginative aspect.

The same author, when studying some traits of students considered to have little ability for mathematics, says that 'though the logical verbal component does not determine flawlessly the mathematical ability, it is a necessary condition' (1991, 84). Besides, he says that a poor development of this component induces difficulties in mathematical comprehension. The ineptness for mathematics means, consequently, that there is feebleness in the logical verbal component of thought. Nonetheless, particular traces of this inability are determined by reciprocal relationship between the logical verbal and visual imaginative components. That demands diverse methodological orientations in the educational process. Such procedure relies on the assumption that mental elaboration is a culturally developed way which humans employ to reflect their experiences cognitively. This process implies both analysis (abstraction) and synthesis (generalising).

Kalmykova (1991) says that all mathematical concepts are similar to any form of thought and, because of that, demand different degrees of difficulty in the process of analysis and synthesis. This process depends basically on the student's ability to acquire objective knowledge and organisation, content, classification and elaboration of knowledge. Such possibilities are presented in the student's interactions, using the word as the mediating instrument.

Kalmykova, however, warns us that words are 'multiform stimuli'. One and the same word in the context of analysis and synthesis of mathematical concept learning can be attached to a certain mental action in one situation, and to another mental action under different circumstances. The mentioned author also points out that analysis and synthesis do not occur isolated, but are rather processed in a dialectic process.

That is why any attempt to artificially isolate analysis and synthesis in the teaching process is doomed for failure. The psychological basis for a correct concept formation is an assimilation that allows the creation of conditions for abstract and concrete components of thought, between word and image. (1991, 12)

Kalmykova suggests that the teacher should resort to adequate use of diverse didactic material, in order to achieve proper mathematical concept formation. These should be presented and used in such a way that the sensorial experience (1) is not abusive and (2) points out the fundamental char-

acteristics at the cost of the less significant ones, to allow that such characteristics must be verbally formulated and the fundamental characteristics of
the concept must be evidenced.

In sum, the theoretical aspects brought to light in this section point out
some categories to be considered in the analysis of mathematical cognition
in the school context, i.e., in mathematics teaching and learning. These categories are: (1) concept of mathematics from the cultural-historical viewpoint, (2) learning and development, (3) the zone of proximal development,
(4) heterogeneity, (5) social interaction, (6) language-speech-dialogue-didac-
tic mediation, (7) contextualising and decontextualising, (8) everyday and
scientific concepts, (9) analysis-synthesis, (10) logical-verbal and imagina-
tive-visual components. These categories will certainly provide the basis to
understand the mathematical discourse in the classroom, in the following
text. Voices and experiences rose, and the careful observation of the discursive plot present in the classroom provides us with elements to identify the
student's particular way of learning, and consequently, to generate pedagogical intervention in order to ensure meaningful improvement in the acquisition of mathematical knowledge. Such concerns are shared by Vygotsky (1989) when he warns about the need to understand the child's scientific concept formation process in order to support proper teaching methods.

The Mathematics Class

In the course of the present study, we observed after a period of ac-
quaintance with the teacher in the school environment, twenty class sessions
of a maths activity which took place in a public school.

In the search to understand how the teacher's intentions are accomplished in these daily sessions that offer the student a more intimate contact
with mathematical knowledge, we remained in the classroom for the period
that corresponded to the study of the content scheduled in the teacher's
planning.

Relative Whole Numbers

The class sessions were conducted in the sixth grade, and the topic of
teaching was relative whole numbers. The study of relative whole numbers
is of great importance to both teacher and students. It is a subject that
expands the concept of number held previously (natural number), and de-

mands rupturing certain epistemological barriers and cognitive conflict.

The difficulty in the acquisition of the concept of relative whole numbers is historical. The history of mathematics shows us that, for many centuries, they stirred doubt in many famous mathematicians, especially in the explanation for the multiplication signs rule. Glaeser (1985) lists six epistemological obstacles that caused trouble in the systematisation of relative whole numbers, and create trouble in the student's learning as well. The obstacles are: (1) ineptness to deal with isolated quantities, (2) difficulties to give meaning to isolated negative quantities, (3) difficulties in joining the numerical axis, (4) ambiguity in the two zeros, (5) stagnation in the stage of concrete operations, (6) desire for an unifying model for both addition and multiplication.

In the mathematical lessons about relative whole numbers in this study, the teacher follows his class plan strictly. He only works with this subject, the first to appear in sixth grade books. The concern is to teach the contents based on the dialogue about situations that were familiar to the students. During most of the classes, when a new concept or a new property of the Z (relative whole numbers set) was introduced, the teacher created a dialogue based on knowledge the students already had.

To introduce the 'relative whole numbers' topic, the teacher starts out with the handball championship that happened the week before, the coal mining workers strike, the average temperature in the town of São Joaquim (the coldest city in Brazil) and the movement of miners to the underground. All of these situations are topics which are part of the student's dialogue at the moment.

Teacher:
— Now we are going to start the sixth grade programme. All of this that happened last week, in this case the championship, what is happening in the strikes, the work of the miners, many of whom are your fathers, the change of temperature, all this has to do with our study.
The students demonstrate anxiety and excitement to start the sixth grade programme and yell: All right!
The teacher proposes:
— Let's check what happened at the handball championship. Shall we draw a table on the board?

In group work, teacher and students draw a table to show the students the topic is already part of their daily life (see Table 9.1).

Team	Points for	Points against	Credit
Quintanilha	+3	−2	+1
Barão	+5	−1	+4
Rainha	+4	−5	−1
Caetano	+7	−4	+3

Table 9.1. Team table.

When filling out the credit column the debate arises. The students participate more than the teacher does. The teacher's role now is to move around some situations that appeared and to write down the conclusions of the group.

It is now that the dialogue that underlies the mathematical speeches establishes itself in the student-student and students-teacher interactions. The language, as the mediating instrument for the personal elaboration of the concept of relative whole number, is presented in two forms: in the oral talk among students and teacher, and in writing (teacher on the board and students in the notebook). All mathematical knowledge demands a specific language. In the case of relative whole numbers, the language to be appropriated by the students becomes clear the moment the teacher fills in the table with the results of the handball championship, which represents an important 'semiotic instrument' for teaching the mentioned subject. In the construction of the table, teacher and students demonstrate the use of visual imaginative and logical verbal components of mathematical thinking. When explaining the points' standings the students use the proper language: plus three, minus two, etc. In this case, the contextualisation allows the student to acquire the language without difficulty.

The teacher's decision to use a situation in the student's context in the beginning of the study reveals his concern in recognising that they use notions of concepts in their daily lives. In Vygotsky's way of thinking, the experience they have out of the school helps them develop shared concepts. So, by constructing the table, a semiotic instrument was created, and it reveals the student's dynamism in shifting from their common concepts (in this case, their actual development level) and the mathematical concept of relative whole numbers (potential development level).

The most intense discussion rises when the credit of the Rainha team is calculated, for it is necessary to subtract a larger number out of a smaller one, since the students do not know +4 > –5.

A student says:
— You cannot subtract a larger number out of a smaller one, in this case plus four and minus five.

This student shows her conviction about numbers: natural numbers. At the same time, she evidences the cognitive conflict of the subject when faced with the object of knowledge. In this speech, the zone of proximal development is outlined, stimulating the teacher and classmates to help her attain her potential development in an interaction process. This interaction is perceived when another student turns the discussion to another situation, that is, the bank account situation.

Another student: I know where the teacher wants to get. If I have 300 dollars in my bank account and issue a 50-dollar check, this is negative.
With a different interpretation, a third student interferes:
— That's wrong, it is not negative. It will only be negative if he issued a 350-dollar check. Then his account would show minus 50.
The teacher does not interfere in this discussion with any comment, nor contribution. Noticing the students already manipulate the language of positive and negative numbers, the teacher leads them towards the need to form a new set that includes the mentioned numbers:
— Now let me tell one thing. Someone said we could not subtract a larger number out of a smaller one, then someone found it possible, but the result would be a negative number. But, do these numbers belong to the numerical set? Does the natural number set contain these negative numbers? The subtraction of two numbers x and y is only possible if x is more than y. So, observe that natural numbers, even though they are formed of infinite numbers, do not solve all mathematical situations that appear in our daily life.
The teacher's intervention seems to rush into decontextualisation, into the logical verbal component, the abstraction, the scientific concept. After that, the students remain in silence for a few seconds, trying to find an answer for the question presented before them. As ideas appear, the students resume the discussion process. The dialogue is re-established when a student says, shyly:
— I think it could be the Q+ set of absolute rational numbers, but there are no negative numbers in it, so it can't be.

The expected answer comes from another student in the form of a question:
— Couldn't we invent another set which would include negative numbers?
Taking advantage of the situation, the teacher writes on the board the set of the relative whole numbers:
$$Z = \{\ldots -6, -5, -4, -3, -2, -1, 0, +1, +2, +3, +4, +5, +6 \ldots\}$$
He draws the student's attention to the name of the set and the placement of elements:
— Z is the set of relative whole numbers which is composed of the zero, the positive numbers and the negative numbers. Note that the zero is the reference point. On its right we have the positive numbers, and on the left, the negative ones.

The teacher always tries, as it can be seen from the above, to generalise and present a systematisation of the topic in a more elaborated form. The teacher's concern is to make the student achieve his potential development. He is aware that his purpose is to provide students with the theory concept learning of relative whole numbers.

At the moment, the students seem uninterested in the representation and symbolisation of the set; they would rather discuss its application in their daily lives. So, the discussion goes back to this issue, with an emphasis on the visual imaginative component of mathematical thought.

Student:
— Teacher, in São Joaquim the temperature varies a lot and sometimes reaches as low as 5 degrees below zero. This means that the temperature there is minus five. Here in Urussanga I have never heard of negative temperature. It's warmer here because the altitude is lower. So, we only have positive temperatures.
The situation created by the student impels the teacher to draw a thermometer on the board with coloured chalk. When representing degrees Celsius in the drawing, he asks the students to help, by saying:
— Here is the zero, so where do we put the first, second and third positive degrees?
Student:
— Above zero?
Teacher:
— And the first, second and third negative degrees?
Students:
— Below zero.
Observing the drawing, a student says:

— How funny! The thermometer looks pretty much like the numbered axis of the set Z elements. Only it's rotated vertically.

The teacher agrees, and asks a student to draw the numbered axis. The student carries out the task with no problem.

But the students are still anxious to find situations where they experienced such numbers. They tell their situations euphorically. New examples appear. One girl:

— In the last year we studied the years before and after Jesus Christ, in History class. I may say, then, that the year of Christ is zero, before him, it's negative and after him, positive.

The teacher explains to the class this situation:

— That's right. Let's see an example. [Pitagoras] was a great Greek philosopher and mathematician, and he was born in 500 BC. We could say in the year of –500. But we could say the discovery of Brazil happened in +1500, instead of AD 1500.

Another student immediately points out a different situation:

— One day I went to the mine to deliver my uncle's lunch. Now I see that in his job there is a relative number too. Do you know why? He gets inside the elevator some 10 meters above ground and goes down in the underground another 30 meters. So, when he is on the surface, it's positive meters, and when he is below, it's negative meters.

The students seek other situations. One of them leads the group to intense questioning:

— With this miner's strike, my neighbour had his chequebook cancelled because he had negative account at the bank. I doubt if the bank manager would cancel the mine owner's check or a politician's one. Poor people and workers don't have a chance.

Another student adds:

— Some people say the miners are bums, drunks, and do nothing but go on strike. These people should realise that the miner's salary won't pay a bottle of whiskey the mine owner drinks.

The opinion is shared by another student:

— The rich man drinks expensive whiskey and no one calls him a drunk, they say he drinks socially. A miner drinks cheap brandy and people call him a drunk.

The political and social questions raised by the students did not deserve particular attention from the teacher and remained more of a commentary than a careful analysis of the situation. The subject being studied, relative whole numbers, offers a great basis for the discussion raised by the students.

The teacher's contribution in this case is:

— People, you know what our politicians are like. One thing I cannot stand is to see a politician being elected by the people and forgetting all about the people the moment he steps in the office.

The discussion is brought to an end and the students start working on the text book activities, in groups. In the next classes, the teacher will recall the situations discussed in the classroom to continue the study of the subject.

For the study of opposed or symmetrical numbers, the teacher simulates the position of the numbers, bank accounts, handball championship points standing and temperature comparisons.

The teacher writes on the board: Imagine these situations: 1. A miner is in the underground three meters from the surface. Another miner is in opposite or symmetrical position. Where would he be? 2. A teacher has five thousand dollars in his account. A miner is in opposite situation. What does the miner's account show? 3. The Barão team has a credit of eight goals positive, while the Rainha team is in the opposite situation. What is their points situation? 4. In Sao Joaquim the temperature now is –2º C, while here in Urussanga it is the opposite. What is the temperature in Urussanga?

The teacher makes comments about each situation, while the students answer the questions cheerfully. The culminating point is the resolution of textbook exercises. During the correction, it is emphasised that the negative is the negation of the positive. For instance, by saying minus five, it means I do not want plus five, that is, I want a situation that is the opposite of plus five.

For the study of absolute value or modulus of a whole number, all the previously exposed situations were used. The analysis of these situations demonstrates a very relaxed atmosphere, making us feel that it was not a maths class. It seemed the students were reviewing the subject rather than having their first contact with it.

The dialogue on absolute value proceeded like this:

Teacher:
— We saw before that the miner was at –3 meters from the surface. The other miner, in the opposite situation, was at +3. Which one was closer to the surface?
The students' answer:
— Both are the same distance from the surface.

Teacher:

— What distance?

Students:

— Three meters.

The teacher speaks and writes down the symbolic notation on the board:

— This situation, in Mathematics, is called Absolute Value or Modulus, and it is represented like this:

$|-3| = 3$, the module of minus three is three.

$|+3| = 3$, the module of plus three is three.

A student says:

— So the module means how many units one is away from zero, but it does not indicate which side it is on. To know the side, you've got to see if it is positive or negative.

Teacher:

— That's it. You got the picture.

Showing he had followed the discussion of the last topic, a student analyses the following situation:

— In the case of the teacher's 5000 dollar positive account and the miner's 5000 negative, both need 5000 dollar units to bring their accounts to zero. The teacher needs to withdraw five thousand and the miner needs to make a five thousand dollar deposit.

Teacher:

— That's right, I had not considered it from this angle, now I understand this situation better.

A student says:

— We taught the teacher something again. That's nice.

Teacher:

— Nobody knows everything. We are learning new things all the time. We will never know everything.

Let's write the absolute value of the teacher's and the miner's accounts.

$|+5000| = 5000 \quad |-5000| = 5000$

To complete the study of the situations raised in the beginning of the class, the teacher recalls the question of the modulus of the two teams points standings.

— How do we interpret the absolute value of the points credit of the two teams?

Showing that they had understood the subjects being studied, the student raised their arms to answer the question, while the teacher sorts one out, but allows contribution from the others.

The chosen student says:

— The module of plus eight, which is Barão's points, is eight. The module of minus eight, Rainha's points, is eight.

A classmate completes:

— This means that both teams have no goal credit. One has to make eight goals and the other must suffer them. In this case, it involves eight units.

A girl, in an attempt to end the discussion, says:

— I think it's time to move on. This subject is well understood. Who wouldn't know, now, that in São Joaquim the temperature needs to rise two units of degrees to reach zero, and that in Urussanga it needs to lower two degrees. This means that, to reach zero from minus two, you need two units, and, to reach zero from plus two, you also need two units. It is also easy to know because the absolute value is when the negative or positive number is between those two bars, so all you need to do is to put the number without the + or – sign, that you know how far you are from zero.

That is the opinion of the other students, so the teacher suggests the students to work with textbook exercises, and then begin the study of the subset of Z.

The teacher's decision when faced with the student's opinion reveals that true dialogue drives the social interaction in the classroom. This interchange does not mean the teacher's question on one side and the student's answer on the other, but rather a relationship of trust that is carried on in the act of knowing. As Freire (1975, 93) puts it, 'the dialogue is not limited by the I-you relationship, the dialogue is a relationship of faith, love and respect between teacher and student'.

In order to study the subset of Z (Z^*, $Z+$, $Z-$, Z^*+, Z^*-) the strategy used was the use of the board and presentation of the subject. No relationship with previous situations was established. Maybe this drastic rupture with context situations was one of the reasons that caused the students to demonstrate difficulty in the identification of such subset, even with more classes than what had been planned beforehand. The majority of the students did not achieve the level of understanding to the point of establishing the relationship of pertinence among the elements of each subset, nor the inclusion relationship. Like Vygotsky (1989, 72) said:

The direct teaching of concepts is impossible and fruitless. A teacher that tries to do that obtains nothing but empty verbalism, a word repetition by the child, like that of a parrot, which simulates knowledge, but only hides a vacuum.

Giving sequence to what had been planned, the focus of study shifts to the order relationship of whole numbers. At first, the study is conducted through the team table (Table 9.1).

The table was assembled by teacher and students. Greater attention will be given to the last column, since the question to be answered is the position of each team considering points credit.

The dialogue among the students leads them to the conclusion that the decreasing order of teams is: 1st place, Barão, 2nd place, Caetano, 3rd place, Quintanilha, 4th place, Rainha. Using mathematical language, the student writes down on the board the decreasing and increasing order:

$$+4 > +3 > +1 > -1$$
$$-1 < +1 < +3 < +4$$

The same discussion is conducted using the numbered straight line. The conclusion of the study is carried out with a series of activities suggested by the teacher and by the textbook.

One fact that attracted our attention was that in the study of the order of the relative whole numbers, no rules were used to identify a larger number from a small one, like the number on the right is more than the one on the left. This type of rule is widely used in schoolbooks.

We noticed that the students demonstrated cleverness in the suggested activities, showing comprehension of all they wrote or spoke to the group.

After that, an examination was conducted, on all topics concerning relative whole numbers.

Operations with Relative Whole Numbers

The subject to be discussed in the next classes refer to operations with relative whole numbers. For the teacher, addition, subtraction, multiplication and division are fundamental topics for the themes that will follow in 6th, 7th, and 8th grades.

The examination of these operations does not flow with the same smoothness as former classes. Through the teacher tried to start out from the student's intuitive concepts to reach systematisation, he is now more concerned with the signs rule.

Contrary to what we had been witnessing until now, where the dialogue was the summit leading the student towards the construction of a new concept, in the study of operations the teacher's monologue obstructed the discussion and debate about doubts. From then on, we observed the routine of definitions, examples and exercises, with the use of structural properties to justify definitions and rules. Due to this routine, we shall not write down what was said during these classes.

Discussion and Conclusion

From this study, we may extract a few considerations. The teacher ceases to evidence relevant aspects for concept formation. Few were the opportunities when the social meaning of the negative number and of the word 'negative' was discussed. According to Vygotsky (1989), the social interaction necessarily presupposes generalisation, and as a result, the meaning of the word.

The same happened for the two zero ambiguity. The notion of a relative zero (as a reference point) as opposed to that of absolute zero (with no number inferior to it) is the foundation of the concept of relative whole numbers.

In the same sense, addition demands the overcoming of the idea of gather and add, present in natural numbers. The mental action of adding whole numbers demands the mental action of adding and subtracting natural numbers. This step is a learning barrier, since the students hesitate to reject something they thought was valid for all addition. Therefore, the teacher-student mediation must be mediated by a dialogue rich in analysis-synthesis, context-decontextualisation and generalisation-abstraction.

Subtraction, multiplication and division present an even wider field of difficulty for the student if the empirical notion of number is not overcome. According to Glaeser (1985), this conception is an obstacle to the understanding of multiplication properties.

The operations in Z, with a few restrictions to addition, were carried on with restricted concepts and confused theoretical notions, being conducted by oral and written questions created by the teacher, leading towards a predetermined answer. The dialogue had changed. The mathematical speech had become traditional speech. The activity taken led students to see in the operations a single meaning: the interiorisation of the signs rule for opertions.

The most controversial topics in this research were: (1) The insistence by the students in dialoguing about their everyday concepts, rejecting the teacher's actions that focused on scientific concepts; (2) The motives and meaning of the teaching and learning activity are not the same for teacher and student.

Another aspect to consider in the present study is that, from subtraction on, the analysis regarding the realistic situations previously discussed was completely abandoned. When they were used, there was a great participation from both teacher and students. The sincere and equal dialogue had been an essential element to construct and understand certain concepts.

We stress that this study included addition, subtraction, multiplication and division of the relative whole numbers. The mathematical speeches were not mentioned, because they are daily ones. From those speeches, we could see the distance between the motives of teacher and students. In the beginning, they had the same purpose, that is, learning and developing the acquisition of the concept. But, then, the students became worried about the evaluation.

The movement of the miners, the handball team points standing, the bank account and the temperature could have been the focus of the discussion so that the students would grasp the logic of addition, subtraction, multiplication and division in Z. Certainly, their understanding would not be restricted to the signs rule of operations.

According to Vygotsky's theory, formal education automatically produces a progressive decontextualisation of instrument mediation, because the student becomes able to use signs in a context independent manner. However, this does not happen abruptly.

Nonetheless, we see the teacher made an improvement, if we compare his effort to the requirements of the textbook used. In the book, each operation is shown with a few examples of 'how to do', followed by the signs rule. The teacher was, at least, concerned about giving a meaning to the signs rule, in each operation.

About the mathematics class where the concept of relative whole numbers was introduced, we could say it had two moments. One of dialogue and one of authoritative behaviour. One of analysis, synthesis, generalisation and abstraction, and one of memorisation. One of historical cultural discourse and one of traditional mathematical discourse. One of logical verbal components and one of visual imaginative components. Cognitively, it can be observed that the students did not overcome the concept of number as an ability to count concrete objects instead of as abstract objects that can be operated independently. In this case, the decontextualisation took place on a very small scale.

The present study is an attempt to begin a study about the mathematics learning process in the classroom, according to a cultural-historical perspective. We are aware of the necessity for a theoretical study of historical philosophic epistemological nature concerning the nature of knowledge and learning, and also concerning the concept of relative whole numbers. This is the necessary step to innovate the teacher's educational specialisation process. The main purpose is to turn the State Education Project effective.

References

Baldino, R.R. (1995). Sobre a epistemologia dos números inteiros. *Educação matemática em Revista*, 3(5), 4-11.

Damazio, A. (1991). *A prática docente do professor de matemática: pedagogia que fundamenta o planejamento e a execução do ensino*. Florianópolis: UFSC. Dissertação de Mestrado.

Fiorentini, D. (1995). Alguns modos de ver e conceber o ensino de matemática no Brasil. *Zetetiké*, 3(4), 1-37.

Freire, P. (1975). *Pedagogia do oprimido*. Rio de Janeiro: Paz e Terra.

Glaeser, G. (1985). Epistemologia dos números relativos. *Boletim GEPEM*, 17, 29-124.

Kalmykova, Z.I. (1991). Pressupostos psicológicos para uma melhor aprendizagem da resolução de problemas de matemática. In Lúria, Leontiev, Vygotsky et al., *Pedagogia e Psicologia II*. Lisboa: Editorial Estampa.

Krutetsky, V.A. (1991). Algumas características do desenvolvimento nos estudantes com pouca capacidade para as matemáticas. In Lúria, Leontiev, Vygotsky et al., *Pedagogia e Psicologia II*. Lisboa: Editorial Estampa.

Leontiev, A.N. (1978). *O desenvolvimento do psiquismo*. Lisboa: Livros Horizonte.

Souza, A.C. et al. (1995). *Novas diretrizes para a licenciatura em matemática*. Rio Claro: IGCE-UNESP.

Vygotsky, L.S. (1973). Aprendizaje y desarrollo intelectual en la edad escolar. In Lúria, Leontiev, Vygotsky et al., *Psicología y Pedagogia*. Madrid: Akal.

Vygotsky, L.S. (1989). *Pensamento e linguagem*. São Paulo: Martins Fontes.

Vygotsky, L.S. (1989). *A formação social da mente*. São Paulo: Martins Fontes.

Vygotsky L.S. (1993). *Obras Escogidas II*. Madrid: Visor.

Vygotsky, L.S. et al. (1988). *Linguagem, desenvolvimento e aprendizagem*. São Paulo: ICONE/EDUSP.

10 From Monologic to Dialogic Learning: A Case Study of Japanese Mathematics Classrooms

Kayo Matsushita

Distinguishing between three theoretical generations in the evolution of activity theory, Engeström (1997) argued that the third present generation, after a dialogical turn in the 1990s, must deal with the questions of dialogue, multiple perspectives, voices and networks of interacting activity systems. Along this line, researchers have done some extensive work and have explored various facets of the questions. In the field of classroom research, for example, Gutierrez, Rymes and Joanne (1995) offered the concept of a 'third space' to represent a place where the two scripts — the teacher's script and the students' counter scripts — intersect, creating the potential for true dialogue to occur. This paper follows along similar lines of research. Here I will examine the possibility of transformation from monologic to dialogic learning in Japanese mathematics classrooms.

I would like to explore three major themes. First, that Japanese classrooms are not homogeneous, but culturally diverse in a very unique way. Second, learning mathematics becomes more monologic when the classroom culture is less homogeneous and when the teacher's control over students is somewhat relaxed. Third, it is difficult but not impossible to transform learning from monologic to dialogic by listening to the students' voices.

My findings are based on analysis of the learning activities in two different mathematics classrooms, one at elementary level and the other at junior high level. The observations indicated that even though the teachers in both classrooms had similar goals, i.e., the students should construct meaning through collaborative learning, the activity resulted in monologic learning in one classroom, and dialogic in the other.

* This study is partially supported by the Ministry of Education, Science, Sports and Culture, Grant-in-Aid for the Encouragement of Young Scientists, 09710182, 1997-98.

Cultural Diversity in Japanese Classrooms

How the Japanese Classroom Culture has Changed

It is generally believed that the Japanese schools are ethnically, linguistically, and socio-economically homogeneous. Consequently, certain pedagogical methods, e.g., cooperative activities in a class or in well-organised small groups have been very effective (e.g., Cummings 1980). However, if the word 'culture' is broadly defined, the premise of the cultural homogeneity of the Japanese classroom is not valid. The Japanese classroom culture has been changing over the last 20 years. Since the late 1970s, a phenomenon known as 'double school phenomenon' has had a major impact. It means that the children go to two schools: the regular school and the coaching schools known as 'juku'. Generally speaking, there are four types of juku (Yuki, Sato & Hashisako 1987), but we can say that the philosophy of juku education is more or less exemplified by the 'Kumon Method', the most popular juku-method in Japan. It uses teacher-proof written material with small steps and makes the children learn in isolation and competition. The Kumon Method is offered through franchised and privately run coaching classes spread all over Japan. According to 1997 data, 1.6 million students in Japan, and 866 thousand students abroad, followed the Kumon Method. After finishing regular school, children go to juku in the evening. It is a common sight in Japan to see children, who attend juku in order to pass entrance exams, returning home as late as 10 p.m. at night.

Three Cultures in a Mathematics Classroom

The double school phenomenon has brought about a kind of cultural diversity in the classrooms. Broadly speaking, there exist three types of culture in a mathematics classroom: 'juku maths', 'inquiry maths' and 'everyday maths' (see Inagaki & Sato 1996). The juku maths stresses rote memorisation and constant drilling of routine procedures, as is typically seen in the Kumon Method. The inquiry maths is characterised by the construction of mathematical meaning and consistent mathematical reasoning. In everyday maths, the acquisition of knowledge is done in an unconscious or involuntary manner, and it uses mathematical ideas embedded in everyday life situations. There are two things to be noted. First, juku maths does not exclusively belong to juku learning. It is true that inquiry maths culture is observed in some jukus whereas juku maths culture penetrates into some schools especially at junior and senior high level. Second, the three cultures are strictly 'ideal types'. The actual culture of each individual student is usually a mixture of all three.

Various studies on mathematical culture and cognition point out that there is a difference between school maths and inquiry maths on one hand (Lampert 1990; Cobb, Wood & Yackel 1993), and between school maths and everyday maths on the other hand (Lave 1988; Nunes, Schliemann & Carraher 1993). There is a reason why I refer to one of the three maths cultures as 'juku maths' not 'school maths' while my typology is based on these studies. Undoubtedly juku maths is an efficient and economic form of teaching school maths whose aim is the achievement of good grades. But juku maths does something more. Going to juku encourages comparison between the pedagogies of school and juku, and cultivates in the young student's mind a different value system, a different way of looking at schools, teachers and education in general. According to one survey (Yuki et al. 1987), students rate juku teachers higher than regular schoolteachers. They think that juku teachers are more earnest, more devoted to teaching and more friendly. Thus, considering children as consumers and education as a commodity, in their view, juku education is a better commodity. Students say: 'School teachers are just average adults, nothing more', 'They earn their pay because we are the ones that go to school. They should thank us' (NHK 1998, April 11).

How do these three maths cultures compare? The juku maths and the inquiry maths have something in common; the acquisition of knowledge is done consciously at least under some teaching programmes. This is not so in everyday maths. But looking at it from the viewpoint of object/motive, the inquiry maths and everyday maths are similar. While juku maths emphasises exchange value, such as good grades, both inquiry maths and everyday maths emphasise use value. The only difference between these two is that the inquiry maths pursues the use value in mathematical practice, while everyday maths does that in everyday practice. In the following, I intend to demonstrate that the conflict between juku maths on the one hand, and inquiry maths and everyday maths on the other, poses difficulties and disturbances for learning.

Monologic Learning and Cultural Differences

Due to the cultural differences and the dominance of juku maths, as I have described above, the mathematics learning in the classroom tends to be monologic. There are two reasons for this.

First, the usual teacher-student relation is unidirectional. This has often been discussed as an indicator of classroom power relations, in which the teacher has the initiative and the students follow. But, interestingly in Japan, this does not imply teacher's power over the students. Even when the teacher's intention is that the students learn by constructing meaning in collaboration, the students are able to convert his classroom teaching into a passive learning of procedures. The reason is the conflict between the teacher's culture of inquiry maths and the students' culture of juku maths. Sometimes, the juku maths students, having already learned the material being taught, cease to be receivers in the transmission process even though some pretend to be so. This reduces classroom instruction into teacher's monologue. Thus it is the students and not the teacher who control the decisions on what is to be learned and how. Karatani (1992), a Japanese philosopher, compares the 'teaching-learning' relation, with the 'selling-buying' relation. He warns us that we should not confuse the 'teaching-learning' relation with a power relation. According to him, the 'teaching' position is never superior to the 'learning' position, because it is the teacher's weak position which is obliged to seek agreement from the 'learning' side.

Second, the classroom space tends to be virtually univocal. While the voices from different cultures do exist in the classroom, there is little cross-cultural communication between them. In some cases, the inquiry maths and the everyday maths act as minor cultures and are suppressed by juku maths as the major culture. In other cases, these cultures develop indifference or 'habitat isolation' to each other. Moreover, since juku maths as the major culture stresses isolation and competition, the students oriented toward juku maths are reluctant to learn cooperatively by dialogue with their peers. For all these reasons, there is little dialogue *between* the cultures as well as *within* a culture, especially the juku maths culture. Thus, as I will describe below, some effective intervention may be necessary.

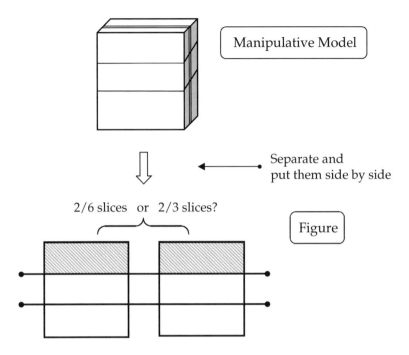

Figure 10.1. A manipulative model and a figure used in the main story problem in case study 1.

Case Study 1

I will now share with you my experience of a learning activity which I observed in a private elementary class in Saitama prefecture in 1997. I observed a two-hour lesson on fractions. The class consisted of 23 fifth and sixth grade students. The teacher was highly skilled and had many years of experience. The teaching material, which was prepared by the teacher and myself, consisted of five problems in story style. The story had two characters, a fat king, and a not-so-intelligent servant. The main problem was like this. 'The servant made a sandwich of two slices of bread for the king. He cut it into three pieces and served them to the fat king. The king ate one of the three pieces and realised that he was on diet. So, he asked, "How many slices of bread did I eat?" The servant does not know the fractions, and needs your help.' The teacher presented this problem to the students using a manipulative model and a figure (see Figure 10.1).

This is a variation of the *tape problem*, which is well known in Japanese mathematics education because it results in a low percentage of correct answers. The problem and its variations are designed so that the children understand the difference between the two concepts of fractions: the fraction as a ratio ('1/3') and the fraction as a definite quantity ('1/3 meter'). In everyday life, we seldom differentiate these two concepts, because in many cases we can communicate the fraction as a quantity by expressing it as a ratio. For example, if someone says 'I used a third' pointing to the tape which is two meters long, we can understand 'a third' means '1/3 of the tape.' However, when one is asked to express in meters the length of the tape he used, he needs to answer '2/3 meters', and not '1/3 meter', thus distinguishing the fraction as a definite quantity from the fraction as a ratio. The teacher's intent was to make the children construct these two mathematical meanings of fractions through analysing the fractions in everyday life.

As the teacher had expected, the children's answers were divided. Among 23 students, 22 said '2/6 slices (or 1/3 slice).' Only one student answered '2/3 slices'. I would now like to focus on the most interesting part of my observation: the speech and behaviour of three students. As I described earlier, the three cultures are ideal types, and the actual culture of each individual student is usually a mixture of the three cultures. However, these three students typically represented three maths cultures. So, let me symbolise them by their appropriate initials IM (inquiry maths), EM (everyday maths) and JM (juku maths) respectively.

IM initially answered '2/6 slices', but after some interaction with the teacher and other students, she changed her answer to '2/3 slices'. The teacher asked her how she got this answer. She demonstrated it with persuasive mathematical reasoning, by adding a drawing to the figure and manipulating the model of a sandwich. Her first explanation was as follows.

(circling the left, whole slice) This is one slice, and (pointing to the left uppermost piece) this is one piece of a slice divided three, so it is 1/3 slice. (pointing to the right uppermost piece) This is 1/3 slice, too. So, 1/3 plus 1/3 is 2/3. (looking at the teacher and tilting her head)

There was no reply from the teacher and other students, and then she moved to the second way of explanation. She showed that '2/6 slices' was an incorrect answer by using the result of the previous problem and using a kind of reductive absurdity.

When the teacher asked the students, 'Do you understand what she said?, ' only EM responded. He partly agreed with IM's explanation while he told the whole sandwich story in his own words. He had correctly concluded that the answer was twice of 1/3 slice, but he made a calculation error by saying $1/3 + 1/3 = 2/6$. Thus, he belonged to the group with wrong answers. Finally, JM's behaviour and speech was most interesting. He showed total indifference to IM's mathematical reasoning, and pressed EM to get on with his explanation and come to a conclusion. He was irritated by the halting way EM spoke and reacted to EM's calculation error with mockery.

After the interaction between EM and JM, IM raised her hand and said 'I'll explain more easily'. She, by moving the right piece under the left piece, illustrated that those two pieces are 2/3 of one slice, namely '2/3 slices'. Her three different ways of demonstration showed that she had constructed the meaning of the fraction as a definite quantity by distinguishing it from the fraction as a ratio. Her reasoning and meaning construction was the result of incorporation in her mind of others' ideas and the internal dialogisation with the self. I felt that her demonstration sounded like a voice asking for more dialogue with other students.

When the interaction came to an end, the teacher asked once again the students for their answer. Unfortunately, nobody but IM altered the answer. The teacher had hoped that he would help the students to construct mathematical meaning by interaction with others. But it did not happen.

One may argue that perhaps the students did not fully understand IM's mathematical reasoning. However, no student ever mentioned what either IM or EM had said. It seems reasonable to assume that most students felt that IM's reasoning and EM's talk was totally irrelevant, and they certainly did not incorporate it in their thinking. There was no true dialogue between the juku maths students who were in the majority and the IM and EM students who were in the minority. Nor was there any dialogue between the juku maths students and the teacher who was oriented toward inquiry maths. My observations made me feel more aware of the divergent behaviour of the different maths cultures and the obstacles they raise for cross-cultural communication. This in turn hinders dialogic learning.

Toward Dialogic Learning

What is Dialogic Learning?

Dialogic learning, as Freire (1973) put it, means that subjects construct-shared meaning of an object through dialogue with each other in a horizontal relation. In contrast to monologic learning, it is necessarily bi-directional, and multi-voiced. There are dialogues at different levels and of different kinds. What I have mentioned is not a dialogue between concrete individual voices, but a dialogue between different voice types (Wertsch 1991) such as juku maths, inquiry maths, and everyday maths. It is a dialogue between the different voices from different cultures. To understand and appreciate the role of dialogue in learning I will now describe my second case study.

Case Study 2

This second activity took place in the ninth grade junior high class in Tokyo in 1996 (see Sato 1997; Matsushita, in preparation). The class was about to study the section on quadratic equations.

In Japan, of all the grades, the ninth-graders are the ones most influenced by the juku maths culture. This is because the tension of passing the high school entrance exam permeates their everyday life, and most of them prepare for this exam with the help of juku education. According to 1997 data, 64% of ninth-graders went to juku (National Congress of Parents & Teachers Association of Japan 1998). In this classroom, more than 70% of the students were juku-goers. They had four maths classes a week at school and, at the same time, maths and other classes for three to five days at juku. Nearly half of the students had already learned about the quadratic equations before the lessons at school, though their learning was superficial and without understanding.

Under the boundary crossing between school and juku, what activity system of learning was generated? Engeström (1987) says that the structure of the activity of school going in capitalism is determined by the inner contradiction of this socio-economic formation, namely, the double nature of commodity as a unity of exchange value and use value (p. 102). The inner contradiction between exchange value vs. use value was embodied he depicted in the form of the inner contradiction between juku maths vs. inquiry

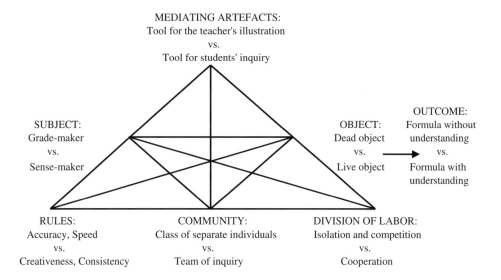

Figure 10.2. A representation of the shift of the students' leaning activity system in case study 2.

maths in this classroom. While most Japanese teachers teach in accordance with the national curriculum and the assigned textbook, this teacher had tried to organise his lessons by focusing on the inquiry process using artefacts. In this respect, his classes have the nature of 'counter-hegemonic activity' (Apple 1993), beyond official knowledge and institutionalised learning. On the other hand, many students had experienced juku maths at juku and brought it into the classroom under the boundary crossing. The students would say to the teacher, 'Just show us how to solve', 'Don't give us complicated mathematical explanations'. One can hardly fail to notice the presence of the conflict between the teacher's inquiry maths culture, and the students' juku maths culture. Thus, the inner contradiction in this classroom can be schematised as shown in Figure 10.2.

This time, when they came to quadratic equations, the teacher changed his strategy. He announced that he was going to give the students only the formula and a set of exercises and nothing else. He neither rendered any explanation nor spiced up the background with historical titbits. Then, interestingly enough, the following remarks came from the students: 'It is a very complicated expression with a square root! How come we got such an ugly expression?', 'Who discovered this formula and how?', 'It is difficult to remember this formula without understanding', 'If I learn it by rote memorisation, I will make calculation errors'. These were the very same pleas from the teacher before, but the students had ignored him. Apparently, the teacher's voice became students' voice, when the teacher turned the tables on them.

The point to be made is the following. That these voices were consciously created inside the students' minds means that the students as *subject* became sense-makers rather than grade-makers. And the content of their voices showed that the quadratic formula, considered as *object*, was reconstructed from a dead object separated from the context of mathematical construction into a live object situated in the context. Along with this, the other constituents of the learning activity system shifted their weight from juku maths to inquiry maths. The classroom as a *community* began to function as a team of inquiry rather than as a class of separate individuals. Even the nature of *mediating artefacts* was switched. Although previously the teacher had brought in various manipulative and figurative models for understanding mathematics, those models often remained just tools for the teacher's illustration. But, once the learning activity changed, the model as mediating artefacts revived from a tool for the teacher's illustration to a tool for students' inquiry.

Finally, using the model, the students devised a remarkable *outcome* on their own, what they named 'four times method'. Figure 10.3 illustrates how the meaning of the quadratic formula is constructed by this method. The characteristic of this method is that the process of solving a quadratic equation is carried out in two stages: the transformation of the given expression into a perfect square, and the solution of the equation with the perfect square. The transformation in the first stage is performed through figure manipulation instead of symbol manipulation. The figure manipulation does not produce the usual perfect square $(x + 2a/b)^2$, but a new one, $(2ax + b)^2$, which makes the subsequent symbol manipulation much easier. In this method, the operation of making the given expression a perfect square is done by combining four of the quadrangles made of the expression and actually constructing a square as figure, and the expression $b^2 - 4ac$ inside the square root sign refers to the area of the square.

The significant fact is that they themselves came up with an idea to understand a mathematical concept, and created their own model to under-

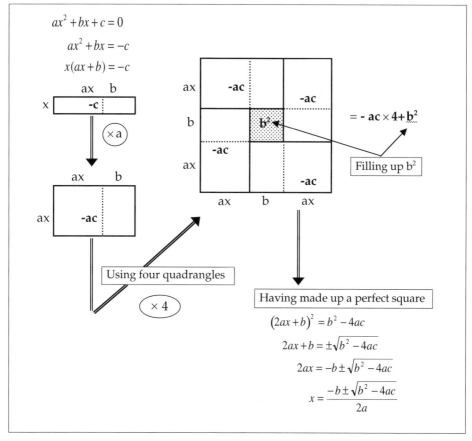

Figure 10.3. A representation of 'four times method' discovered by the students in case study 2.

stand it. The textbook did not have this kind of explanation, and neither had the teacher anticipated this outcome from the students. At least for that moment in time learning became a process of rediscovering and understanding for both the students and the teacher. In other words, the students and the teacher took joint participation in the practice of mathematical inquiry and formed shared meaning through cross-cultural dialogue. This can only be regarded as a fine example of dialogic learning.

This process repeated itself. In three out of four classes taught by this teacher, the students discovered the four times method on their own. It is therefore reasonable to suppose that, in this episode, some factors do exist which made dialogic learning possible. Let me focus on two such factors that helped the emergence of dialogic learning.

First, there was an inner voice of inquiry maths inside the students' minds. The students were seemingly drowned by the dominant voices of juku maths culture. But, in fact, a different voice was hidden inside them. In other words, different voices from different cultures echoed in one person's internal dialogisation (Bakhtin 1984). We can suppose that this inner voice had been internalised through interactions with the teacher and other inquiry maths students, mediated by various cognitive artefacts. As Vygotsky (1978) put it, the mental functioning in the individual originates with social communication processes.

Second, the teacher's action brought that hidden, inner voice outside. When he said, 'Here is the formula, and here is the set of exercises to do', he caught the students' voice and made it his own. The teacher's intervention set the stage for the beginning of a cross-cultural dialogue. More than regarding the teacher's utterance as a strategy for bringing students into his own programme, we should consider this as an exposure of his own internal dialogisation. The teacher had mentioned to me that he had faced criticism of his curriculum and lessons from one juku teacher as well as some juku maths students. In his mind, there would be an internal dialogisation between different voices from two contrasting cultures.

When both the students and the teacher expressed their own internal dialogisations, the two different types of voices met and the dialogue began. We can regard the very place as the third space (Gutierrez et al. 1995), in which true dialogue between different voices is possible (see Figure 10.4). It is also the place where learning activity system begins to change.

Conclusion

Cultural diversity and dialogue are the dual challenges of the third generation of activity theory. However, although at present we find cultural diversity in Japanese classrooms, we find at the same time an absence of dialogue.

Many classroom researchers have reported on the absence of dialogue and the monologic learning in classrooms as a reflection of the teacher's power over the students: a teacher has the initiative and the students follow passively. What has to be noticed is that monologic learning in present day Japanese classrooms occurs when the traditional power relations have col-

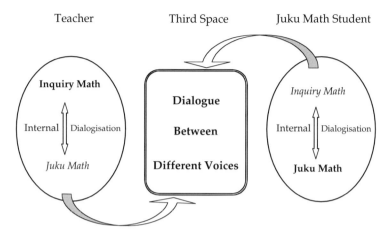

Figure 10.4. A representation of the structure and process of dialogic learning in case study 2.

lapsed due to the double school phenomenon. The nature of the juku maths culture and its dominance in the classrooms make it difficult for a meaningful dialogue to take place between the students and teacher and also among the students themselves. The first case study clearly illustrates that.

The second case study episode suggests that it is possible to intervene in students' learning activity and revive dialogic learning. The teacher had tried to orient the class toward inquiry maths, which meant a 'counter-hegemonic activity'. The boundary crossing between juku and school by the students had caused the conflict between the teacher's inquiry maths culture and the students' juku maths culture in the classroom. It had aggravated the inner contradiction within the learning activity system. What changed this situation was the teacher's utterance given in the voice of juku maths. It brought out the voice of inquiry maths that would have remained hidden inside the students. Thus, the third space was created where the voices from the teacher and the students met and dialogic learning took place. This, in turn, caused the change in the learning activity system and eventually a fruitful outcome.

The third space is often transitory, as Gutierrez et al. (1995) put it. To maintain the initiated dialogic learning, another effort is needed. In the second learning activity, the teacher guided the students' discovery by a series of tasks which he devised in reaction to students' learning, and he continued his attempts to reconstruct the object/motive for the students, who liked to retreat to their juku maths culture. In my opinion, this is an important matter that I plan to discuss more fully in another paper (Matsushita, in preparation).

It is not my intention here to generalise one teacher's action as a universal teaching strategy. But it is a good example illustrating what kinds of interventions are more effective for dialogic learning to occur. These interventions will also help us to understand the structure and the process of dialogic learning.

References

Apple, M. (1993). *Official knowledge: Democratic education in a conservative age*. New York: Routledge.

Bakhtin, M.M. (1984). *Problems of Dostoevsky's poetics* (C. Emerson, ed. and trans.). Minneapolis, M.N.: University of Minnesota Press.

Cobb, P., Wood, T. & Yackel, E. (1993). Discourse, mathematical thinking, and classroom practice. In E.A. Forman, N. Minick & C.A. Stone (eds.), *Contexts for learning: Sociocultural dynamics in children's development*. New York: Oxford University Press.

Cummings, W.K. (1980). *Education and equality in Japan*. Princeton, N.J.: Princeton University Press.

Engeström, Y. (1987). *Learning by expanding: An activity-theoretical approach to developmental research*. Helsinki: Orienta-Konsultit.

Engeström, Y. (1997). Learning by expanding: Ten years after. In Y. Engeström (F. Seeger, trans.), *Neuland des Lernens: Entwicklung und Perspektive der Tätigkeitstheorie* (the German edition of *Learning by expanding*). Marburg: BdWi-Verlag.

Freire, P. (1973). *Education for critical consciousness*. New York: Seabury Press.

Gutierrez, K., Rymes, B. & Joanne, L. (1995). Script, counterscript, and underlife in the classroom: James Brown versus Brown v. Board of Education. *Harvard Educational Review*, 65, 445-71.

Inagaki, T. & Sato, M. (1996). *Zyugyô kenkyû nyûmon* [Introduction to research on teaching and learning]. Tokyo: Iwanami syoten.

Karatani, K. (1992). *Tankyû (I)* [Inquiry (1)]. Tokyo: Kôdansya.

Lampert, M. (1990). When the problem is not the question and the solution is not the answer: Mathematical knowing and teaching. *American Educational Research Journal*, 27, 29-63.

Lave, J. (1988). *Cognition in practice: Mind, mathematics and culture in everyday life*. Cambridge: Cambridge University Press.

Matsushita, K. (in preparation). *Generating contexts for learning in a Japanese class-room of diverse cultures: The dilemma of two interacting activity systems.*

National Congress of the Parents & Teachers Association of Japan (1998). *Heisei 9 nendo Gakusyû-juku ni kansuru ankêto chôsa kekka hôkokusyo* [Report on Juku 1997].

NHK (1998, April 11). *Kyôiku today 98* [Education today 98]. Tokyo: NHK (Japan Broadcasting Corporation).

Nunes, T., Schliemann, A.D. & Carraher, D.W. (1993). *Street mathematics and school mathematics.* Cambridge: Cambridge University Press.

Sato, N. (1997). Nizihôteisiki '4 bai hô' hakken eno miti: Mietazo! 'b^2– 4ac' [Way to 'four times method' in quadratic equations: We've got the meaning of 'b^2–4ac'!]. *Sûgaku Kyôsitu,* 43(11), 51-66.

Vygotsky, L.S. (1978). *Mind in society: The development of higher psychological processes* (M. Cole, V. John-Steiner, S. Scribner & E. Souberman, eds.). Cambridge, Mass.: Harvard University Press.

Wertsch, J.V. (1991). *Voices of the mind: A sociocultural approach to mediated action.* Cambridge, Mass.: Harvard University Press.

Yuki, T., Sato, A. & Hashisako, K. (1987). *Gakusyû-juku* [Juku]. Tokyo: Gyôsei.

Diversity in Learning Modes

11 How School Students Become Subjects of Cooperative Learning Activity

Galina A. Zuckerman

Introduction

The learning task gives rise to a particular kind of student activity: the independent search for new ways of acting in a situation where an adult does not provide any ready models of action. Who sets the learning task? A genuine learning task is conceived from an encounter of two initiatives: (1) that of a teacher trying to reorient the student from a pragmatic result to a general method of reaching such results, and (2) that of the students, who are so eager to reach their goal that a trap, created by the teacher to make them reflect, will only excite their interest. We have studied the difference between this 'breakthrough group' and their classmates who do not participate in the search for new methods of actions.

Everyone who has observed the process of setting the learning task in the classroom knows that the major part of the job will inevitably be carried out by two groups of children (Zuckerman 1993). One group is particularly active at the starting point of the search for something new. These students seem to be extremely mobile when wild ideas are requested; they take risks to suggest hypotheses and to try new ways of action. However, members of this 'breakthrough group' are not usually successful in applying newly invented methods to a wide variety of specific situations. When a general decision has been reached, they may lose interest in the lesson, but will immediately wake up again as soon as a search for new ideas is demanded.

The second group of participants in the cooperative activity of solving a learning task can be discerned as soon as the breakthrough group comes up with some general and vague suggestions and the teacher authorises all or some of these suggestions. This *group of developers of initial hypotheses* elaborates the new method to the level of foolproof technical application. What constellation of psychological characteristics predisposes a child to choose a particular role in the cooperative activity of solving learning tasks? To answer this question, I have started a longitudinal study of fifty first-graders in the Moscow school no. 91, where the 'Davydov type' of curriculum is implemented. The first results of this study are reported below.

Goal

To teach oneself, with the help of a grown-up, to become the initiator, the subject of one's own learning activity — such is the projected effect of development in elementary schoolchildren. The cooperative learning activity is the means to achieve this goal. 'What essential features must a group of people engaged in cooperative activity possess to be defined as a collective subject?' (Davydov 1996, 27) — that was the starting question of our analysis of a group of fifty seven-year-old first-graders.

The designers of learning activity hope each elementary schoolchild to be, at first, part of the collective subject of this activity, and later, beyond the elementary school age, to become an individual subject of self-education. It is, however, well known that almost no one has as yet been able to achieve this. There are children in any class who never become subjects of learning activity, though they attend lessons and diligently and quite successfully carry out most of the teacher's assignments. Such children are the subjects of other activities, which coexist alongside learning activity (first and foremost, imitation and communication); they feel happy and content at school and sense no loss in the fact that they do not serve psychologists as the model of the top achievements of an elementary schoolchild's psychological development. Yet, the very existence of such a group of students keeps the designers of learning activity in a constant state of steady exploration and discontent. In every class engaged in learning activity, we find children that, despite the zeal of teachers, do not become the subjects of this activity. This evidence presumes a deficiency either in these students, or in the existing design of learning activity. Both approaches to the problem of ensuring conditions for developing students as subjects of learning activity seem equally important: to consider the individual variations in child development and to modify the design of learning activity. Our present study is an attempt to combine these two approaches. The study is based on the following notion of a subject of learning activity.

A subject is a source of energy and action, an author, a creator, a master initiating transformations of reality, people and him/herself. Present-day

psychological writings are full of such semi-poetical, metaphorical definitions of the subject (Brushlinskii 1994; Petrovskii 1996; Slobodchikov & Isaev
1995). Undoubtedly, however, although these definitions are valid, they are
much too general to serve as a basis for answering one practical question: is
a child a subject of learning activity if he or she is full of energy and initiative at a lesson? One cannot answer 'yes' straightaway. One must first determine at what the child's activity is directed. It can, for instance, be directed
at winning the teacher's approval or favour. Unmistakably, such a student is
a subject, but of an activity that is by no means a learning activity. It can be
communicative activity with its own rules in the classroom: if you want the
teacher to like you, raise your hand as often and as high as possible and give
clear and intelligible answers.

'To search for something that is as yet missing but is, nevertheless, feas-
ible and is presented to an individual only as a goal — such is the basic
characteristic of the vital activity of any subject' (Davydov 1986, 27). On the
basis of this general definition of the subject, one can form a working criterion for coining a more specific definition of whether or not a child acts
as a subject of the learning activity *per se*. When students are confronted
with a new learning problem and participate in the search for new ways of
action, they become the subjects of learning activity. For the subject himself,
the result of his activity takes the form of a variety of hypotheses (Magkayev 1995).

The method of longitudinal research described in this paper is based on
this very concept: the core of a subject's behaviour in learning activity is the
search for new ways of action in a situation when the old way is inadequate,
while the solution of the new problem is already motivated. I should not attempt a pseudo-Freudian denouncement of children who take an active part
in this search, who come up with hypotheses, suggestions or conjectures,
which may serve as a basis for the joint discovery of the new ways. Children
may be covertly or openly ambitious, striving to assert themselves, and har-
bouring other motives apart from learning. The motivation of human activity is polyphonic, and the seven-year-olds are no exception. Children who
launch eagerly into the search for new ways of action can be regarded as
subjects of learning activity even when they are motivated not only by a self-
less yearning for knowledge. Who are our heroes that constitute the breakthrough group in the conventional slang of educators? How do they differ
from their classmates? What helps and hinders each child from becoming a
member of this group? It is to answer these questions that we have undertaken this five-year-long project.

Teachers' assessment	School schedule	Psychological indices and tests
	September	Imitative and motor skills (Kern)
	October	Nonverbal intelligence (Raven)
First	Vacation	Verbal intelligence (Jirasek)
	November	School anxiety (Amen – Dorky)
	December	Personality (drawing tests)
	Vacation	School achievements
	January	Self-esteem (Dembo – Rubinstein)
Second	February	Sociometric test (Moreno)
	March	Creativity (Torrence)
	Vacation	
	April	School achievements
	May	Value orientation (Yurkevich)
Third	Summer vacation	

Figure 11.1. Design (The first grade, Moscow school no. 91, 1996/97).

Methods

The research was commenced in 1996 in two first grades of the Moscow school no. 91, where learning activity was systematically and very professionally perfected in maths and language and literature lessons (teachers L.A. Sukhoversha and N.L. Tabachnikova), and somewhat less successfully at science and art lessons. Fifty first-graders (22 girls and 28 boys) were put through a number of tests; their work in maths and language lessons was systematically followed and regularly recorded on video and in the diary. The individual characteristics of the students were studied as the major behavioural manifestations of the subject in three spheres: cognition, communication and self-consciousness. The experimental design of the first year of our longitudinal study is presented in Figure 11.1.

The quantitative and qualitative characteristics of a child's behaviour as a subject of cooperative learning activity became the basis for the first-graders typology, with the help of which we plan to study their individual peculiarities. Since we have no reliable objective methods to diagnose the level and quality of involvement of each child in the learning activity, we used the expert evaluation method. The subjectivity of this method is compensated by the fact that it was the child's teacher who was the expert eval-

Measured at:	Correlation coefficients*:		
	Search activity	Activity in discussion	Reproductive activity
The beginning of the school year	0.57	0.59	0.58
The middle of the school year	0.72	0.67	0.61
The end of the school year	0.75	0.62	0.64

*All coefficients are significant at 0.1% level.

Table 11.1. Correlation between the assessments of each activity index by two experts in the course of the first grade.

uating his or her behaviour, and the subjective teacher-child relation is for the latter an objective reality forcibly influencing the student's performance.

Two independent experts: maths and language teachers — gave scores to each student three times during the school year. A sample of the protocol of experts' assessment can be seen in Figure 11.2. The scores by two experts are closely correlated as shown in Table 11.1.

Eight indices were chosen for the expert evaluation to elucidate various aspects of student's activity at the lesson. Three major indices assessed were (1) general activity in the classroom discussion; (2) reproductive activity; (3) search activity.

The index of 'general activity in the classroom discussion' describes the level of student's involvement in social interaction with a teacher and class-mates related to maths and language. This type of student's activity is not immediately related to the learning activity per se. It can be motivated by a craving for appraisal, attention, recognition, by easy emotional involvement into any common affair and so on, rather than by any interest in a new problem.

The index of 'reproductive activity' evaluates the industriousness and diligence of each student.

The index of 'search activity' shows the level of initiative taken by each student when encountering a new learning situation. It is this particular situation that calls for risky actions: students must try out something new, untested, unsanctioned. In this situation, any guess is valuable, any observation, question, comment, anything that helps break the stereotype of the old

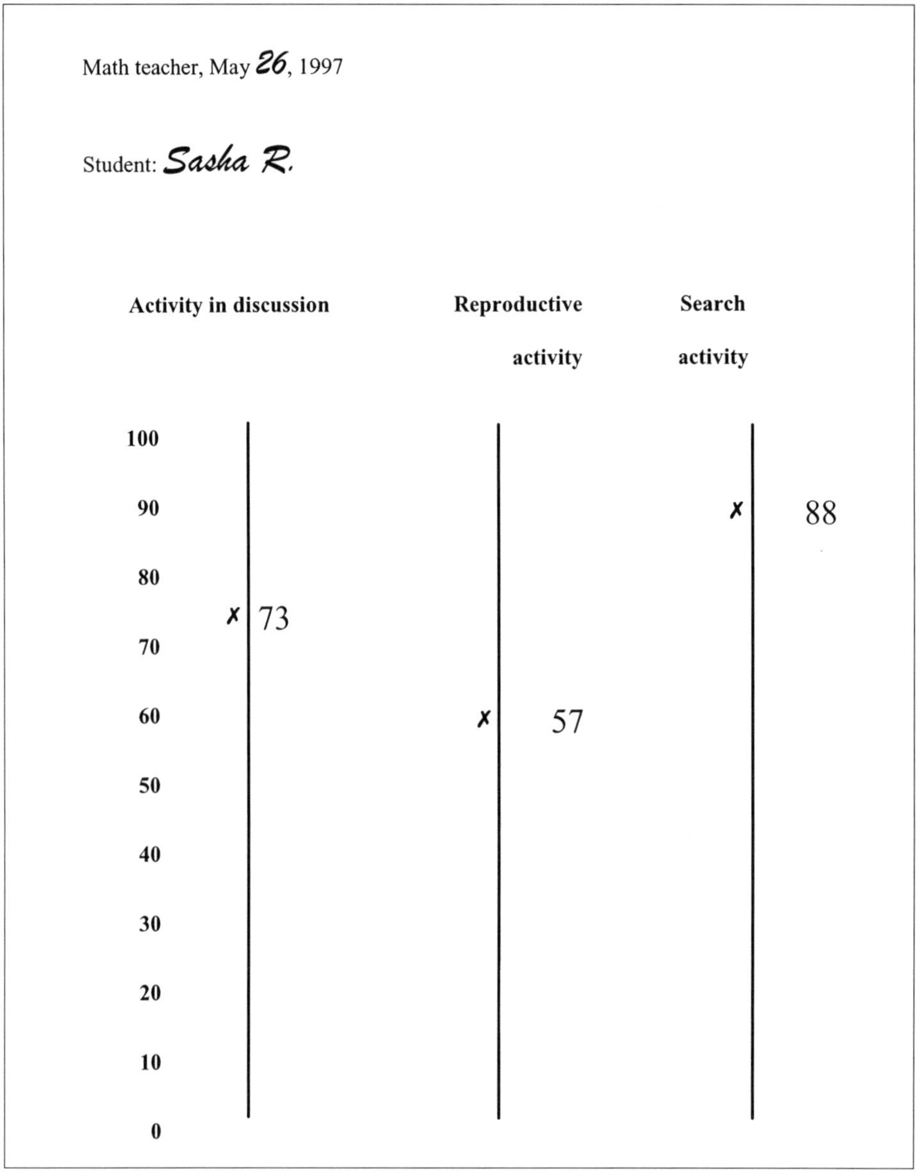

Math teacher, May **26**, 1997

Student: **Sasha R.**

Activity in discussion	Reproductive activity	Search activity

100

90   ✗ 88

80

✗ 73

70

60   ✗   57

50

40

30

20

10

0

Figure 11.2. A sample of the protocol of expert's assessment.

way of acting and thinking. The teachers were instructed to ignore whether a student's suggestion was right or wrong: only the initiative to question or suggest was scored.

Groups of first-graders	The number of students (% of the total) at:		
	The beginning of the school year	The middle of the school year	The end of the school year
	Boys and girls		
Subjects of learning activity	40a	73b	71b
All the other students	60a	27b	29b
	Boys		
Subjects of learning activity	39a	86b	72b
All the other students	61a	14b	28b
	Girls		
Subjects of learning activity	41a	55a	68a
All the other students	59a	45a	32a

Within each row, the data accompanied by unlike letters differ significantly at 5% level by chi-square criterion.

Table 11.2. The size of two groups of first-graders classified on the basis of teachers' assessment.

The teachers evaluated each student with the aid of a scale, the top point of which corresponded to the highest manifestation of the evaluated quality, and the lower point to the absence of this quality. The top score was 100. Figure 11.2 gives an example of an evaluation of one boy by his maths teacher.

Fifty students were categorised into two major groups on the basis of the teachers' evaluation: (1) subjects of learning activity/ the breakthrough group; and (2) the rest of the students. The breakthrough group comprised those students with search activity scores in the upper quarter of the scale (over 75), as assessed by one of the experts at least. Data presented in Table 11.2 show that this group significantly expanded in the course of the first grade.

The breakthrough group revealed itself most notably at the lessons where learning problems were set. Usually, it was these children who led in the search for solutions, who heatedly exchanged opinions, suggested and checked every possible conjecture, and remained in a state of happy excitement until the moment where a solution was found. These external manifestations could be observed with remarkable permanency. Apparently, it is the very situation of intellectual quest, which is highly significant and impelling for this breakthrough group.

This observation was confirmed by the students themselves. By the end of the first grade, our students wrote a composition describing the important events of their first school year. They listed various happenings: the first day at school, the first success at a lesson, the first whole-class trip to the country, the first friendships ... Volodya V., one of the leaders of the breakthrough group, formulated his cognitive values concisely: 'The most important thing in first grade was when I learned about spelling vowels.' His more ambitious classmate belonging to the same breakthrough group, Gleb S. also focused on a moment of discovery, however, he emphasised his authorship:

Once in a Russian language class our teacher explained a difficult rule and asked for an explanation. All the proposed answers were wrong. But my explanation turned out to be the right one.

Quite a different set of values was manifested by the students who did not belong to the breakthrough group, who were diligently engaged in reproductive activities rather than in the search for new solutions to the learning tasks (above, these student were referred to as the 'group of developers of initial hypotheses put forward by the breakthrough group'). Their statements prove that their interest is focused on following the school rules rather than discovering new laws of maths, linguistics, etc.

The most important thing in first grade is to respect your teachers, study hard, understand what they want and make sure you pay attention in class. I love our Lyudmila Andreevna! (Tamara E.)
I really want to have perfect handwriting, but I can never do it. I think the most important thing in first grade is beautiful writing. I will keep trying! (Irina S.)

The common sense suggests two hypotheses about the students, who were pinpointed as the subjects of learning activity: (1) they seem to be smarter than the rest of the class and (2) they are cognitively oriented.

Groups of first-graders	The number of problems solved (% of the maximum score)* at:		
	The beginning of the school year	The middle of the school year	The end of the school year
	Verbal Intelligence Test (the maximum score – 68)		
Subjects of learning activity	54.2a	52.4a	52.3a
All the other students	49.7b	49.2b	49.6b
	Nonverbal Intelligence Test (the maximum score – 36)		
Subjects of learning activity	29.5 a	28.2 a	28.6 a
All the other students	25.5 b	24.2 b	23.7 b

*Within each column, the data for each test when accompanied by unlike letters differ significantly at 5% level by chi-square criterion.

Table 11.3. Comparison of the intellectual development in two groups of first-graders classified on the basis of teachers' assessment (average test scores).

The first hypothesis maintained that the breakthrough group comprised the intellectually advanced children. To examine this hypothesis, two tests were used: (1) the Progressive Raven Matrix to assess the nonverbal intelligence and (2) test of verbal intelligence designed by Jaroslav Jirasek (Švancara 1978). The breakthrough group demonstrated a significantly higher level of preschool development of nonverbal and verbal intelligence (Table 11.3). This result could be easily predicted.

The most interesting result of testing intelligence in our students is presented in Table 11.4. In the subjects of learning activity, nonverbal intelligence dominated over verbal intelligence, with the opposite pattern in the rest of the students. It means that the students from the breakthrough group base their judgments primarily on real or mental experimenting with objects rather than on the verbal definitions. The rest of our students tend to treat the verbal definitions as a real explanation without any attempt to verify them experimentally.

Groups of first-graders	The difference between the scores of verbal and nonverbal intelligence tests, %		
	The beginning of the school year	The middle of the school year	The end of the school year
Subjects of learning activity	−2.3	−1.4	−2.5
All the other students	+2.3	+5.1	+7.2

Table 11.4. Index of verbalism in two groups of first-graders classified on the basis of teachers' assessment.

The second hypothesis presumed that the breakthrough group comprised the students with a higher level of search activity. The method of revealing children's cognitive orientations was devised by V.S. Yurkevich (as yet unpublished) and represents a semiprojective conversation based on a fairy-tale plot. The experiment is conducted individually. The child is invited to step into a fairy tale in which s/he is to have five encounters. At the very start, s/he is met by a magician who offers five wishes and promises that sooner or later they will come true. The second encounter is with a sage who knows everything that everyone knows and even things people will only learn in the future. The sage suggests that the child ask any five questions, to which answers will undoubtedly come, but not necessarily at once. Then a flying carpet sweeps up beside the child, ready to carry him anywhere he wants to go, and he is told to choose five trips. The fourth encounter is with a magic book, which is a collection of every story written to this day and even those that will be written in the future. The child can make the choice of any five books. The fifth and last encounter is the most modern one: a miraculous computer-factory, which can produce anything displayed on its screen, suggests that the child make five orders. In the course of the conversation the adult undertakes the role of 'the magician's secretary' and writes down all the child's wishes, questions and orders, specifying them if the child's wording is not explicit enough.

These specifications are necessary, because later, during the content analysis, children's answers are classified into one of the three categories marked out by the author of the method, V.S. Yurkevich:

1) cognitive, for instance, 'I wish to read a book about truth, I wonder what truth is';
2) social, for example, 'I would like my father to spend more time with me, and my mother to be always in a good mood';
3) consumer, for instance, 'I wish all the toys in the world were mine'.
   When V.S. Yurkevich and I made the content analysis of the statements we had recorded in the group of first-graders described above, we established one more category, a rare one, not covered by the previous three:
4) wishes and questions directed at self-changing, for example, 'I wish I could compose interesting stories' or 'I want to be less lazy'.

A considerable part of the children's answers were, of course, of a mixed nature, and we coded them simultaneously in several categories.

Table 11.5 lists the entirely unexpected results of this experiment. Forty-eight students tested were divided into three groups. The group of 'the permanent subjects of learning activity' includes those 11 students who showed the highest level of the search activity (over 75 points on the 100-point scale) from the very beginning of school and throughout the whole school year, both in maths and language lessons. The group defined as 'New wave' subjects of learning activity comprised those 10 students, who did not exhibit any predisposition towards the search activity at the first months of schooling, yet towards the end of the first class, showed the highest level of search activity both in maths and language lessons.

Wishes and questions of a cognitive nature from all groups of children were the most numerous, followed by those of a consumer nature and those directed at social, personal contacts.

The category of 'self-change' was the least numerous, but it was precisely in this category that the most striking differences were noticed between those children who took an active part in the solution of learning problems, and their classmates.

These results make us recollect one of D.B. Elkonin's ideas — often quoted but not really comprehended — that learning activity is an activity directed at self-changing (Elkonin 1974). In the broad sense of the words, 'the ability to teach oneself', i.e., to be the subject of individual learning activity, presumes that the student can overcome his/her own limitations not merely in the sphere of cognition, but in every other sphere of human existence (Davydov, Slobodchikov & Zuckerman 1992): for instance, 'to be a merrier

Groups of first-graders (the number of students)	Distribution of students' answers (% of the total)* oriented at:			
	Cognition	Self-change	Social	Consumer values
Permanent subjects of learning activity (11)	40ab	17a	18a	25a
'New wave' subjects of learning activity (10)	50a	6b	20a	24a
All the rest (27)	38b	8b	21a	33b

*Within each column, the data accompanied by unlike letters differ significantly at 5% level by chi-square criterion.

Table 11.5. The value orientation of first-graders classified on the basis of teachers' assessment.

person' (the wish by Sasha M). or 'to know what to do when someone hurts your feelings' (as Olya P. answered).

It is, obviously, far from incidental that the children most involved in learning activity manifested the greatest orientation possible for first-graders towards self-changing. However, the issue of cause-effect once again remains undecided. The tests were conducted towards the end of the school year, and we knew nothing about the initial orientation of the children. Therefore we do not know why some children threw themselves so readily into the learning activity: 1) was it because of individual, personal orientation born in their preschool days, or 2) was it because their participation in the learning activity was motivated by some other reasons that these children acquired the taste for self-change?

Our data show that the first hypothesis is more likely to be true. The group of children (ten of them) who joined the original breakthrough group towards the middle of the school year, that is, had sufficient practice in quest activity in the situation of learning problems, did not by the end of the year show any orientation towards self-changing. On the contrary, it is precisely in this index that the group of new wave subjects of learning activity slightly lagged behind the rest of their classmates, though they were considerably ahead of them in cognitive orientation.

We tend to interpret these data in the following way. The group of children with preschool self-change orientation launches into the learning activity from the very start of the school year. This activity appeals very positively to their emotional experience, giving them the possibility to constantly test and expand their potential. By the efforts of this group, the puzzles and contradictions show through the mathematical and linguistic games and amusements of the first weeks of schooling. When this pioneer group discerns the first problems in maths and language, the group of cognitively oriented students comes to the forefront.

Conclusion

As the teacher starts building up the cooperative learning activity in class, not all the first-graders who enter the breakthrough group, become the subjects of learning activity engaged in the quest for new solutions to learning tasks. When these children find themselves in a situation of uncertainty and discover that the ways of action they already know do not work, while new ones have not yet been created, they begin excitedly to search for these new ways, coming up with all sorts of guesses and observations. It is precisely through the efforts of these children, none of whom is capable of solving the learning problem independently, that the 'body' of the collective subject of learning activity takes shape. This study was undertaken to discern the individual and typological traits of the first-graders that form the collective subject of learning activity. Let us consider the preliminary results of this study.

1) The breakthrough group expands in the course of the whole first school year: the number of children constantly or partially participating in the search for new ways of action increased from 40 to 70 percent of the total sample. A large part of the children (about 80%) who joined the breakthrough group stay in this group. In other words, students' participation in learning activity as its subjects becomes self-perpetuating.
2) The initial preschool indices of children's intellectual development imply that students who constitute the breakthrough group significantly surpass their classmates. Does this mean that it is the cleverest children who help the teacher expand the learning activity?

Our data indicate that higher intellectual development is neither necessary nor sufficient for the first-graders' behaviour as subjects of the learning activity. An intellectual development substantially lower than the average in the class may impede joining the breakthrough group. Yet, with an intellectual development substantially higher than the average, the students are not guaranteed 'membership' of that group. It seems that the emotional and personal traits of a child become crucial factors, determining the form of a child's participation in the learning activity. Among these traits are, undoubtedly, the following:

a) the first sprouts of orientation towards self-changing, of the ability to set problems of changing one's own potential, at least in the imagination;
b) reflective, slightly underestimated self-evaluation exemplified by the following formula for the child's behaviour: 'I don't know whether I can do it, but I'll risk trying it';
c) reflection in both intellectual and emotional spheres of life (understanding emotional ambivalence), as well as in communication and cooperation (considering other points of view).

The method of our study (discerning typological groups of children on the basis of their interpsychological characteristics and elucidating the predominant intrapsychological traits of the members of these groups) repeatedly brings us face to face with the unsolvable problem of the hen and the egg. Indeed, do children become involved in learning activity, which requires at least rudimentary reflection, because they have appropriate reflective prerequisites, or is the involvement in such activity a crucial factor for the reflective development of a child? This 'blind-alley' question is eliminated by the idea of paradoxical interaction in the zone of proximal development. As wittily expressed by A.V. Brushlinskii (1994), the nearer an individual is to a successful solution to a problem, the less he needs help from outside, yet the easier he acquires it. And vice versa, the further he is from a correct solution, the more necessary it is to have help from outside, but the harder it is to attain it.

In other words, those children who due to their preschool development need minimum help from their teacher when they search for new methods of solving learning tasks, will be the first to become subjects of cooperative learning. However, when the collective subject of learning activity has already begun to take shape in the class, other children may also become involved in this search for new methods. The involvement of this second wave of subjects of learning activity is especially successful when the teacher provides them with the experience the breakthrough group has received before school: first and foremost, the ability to independently set the task of self-changing.

Speaking of self-consciousness as the priority direction in the work of the designers of learning activity, I proceed from the fact that the conditions for development of reflection in the spheres of action, thinking and cooperation have, to a sufficient extent, already been elaborated. And yet, the question of how to objectify for a child the change that takes place within him/her in the process of education is still an open one (Davydov et al. 1992). The data accumulated in our research explicitly proves that the key solution to the problem of developing students' learning activity is to provide them with cultural tools for identification and planning self-changes.

References

Brushlinskii, A.V. (1994). *Problemy psikhologii sub'ekta* [The problems of subject psychology]. Moscow: Institute of Psychology, Russian Academy of Sciences.

Davydov, V.V. (1986). *Problemy razvivayushchego obucheniya* [The problems of developmental education]. Moscow: Pedagogika.

Davydov, V.V. (1996). *Teorya razvivayushchego obucheniya* [The theory of developmental education]. Moscow: Intor.

Davydov, V.V., Slobodchikov, V.I. & Zuckerman, G.A. (1992). Elementary schoolchild as the subject of learning activity. *Voprosy Psikhologii*, 2, 14-19.

Elkonin, D.B. (1974). *Psikhologiya mladshego shkol'nika* [Psychology of the elementary schoolchild]. Moscow: Znaniye.

Magkayev, V.Kh. (1995). Theoretical prerequisites of designing the methods for studying and assessing the basic metacognitive thinking. In V.V. Davydov & V.V. Rubtsov (eds.), *Razvitie osnov reflektivnogo myshleniya shkol'nikov v protsesse uchebnoi deyatel'nosti* [Development of the basic metacognitive thinking in the course of learning activity]. Novosibirsk: Psychological Institute, Russian Academy of Education.

Petrovskii, A.V. (1996). *Lichnost' v psikhologii* [The personality in psychology]. Rostov-na-Donu: Feniks.

Slobodchikov, V.I. & Isaev, E.I. (1995). *Psikhologiya cheloveka* [Human psychology]. Moscow: Shkola-Press.

Švancara, J. (ed.) (1974). *Diagnostika psychického vývoje* [Diagnostics of psychological development]. 2nd ed. Praha: Avicenum.

Zuckerman, G.A. (1993). *Vidy obshcheniya v obuchenii* [Communication types in learning]. Tomsk: Peleng.

12 Construction of Distance, Time and Speed Concepts: A Cultural-Historical Approach

Paulo R. de Oliveira Frota

At first, touching and manipulating his own body, the child discovers his senses. Gradually, through spoken and written (symbolic) language, s/he evolves from concrete operations to formal thinking, from animist and ingenuous symbolic representation to more complex formal thinking operations (Inhelder et al. 1977; Ferreiro & Teberosky 1979, 1981; Luria & Yudovich 1987), constituting concepts in the eternal pursuit to represent the world.

Among different concepts acquired by man during his development in informal interactions with the environment, speed, distance and time became essential for the formal learning in disciplines such as physics. It is through them that adolescents start the study of physics, as well as of other subjects, such as history, biological evolution, geochronology (time), architecture, theatre, dance, painting and geography (space/distance), they are fundamental to one's formation of a worldview.

In classical mechanics, concepts of space (which will be treated in this text in the sense of distance, in the form of the distance travelled) and time exist independently, so that it is possible to calculate anyone of them without direct dependence on the other, velocity (v) can be construed as distance (d) per unit time (t), that is $v = d/t$. Yet, in the 'theory of relativity', space and time make a new entity, not allowing to separate one variable independently of the other. Einstein questioned himself: What happens in the child's mind? How is this conceived? These questions have been raised by Albert Einstein in 1928 and later by Jean Piaget, and have not yet been answered.

These concepts are constituted in a network of organised and established ideas, through the logic of space-time structure, to which action and thinking are related, constituting and incorporating new knowledge.

Davidov and Márkova drew attention to the fact that the acquisition of concepts within a cognitive domain is not a passive adaptation of the individual to the existing social life conditions:

[This process] is not a mere copy of the social experience and it represents the individual activity result aimed at dominating socially elaborated procedures of orientations in the material world. (1987, 323)

Vygotsky's main thesis states the existence of a unit between the activity — which mediates the act of assimilation — and the psyche, which is reflected through the guiding activity in the materialisation of a scientific concept. These, in turn, go through a descending development while the spontaneous concepts go through ascending development, to a more elementary and concrete level (Vygotsky 1993).

It is possible to discover that children who study in the periphery of the cities (which in Brazil almost always concentrate the lowest income groups) show uncommon sharpness in everyday functioning when they enter school, as they are more directly exposed to the world. Those children develop survival strategies and elementary psychological functions earlier than middle class children, protected from violence by their families.

Thus the existence of two cultural systems can be inferred from this, two distinct worlds in the same community: a life culture, in which the subject is fully conscious of his actions, aiming at the survival (everyday concepts world), and another, from school, which offers no practical and social experience (scientific concepts world), in which the subject usually fails.

These children and teenagers seem to develop a group of proto-ideas, based on commonsense, which challenge the scientific knowledge offered by the school, as Carraher (1988) would say. But the school does not consider this as a lack of interest or as an incapability on the part of the children to explain.

As to the scientific concepts in the evolution of higher psychological functions, Vygotsky, states that:

The power of the scientific concepts is evident in the sphere that generally defines the ultimate domain of concepts: conscious achievement and voluntary action. At the same time, in this same sphere we can observe the fidelity of the child's concept, concepts that are powerful in the sphere of concrete application, in the situation specific, spontaneous sphere of experience and empiricism. (Vygotsky 1993, 254)

Being interrelated in the human mind, speed, distance and time are a concern for teaching. It must particularly concern elementary school teachers, since the awareness of such concept acquisition may facilitate their jobs.

The Empirical Study

The present study investigates the integration of physical concepts of distance, time and speed.

The objective was to verify, empirically, how mind is organised regarding aspects related to space-time concepts. The physical-mathematical model of the integration of these concepts (distance = speed x time) impose, according to Wilkening (1981), that the graphic representation indicates an opening fan shape that is constantly growing, as a function of the understanding of the difference in speed and time.

The idea of activity is used as a reference for mental and external operations in a research that could be profiled as transversal.

The students' acquisition process was observed through quantitative analysis by internal comparison between two samples, and, especially, through dynamic structural analysis on the evolution of the activity level. We analysed the transition from everyday concepts to a second system of signs by instrumental mediation, consolidating the scientific concepts in the study through graphical representation.

The theoretical approach of cultural-historical psychology, especially the concept of the 'Zone of Proximal Development' (ZPD), 'activity', 'instrumental and social mediation' were all used in the planning of the research and in the analysis of the empirical material.

Subjects, material and method

The subjects studied were 96 students from a public junior high school, located in a very poor suburb (where the average family income does not exceed approximately US$ 120 per month) and 96 students from a private school in a middle class suburb — Teresina in the state of Piaui, in Brazil's Northeast — with a much higher average family income. The overwhelming majority of the students in the public school come from families headed by single-mothers.

The sample was divided into groups of 12 students, of the same age (from 7 to 14 years old) according to school grade (from first to eighth), as homogeneous as possible in terms of sex, and chosen randomly to avoid any sort of selective character of the sample.

The experiment consisted of estimating the distance travelled (space) by a person on foot, on a bicycle and in a car (speed) as a function of the repeated sounding of a horn in three different intervals (lengths of time): a short two-second interval; a medium five-second interval; and a long eight-second interval.

The interactive distance-time-speed effect was perceived in private school students from eight years old on, thus in second grade. While in the public school it was noted only in children older than eleven, from sixth grade on, without significant discrepancies relating to sex.

The material used for the main task consisted of a 300 cm tape measure, a race track, a tape recorder with a tape with the sound of an intermittent siren recorded on it, in the lengths of time: short (2 sec.); medium (5 sec.) and long (8 sec.); three plastic miniature toys (a man, a bicycle and a car), of nearly 6 cm long; information sheets; two patterned psychometric tests (Raven's colourful matrix and the Wisc's Arithmetic sub-test).

The design had three phases. Two of them concern the control test application (Wisc and Ravel), and the third, consisted of the experimental task which concerned the children's acquisition of the integrated concepts of distance, speed and time, represented by a simulated race, a kind of game. This design led to a cross-sectional study, in which the subjects were evaluated individually only once, in the presence of an investigator and an assistant. The assistant recorded the measurements of distance in the realisation of the experiment. She also noted the gestures and reactions of the children for later analysis and to provide a better description.

In this phase, putting the miniature toys on the track, the researcher would say to the interviewee:

You will take part in a race. We have our 3-meter-long track and you will be our racer. We want to know how you would win the race most easily. A siren will begin. You must listen to it very carefully, as noting its length, put the miniature on the spot where you think it would get to, if running, riding a bicycle or racing a car.

Once the requested activity was understood, the test would start. Otherwise, the explanation would be repeated, in an attempt to articulate the experienced logical verbal mediation with the visual imaginativeness of the student (Krutstsky 1991).

The subject was then invited to take part in the test, for which the presentation of tasks was done using a 'Latin square' in order to avoid an order effect. The tests were then initiated and the siren sounded 27 times, alternately and randomly accordingly to length and speeds. The subject moved the three miniatures for the same number of times, estimating the resulting distances of the combination of the three timings and three speeds (man running, riding and racing). The individual data gathering was done by the researcher and recorded by the assistant, seeking to record quantitatively and qualitatively the development of the activity.

During the testing phase, the researcher inquired if the subjects needed some clarification on the actions accomplished. Also, after the testing, the subjects went on a socialisation process. Such a procedure provided a kind of ZPD guidance, with 10 groups of two students in each, consisting of five students who had succeeded well, and five who had problems in performing the interaction task.

Results

The student's acquisition process was observed through a quantitative analysis comparing two samples, and, especially, through a dynamic structural analysis on the evolution of the activity level. We analysed the transition from everyday concepts to a second system of signs by instrumental mediation, consolidating the scientific concepts in study through graphical representation.

The performance in the control tasks (Wisc and Raven), in general, was better for older subjects and higher grades. And, in the case of the private school, slightly better results were noticed. With these standard tests, we sought to identify the levels of development of general psychological functions in both groups.

In theoretical terms, the basic question concerned the assessment of the subject's understanding of the interaction of both variables — speed and time, in a multiplicative way, e.g., judging the distance as a product of speed by time.

Eventually, according to the theoretical model (distance = speed x time), the graphs of the evaluation means of distances should form a series of lines, opening widely (Wilkening 1981), representative curves of the speeds.

Considering the distance represented according to time, the level curve representing the lowest speed (running) will, probably, present the lowest

Grade	F	Sig. F	p
5th grade	$F_{(4,44)}$	2.97	$p < .030$
6th grade	$F_{(4,36)}$	2.70	$p < .046$
7th grade	$F_{(4,44)}$	5.61	$p < .001$
8th grade	$F_{(4,48)}$	5.60	$p < .001$

Table 12.1. The sample effect of integration.

inclination, whilst the curve representing the highest speed (by car), will, probably, present the highest inclination.

The State School

The search for the relationship between speed and time, through the assessment of distance, was the main concern of this study. Therefore, the multiplicative model must be the objective that is sought in the graphs plotted by means of the observed values.

The data gathered — estimation of the covered distances — allowed the construction of eight graphs, representative of the studied grades.

Drawn from the results presented by the fifth-grade-subjects, the interactive effect represented by a branching out of the three speeds due to the three timings was noticed, but was actually first consolidated in the eighth grade. In effect, only the seventh and eighth grade children seem to be able to take into consideration both variables and also to integrate them in a multiplicative way.

To assess the significance of these differences both in terms of the main effect (integration of distance as a function of the speed of time), and, especially, in terms of the interactive effects (speed versus time and time versus speed), the data underwent an analysis of variation for each age group. Each analysis also included a post test (Sample Effect) of the interactive effect of the two conditions: time and speed, presenting values for speed versus time and time versus speed. The interactive effect of the integration of distance as a function of speed and time was first observed in subjects from the 5th grade, i.e., more than 11 years old (see Table 12.1).

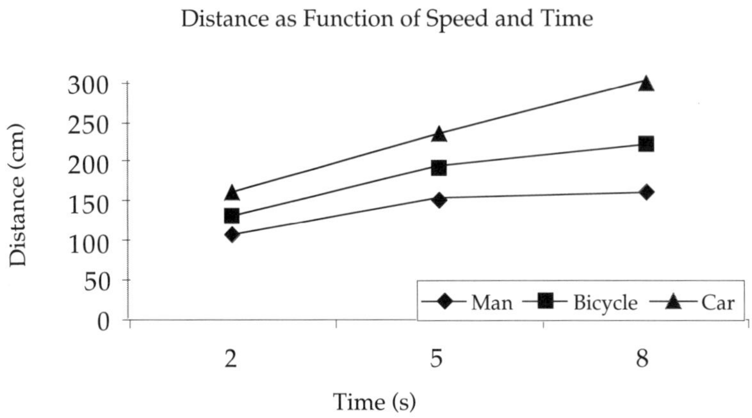

Distance as Function of Speed and Time

Figure 12.1. Graph over distance understood as a function of speed and time in the 5th grade by 11-year olds in the State School.

The subsequent analysis of the differences in the means — the time variable versus speed and the speed variable versus time — confirms the hypothesis that children understand them as integrated in a multiplicative way, from the age of 11 years old, as shown in Figure 12.1.

The major effects of the variables time and speed for all the age groups were also observed except for the 8-year-old group, F (2.22) = 2.42 in p < .01. The multivariational analysis examined the weight of each variable in the integration of the concept of distance as a function of speed and time.

The interactive effects between gender experimental results, performance in the Raven's test, performance in the Wisc's test and school grades were examined but only performances in the Raven test were significant p < .001. The variable that had the highest correlation with the concept acquisition was the performance in the Raven's test — which tested the children's skills in relating individual parts to the whole, differentiating geometric forms and metric and topology concepts.

The variable schooling, represented here by the school grades and by the classroom environment, did not present any significant prediction value. We assume that this may be due to the levelling value that formal education has and that the individual differences, particularly those of a psychometric character, are responsible for the differentiation of students in the same age group and school grade.

The Private School

The analysis of the private school student graphs showed that the variables — distance, time and speed — were understood by all the groups, except for the 1st grade students, at the age of seven.

As in the public school, in the private school also the distance covered by the man running received lower level judgement than the man cycling and driving, in regard to time grading.

However, the evaluation by the 1st grade subjects presented a higher estimation for the mean time, than for the maximum time. Yet, the differences among the results obtained at the private school showed values that increased as judgements of various speeds were conducted, for the same time variable.

To check the significance of these differences, particularly as interactive effects, the data were analysed by variance analysis, for each age group, in the mixed experimental planning described above.

The results of the analysis showed the main significant effect of the variable time from the 2nd grade onwards, in $F_{(2.22)} = 10.91$, $p < .001$. However, the effect of the variable speed was observed in all grades, with no exceptions.

Concerning the effect of the integration of speed and time, which provides us with an understanding of distance as a function of speed and time ($d = v \times t$), it was significant for all the grades assessed, except for the 1st grade (see Table 12.2).

Grade	F	Sig. F	p
1st grade	F (4.44)	1.07	p < 0.384
2nd grade	F (4.44)	4.65	p < .001
3rd grade	F (4.40)	49.58	p < .001
4th grade	F (4.44)	35.58	p < .001
5th grade	F (4.44)	3.70	p < .001
6th grade	F (4.44)	8.28	p < .001
7th grade	F (4.44)	7.71	p < .001
8th grade	F (4.44)	6.00	p < .001

Table 12.2. The sample effect of integration.

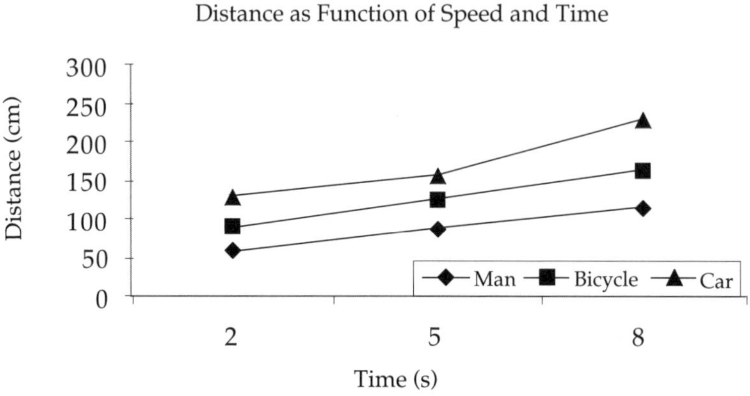

Distance as Function of Speed and Time

Figure 12.2. Graph over distance as a function of speed and time in the 2nd grade by 8-year olds in the Private School.

The subsequent analysis of the differences between the means — time versus speed and vice versa, confirm the hypothesis that this interaction corresponds to an understanding of these variables as integrated, in a multiplicative way, from the 2nd grade onwards (8 years old), as shown in Figure 12.2.

As for the influence of the variable gender, identical procedures as previously used were applied, through MANOVA, checking the non-significant differences in the students' performance of both schools.

Concerning the greater influence of the variables in the constitution of the integrated concepts, the logistic analysis presented significant effect of the schooling variable.

Thus, the important weight of schooling became evident for the acquisition of the concepts of speed, distance and time, particularly in terms of distance integration as a function of speed and time. All these aspects — school grade, kind of school, daily experiences in the classroom — were considered essential for the constitution of such concepts, which accounts for the fact that they should be a priority for the individual's critical and psychical education.

This is, undoubtedly, a major objective to be pursued by modern elementary schools.

Conclusions and Suggestions

Due to the quantitative (variance analysis) and qualitative (graph analysis) analysis, we may come up with the following plausible conclusions:

Integration of distance as a function of speed and time occurs for the subjects at the state school from the 5th grade, i.e., at the age of 11 upwards, and it consolidates between the ages of 13 and 14, whereas for the private school, from the 2nd grade, i.e., the age of 8 upwards.

This result should not, however, be understood as a demonstration of the superiority of the scientific thought of private school students, nor a demonstration of a lag in the psychological development of public school children.

However, the actual reality of the material is diverse. The samples from different schools conform with their respective surroundings and experience of different social practices that result from going through different challenges in life and in school, that is, in their concrete social cultural and historical contexts.

In this scenery, it is important to consider the influence of the subject's background, because:

the natural processes regulate the growth of elementary psychological functions in the child — forms of memory, perception, and practical tool — using intelligence, for example, that are continuous with the mental life of apes and other species. Social and cultural processes regulate the child's acquisition of speech and other sign systems, and the development of 'special higher psychological functions' such as voluntary attention and logical memory. (Vygotsky 1978, 19)

Leontiev states that the child's interpretation of real phenomena, and here we have the representation of a real phenomenon, happens in connection with the child's activity. It should be noted that the activity is related to objectives, goals and aims that are dictated by the surroundings — material and social — limiting the child to his/her sphere of activity.

It is important to note that, after socialisation, public school children also succeed academically, due to the opportunity of being guided within the 'zone of proximal development'. The zone is defined as the difference between the level of problem solving that a child can engage in independently, and the level that can be accomplished with the help of an adult (Vygotsky 1978).

Through interaction between more competent subjects and the less competent ones, it became possible to increase the general performance.

The variable of gender did influence the formation of the concept of distance as a function of speed and time. In communities such as this one, where single women are typically the heads of households, there is no distinction between the work of men and women, and for this reason women typically assume roles considered to be those of men. Thus gender differences will be found on other levels, but not in the differences of performance between boys and girls. The results are perhaps an indication of the positive role that the school has in reducing the traditional role differences of men and women.

One could speculate that age itself supported a subject's ability to integrate studied concepts, in that the older the student, the better his/her performance is in evaluating distance as a function of time and speed. However, as research has pointed out, even literate adults may have difficulties when dealing mentally with the logical structures conceptualised in Piaget's theory. It is therefore worth noting that, though significant, age was not significant enough to predict the presence of the examined abilities.

As Davidov & Márkova state:

age is not characterised by a correlation between isolated psychic functions, but by the specific tasks that are carried out and solved by the person, [... and assimilation aspects of reality] and also by the evolutionary neo-formations, of the activity, of consciousness and of personality that appear in a given stage of development. (1993, 332)

Understanding the variables of speed, distance and time respectively, during the experiment, has not proven to be a sufficient condition for accomplishing concept integration.

Grade represented a highly interactive variable concerning students' ability to achieve concept integration. This, though, requires further study insofar as school grade and type of school — state or private — were bound to a variable which is hard to describe and allows for individual abilities such as the ones in Raven's and Wisc's tests. Once these aspects are discarded through the variance analysis, the importance of school grade nearly disappears.

Undoubtedly, schooling — consisting of many aspects such as school grade, and the experiences derived from the home and the school (real personal development as a sum of all aspects, of the educational process) — represented the most significant contribution to the occurrence of the ability to integrate distance as a function of speed and time.

Evidently, the daily experimental conditions of the private schools are better, once varied strategies and actions are used in the teaching (use of computers, libraries, games, science fairs). It is clear that the child's intellectual capacities are stimulated in many ways. In this sense, Rubinshtein states that:

the nucleus of general intellectual abilities is the quality of the processes of analysis, synthesis and generalisation (especially generalisation), which allows the subject to transfer acquired knowledge to face new and/or similar situations ... (1987, 157)

At this point, therefore, the importance remains of the type of school as a mediator of acquisition. School learning, centring children's orientation efforts, stimulates development of internal processes.

Children are sources of distinct social and instrumental mediation in school, and as they have different social and cultural relationships in the family and other social contexts, this enables them to develop the ability to understand the logical articulation between time, distance and speed.

We also point out that the gap in the acquisition of integrated concepts between subjects from public and from private schools is due to the schooling, and to aspects related to the social and cultural background of the children and the teenagers who were sampled.

The results suggest that such physical concepts may be taught to children as young as eight years old, and that formal school procedures may contribute to its acquisition. One will also notice that a social and cultural context which is rich in mediations (social interaction outside of school) may positively alter the thinking process and the integration of the concrete and abstract aspects of time and distance into a united concept earlier in the development of children and teenagers.

So, taking all this into consideration, we believe that the importance of this study lies in the contribution it offers to science teachers, particularly, elementary school physics teachers, seeking relationships between the teaching-learning processes of physics' concepts and the psychological principles on cognition. The need for a better understanding of the activities of the school, of teaching and studying, is also pointed out.

Davidov & Márkova state, that the main content of the studying activity is the assimilation of generalised action procedures in the sphere of scientific knowledge which leads to quality changes in the child's psychic development.

Study is not only the domain of knowledge nor those actions or transformations carried out by the student in the course of knowledge acquisition, but also the changes, or restructurations, the enrichment of the child. Such a model paves the way to assess the activity of the subject in the process of study, and allows at each measure the student to overcome intellectualism in the understanding of such process. (1987, 324)

Furthermore, it is particularly important, in physics and geography, to know, to understand and to interpret the space surrounding us, in that our sense of orientation depends on cinematic-mechanic relationships. Relationships derived from the understanding and employment of speed, distance and time, might be useful for individuals, not only in an ordinary person's daily life, but also in the scientific one, through physical and logical-mathematical experiences, which promote adaptation to the environment.

Concerning the school function as an educating institution, it is noteworthy that school actions leave a gap between the exploration of the formation of rudimentary notions of distance, time and speed, elicited in the first school years, and the concepts themselves which are dealt with — at least in physics — as late as in the eight grade of elementary school.

There are possible solutions to these predicaments, but the Brazilian educational system has not yet considered the language paradigms (Wertsch 1992) for semantic learning (e.g., velocity as speed, reason, rate, flow; time as yesterday, today, tomorrow, past, present, future, before, after, early, late, etc.), nor the utilisation of ZPD as an instruction basis (Hedegaard 1996).

References

Bachelard, G. (1977). *O racionalismo aplicado*. Rio de Janeiro: Zahar.

Carraher, T.N et al. (1988). *Na vida dez, na escola zero*. São Paulo: Cortez.

Carvalho, A.M.P. & Teixeira, O.P.B. (1985). O conceito de velocidade em alunos de 5ª série do primeiro grau — Um estudo a partir de questões típicas de sala de aula. *Revista da Faculdade de Educação (SP)*, 11, 173-91.

Davidov, V. & Márkova, A. (1987). La concepción de la actividad de estudio de los escolares. In V. Davidov and M. Shuare (eds.), *La psicologia evolutiva na URSS*. Muscú: Editorial Progreso.

Ferreiro, E. & Teberosky, A. (1985). *Los Sistemas de escritura em desarollo del niño*. México: Siglo XXI.

Frota, P.R. de O. & Roazzi, A. (1993). Distância como integração do tempo e da velocidade. Resumos. Universidade Federal de Santa Catarina.

Galperin, P.Ya. (1986). Acerca de la investigación del desarrollo intelectual del niño. In I.I. Iliasov, V.Ya. Liaudis (eds.), *Antología de la psicología pedagógica y de las edades*. La Habana: Pueblo y educación.

Hedegaard, M. (1996). A Zona de Desenvolvimento Proximal como base para a instrução. In L.C. Moll, *Vygotsky e a educação*. Porto Alegre: Artes médicas.

Inhelder, B. & Bovet, M. (1977). *Aprendizagem e estrutura do conhecimento*. São Paulo: Saraiva.

Krutstsky, V. (1991). Algumas características do desenvolvimento nos estudantes com pouca capacidade para a matemática. In Lúria, Leontiev, Vygotsky et al., *Pedagogia e Psicologia II*. Lisboa: Estampa.

Luria, A.R. (1994). A psicologia e o desenvolvimento infantil. In L.S. Vygotsky, A.R. Luria & A.N. Leontiev, *Linguagem, desenvolvimento e aprendizagem*. São Paulo: Icone.

Luria, A.R. & Yudovich, F.I. (1987). *Linguaguem e desenvolvimento intelectual na criança*. Porto Alegre: Artes médicas.

Vénguer, L. (1987). La asimilación de la solución mediatizada de tareas cognoscitivas y el desarrollo de las capacidades cognoscitivas en el niño. In V. Davidov and M. Shuare (eds.), *La psicologia evolutiva na URSS*. Muscú: Editorial Progreso.

Vygotsky, L.S. (1978). *Mind and society: The development of higher mental process*. Cambridge, Mass.: Harvard University Press.

Vygotsky, L.S. (1993). *Pensamento e linguagem*. São Paulo: Martins Fontes.

Vygotsky, L.S., Luria, A.R. & Leontiev, A.N. (1994). *Linguagem, desenvolvimento e aprendizagem*. São Paulo: Icone.

Wertsch, J.V. (1992). *Voces de la Mente*. Madrid: Visor.

Wilkening, F. (1981). Integrating velocity, time, and distance information: A developmental study. *Cognitive Psychology*, 13, 231-47.

13 Teacher-Student Interaction, Text Comprehension and Memory: A Semiotic Analysis of Instructional Actions

Manuel L. de la Mata and Andrés Santamaría

Introduction

The aim of this paper is to study the role of teacher-student inter-action in the acquisition of text comprehension and memory skills from a sociocultural perspective.

In our view, one of the most important lacks of cognitive research in this area is the neglect of the interactive nature of that development. Our paper attempts to focus on this issue.

We intend to establish the way in which teacher-student interaction may facilitate the acquisition and internalisation of general strategies for under-standing and remembering expository texts, in particular, the socalled struc-ture strategy (Meyer 1984). This strategy is conceived as a type of action that is associated with the context of formal education.

Our analysis is centred on instructional activity, and, more specifically, the nature of instructional actions that teachers displayed through the task.

Data from a study on teacher-student interaction in adults are presented. In this work, the participants' task was to study four expository texts that were similar in their structure. The content of the texts was analysed in terms of idea-units (Meyer 1984). Each text was formed by idea-units from three different hierarchical levels: main ideas, secondary ideas and details.

A category system for the analysis of study and recall of the text was de-

* This paper was supported by a grant from the Dirección General de Enseñanza Super-ior (DGES), PB96-1325.

veloped. In the study phase the analysis focused on the actions employed by teaches and students to study the texts and on the forms of instruction. Recall data were also considered.

The Cognitive Approach to Text Comprehension and Memory

Cognitive research on text comprehension and memory has become an important field in cognitive psychology. In this field it is possible to distinguish two major research lines: theoretical studies of cognitive structures and processes involved in text learning, and studies whose objective is to develop instructional procedures for improving comprehension and memory. In general, researchers assume that the learning strategies employed by the reader to understand and remember the text (Palincsar & Brown 1984; Gutiérrez Calvo 1992; Sánchez Miguel 1993) are some of the most important factors which determine text comprehension and memory. Researchers usually begin by identifying the differences between good and poor comprehenders. Then, they try to teach poor comprehenders the strategies employed by good readers, intending to improve their comprehension and memory (León 1991).

One of the most outstanding differences between expert and less skilled readers is that good readers employ their knowledge of text structure to monitor comprehension, facilitating the construction of an organised and coherent representation of the text. They are able to recognise the global organisation of the text and employ the *structure strategy* (Meyer 1985). According to Meyer, they seek and use the top-level structure in a particular text as an organisational framework to facilitate encoding and retrieval. Subjects recognise the cues in the text, the dominant rhetorical relationships, which make it possible to organise propositions in an integrated mental representation of the overall content of the text. Poor readers, in turn, employ *default list strategy* (Meyer 1985). This strategy is characterised by a non-systematic approach to text content. The reader enumerates different ideas without using any systematic organisation or plan. Ideas are remembered as separate units and the only link between them is their common reference to a given topic. Subjects that employ this strategy are not able to recognise the basic organisational patterns of texts or, conversely, they do not use them efficiently (Sánchez Miguel 1993).

In order to overcome the difficulties experienced by poor readers in understanding texts, an important volume of instructional programmes has been developed (Brooks & Dansereau 1983; Cook & Mayer 1988). Many of these studies have applied Meyer's *strategic plan*, developed by herself and her colleagues for instructing structure strategy (León 1991).

Despite their unquestionable interest, cognitive studies of text comprehension and memory have some important limitations in our opinion. They assume that comprehension and memory are processes located in the individual. They take place 'inside' the subject, as a result of the operating of cognitive processes and structures.

Another important limitation of these studies is that they usually overlook contextual constraints of remembering. As Edwards and Middleton (1986) stress, cognitive researchers tend to forget the pragmatic nature of any situation in which people remember a story or text, including the experimental lab.

In recent years, however, it has been possible to find studies that pay attention to some of the issues mentioned above and intend to overcome their limitations, especially in the field of instructional psychology. In these studies, there is an increasing interest on the interpersonal determinants of text memory. Since the work by Palincsar and Brown (1984) on reciprocal teaching, other authors are becoming aware of the social nature of the acquisition of comprehension and memory skills (Golden 1988; Sánchez Miguel 1993). At the same time, some authors recognise the need that instructional procedures include, as an essential step, the guided practice of strategies by subjects (Mateos 1991). Paris, Lipson and Wixson (1983), for example, explicitly refer to the notion of *zone of proximal development* (Vygotsky 1978) in order to take into account this kind of practice that involves the transfer of responsibility from expert to learner. Guided practice (*guided participation*, according to Rogoff 1990) let the students learn the utility of procedures and the conditions of their proper use (Paris, Lipson & Wixson 1983).

Instructional studies also recognise the need for instructed procedures to be inserted and applied in everyday school activities. Paris and Cross (1983) point out that learning is not just a cognitive but also a social-motivational phenomenon. From our perspective, this means that we have to take into account the nature of the activities in which text comprehension is involved. More specifically, the *motives* (see Leontiev 1981) that guide the use of text learning actions. If we do not pay attention to motives, problems related to the generalisation and applicability of learnt skills will continue.

The Role of Instruction in the Process of Appropriation of Text Comprehension and Memory Skills

In a sociocultural perspective, the instruction of a learner by a more expert member of the cultural group is one of the key situations for understanding learning and ontogenesis. In recent years, research on instruction has focused on communicative issues and on the instructor-learner dyadic interaction (Elbers 1987; Elbers, Maier & Hoogsteder 1992; González 1996). As we shall cover in more detail further on, a sociocultural approach understands that this process and the subsequent progress of the learner takes place in the zone of proximal development constructed in joint activity.

In our work, we develop a consideration of instruction in terms of semiotically mediated actions. Instruction, and thus internalisation, are considered to be the result of 'inter-actions' that instructors and learners develop in joint problem solving (Santamaría 1997). As these actions have a semiotic nature, instruction is mediated by signs. Semiotic mediation shapes instructional actions in a way that is linked to the nature of the sociocultural activities in which these actions are being employed.

From this view, instructional actions are not merely individual. Instead, they move from an interpsychological to an intrapsychological plane. Changes in the zone of proximal development have traditionally been characterised as individual changes that imply that the learner may do today what s/he could only do yesterday with help. This led to an understanding of internalisation as the transfer of social factors to the individual, in which the learner is conceptualised as a passive receiver of the social material. However in our work, the central aspect of changes in the zone of proximal development is centred around the appropriation and mastering of new forms of mediation. This appropriation does not just refer to individual learning after guided joint practice, but instead to the capacity of the learner to participate in new collaborative activities (Newman, Griffin & Cole 1989). As we shall see, the focus will not be on the transfer of skills from those who know more to those who know less, but instead on the shared use of new forms of communication for creating and communicating meaning (McLane 1987; McNamee 1987).

From a Vygotskyan perspective, internalisation refers to the process through which social factors are transferred to the intrapsychological domain. In this process, the 'social others' may be people, social institutions or culturally constructed mechanisms of mediation. What was originally part of the interpersonal (intermental) domain, moves to the intrapersonal (or intramental) domain during the course of development. Or in other words, certain aspects of the structure of the activity that have been carried out on an external plane are performed on an internal one (Vygotsky 1978).

However, this general approach to the notion of internalisation is neither sufficient theoretically, nor does it facilitate the development of methodologies of empirical research. To go beyond these generalities one has to specify more concrete aspects of this notion. Perhaps the main attraction of the socio-historical theory lies in the importance given to the analysis of cognitive development in sociocultural activity. The basic unit of analysis is not the individual, but the sociocultural activity insofar as this activity implies the active participation of individuals in practices that are socially established and maintained (Vygotsky 1981).

The Notion of Memory

Our analysis of text comprehension and recall is grounded in a notion of memory that is quite different from the one that is predominant in cognitive studies. This notion of memory relies on contributions from authors like Vygotsky and Bartlett, and can be summarised in the following points:

— The study of memory must involve the study of everyday activities in which remembering and forgetting take place. One important contributor to this notion of memory is F. Bartlett (1932/1961). Bartlett focused on the activity of remembering rather than on the faculty of memory. Remembering was conceived as a functional activity (Edwards & Middleton 1987).
— Action is the unit of analysis. The problem of the unit of analysis was specifically addressed by Vygotsky (Davydov & Radzikhovskii 1985). However, the unit selected by Vygotsky himself, word meaning, did not accomplish all the requirements that he had previously established. For this reason, authors like Zinchenko (1985) and Wertsch (1985, 1991, 1997) have proposed the concept of tool-mediated action as a unit of analysis for human mental functioning. This concept is based upon Leontiev's (1981) notion of action. For Leontiev, an action is a process subordinated to a conscious goal; actions are defined by goals.

— Memory actions are semiotically mediated. Starting from the concept of goal-directed action, Zinchenko and Wertsch emphasise that human actions are mediated by signs. This kind of mediation is considered, according to Vygotsky, the most distinctive feature of human mental functioning.

— Memory actions are embedded in sociocultural activities. In Leontiev's theory of activity, the first level in the analysis of the structure of human mental functioning. The first level corresponds to the *unit of activity*. This unit is associated to the notion of *motive* (Leontiev 1981; Wertsch 1985). According to Wertsch (1985), this notion focuses on a socioculturally de- fined context in which human functioning occurs. Among the activities mentioned by Leontiev are play, formal education and labour. Wertsch defines the unit of activity in terms of a social institutionally defined set- ting. This setting is not determined nor strongly circumscribed by the physical or perceptual context. Rather, it is a sociocultural interpretation that is imposed on the context by the participants.

Thus, from this theoretical perspective formal education is defined as a form of sociocultural activity and memory in terms of semiotically mediated actions. We are interested in teacher-student interaction as a relevant situ- ation that allows us to observe the relationship between memory actions and sociocultural activities, and, specifically, the appropriation of new forms of understanding and the remembering of texts by a student as a result of inter- action. These new forms of understanding and remembering are specific to institutional settings such as formal education.

As we said before, cognitive research on text processing conceives com- prehension and memory as the result of a process of interaction between text information and a subject's knowledge and strategies. In general, it is as- sumed that s/he must construct a semantic representation of text content. In order to do that, s/he applies several forms of schemata and knowledge rep- resentations related to different domains: general knowledge about the world and human actions, knowledge about text structure, knowledge about his or her own abilities of comprehension and memory (metacompre- hension and metamemory), etc. All these forms of knowledge are attributed to the subject and described in terms of representations stored in memory. Thus, from this perspective, text comprehension and recall are conceived as essentially individual processes.

In contrast to that conception, we start from a different view of text comprehension and memory. The elements involved in cognitive approach are reinterpreted according to the basic notions of our approach. So, for instance, knowledge structures and schemata are defined as a semiotic means that mediate actions. As some authors have pointed out (i.e., Gee 1992), the so-called textual superstructures should be understood as sociocultural semiotic means that mediate the construction of narratives. In the case of school activities, we can observe the importance of expository superstructures. School texts are usually elaborated in accordance with them. Following Bakhtin (1986; Wertsch 1991), they represent a speech genre that is characteristic (although not exclusive) of formal education.

Empirical Study

The theoretical framework described above was applied to an empirical study on teacher-student interaction.

The aim was not to establish causal relationships between variables but to elaborate a detailed description of the elements involved, as well as of the changes in those relationships across phases.

The situation designed for this work consisted of four phases. In all of them, the task was to study and recall an expository text. Each phase was divided into two sub-phases, presentation (study) and recall. Texts had to be recalled at two points, at the end of the study phase and one day later.

The first and fourth phases were labelled *individual* phases and the student was asked to study and recall the text alone, without any assistance. During the second and the third phase (*interactive* phases), the student was assisted by a teacher and the task was carried out jointly.

The analysis of interactive presentation sub-phases started by identifying study actions, that is, strategies that were oriented to comprehension and memorisation of different pieces of text information (the whole text, a paragraph or, even part of a paragraph). Those actions were described according to several criteria, including the complexity (in terms of the topic of the action: the part of the text studied) and the plane of regulation (who performed the action).

The analysis of recall sub-phases was similar to other studies of text recall. Three measures were used: global recall, recall of main ideas, secondary ideas and details. In interactive sub-phases, a new aspect was added to the analysis: assisted and non-assisted recall. The former referred to ideas recalled by teacher and student jointly, so that both participants assumed some role in their recall, whilst the latter to ideas recalled by the student without the teacher's intervention.

Several hypotheses about the relationships between explanatory variables, associated with genetic domains (Wertsch 1985), and the actions performed by teachers and students to understand and remember the texts were formulated. In general, the analyses considered two explanatory factors: the *educational level* of the students (beginning and advanced level), and *phase* (comparison between individual phases 1 and 4 or between interactive phases 2 and 3). The first was associated with the macro genetic domain of sociocultural development (experience in activities of formal education). The second factor was associated with the microgenetic domain.

Explanatory factors were related to study actions and recall of the texts through two sets of hypotheses.

The first set of hypotheses were about the complexity and the regulation of study actions and the types of instruction. It was expected that study actions employed at the advanced student level would be more complex (in terms of the topic) than those observed at the beginner student level. Differences regarding the degree of responsibility assumed by students in the regulation of study actions were also expected. A higher degree of responsibility was expected in advanced students. At the same time, differences in the complexity and regulation of study actions between phases were expected: changes across phases (between phase 1 and 4 and between phase 2 and 3) in the complexity of study actions and in the responsibility assumed by students.

Finally, we expected to observe differences between educational levels and phases in the types/forms of instruction. These differences would show more indirect forms of instruction (which give more initiative to the student) in advanced than in beginner students, and in phase 3 than in phase 2.

The second set of hypotheses was concerned with text recall, the educational level and phases. It was expected that advanced students would recall a greater proportion of text ideas than beginner students and a greater proportion of text ideas recalled in phase 1 than 4 and in phase 3 than 2. A superiority of immediate recall over delayed recall was also expected. In this case, it was expected to find more difference between immediate and delayed recall at the beginner level than at the advanced students' level, and in the sessions 1 and 2 than 3 and 4, respectively.

Method

Participants. Twenty dyads of teacher and students from two educational levels (beginner students and advanced students) in adult education participated in the study. The students attended the Adult Education Programme developed by the Regional Government of Andalusia. They completed the task with their regular teachers.

Materials. Four expository texts about ancient peoples (Celts, Incas, Phoenicians) were employed. Two of them (employed during phases 1 and 4) were about 300 words long and contained information about the economy, society and culture of the people. The other two texts (employed in phases 2 and 3) were about 200 words long and contained information about only one of the former topics (economy and society in this order). The texts were constructed by the authors of the paper. Texts used in phases 1 and 4, on the one hand, and in phases 2 and 3, on the other, shared a similar organisation, in terms of idea-units. They were hierarchically organised and consisted of idea-units from three different hierarchical levels:

— Main ideas from each paragraph. All information in a paragraph was subordinated to one of these ideas. For instance, 'Economy' in the text entitled 'The Celtics'.
— Secondary ideas from each paragraph. These ideas gave further information about some main ideas. For instance, '... they were the inventors of the alphabet' in the text entitled 'The Phoenicians'.
— Details. The lower level of importance. These ideas added some information to main and secondary ideas. For instance: '... they made drinking vessels', referring to products of ceramics (secondary idea) in the text entitled 'The Phoenicians'.

Procedure. The procedure was the same for all the participants and consisted of four successive phases:

— Individual study and recall 1. It consisted of two sub-phases. In the first sub-phase (presentation or study), one of the 300 word texts was presented. Subjects were asked to study the text for as much time as he or she needed. Once they finished, they were asked to recall it (sub-phase 2). They had to recall the text immediately after presentation (immediate recall) and the day after (delayed recall).

— Interactive (teacher-student) study and recall 2 and 3. In these phases two different texts about the Inca people were presented. In presentation sub-phases, teachers were asked to assist students to study. Again, there was no time limit. Once they finished, they were asked to recall the text. In this sub-phase, the teacher could also assist the student. As in the individual phases, recall was measured at two points (immediate and delayed recall).

— Individual study and recall 4. Procedure of phase 1 was repeated employing a different but similar text.

Criteria for Data Analysis

Sessions were videotaped in order to carry out an exhaustive analysis of actions. This analysis adopted the general approach used by Wertsch, Minick and Arns (1984), with some differences because of the different nature of both tasks. The steps of the criteria of our analysis were the following:

Study Actions

This analysis was only applied to phases 2 and 3 during text presentation.

Topic. The categories employed were the following:

1. Whole text. Action refers to the whole text.
2. Paragraph. The main idea in a paragraph was explicitly produced by a teacher and/or a student or they referred to it by using an expression.
3. Part of paragraph. Some explanation or reading about ideas in a paragraph is provided.

Plane of regulation. This criterion corresponded to the distribution of responsibility between teacher and student in the control and performance of action. According to this criterion, actions could be regulated by the student, by teacher and student jointly or by the teacher alone.

Type of instruction. This analysis was concerned with the nature of instruction, the amount of responsibility given by the teacher to the student in the control of the study action. According to this criterion, we distinguished three categories of instruction: guide, indication and demonstration.

Recall

Measures employed individual and interactive recall sub-phases were similar. Three types of measures were distinguished:

— *Global recall.* The percentage of ideas, regardless their hierarchical level, was scored.
— *Recall of* main *ideas.* The percentage of ideas recalled from level 1.
— *Recall of secondary ideas and details.* The percentage of ideas from levels 2 and 3.

Results

Differences Between Beginner and Advanced Students

Study actions were analysed according to three dimensions of the actions: topic, plane of regulation and type of instruction.[1] Table 13.1 shows the results of these analyses.

Interaction	df	Pearson Chi-square
Educ. level and topic of study actions	2	21.704**
Educ. level and plane of regulation	2	18.808**
Educ. level and type of instruction	2	19.804**

Table 13.1. Analyses of study actions. Chi-square analyses of the interaction between educational level and dimensions of study actions (** = $p < 0.01$).

1. Hi-Log Linear technniques (Kennedy 1983) are particularly suitable for showing relationships between factors in multiple-entry tables. These techniques start by considering all variables as independent factors, and the dependent variable is the number of cases per cell. In our work, some specific procedures of analysis were applied. They are called Logit-Models. These models treat some factors as explanatory and others as variables of performance.

The topic of action results showed significant differences between educational levels (L^2 = 21.70; p < 0.0001). At advanced student level we found a significantly greater proportion of actions whose topic was the whole text or more than one paragraph. At the beginner student level, in contrast, there was a higher proportion of actions oriented to the study of a single paragraph.

The plane of regulation results showed evidence of a significant relation between the educational level and the plane of regulation (L^2 = 18.808, p < 0.0001). At the advanced level we observed a higher proportion of actions regulated by the student or by the teacher and the student jointly, than at the beginner level. At the beginner level, the proportion of actions regulated by the teacher was higher than at the advanced level.

The type of instruction results showed a significant relation between educational level and type of instruction (L^2 = 19.804, p < 0.0005). At the beginner level there was a greater use of demonstration than at the advanced level. More than half of the instructional actions involved giving support and clues to help the students perform the task. We found interesting changes across phases in advanced students. While type of instruction did not change from phase 2 to 3 at the beginner level, there were significant changes at advanced students' level. Thus, guiding increased significantly from phase 2 to phase 3 while indication decreased.

Educational Level Combined with Interactive and Individual Recall

Finally, our analysis focused on text recall. We conducted two separate analyses regarding individual and interactive recall. In all cases, data were analysed by using Multivariate Analysis of Variance (MANOVA) tests. Three factors were considered: educational level (between-subjects factor), recall phase (within-subjects factor) and delay (within-subjects factor). In this section we shall present data, starting by interactive recall and following with individual recall.

The first analysis concerned interactive recall of the texts. The analyses distinguished between global recall and recall of main ideas (see Table 13.2).

In the analyses of global recall, data showed only a significant effect of phase (F = 17.94; p < 0.0001). The effect of the other two variables, educational level and delay was not significant. No one interaction between independent variables was significant.

	Global recall		Recall of main ideas	
Effect	df	F	df	F
Educ. level	1	2.46	1	10.44**
Phase	1	17.94**	1	.96
Delay	1	3.59	1	.43
Educ. level x Phase	1	.06	1	.03
Educ. level x Delay	1	.72	1	.69
Phase x Delay	1	.26	1	.03

Table 13.2. Interactive recall. Phases 2 and 3 (** = $p < 0.01$).

The analysis of the effect of variance between individual and interactive recall phases evidenced a drop in the recall of text ideas in the third phase when compared to the second phase. Figure 13.1 shows data from this analysis.

The tests of interactive recall of main ideas provided different results. There was a significant influence of the variable educational level ($F = 10.44$; $p < 0.005$). The other two variables: recall phase and delay had no significant influence on recall. No significant interactions between independent variables were observed.

The last set of analyses was carried out on data from individual recall (see Table 13.3).

In the analyses of global recall we observed significant effect of respectively phase ($F = 8.26$; $p < 0.01$) and recall delay ($F = 10.88$; $p < 0.005$). No significant effect of educational level was observed. Neither was there significant interaction between factors.

As we can see in Figure 13.2, students recalled more ideas in phase 4 and in immediate recall than in phase 1 and delayed recall, respectively.

Results of recall of main ideas showed the significant effect of educational level ($F = 6.51$; $p < 0.05$) and recall phase ($F = 25.37$; $p < 0.001$). Students from the advanced level recalled more main ideas than beginner students and they all recalled more ideas in phase 4 than in phase 1). No significant effects of recall delay or of interactions between factors were observed.

Discussion

With regard to *the first set of hypotheses*, we found the expected differences between educational levels both in the complexity and in the regula-

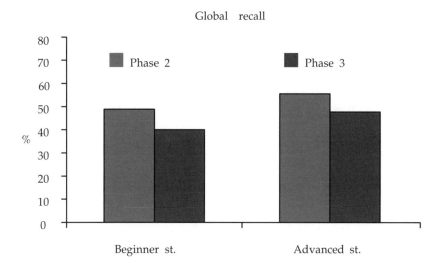

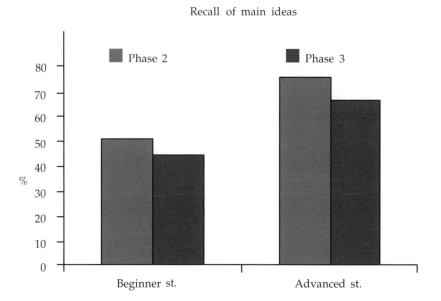

Figure 13.1. Interactive recall: Phases 2 and 3.

	Global recall		Recall of main ideas	
Effect	df	F	df	F
Educ. level	1	3.35	1	6.51**
Phase	1	8.26*	1	25.37**
Delay	1	10.88**	1	3.29
Educ. level x Phase	1	.11	1	.00
Educ. level x Delay	1	.13	1	1.32
Phase x Delay	1	.02	1	.85

Table 13.3. Individual recall. Phases 1 and 4 (* = $p < 0.05$; ** = $p < 0.01$).

tion of study actions. Differences in the school experience of students were associated to different general patterns of studying texts. The actions employed at advanced level were more complex since they referred to wider sections of information in the texts than the actions employed at beginner level, which focused most on single text paragraphs. Advanced students also assumed greater responsibility in controlling and performing study actions. We can observe, thus, how formal education was associated with more complex actions, oriented to memorisation of the text as a whole. These kinds of study actions put the focus of attention on structural aspects of the text, and on the main ideas. These data coincide with data from most of the research into the relationship between culture and memory. These studies show that subjects with more school experience tend to use more complex memory strategies (actions) than less experienced individuals in different kinds of tasks (Cole 1990; Rogoff 1990). In our case, the task was the recall of expository texts. In these kinds of texts, logical relations between concepts, objects and events are very important (Brewer 1980). Given the nature of these texts and their extended use in formal education, it is not surprising that people more experienced in these activities are able to perform more complex actions for studying expository texts and to assume more responsibility in their control. The comparison between the two educational levels enables us to see a greater degree of appropriation of study actions in advanced students.

Data from the analysis of the type of instruction were consistent with these results. As the educational level of the students increased, teachers used less directive guidance in their participation, leaving more room for the initiative and responsibility of the students. At beginner student level, teach-

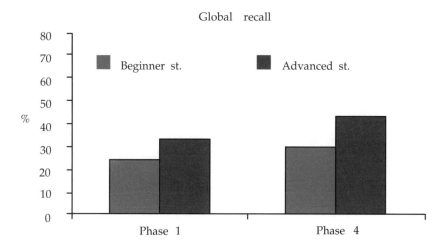

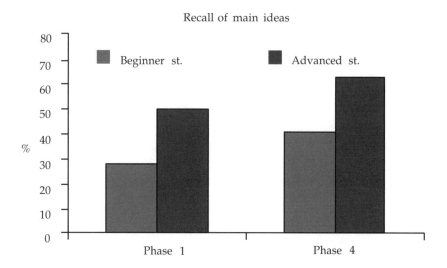

Figure 13.2. Individual recall: Phases 1 and 4.

ers preferred to use instructional actions that involved a very direct instruction (demonstration) of the study action used in text comprehension, while only 14.5% of their instructional actions involved a more indirect form of guidance. The data observed at advanced level were quite different. Teachers usually limited their role to indirectly guiding the performance of the students. More than half of their instructional actions involved giving support and clues to help the students perform the task (guide and indication), while those that involved the greatest possible level of directivity, demonstration, were less frequent. These data showed the expected relationship between students' appropriation of study actions and the use of indirect forms of instruction by the teachers.

Apart from educational level, the second explanatory factor of our study was teacher-student interaction. The analysis of this factor should enable us to examine some mechanisms in the microgenetic evolution of text comprehension and memory actions and relate them to teacher-student interaction. Data showed that at advanced student level there was an accentuation of the tendency to study the text as a whole, with actions oriented to its global organisation. They also involved a selective attention to main ideas. This kind of study action is quite similar to Meyer's structure strategy (Meyer 1985). According to this author, subjects with good skills in reading comprehension employ processing strategies that rely on the recognition and use of text structure. From our perspective, these strategies should not be understood as types of individual strategies that are valid for processing any text, but as memory mediation procedures that are specific of the activities of formal education.

This form of selective study of the text at advanced level seemed to be instructed by teachers through the use of indirect forms of support/guidance. The increase of the use of this type of instruction and the decrease of indication from phase 2 to phase 3 seems also to suggest that teacher-student interaction may promote the appropriation of these strategies for text comprehension and memory.

The second set of hypotheses referred to text recall. In our analysis we distinguished between interactive and individual recall. In these two measures we found different recall patterns at the two educational levels. At advanced student level, recall was more selective than at beginner student level. The participants from the advanced level obtained better results than the beginners in the measure of recall of main ideas of the texts, but not in global recall. At the same time, at the advanced level the recall of main ideas was also more persistent, since we found significant difference between immediate and delayed recall results at beginner student level but not at the advanced level.

The differences between the data of interactive and individual recall were related to the effect of the variable phase. In the interactive recall we observed a descent in the proportion of ideas remembered during the third phase. This descent, nevertheless, was selective and did not affect the recall of main ideas of the text, the recall of which did not change significantly from one phase to another. From our point of view, these results could be attributed to the more selective study of texts carried out during the third phase. In individual recall, however, we found an improvement from the first to the fourth phase. A detailed analysis of this effect showed that this microgenetic tendency had a selective character, since it affected the main ideas of the texts. In this measure we could observe a significant increase in recall score in the fourth phase.

Conclusion

As a whole, these data have offered some evidence of the acquisition of the structure strategy (Meyer 1985) in teacher-student interaction. The use of this structure strategy points to a selective way of studying and remembering the texts. This selective way focuses on the structure of the texts rather than their content. Main ideas, which occupy the highest level in this structure are enhanced. From a theoretical perspective, we think it is necessary to underline that the structure of recalling these 'main ideas' is not a form of memorisation which is intrinsically better than others, as many cognitive studies may imply. Rather, this structure strategy represents the form of memory characteristic of formal education. The fact that the structure strategy method used to be considered (explicitly or implicitly) the best form of memorisation does not deny cultural specificity. It rather reflects the importance of these activities being conferred on our culture.

Our results also offered evidence of the role of teacher-student interaction in the acquisition of structure strategy. We have observed some mechanisms through which this interaction might facilitate students' appropriation of this form of memorisation, which are specific in formal educational activities. Notions such as zone of proximal development (Vygotsky 1978, 1987) or guided participation (Rogoff 1990) may be useful to account for the manner in which this transfer is produced.

It seems to us that, from a theoretical point of view, it is necessary to highlight the importance of the use of forms of instruction that let the students assume an increasing level of responsibility in the control of actions.

These forms of instruction seem to promote the subsequent learner's appropriation of the skills necessary for solving the task. Guided participation in activities of formal schooling (Rogoff 1990) may again constitute a basic condition for this appropriation.

We think that one of the most important problems for the study of instructional processes is the separation from sociocultural activities within which they take place. In our work we have observed the relationship between students' experience in activities of formal education and the form of instruction that teachers selected. At the advanced students' level we observe the prevalence of forms of instruction that gave more responsibility to the learner than at the beginner student level, where a predominance of very directive instructional actions (demonstration) was observed. These data are very consistent with results from a previous study conducted by one of us (Santamaría 1997) with a quite different task. In both cases, as in most research about instructional interactions, the greater experience in activities of formal education was associated with forms of instruction which are characterised by a progressive decrease in instructors' control and regulation of the task. We do not wish to say that this constitutes the 'best' form of instruction, but instead that this represents a mode of instruction characteristic of the activities of formal education (Wertsch 1991).

From a more general theoretical perspective, teacher-student interaction seems to facilitate the acquisition of new forms of remembering. As we have defended in this paper, these (and other) forms of remembering can be defined as (mediated) actions. We assume that structure strategy constitutes, from a sociocultural perspective, a speech genre, a particular semiotic tool for mediating text comprehension and memory. This semiotic mediational means focuses on structural aspect of texts and is privileged (Wertsch 1991, 1998) in the sociocultural activity of formal education.

Finally, we must comment on some of the problems that may arise from this study. First, it is necessary to develop in greater dimension new studies for analysing teacher-student interaction. Furthermore, the comparative analysis of the development of teacher-student interaction with regard to individual activity and assisted activity, respectively, should be continued. Both forms of analysis, the one that results from increasing the number of interactive phases of study activity and those that involve a detailed analysis of how task accomplishment within phases of individual and interactive study activities, are complementary. These types of analyses can provide a more complete microgenetic perspective of the way in which teachers and students memorise and recall the texts.

References

Bakhtin, M.J. (1986). *Speech genres and other late essays* (C. Emerson and M. Holquist, eds.). Austin: University of Texas Press.

Bartlett, F.C. (1932/1961). *Remembering. A study in experimental and social psychology.* Cambridge: Cambridge University Press.

Brewer, W.F. (1980). Literary theory, rhethoric and stylistics; implications for psychology. In R.J. Spiro, B. Bruce & W. Brewer (eds.), *Theoretical issues in reading comprehension.* Hillsdale, N.J.: Erlbaum.

Brooks, L.W. & Dansereau, D.F. (1983). Effects of structural schema training and text organization on expository prose processing. *Journal of Educational Psychology,* 75(6), 811-20.

Cole, M. (1990). Cognitive development and formal schooling: the evidence from cross-cultural research. In L.C. Moll (ed.), *Vygotsky and education.* New York: Cambridge University Press.

Cook, L.K. & Mayer, R.E. (1988). Teaching readers about the structure of scientific text. *Journal of Educational Psychology,* 80(4), 448-56.

Davydov, V.V. & Radzikhovskii, L.A. (1985). Vygotsky's theory and the activity-oriented approach in psychology. In J.V. Wertsch (ed.), *Culture, communication and cognition: Vygotskian perspectives.* Cambridge, Mass.: Cambridge University Press.

Edwards, D. & Middleton, D. (1986): Conversation with Bartlett. *Quarterly Newsletter of the LCHC,* 8(3), 79-89.

Edwards, D. & Middleton, D. (1987). Conversation and remembering: Bartlett revisited. *Applied Cognitive Psychology,* 1(77), 92.

Elbers, E. (1987). Interaction and instruction in the conservation experiment. *European Journal of Psychology of Education,* 1, 77-89.

Elbers, E., Maier, R., Hoekstra, T. & Hoogsteder, M. (1992). Internalization and adult-child interaction. *Learning and Instruction,* 2, 101-18.

Gee, J.P. (1992). *The social mind: Language ideology and social practice.* New York: Bergin & Garvey.

Golden, J.M. (1988). The construction of a literary text in a story-reading lesson. In J.L. Green & J.O. Harker (eds.), *Multiple perspective analyses of classroom discourse.* Vol. XXVIII. Norwood, N.J.: Ablex.

González, M.M. (1996). Tasks and activities: A parent-child interaction analysis. *Learning and Instruction,* 6(4), 287-306.

Gutiérrez Calvo, M. (1992). Comprensión y memoria de textos. In J. Mayor & M. de Vega (eds.), *Tratado de psicología general. Vol. 3. Memoria y representación.* Madrid: Alhambra.

Kennedy, J.J. (1983). *Analyzing qualitative data: Introductory log-linear analysis for behavioral research.* New York: Praeger.

León, J.A. (1991). La mejora de la comprensión lectora: un análisis interactivo. *Infancia y Aprendizaje*, 56, 5-24.

León, J.A. & García Madruga (1991). Comprensión y memoria de textos. In J.M. Ruíz-Vargas (ed.), *Psicología de la memoria*. Madrid: Alianza.

Leontiev, A.N. (1981): The problem of activity in psychology. In J.V. Wertsch (ed.), *The concept of activity in Soviet Psychology*. New York: Sharpe.

Mateos, M.M. (1991). Entrenamiento en el proceso de supervisión de la comprensión lectora: Fundamentación teórica e implicaciones educativas. *Infancia y Aprendizaje*, 56, 25-50.

McLane, B. (1987). Interaction, context and the zone of proximal development. In M. Hickman (ed.), *Social and functional approaches to language and thought*. Orlando, Fla.: Academic Press.

McNamee, G.D. (1987). The social origins of narrative skills. In M. Hickman (ed.), *Social and functional approaches to language and thought*. Orlando, Fla.: Academic Press.

Meyer, B.J.F. (1985). Prose analysis: purposes, procedures and problems. In B.K. Britton & J.B. Black (eds.), *Understanding expository text. A theoretical and practical handbook for analyzing explanatory text*. Hillsdale, N.J.: Erlbaum.

Newman, D.; Griffin, P. & Cole, M. (1989). *The construction zone: working for cognitive change in school*. New York: Cambridge University Press.

Palincsar, A.S. & Brown, A.L. (1984). Reciprocal teaching of comprehension-fostering and comprehension-monitoring activities. *Cognition and Instruction*, 1(2), 117-75.

Paris, S.G. & Cross, D.R. (1983). Ordinary learning: Pragmatic connections among children's beliefs, motives and actions. In J. Bisanz, G. Bisanz & R. Kail (eds.), *Learning in children*. New York: Springer-Verlag.

Paris, S.G., Lipson, M.Y. & Wixson, K.K. (1983). Becoming a strategic reader. *Contemporary Educational Psychology*, 8, 293-316.

Rogoff, B. (1990). *Apprenticeship in thinking: Cognitive development in social context*. New York: Oxford University Press.

Rogoff, B. (1993). Children's guided participation and participatory appropiation in sociocultural activity. In R.H. Wozniak & K.W. Fisher (eds.), *Development in context*. Hillsdale, N.J.: LEA.

Rogoff, B., Gauvain, M. & Ellis, S. (1984). Development viewed in its cultural context. In M.H.Bornstein & M.E. Lamb (eds.), *Developmental psychology: An advanced textbook*. Hillsdale, N.J.: Erlbaum.

Sánchez Miguel, E. (1990). Estructuras textuales y procesos de comprensión: un programa para instruir en la comprensión de textos. *Estudios de Psicología*, 41, 21-40.

Sánchez Miguel, E. (1993). *Los textos expositivos. Estrategias para mejorar su comprensión*. Madrid: Santillana.

Santamaría, A. (1997). Mediación semiótica, acciones instruccionales e interiorización. Un estudio de interacciones en educación de personas adultas. Unpublished Doctoral Dissertation.

Vygotsky, L.S. (1978). *Mind in society. The development of higher psychological processes* (M. Cole, V. John-Steiner, S. Scribner & E. Souberman, eds.). Cambridge, Mass.: Harvard University Press.

Vygotsky, L.S. (1981). The genesis of higher mental functions. In J.V. Wertsch (ed.), *The concept of activity in Soviet Psychology*. Armonk, New York: Sharpe.

Vygotsky, L.S. (1987). *Thinking and speech* (Norris Minick, ed. and trans.). New York: Plenum Press.

Wertsch, J.V. (1984). The zone of proximal development: some conceptual issues. In B. Rogoff & J.V. Wertsch (eds.), *Children's learning in the 'zone of proximal development'*. San Francisco: Jossey-Bass.

Wertsch, J.V. (1985). *Vygotsky and the social formation of mind*. Cambridge, Mass.: Harvard University Press.

Wertsch, J.V. (1991). *Voices of the mind: A sociocultural approach to mediated action*. Cambridge, Mass.: Harvard University Press.

Wertsch, J.V. (1998). *Mind as action*. New York: Oxford University Press.

Wertsch, J.V., Minick, N. & Arns, F.J. (1984). The creation of context in joint problem solving. In B. Rogoff & J. Lave (eds.), *Everyday cognition: Its development in social con-text*. Cambridge, Mass.: Harvard University Press.

Zinchenko, V.P. (1985). Vygotsky's ideas about units for analysis of mind. In J.V. Wertsch (ed.), *Culture, Communication and Cognition: Vygotskian perspectives*. Cambridge, Mass.: Cambridge University Press.

14 Children's Self-Concept as Gendered and Contextual: Socio-Moral Self-Concepts among 12-year-old Finnish Girls and Boys

Airi Hautamäki and Jarkko Hautamäki

A Developmental Perspective on the Self-Concept

Previous research on the development of the self-concept has focused on the nature of the dynamics of such development. The implication drawn on the basis of developmental theory (Werner 1957) and self-concept research that has taken a developmental perspective (Harter 1988; Harter 1990a, 1990b, 1990c) is that a progressive increase in the differentiation of the domains of activity of the self-concept is paralleled by a hierarchical ordering of the structure of the self-concept. According to this line of reasoning, the developmental outcome is a multi-dimensional and hierarchically ordered self-concept (Marsh 1990; Shavelson et al. 1976; Shavelson & Marsh 1986). Byrne & Shavelson (1996) demonstrate this presumed developmental pattern also in regard to the social self-concept.

Developmental factors are also associated with shifts in the salience of the particular dimensions of the self-concept at various stages in the life cycle (Harter 1990a). In early and late childhood, the focus is on the physical and active self, which subsequently shifts in pre-adolescence to the social and psychological self (Damon & Hart 1982). On the basis of previous research (Montemayor & Eisen 1977), Byrne & Shavelson (1996, 611) stress that children do not simply add new facets, which are relative to new domains, to their self-conceptualisations: 'but rather that they evaluate themselves in different terms relative to the ontogenetic development of their social cognitions'. Thus, there is a gradual, progressive shift during the primary grades from describing the self in physical terms, and in terms of outer activities, to the description of self in psychological terms during adolescence (Harter 1988; Harter 1990c; Pölkki 1978).

The Socio-Moral Self-Concept of the Latency-Aged Child: The Conventional 'Good Girl/Boy' Morality

This study analyses and elaborates on the salience of the particular dimensions of the self-concept during various life-cycle stages using the concept of 'developmental task' (Erikson 1951/1977; Havighurst 1948/1972). With this concept, it is possible to situate the developing individual in the age-graded sociocultural context. The transition to the role of the pupil represents a new developmental task for the 7-11 year old children. As the child starts primary school s/he is embarking on a new institutional career (Mayer 1986), being surrounded by a complex set of new interrelated expectations (Hautamäki, A. 1982, 1986; Hautamäki, A. & Hautamäki, J. 1997; Nurmi 1993). The child is therefore confronted with new developmental standards (Caspi 1987; Nurmi 1993) and norms for age-appropriate behaviour according to which s/he is evaluated (usually in comparison with his classmates) especially, his/her capacity to learn and work industriously (Hautamäki, A. 1982, 1986) as a means of gradually acquiring, what Erikson (1951/1977, 234) has termed 'the technological ethos of a culture'.

It is posited that the pupil reacts to challenge by developing skills and by gradually generalising his/her beliefs concerning him/herself as an achiever in relation to the requirements of the school, e.g., that schooling does matter; it is a serious issue to achieve well in school. It is also assumed that coping with this task is reflected in the development of a more generalised self-concept, including the socio-moral self-concept, e.g., how the child relates to him/herself as an object in a socio-moral sense. What kind of images and representations does the child maintain about him/herself as a moral and socially interconnected person? It is also posited that the development of the conventional morality of the latency-aged child — 'good girl/boy' (Kohlberg 1976) — forms the core of the acquisition of the role expectations of the pupil.

The Unitary Individual as a Multi-Layered and Multi-Voiced Subject?

The post-modern stance of decentring has tended to deny psychological subjectivity and the possibility to postulate generalizable features of the psyche, as stated by Gergen (1991, 7):

processes such as emotion and reason cease to be real and significant essences of persons; rather, in the light of pluralism we perceive them as impostors, the outcome of our ways of conceptualizing them. Under post-modern conditions, persons exist in a state of continuous construction and reconstruction; it is a world where anything goes that can be negotiated. Each reality of self gives ways to reflexive questioning, irony, and ultimate playful probing of yet another reality. The centre fails to hold.

The unitary subject or, analogously, the self, is rejected on the grounds that such an assumption would represent an essentialist stance (Butler 1990).

Two points are, however, confused in this polarisation of presumed opposites. The rejection of 'self' as essentialist is criticised by Benjamin (1995, 12) as follows: 'it seems to confuse the category of the epistemological, thinking subject with that of the self as a locus of subjective experience, unconscious as well as conscious, when, in fact, these operate on very different registers'. The minimum assumption made by psychology, as the science about the individual is the self-consciousness of the human being. According to this line of reasoning, a subject has to be postulated as a locus of experience to give existence for the individual, a subject that is more or less centrally organised and, a subject, that need not be either unified or coherent (Benjamin 1995, 13). Thus, individuality in terms of the psychology of the self denotes a subject's experience of continuity and his/her awareness of different states of mind, including his/her recognition of the impact that s/he has on another person and of his/her moderation of his/her affects in accordance with the recognition of his/her impact. The other side of the coin is, stressed by Benjamin (1995), the recognition of the impact of the other on oneself.

As Giddens (1991) suggests, the fragmented subjectivity of post-modern times need not be a representative of 'shattered selves' (Glass 1995), but may also be harmoniously functioning and well integrated. Thus, if a developmental perspective of a gradual progressive differentiation, paralleled by a hierarchical ordering (and structuralisation) of the self-concept is posited, there does not necessarily exist a conflict between the trait approach, broadly taken and a more context-tied, dynamic approach to the self-concept. The self-concept is looked upon as, on the one hand, a multi-layered and a multi-voiced and, on the other hand, in a complex way orchestrated self.

Short-Term Microgenetic and Long-Term Cumulative Ontogenetic Changes

In addition, short-term microgenetic and long-term ontogenetic processes of change have been confused, i.e., studying short-term changes induced by the ongoing situation, in contrast to studying long-term developmental, ontogenetic changes producing more generalised and stable, complex structures of self-regulation (Hautamäki, A. 1982; Peters 1996). In this study, it is assumed that particularly the culturally valued features of the socio-moral self-concept (as mediated through the developmental task) are generalised across the different domains of activity during the early school years on the basis of the experiences of the child, as s/he is trying to cope with the role expectations of the pupil.

The General Self-Concept vs. Contextual Selves

The question of a more general self-concept vs. contextual (more context-bound) selves is analysed from a developmental perspective. According to a developmental perspective of the progressive differentiation and hierarchical ordering of the self-concept, the trait-approach, which assumes temporal stability and internal consistency of self-beliefs, is not radically opposed to the context-specific state-approaches to the self-concept (the dynamic self-concept, Markus 1977; Markus & Wurf 1987). According to the classical trait-approach, the self-concept is considered a unitary, monolithic entity, a general(ised) view of self, which is cross-situationally and internally consistent (Gergen & Morse 1967), which is also relatively stable. Current conceptualisations inspired by social constructionism stress the nature of self as a multifaceted dynamic construct, a state rather than a trait. The self-concept is thus defined as a cognitive schema. Campbell et al. (1996, 141) maintain that this organised knowledge structure '... contains traits, values, semantic and episodic memories about the self and controls the processing of self-relevant information'. As such, situational determinants of behaviour, e.g., demands implicit in social scripts and put on the actors, are emphasised.

Gender-Related Orientations for Moral Decisions

Gilligan has postulated gender-related orientations for moral decisions (1982, 16-17): rights/justice vs. response/care. Even though Gilligan's conclusions have been contested (Walker 1988, 1991), some of their implications are interesting. The moral reasoning of girls is, according to Gilligan (1982, 16-17) based on an ethic of care, assumed to be 'inseparable from women's moral strength, an overriding concern with relationships and responsibilities', resulting, among others, in that girls would be more sensitive to contextual cues. Gilligan (1982, 17) emphasises that, in accordance with Chodorow's (1978) thinking of the reproduction of mothering and gender identity, girls/women tend, to a higher degree than men, to define themselves in the context of human relationships and judge themselves in terms of their caring abilities (see also, Stein, Newcomb & Bentler 1992). The boys/men, in turn, would express the more general, principled moral reasoning, as described by Kohlberg's (1976) structural model of development, assumed to be anthropologically universal.

Miller (1976) has also postulated the more relational structure of the female self-aiming at establishing and maintaining interdependent connections. According to Miller (1990), the feminine 'self in relation' is a mental representation of the self, characterised by more permeable boundaries and a more encompassing sense of self, in contrast to the more bounded self encouraged in boys. In contrast, the 'positional self' (Hautamäki, A. 1995, 1998) of the boy/male aims at separateness, autonomy and sense of agency. Connell (1987, 183), from a sociological and social constructionist point of departure defines current masculine hegemonic practice in terms of (the right to) heterosexual power, authority, aggression and technical competence, these features constructing together a powerful investment in autonomy. As succinctly put by Griffiths (1995): 'Learning to be autonomous — learning to be cruel'.

Daniels (1996; Daniels et al. 1996; Daniels 1998) proposes that a 'male disadvantage' currently exists in primary school and that boys' educational under-performance in these schools is based on the contradiction between the practices related to hegemonic masculinity, including many cultural subvariants, and teaching practices within primary schooling. Daniels (1998) states that a contradiction arises: 'viz. group and team work, in short collaboration — presume peer co-dependency', which are in contrast to the powerful investment in autonomy typical to hegemonic masculinity. Thus, among certain groups of boys (e.g., working-class boys; Willis 1980) a mismatch may exist between the way of being a boy in accordance with the demands of hegemonic masculinity and ways of being an effective learner. For this reason, it is assumed firstly that girls, on the average, express a greater general sensitivity than do boys to the normative pressures of the school, which is reflected in the girls' more consistent acquisition of the socio-moral expectations. Moreover, this hypothesised gender difference that favours girls in the socio-moral self-concept may also be rooted in the proposed 'male disadvantage' (Daniels et al. 1996). It is therefore suggested that if the primary classroom practices and discourses place more boys than girls in the position of ineffective learners (Daniels 1998), it may be more difficult for the boys to attach personal meaning to the normative expectations of the school.

The Empirical Study

The study is part of a large-scale cross-sectional assessment of 'Learning-to-Learn-Competencies' of the 6th formers at the end of the Finnish primary school. The research project is situated at the University of Helsinki. The sample is representative of Finland (Hautamäki, J. et al. 1999). The data consist of 2717 pupils from the 6th form, which is the last form of the Finnish primary school. On average, the pupils are 12 years old.

Methods

The 'Vidnoie Scale' has been developed in the joint Dutch-Russian research project, 'Socio-moral competencies of adolescents in Russia' (Heymans et al. 1996); our adaptation is referred to by the name 'Socio-Moral Selves Scale'. The aim is to tap aspects of developmental tasks, the content and mental representation of developmental tasks, particularly salient socio-moral issues (Hautamäki, A. 1994; Heymans 1994; Heymans et al. 1996) by studying the socio-moral self-concept of the latency-aged children ('good boy-good girl', Kohlberg 1976). In studying the socio-moral self-concept, the

	Descriptor	Factor
1.	Fair	I
2.	Behaving well	I
3.	Brave	IV
4.	A liar	II
5.	Hard working	IV
6.	Self-confident	III
7.	Tactful	I
8.	Indifferent	II
9.	Lazy	II
10.	Honest	I
11.	Helpful	I
12.	Responsible, reliable	I
13.	Open, communicative	III
14.	Thoughtless, reckless	II
15.	Friendly	I
16.	Modest	I
17.	Sensible	IV
18.	Reserved, quiet	I
19.	Empathetic	I
20.	Harsh, blunt	II
21.	I leave things unfinished	II
22.	Intelligent	IV
23.	I know what I want to do	III
24.	I can be myself	III

Table 14.1. The items of the Socio-Moral Self-Scale.

scale differentiates between five contexts: being alone, with one's parents, with siblings, with friends, at school. As the Socio-Moral Selves Scale aims at tapping the socio-moral aspects of the self-concept, it is less oriented at a formal, context-free description of personality and human functioning and more oriented at the contents of activities. Elkonin distinctly spelled out this position (1977; Hautamäki, A. 1982) in his objective-contextual approach to human development as follows: 'With what particular aspects of reality does the child interact — and consequently, towards which aspects does he become oriented — in performing this or that activity?'

The Socio-Moral Selves Scale is a Likert-type self-assessment scale of the 'present self' (Markus & Nurius 1986), in which each descriptor is given a value on a 5-point scale ranging from strongly disagree (1) to strongly agree (5). Some of the 24 descriptors are highly socio-morally saturated, implying, and allowing, skewed (skewness high) and peaked (kurtosis high) distributions. Some more cognitively oriented descriptors (e.g., sensible, intelligent) were added by us to the original Vidnoie Scale in order to have a bridge to other, more cognitive or motivational self-concepts and self-conceptions, or generally to beliefs and orientations (Hautamäki, J. et al., 1997, 1999).

The pupils were asked to assess themselves with the 24 descriptors in five different contexts: as myself (e.g., alone), with parents, with friends, at school and with siblings. A total of 5 times 24 variables (see Table 14.1) were analysed.

In most of the present analyses, four contexts were used: with parents, at school, with friends and with siblings. The context 'sibling' is not always included. The analytical tools were exploratory factor analysis used for the scale construction and the repeated and one-way analyses of variance. The different contexts were combined into compound variables, and were treated as repeated measures of the analysis of variance. The other main categorical variables were gender, father's educational level (I, lowest, II, or III, highest or university based, degree of education) and grade-point-average (in Finland, from 4, failed, to 10, highest, GPA. The pupils were divided into three groups: < 7, low; ≥ 7 < 9; ≥ 9, high).

Results

Construction and Structure of the Socio-Moral Self-Concepts Scale

The Socio-Moral Self-Scale was factor analysed (firstly, principal components, and secondly, with varimax rotations and orthogonal and oblique solutions). The exploratory factor analyses yielded two possible solutions, either one strong principal component (PC) score or a four-factor score. This result is the same in all the contexts, except with siblings, in which case the two-factor score would have been the best one. The same four-factor-score was found also in an independent Helsinki City sample (Hautamäki, A. & Hautamäki, J. 1999). In the four-factor model the factors eigenvalues and alfa reliabilities in the school context are presented in Table 14.2.

	Eigenvalue	Reliability
Factor I 'Good Boy/Girl'	7.85	.73
Factor II 'Sloth'	2.47	.75
Factor III 'General Self-Confidence'	1.53	.73
Factor IV 'Rational Self'	1.14	.80

Table 14.2. The four-factor model.

The one-factor PC-score was termed 'Socio-Moral Self-Concept'. In the context 'Sibling' the two factors were the factors I and II. The eigenvalues of the factors III and IV were lower for siblings and accordingly were not included in certain analyses (see later figures).

Factor I: Good Girl/Good Boy can be interpreted as the core of the socio-moral self, i.e., as an essential indicator of the degree to which the child has accepted the requirements of the pupil role and the learning expectations of the school.

Factor II: Sloth may be interpreted as the shadow of Good Girl/Good Boy, indicating a kind of protest against and denial of the socio-moral values of the school as being expressed by conventional morality of the latency-aged child. As this kind of protest is related to some subvariants of hegemonic masculinity, such as just being reckless, one of the daring guys who really shows off by standing up to authorities (Connell 1987; Daniels 1998; Griffiths 1995; Willis 1980), the results in regard to this factor should be interpreted with some caution. Parallels may be drawn by citing two classic literary heroes, Mark Twain's Tom Sawyer and Astrid Lindgren's Emil in Lönneberga. Twain depicted Sawyer as a young boy fighting for his autonomy against the admonition of his Aunt Polly. This quest for independence even drove Sawyer to run away with a negro slave to the freedom of the Mississippi River. Another literary hero is Lindgren's Emil in Lönneberga, who only learnt by doing, i.e., who only knew he had done a mischievous thing by doing it and being confronted with the consequences of his actions. Thus, Sloth seems to encompass a large range of behaviours from current hegemonic masculinity practices (Connell 1987; Griffiths 1995) to boys just behaving badly.

Factor III: General Self-Confidence seems to be related to both global positive self-esteem (Dutton & Brown 1997) (I know what I want to do, I can be myself) and being assertive and open (paralleling extraversion) in social interchanges.

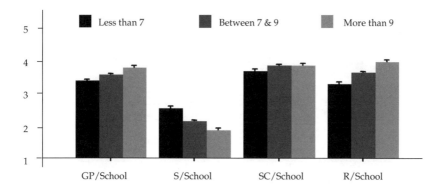

GP = good pupil, S = sloth, SC = self-confidence, R = rational.
Y-axis values depict the full Likert-scale (1-to-5). Error bars indicate 95% confidence intervals.

Figure 14.1. Interaction bars for Socio-Moral Self-Concepts at school context (four-factor-solution, average sum-scores) in three GPA-groups.

Factor IV: Rational Pupil taps how the child evaluates his/her capacity for rational and intelligent, sensible action in order to attain his/her goals.

The General Level of the Socio-Moral Self-Concept

Have Finnish pupils, in general, accepted the dominant socio-moral values as expressed by their Socio-Moral Self-Concept? To answer this question, the average sum scores of the factors were calculated. The distributions of the average sum scores were then grouped according to grade-point averages (GPA) into three categories — 1: GPA higher than 9: high-achievers ($\approx$ 15%); 2: GPA more than or equal to 7, but less than or equal to 9: medium-achievers ($\approx$ 72%); GPA less than 7: low-achievers ($\approx$ 13%). The average level of the moral self-concept dimensions (Good Girl/Good Boy; Rational Self; General Self-Confidence) is rather high for Finnish sixth formers (Figure 14.1), whereas the average value of the Sloth category is low. The self-descriptions are related to the grade-point averages of the pupil. The high-achieving pupils describe themselves as the most sensible and intelligent, most like the Good Girl/Good Boy and the least like Sloth, expressing also

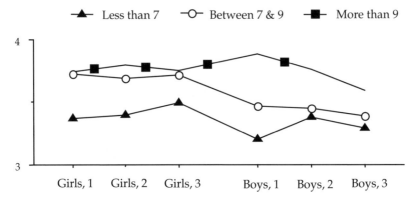

Fathers' educational level 1, low; 2; 3, high.

Y-axis values vary from 3 to 4 (the full scale being 1-5).

Figure 14.2. Interaction line plot for Good Boy/Girl at School in relation to GPA, gender and the educational level of the fathers.

the highest self-confidence levels. The medium-achieving pupil is in the medium range in regard to self-descriptions. The low-achieving pupil defines him/herself as the least rational, the least like the Good Girl/Good Boy, most like Sloth and expresses the lowest self-confidence.

If the average sum scores are also grouped according to gender, and the educational level of the father, a more nuanced picture emerges. Both the high-achieving and medium-achieving girls define themselves very clearly in terms of a 'Good Girl'. This is less typical for the low-achieving girls. The boys define themselves as 'Good Boys', only if they are high-achievers, otherwise their values are markedly lower than those of the girls (Figure 14.2), and the medium achieving boys are close to the low-achieving boys.

In regard to 'Sloth' the picture is the reverse. In general, the highest values on 'Sloth' are related to lowest school performance. The same gender differences appear. High- and medium-achieving girls define themselves the least in terms of Sloth, whereas this is not the case for medium-achieving boys. Only high-achieving boys have low values on Sloth (Figure 14.3). The result raises the question of whether or not only high-achieving boys can free themselves from the code of such reckless hegemonic masculinity, which stands in opposition to some socio-moral values of the school.

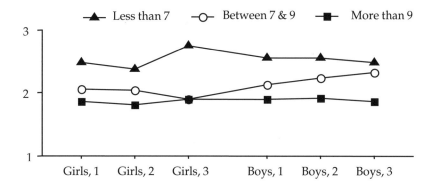

Fathers' educational level 1, low; 2; 3, high.

Y-axis values vary from 1 to 3 (the full scale being 1-5).

Figure 14.3. Interaction line plot for Sloth in relation to GPA, gender and the educational level of the fathers.

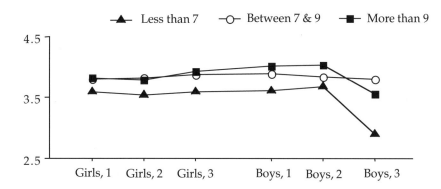

Fathers' educational level 1, low; 2; 3, high.

Y-axis values vary from 2.5 to 4.5 (the full scale being 1-5).

Figure 14.4. Interaction line plot for General Self-Confidence in relation to GPA, gender and the educational level of the fathers.

General Self-Confidence is relatively high for high- and medium-achieving boys and girls. The only problematic group seems to be low achieving boys with academically educated fathers (Figure 14.4).

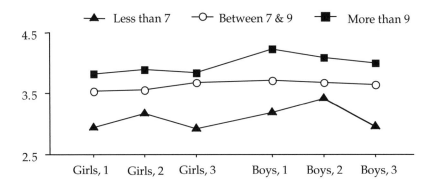

Fathers' educational level 1, low; 2; 3, high.

Y-axis values vary from 2.5 to 4.5 (the full scale being 1-5).

Figure 14.5. Interaction line plot for Rational Self in relation to GPA, gender and the educational level of the fathers.

Apparently, these boys are confronted with a humiliating social comparison situation with their academically educated fathers. There are no gender differences in self-confidence at school (see, however, later). Values on Rational Self are related to the grade point average level; the better the school performance, the more sensible the child thinks s/he is. But at each grade point average level, the boys define themselves as somewhat more sensible and intelligent than the girls (Figure 14.5).

The Effect of Context and Gender: The Grid of the Socio-Moral Self

The children's socio-moral self-concepts were analysed by context and gender, firstly, in relation to Socio-Moral Self-Concept, and, then, in relation to the four average sum scores.

Socio-Moral Self-Concept. As the variable is constructed as a 1PC-factor score there is no context effect for the scores in all the context areas, that means that the absolute value of the scale is not taken into account. A gender effect occurs indicating that contexts have varying effects for boys and

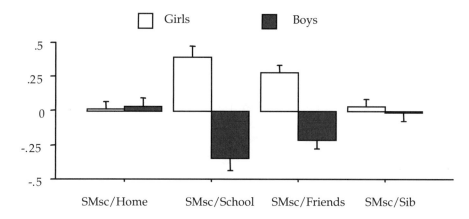

First principal component, scaled to x = 0, SD = 1.
Error bars indicate 95% confidence intervals.

Figure 14.6. Socio-Moral Self-Concept in relation to context (at home with parent, at school with teachers, with friends and with sibling) and gender.

girls (F = 80.9, p < .0001) (Figure 14.6). No differences emerge between the Socio-Moral Self-Concept of the two sexes, when the contexts are with siblings or with parents. The boys are, however, at their worst at school, and there is, of course, a strong interaction effect (F = 102.6, p < .0001).

The result is in accordance with the proposed thesis of the mismatch between the demands of some cultural subvariants of hegemonic masculinity, and the demands of teaching practices at school. The girls, in contrast, assess themselves as the most socio-moral at school, which is in accordance with earlier Finnish research (Takala 1978). The girls also attain higher values on Socio-Moral Self-Concept in the context of being with friends, than is the case for the boys. The results seem to lend support to the thesis of the hypothesised feminine 'self-in-relation' (Chodorow 1990; Gilligan 1990; Hautamäki, A. 1995; Miller 1990), i.e., the greater concern of the girls with relationships and taking responsibility for the relationships and the well being of other persons. The girls therefore seem to be more sensitive to the socio-moral demands of school. This may explain why the girls seem to have acquired the requirements more thoroughly as a regulative part of their self-concept than the boys.

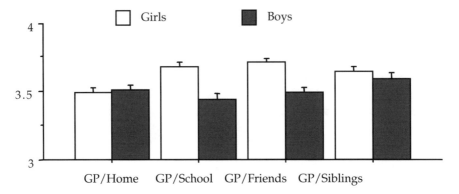

Y-axis values vary from 3 to 4 (the full scale being 1-5).
Error bars indicate 95% confidence intervals.

Figure 14.7. Interaction bars of Good Boy/Good Girl in relation to context (at home with parents, at school with teachers, with friends and with sibling) and gender.

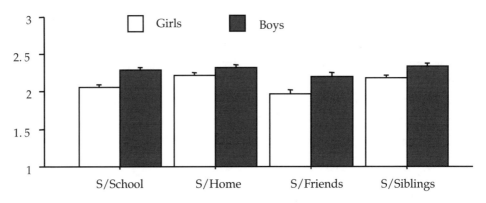

Y-axis values vary from 1 to 3 (the full scale being 1-5).
Error bars indicate 95% confidence intervals.

Figure 14.8. Interaction bars of Sloth in relation to context (at home with parents, at school with teachers, with friends and with sibling) and gender.

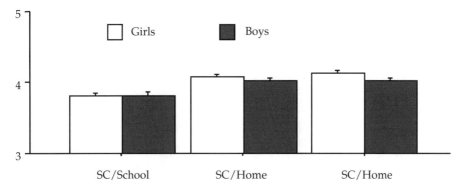

Y-axis values vary from 3 to 5 (the full scale being 1-5).
Error bars indicate 95% confidence intervals.

Figure 14.9. Interaction bars of General Self-Confidence in relation to context (at home with parents, at school with teachers, with friends) and gender.

More detailed results can be obtained from the analyses of the four average sum scores:

1) Good Girl/Good Boy — there are significant context differences (F = 45.5, p < .0001), gender differences (F = 34.4, p < .0001) and interaction effects (F = 60.8, p < .0001) (Figure 14.7). Girls define themselves more in terms of Good Girls than the boys as Good Boys, but the estimates of both sexes vary in accordance with the situation.

2) Sloth — significant differences emerge in terms of context (F = 93.9, p < .0001), gender (F = 51.5, p < .0001) and interaction effects (F = 11.9, p < .0001) (Figure 14.8). The results agree with schematisations formed on the basis of previous research: the notion of the adaptive, even docile girl, reacting sensitively to the demands imposed by the teaching practices, and the robustly acting (even acting out) boy, learning by doing and aiming at mastery. As cultural practice, moderate forms of 'Sloth' may be connected to some cultural subvariants of hegemonic masculinity, especially those analysed by Willis (1980).

3) General Self-Confidence — there is a strong context effect (F = 317.2, p < .0001), and a significant, but small gender effect (F = 5.1, p < .0001) and

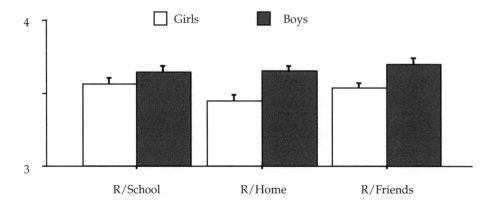

Y-axis values vary from 3 to 4 (the full scale being 1-5).
Error bars indicate 95% confidence intervals.

> Figure 14.10. Interaction bars of Rational Self in relation to context (at home with parents, at school with teachers, with friends) and gender.

a significant interaction (F = 10.6, p < .0001) (Figure 14.9). The context 'siblings' is not incluced.

4) Rational Self — all effects are significant (gender F = 29.9, p < .0001; context F = 17.1, p < .0001; interaction F = 14.4, p < .0001) (Figure 14.10). The gender differences are striking. Boys define themselves as rational in all contexts, whereas girls define themselves as most rational at school, a context in which teaching practices also demand rational and instrumental action. The girls define themselves as the least rational at home. Home also is a place where girls are allowed, sometimes even encouraged, to be more expressive (Rauste-von Wright 1975). The context 'sibling' is not included.

The results based on the F-values from the analyses of variance expressing the strength of the gender and context differences are summarised in the following grid (Figure 14.11). The most generalised feature is the 'Rational Self' and in this regard boys and girls differ, boys defining themselves as more rational. 'Good Girl/Good Boy' and 'Sloth' are less generalised and are more context-bound.

Context sensitivity

	low	high
high	Rational self	Good Boy/Girl Sloth
low		Self-Confidence

Gender effects

Figure 14.11. The grid generalising the results of the effect of context and gender.

In regard to these dimensions, the sexes differ in line with previous research and with the assumption of the more relational self of the girl and positional self of the boy (Chodorow 1978; Gilligan 1982; Hautamäki, A. 1995; Miller 1976; Stein, Newcomb & Bentler 1992). Boys and girls do not differ yet at this age (see Josephs, Markus & Tafardi 1992), in regard to the more context-bound general self-confidence.

More Detailed Analysis

The extended grid (Figure 14.12) presents the 24 descriptors. This grid is formed by summarising the F-values for the descriptors from the analyses of variance, gender and context being the independent variables. The contextual F-values from the analysis of variance are classified into three classes: F-value either non-significant, equal to or less than 10; F-value higher than 10, but equal to or less than 100; and F-value more than 100. The gender dimension is also classified into three classes: F-value either non-significant or equal to or less than 10, F-value higher than 10, but equal to or less than 50, and F-value, higher than 50. The two dimensions are 'context specific' vs. 'generalised across situations', and 'gender specific' vs. 'generalised across the sexes'. The interaction terms are marked with *, when the F-value of a respective term exceeds 20.

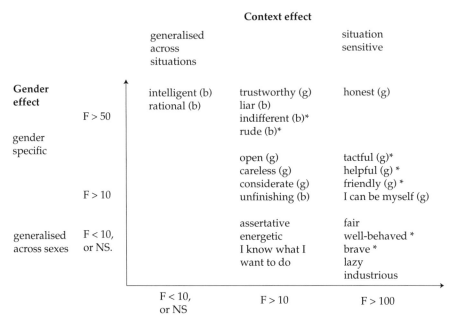

F refers to ANOVA results, the items have been cross-tabulated using values defined
by ANOVA results; item (b, or g), b = boys have a higher mean, g = girls have a higher mean,
* means that Gender x Context interaction is significant (F > 20).

Figure 14.12. The extended grid detailed analysis of the results of the effect
of context and gender on Socio-Moral Self-Concept.

Discussion

Gender differences are found in regard to rationality at each level of
school performance. Twelve-year-old boys define themselves as more rational which is in accordance with earlier research on Finnish youth (Rauste-
von Wright 1975). By contrast, girls express that they can be themselves significantly more often than boys, but boys report, in turn, that they know
what they want to do, i.e., the girls are feeling/being more expressive, the
boys are feeling/being more instrumental. This is in accordance with the old
distinction proposed in 1955 by Parsons & Bales, based on the distribution
of labour between the sexes in the Bourgeois-Patriarchal family. One psychological consequence of this distribution of labour has been the predominance

of relational (communality) themes in the feminine self and the predomin-ance of positional (agency) themes in the masculine self (Bjerrum Nielsen & Rudberg 1991; Stein, Newcomb & Bentler 1992). Yet, as the progressive ten-dency of individualisation also encompasses girls/women (see Bjerrum Nielsen & Rudberg 1994), the question remains: will this complementary and polar relation between the sexes — in regard to both the tasks and the themes of self — change, and will it be replaced by a greater similarity of the tasks and themes of the self of the two sexes?

This seemingly greater acquisition of predominant socio-moral values by girls as expressed by the self-concept may also stem from biased response sets. The socio-moral behaviours described by the items of the Socio-Moral Selves Scale express socially desirable attributes to which girls, according to dominant values in society, should, to a higher degree, be attuned and which the boys do not have to take too seriously. The girls seem to have been more sensitive to the social scripts and have acquired the socio-moral demands of school more thoroughly as a regulative part of their self-concept; they define themselves more in terms of 'Good Girls' than boys define themselves as 'Good Boys', but the estimates vary in accordance with the situation. As a result, the boys are more prone than the girls to express that they oppose prevailing socio-moral values (from reckless to sloth) and this is probably also rooted in the mismatch between some cultural subvariants of hegemonic masculinity and the demands stemming from the teaching practices of pri-mary school. But the estimates vary according to the situation. Self-confi-dence is still the same for the sexes at the age of twelve, but the estimates vary in accordance with the situation. The question of self-confidence is par-ticularly interesting in this sample of Finnish pre-adolescents, as the cog-nitive skills and the school performance of the girls are better than those of the boys (Hautamäki, J. et al. 1999). Will the self-confidence of the girls deteri-orate gradually from pre-adolescence onwards, as Finnish studies from the seventies (Rauste-von Wright 1975) indicate? Or does this generation of girls represent a more individualised generation who have freed themselves from the traditional complementary gender roles (see Bjerrum Nielsen & Rudberg 1994, for an analysis of the process of individualisation and gender roles across three Norwegian generations of women) and who are more flexible and capable than earlier generations of women in combining home and career (Farmer & al. 1980), thus making possible the peaceful coexistence of what were earlier conflicting desires and themes of self?

References

Benjamin, J. (1995). *Like subjects, love objects. Essays on recognition and sexual difference.* New Haven, Conn.: Yale University Press.

Butler, J. (1991). *Gender trouble.* London: Routledge.

Byrne, B.M. & Shavelson, R.J. (1987). Adolescent self-concept: Testing the assumption of equivalent structure across gender. *American Educational Research Journal*, 24, 356-58.

Byrne, B.M. & Shavelson, R.J. (1996). On the structure of social self-concept for
pre-, early and late adolescents: A test of the Shavelson, Hubner, and Stanton
(1976) Model. *Journal of Personality and Social Psychology*, 70(3), 599-613.

Campbell, J.D., Trapnell, P.D., Heine, S.J., Katz, I.M., Lavallee, L.F. & Lehman, D.R.
(1996). Self-concept clarity: Measurement, personality correlates, and cultural
boundaries. *Journal of Personality and Social Psychology*, 70(1), 141-56.

Caspi, A. (1987). Personality in the life-course. *Journal of Personality and Social Psychology*, 53, 1203-13.

Chodorow, N. (1978). *The reproduction of mothering.* Berkeley: University of California Press.

Connell, R.W. (1995). *Masculinities.* Cambridge: Polity Press.

Damon, W. & Hart, D. (1982). The development of self-understanding from in-
fancy through adolescence. *Child Development*, 53, 841-64.

Daniels, H. (ed.) (1996). *An introduction to Vygotsky.* London: Routledge.

Daniels, H. (1998). Research proposal. An unpublished paper. Birmingham: University of Birmingham.

Daniels, H., Hay, V., Leonard, D. & Smith, M. (1996). 'Underachievement' and
'special educational needs': the gendering of special needs practices. Paper
presented at 'ESRC Seminar Series on Gender and Schooling: Are Boys now
Underachieving?' Institute of Education. University of London, May 17th,
1996.

Dutton, K.A. & Brown, J.D. (1997). Global self-esteem and specific self-views as
determinants of people's reactions to success and failure. *Journal of Social and
Personality Psychology*, 73, 139-48.

Elkonin, D.B. (1977). Toward the problem of stages in the mental development of
the child. In M. Cole (ed.), *Soviet developmental psychology.* New York: M.E.
Sharpe Inc.

Erikson, E.H. (1977). *Childhood and society.* Frogmore, St. Albans: Herts.

Farmer, H.S. & Fyans, Jr., L.J. (1980). Women's achievement and career motivation:
Their risk taking patterns, home-career conflict, sex role orientation, fear of
success, and self-concept. In L.J. Fyans, Jr. (ed.), *Achievement motivation. Recent
trends in theory and research.* New York: Plenum Press.

Gergen, K.J. (1991). *The saturated self. Dilemmas of identity in contemporary life*. New York: Basic Books.

Gergen, K.J. & Morse, S. (1967). Self-consistency: Measurement and validation. *Proceedings of the American Psychological Association*, 75, 207-8.

Giddens, A. (1991). *Modernity and self-identity: Self and society in the late modern age*. Cambridge: Polity Press.

Gilligan, C. (1982). *In a different voice: psychological theory and women's development*. Cambridge, Mass.: Harvard University Press.

Glass, J. (1995). *Shattered selves*. Ithaca: Cornell University Press.

Griffiths, M. (1995). Learning to be autonomous: Learning to be cruel. Paper presented at the 'Women's Studies Network Conference', University of Stirling, 23-25th June, 1995.

Harter, S. (1988). Developmental processes in the construction of the Self. In T.D. Yawkey & J.E. Johnson (eds.), *Integrative processes and socialization: Early to middle childhood*. Hillsdale, N.J.: Erlbaum.

Harter, S. (1990a). Issues in the assessment of the self-concept of children and adolescents. In A.M. LaGreca (ed.), *Through the eyes of a child: Obtaining self-reports from children and adolescents*. Boston: Allyn & Bacon.

Harter, S. (1990b). Causes, correlates and the functional role of global self-worth: A life span perspective. In R.J. Sternberg & J. Kolligian (eds.), *Competence considered*. New Haven, Conn.: Yale University Press.

Harter, S. (1990c). Processes underlying adolescent self-concept formation. In R. Montemayor, G.R. Adams & T.P. Gulotta (eds.), *From childhood to adolescence: A transitional period*. Newbury Park, Calif.: Sage.

Hautamäki, A. (1982). *Activity environment, social class and voluntary learning. An interpretation and application of Vygotsky's concepts*. Research Reports, Series A, 22. University of Joensuu.

Hautamäki, A. (1986). Activity environment, social class and educational career: Development of mastery among 11-17-year-olds. *Scandinavian Journal of Educational Research*, 30, 1-16.

Hautamäki, A. (1987). Ungdom och dens kultur i spänningsfältet mellan individ och samhälle — sett i systemperspektiv. In I. Bo (ed.) *Ungdom i systemperspektiv. Nordiska forskningsbidrag*. Bergen: Sigma forlag.

Hautamäki, A. (1995). *Masochism — the riddle of femininity? A developmental perspective*. Swedish School of Social Science, Research Reports 6. Helsinki: University of Helsinki.

Hautamäki, A. (1997). Postmoderni perhe toimintaympäristönä — kodin ja koulun vuorovaikutussuhde. In Jakku-Sihvonen (ed.), *Onnistuuko oppiminen? Oppimistuloksien ja oppimisen laadun arviointiperusteita peruskoulussa ja lukiossa*. (Arviointi 3). Helsinki: National Board of Education.

Hautamäki, A. (1998). Mistä on pienet tytöt tehty, mistä on pienet pojat tehty? — Sukupuolilinssi ja sukupuoli-identiteetin kehitys. In E. Saarinen (ed.), *Sairaan ja vammaisen lapsen hyvä elämä*. Lastensuojelun keskusliitto. Helsinki: Edita.

Hautamäki, A. & Hautamäki, J. (1997). Koululaispersoonallisuuden kehitys ja oppimaan oppiminen. In R. Jakku-Sihvonen (ed.), *Onnistuuko oppiminen — oppimistulosten ja opetuksen laadun arviointiperusteita peruskoulussa ja lukiossa*. (Arviointi 3). Helsinki: National Board of Education.

Hautamäki, A. & Hautamäki, J. (1998). Establishing the seriousness of learning — Generalization of the self-conceptions of the self-regulated learner. Paper presented to the '4th Congress of the International Society for Cultural Research and Activity Theory', Symposium: Learning Activity and Development, June 9-11, 1998, Århus, Denmark.

Hautamäki, A. & Hautamäki, J. (1999). Minä koulussa ja omat koulutavoitteet — sosiomoraalinen minäkäsitys ja usko koulutehtävien suorittamiseen. In J. Hautamäki, P. Arinen, B. Bergholm, A. Hautamäki, S. Kupiainen, J. Kuusela, J. Lehto, M. Niemivirta & P. Scheinin (eds.), *Oppimaan oppiminen ala-asteilla*. (Oppimistulosten arviointi 3). Helsinki: Finnish Board of Education.

Hautamäki, J. (1994). Developmental tasks and school learning: Why and how to assess and promote the development of thinking by setting matched tasks for primary school pupils. In Jan ter Laak (ed.), *Voronovo thoughts on developmental tasks*. Utrecht: Utrecht University.

Hautamäki, J., Arinen, P., Bergholm, B., Hautamäki, J., Kuusela, J., Lehto, J., Kupiainen, S., Niemivirta, M. & Scheinin, P. (1999). *Oppimaan oppiminen ala-asteella*. Oppimistulosten arviointi 3/99. Helsinki: National Board of Education.

Hautamäki, J., Arinen, P., Hautamäki, A., Lehto, J., Kupiainen, S., Niemivirta, M. & Scheinin, P. (1997), *Oppimaan oppiminen Helsingissä*. Research Publications of Helsinki City Board of Education A:10:1997. Helsinki: Helsinki City Educational Board.

Havighurst, R.J. (1948/1974). *Developmental tasks and education*. (3rd ed.). New York: McKay.

Heymans, P. (1994). Developmental tasks: Towards a cultural analysis of human development. In J. ter Laak, A.I. Podolskij & P.G. Heymans (eds.), *Developmental tasks: a cultural analysis of human development*. Dordrecht: Kluwer.

Heymans, P., Karabanova, O., Podolski, A., Zacharova, H. & Polivanova, K. (1996). *The acquisition of socio-moral competencies. Part 2: Personal development in Vidnoie's adolescents*. EEC/INTAS Project report #93-2576.

Josephs, R.A., Markus, H.R. & Tafardi, R.W. (1992). Gender and self-esteem. *Journal of Personality and Social Psychology*, 63, 391-402.

Kohlberg, L. (1976). Moral stages and moralization: the cognitive-developmental approach. In T. Lickona (ed.), *Moral development and behavior: Theory, research and social issues*. New York: Holt, Rinehart & Winston.

Markus, H.R. (1977). Self-schemata and processing information about the self. *Journal of Personality and Social Psychology*, 35, 63-78.

Markus, H.R. & Nurius, P. (1986). Possible selves. *American Psychologist*, 41, 954-69.

Markus, H.R. & Wurf, E. (1987). The dynamic self-concept: A social psychological perspective. *Annual Review of Psychology*, 38, 299-337.

Marsh, H.W. (1990). A multi-dimensional, hierarchical self-concept: Theoretical and empirical justification. *Educational Psychology Review*, 2, 77-172.

Mayer, K.U. (1986). Structural constraints on the life-course. *Human Development*, 29, 163-70.

Miller, J.B. (1976). *Toward a new psychology of women*. Boston: Beacon Press.

Miller, J.B. (1990). The development of women's sense of self. In C. Zanardi (ed.), *Essential papers on the psychology of women*. New York, London: New York University Press.

Montemayor, R. & Eisen, M. (1977). The development of the self-conceptions from childhood to adolescence. *Developmental Psychology*, 13, 314-19.

Nielsen, H. Bjerrum & Rudberg, M. (1991). *Historien om pojkar och flickor*. Lund: Studentlitteratur.

Nielsen, H. Bjerrum & Rudberg, M. (1994). *Psychological gender and modernity*. Oslo, Copenhagen, Stockholm: Scandinavian University Press.

Nurmi, J.E. (1993). Adolescent development in an age-graded context: The role of personal beliefs, goals and strategies in the tackling of developmental tasks and standards. *International Journal of Behavioural Development*, 16, 169-89.

Parsons, T. & Bales, R.S. (1955). *Family, socialization and interaction process*. Illinois: Free Press.

Peters, H. (1996). *Psychology: The historical dimension*. Tilburg: Syntax Publishers.

Pölkki, P. (1978). Koulutulokkaiden minäkäsitys eri kasvuympäristöissä. *Reports from the Department of Psychology, 210*. Jyväskylä: University of Jyväskylä.

Rauste-von Wright, M-L. (1975). The image of man among Finnish girls and boys on the basis of material from Helsinki and North Karelia. *Reports from the Department of Psychology, University of Turku, 41*.

Shavelson, R.J., Hubner, J. & Stanton, G. (1976). Self-concept: Validation of construct interpretations. *Review of Educational Research*, 46, 407-41.

Shavelson, R.J. & Marsh, H.W. (1986). On the structure of self-concept. In R. Schwartzer (ed.), *Anxiety and Cognition*. Hillsdale, N.J.: Erlbaum, 305-30.

Stein, J.A., Newcomb, M.D. & Bentler, P.M. (1992). The effect of agency and communality on self- esteem: Gender differences in longitudinal studies. *Sex Roles*, 26, 465-83.

Takala, M. (1978). Koulutulokkaiden tottuminen kouluympäristöön opettajien havaitsemana. *Reports from the Department of Psychology, 205*. Jyväskylä: University of Jyväskylä.

Walker, L.J. (1988). The development of moral reasoning. *Annals of Child Development*, 5, 33-78.

Walker, L.J. (1991). Sex differences in moral reasoning. In W.M. Kurtines & J.L. Gewirtz (eds.), *Handbook of moral behavior and development: research: Vol.2.* Hillsdale, N.J.: Erlbaum.

Werner, H. (1957). The concept of development from a comparative and organismic point of view. In D.B. Harris (ed.), *The concept of development*. Minneapolis: University.

Willis, P. (1980). *Learning to labour. How working class kids get working class jobs.* Westmead: Gower.

Classroom Interaction and Discourse

15 The Construction of Contemporary Subjectivity: Interactions between Knowledge and School Environment

Solange Jobim e Souza

The aim of this article is to search for an understanding of the experience that children have with school in the contemporary world. To achieve this, we have taken into account the dialogue that occurred between adults and children in the context of research into the subjects of school environment and knowledge. It is important to say that we consider language as the locus in which we produce meaning from our experience, which in turn can be shared with others.

In this study we found that ambiguousness and the verging and diverging which characterise both the child and adult discourses, show us, on the one hand, an idealisation of this place called school but, on the other hand, discards the classical vision of the ideal place. We grasp in the spoken word the movements of building and unbuilding the meanings attributed not only to the school, but also to the institutions which form the scenery of political and cultural experiences in a given society. Nevertheless, it is also in and by the word that we can engineer the most significant social changes which will give a new meaning and transform human experience, introducing new challenges to be successfully overcome in the near future.

* This text was produced during the research project 'Contemporary Subjectivities — Childhood and Adolescence in Consumer Society', financed by CNP (National Research Council) and FAPERJ (State of Rio de Janeiro Research Council). The first part of the project, 'Childhood in Modern Times', was written in partnership with Rita Marisa Ribes Pereira, with whom I have worked and studied on this theme, both in research and in a course for pre-school teachers which we held together at PUC-Rio (Catholic University of Rio). I would like to explain that the dialogues with the children that are presented in this study were taken from interviews made for the video-text 'Once Upon a Time … a School', produced in 1997 by the Psychology Department at PUC-Rio. This video-text was written and directed by Solange Jobim e Souza, Maria Florentina Camerini and Maria Cecília Morais.

First, we discuss and criticise the rationalised concept of childhood which, due to the Enlightenment approach, has greatly influenced developmental psychology in modern times. Afterwards, as a way of building new paradigms to answer our questions in a more satisfactory way, we took up the challenge of assuming a social and historical concept of the child, and used the dialogical approach in our interview with children. It is understandable that the child needs the adult, but it is essential that we recognise that the adult also needs the child, because only then will it be possible to build up a better and deeper understanding of the vicissitudes of the contemporary world. We are convinced that talking with the child presents an opportunity for us to recover, by way of the child's point of view, a critical view of all that is lacking in our culture.

Childhood in Modern Times

The production of knowledge about childhood is closely linked to the social place the child holds in relation to 'other people'. Our initial concern, therefore, is to reveal and emphasise transformations and orientations on the concept of childhood throughout time. Only then, can we grasp the necessary theoretical tools to help understand the experience of 'being a child' and the vicissitudes that childhood represents in the contemporary world. Of course, each period of time expresses its ideals and expectations in relation to children, and this will bring consequences in the formation of the individual. To make it clearer, the production and consumption of concepts about childhood by society as a whole will interfere directly with the behaviour of children, adolescents and adults. Their acts and attitudes will be modelled in accordance with the expectations generated by this discourse which will exist among people. These expectations will correspond to the cultural, political and economic interests of a broader social context (Jobim e Souza 1997).

In the Enlightenment approach, the child is seen in a paradoxical way. Although childhood is the time and place for the passions, desires and experience itself that precede the limits imposed by word and reason, it is also a potential depository for something which will be revealed in the future, that is, the way in which we become adults endowed with reason. As a consequence, the task of transforming these small 'imperfect' beings into men/women endowed with language and logos — future citizens who are responsible, independent and self-sufficient, is left to education. Let us explain, however, that although the Enlightenment has placed the child in a conflicting situation between incompetence and at the same time the denial of his/her presumed condition of incompleteness, it is thanks to the Enlightenment ideas that the child was actually recognised as a subject of study by science. The modern concept of science admits truth as certainty, and takes responsibility in explaining, organising, filing and rationalising the 'real' and the 'being' in their wholeness. It is within this context that science radically transforms the feelings of modern people in relation to childhood, and make it an object of research.

When trying to free men from the evil that ignorance or 'not knowing' represents, and transforming them into lords of the world via reason, the Enlightenment also inaugurated concern with the child and his/her formation. This concern, although at a pioneer stage, had no intention of dealing with the peculiarities of this period of life; on the contrary, it is denied, since the real interest was the 'small adult', the man of tomorrow. Therefore, at that time, childhood was understood as an ephemeral, temporary and transitory stage that must be accelerated. To grow up means to become a being of reason, and this maturation, like fruit in a hothouse, must be hastened (Nunes & Pereira 1996).

The so-called modern life is structured under the sign of reason. The idea of progress, brought forward by the industrial revolution and by Darwin's theory of evolution, is strengthened by monopolist capitalism and supported by positivist theories. History is seen as a chain of successive well-defined dimensions — past, present and future — crystallised by the laws of casualness and unfolded by the concepts of cause and consequence. Therefore, 'social reality is submitted to a method which claims to be universal and unitary: the scientific method, organised by non-social procedures' (Matos 1989). The idea of a directive science will take us, necessarily, to forecasting time, history and life, because, if the human social experience allows itself to be held captive by an objective science, what is settled is the idea that any process can be decided beforehand (Horkheimer and Adorno 1986). When we try an approximation between the course of the psychology of development and the Enlightenment ideas, we come to a fundamental question: up to which extent would the phases or stages in the development of the child, described according to the psychological theories, be forging an excessive rationalisation of childhood and, in this manner, engineering a developmentalist speech, supported by psychological science, that establishes ways and possibilities on whose basis human life might make sense.

The way in which we relate to childhood reveals the forms of control of the social history of contemporary individuals. The need to control the future causes existence itself to be absolutely submitted to foreknowledge. Past, present and future unfold in phases, reinforcing the idea of a previously decided linear process. Each phase corresponds to a precise behaviour and through this timely relationship the criteria of 'normality' and of the 'good course' of development itself are constructed. Science and specialised knowledge take on the role of 'explaining' childhood and establishing the criteria to legitimate 'good' education for the child. Therefore, the psychologist, the psycho-pedagogue, the language therapist, the psychometrist, the paediatrician, and even the media professionals, take on the role of characterising the child and his/her needs, defining educational goals and offering essential subsidies for social regulation to discipline the course of life. As a continuation of the principle according to which science is the criterion of truth, the authority is given to the specialist to produce 'truths' about child education in modern times. The family is left with a growing insecurity and uncertainty about their role in the orientation of the education of their children.

The psychology of development has taken charge of supporting and divulging this position, as Buck-Morss (1987) exposes, as well as 'invigilating' human development, through pre-conceived rules which stimulate maturation, selecting and adapting the 'proper' activities for each stage in the development of the child. What becomes evident, much more than understanding and explaining human development, is the rationalisation of childhood legitimated by scientific knowledge. That which could be understood as the building-up of the individual by means of his/her social-historical insertion, is adulterated in a process of 'submission' of the child to a scientificist, universalising and a-historical model of development. And, although we question the limitations imposed by this position, we admit the difficulty in escaping it, as we are constantly surprised and concerned when life challenges the rule: 'Two years old and still can't talk?', 'Still can't pee in the potty!', 'This is no child business', 'You're too old for that ...', 'What will you be when you grow up?' etc. These and many other sentences follow us since birth and threaten us as an accelerator that *tic-tacks* time. Grow up. Future. Hurry, a lot of hurry ...

To understand contemporary experience we must go back to the historical and philosophical paradigms that orient the different concepts of childhood throughout time. The more everyday life becomes complex, the more we feel the need to equate it or make a problem out of it, taking into consideration the increasing number of types of behaviour and social practices that feed the emerging culture. Our concern is to build up an understanding of the contemporary experience of childhood which will allow us to redefine the social place occupied by the individuals in the complex web of intersubjective and social-ideological relationships of which they are made.

Using a Dialogical Approach to do Research with Children

The child is not tomorrow: he/she is today — now — a being who participates in the construction of the history and culture of the time. Nevertheless, one of the main problems we have to face today is the crystallisation of concepts, world views and interpretations of the child which consider him/her as an abstract form, a category separated from social context, resistant to class relations, nothing but an organism in the process of development and socialisation, a 'someone to-be' in the distant future.

To think of the child in this way makes it impossible to have a true dialogue with him/her, or better, makes it impossible to have that dialogue in which he/she shows the social and cultural spaces from whence his/her voice and desire arise in confronting the experience gathered to date. The child must not be seen as an object but, rather, as an individual who will build up a new knowledge from her interaction with adults.

Our analysis takes into consideration that the child's oral manifestation, as well as the adult's, is a result of conversation between the two. It is influenced by the context of its production, apart from other factors that precede the meeting between the child and the adult, but which, in a certain sense, become present at the time of the interview, and are up-dated by the tension of that moment. We understand each interview as the expression of a discourse, both singular and collective. We try, in this way, to unbuild the polarity *individual versus social*, since the individual is made *of* and *by* the language and is, therefore, a being who is built up in the confrontation with the other and with the cultural productions of his time.

As we reflect upon this understanding of childhood, we come to a methodological question related to research in the area of psychology and, consequently, with the need to redefine the social place the child holds in his/her interaction with the adult within this context. The way in which we think and understand the discourse that arises from an interview, shows us that this material does not come in a unilateral way, as it is not offered as a product from the child or the adult alone and, therefore, made of 'data' or simple information that will build a model to explain childhood. On the contrary, we understand the situation of the interview as a moment in which the construction of a conversation happens, and it will reveal the various senses which arise in that specific dialogue situation, and in that way setting limits to part of the aspects which exist in the everyday experience of the interlocutors regarding the theme in question. So, the analysis itself of this discourse material represents a mode of conversation that, far from trying to find absolute interpretations in the selected fragments, will try to unveil the possible senses which arise from this meeting of child and adult, and, in this way, amplify and diversify the ways of understanding a specific cultural phenomenon. Our proposal for analysis is, more than anything, an attempt to feed the discussions about the contemporary and the social, political and ideological place that the individuals — adults and children — hold in this configuration. It is during the flow of verbal interaction that the word is changed and gains different meanings according to the context in which it appears. Constituted by the phenomenon of social interaction, the dialogue reveals itself as a kind of link between language and life (Bakhtin 1981, 1985).

All spheres of human activity are related to the use of language. Even when the character and the form that the language takes in everyday social relations are as multiple as the human activities themselves, one cannot deny the existence of systematic ways of using the language in daily social life, which we call 'discoursive styles' (Bakhtin 1985). Therefore, to apprehend and interpret the 'discoursive styles' which appear in everyday life is to admit language as a mediator of the historical and cultural movements and of the place the individual holds in this intermediation.

The child holds a knowledge which must be taken into consideration. Therefore, the first step for the adult would be to invert the position in relation to the child, that is, have the child as a partner in the search for a deeper understanding of the experience that both of them share every day. This means that instead of assuming that adult knowledge is necessarily superior to that of the child, one assumes that both the child and the adult bear distinct possibilities of understanding the shared experiences. These differences enrich our understanding and broaden our critical view of daily life in the intersubjective relations between children and adults. The building-up of the individual, within this perspective, is a consequence of the meanings that are built through verbal exchanges in various everyday situations.

However, we must say that each specific context is responsible for the course the dialogue takes in a given interview, and that both the child's and the adult's utterances are always situated in the context which originated them. Each period in time and each social group have their own types of discourse which work as a mirror, reflecting and refracting everyday life. The word is the revelation of a space in which the fundamental values of a given society explain and confront each other. The text of the interviews puts us face-to-face with the world as we have built and idealised it, whether in its perverse or stigmatised aspects, or in its critical and transforming dimension of the established order. Therefore, to talk with the child is an opportunity for us to recover, through the child's viewpoint, a critical view of the deficiencies in our culture.

The interviews that we have done during the research work will be analysed in the next section. The children who were interviewed are aged between 7 and 12, come from different social layers and study at state or private schools. We have chosen to leave this information open, since we believe that the children's texts make the reader ask this kind of question and stimulate his interpretation of the dialogues. We do not intend to place the children's discourses into pre-established categories, limiting the origin of these utterances by formal socially settled aspects, and thus weakening the interpretation. Our analysis aims at interpreting the flow of the social discourse, and the interpretation it involves tries to save what 'is said' from the possibility of becoming extinct and fixing it in researchable forms. It is important to say that we are not looking for a consensus, but a refining of the debate (Geertz 1989).

What Children and Adults Say About School and Knowledge

During the interviews, the issue of school is inevitably present in conversations between adults and children. If we find what should seem so obvious to be strange, it would be relevant to ask why the issue is so recurrent. This issue of school was sometimes brought up by the child, but, when this did not happen, the adult would always end up talking about it. Since the interviews did not follow a pre-determined or fixed route, we find the recurrence of a certain subject quite significant. The dialogue that takes place, whether it was started by the adult or the child, in this specific context, takes us to a position which is clearly identified by the interlocutors — 'a child's place is in school'. We are not questioning the necessity of school, but calling attention to the fact that this imposition is not enough to ensure that it fulfils its function. Today, the decreased interest we witness in relation to the school experience is as evident as the school being obligatory. Perhaps, because school is compulsory, meaning the individual cannot exert his 'free will', conversation on this subject almost inevitably ends up dealing with whether one 'likes' or 'doesn't like' school and the activities that take place there every day.

Adult 1:   Do you like to study or do you think it is boring?
Child: Oh, so-so. I like it. I mean, I don't really like it, but I study. I don't like and like it.
Adult: How is that?
Child: It's like this: sometimes I have a class that's good, sometimes it's a difficult class …

…

Adult: When you are at school, what is your day like?
Child: Everything's boring.
Adult: Is that so? Why?
Child: Because I don't like to stay in school.
Adult: Don't you?
Child: No. It's very boring to do school work.

…

Adult: Do you like to study?
Child: Is this some kind of joke? I hate to study. I detest it.

…

Adult: Your school, what's it like? Do you like it there?
Child: Yes.

In these dialogues, it becomes evident that the adult wishes to find out how the child feels about and interprets 'school obligation'. He wants to know if in that space the opportunities of pleasure and of play are preserved, or if pleasure and obligation are compatible experiences. On her part, the child is clear about it: the school becomes negative, a place of displeasure, when associated with study, but positive, when seen as a space where you can make friends, play and subvert the established order. In that sense, pleasure is often related to school activities when it arises from friendship and games.

Adult 2:	What is your class at school like?
Child:	A real mess. I like it.
Adult:	Do you like messing around?
Child:	Love it.
Adult:	Do the teachers complain?
Child:	They do, but we don't care (laughter).

...

Adult:	What do you like best at your school? What's the best?
Child:	Friends, of course.

...

Adult:	And what is it like in school?
Child:	Oh, it's very good.
Child:	I play ping-pong, ball, volleyball ...
Child:	I play football.

Notice that a series of activities are mentioned which are part of children's life both in and out of school. However, whilst the emphasis during the conversation should be on the school activity. The interview, at some moments, goes down other paths and the conversation gets 'off the track'. We get the idea that, despite the effort the adult makes to keep the conversation in a certain direction, the other topics finally take the place which 'should' belong to the school.

Adult 3:	Talk a little about your day. What do you do?
Child:	I study, mm ... on Tuesday, I play ball at half-past-one, mm ... on Wednesday I play ball at five on the indoors field (...) Sometimes I go to the street market, then I give some money to my mother (...) I play capoeira at half-past-seven with mestre Garrincha. Sometimes I make a show, the guys call me (...)
Adult:	Oh! And where do you study?

...

Adult:	Would you like to say something about school. You've said almost nothing about what you think of your school?
Child:	I always when ... on Fridays and Saturdays, I go to parties. I like funk parties. They are very good.
Adult:	I had asked about school (laughter). Your talked about parties ...
Child:	School? Oh, school isn't very good, no. Nearly every day we get rice-meal as a snack. That's a horrible snack. Tasteless rice.

The adult asks the child about her studies, which indicates the value he places on knowledge and intellectual development. The child, however, wants to show the adult the social and affective spaces from where she extracts her desires and her pleasure. In the emotions which arise, adult and child struggle to establish a basis of mutual understanding, but unsuccessfully. Therefore, in the interview situation, the theme is not an isolated manifestation from the interlocutors' point of view; it takes on the form that was possible in that specific context.

An issue that stands out is the fact that everyday school activities are felt and explained within a fundamental scission: studying versus playing, making friends, practising sports, etc. At certain moments during the interviews, it becomes evident that the decision as to whether the school is good, bad or indifferent is much more a question related to social contacts, leisure activities or the guarantee of a concrete subsistence (to feed the children at school) than to the, let's say, more official function of the school, which is to teach specific syllabuses and allow a certain social upgrading through study. However, even if 'studying' does not mean personal pleasure, we visualise in the discourse, both by the adult and by the child, that it means the 'promise of a future'. Study is worshipped as being a means of access to the place held by the adult, further on, since it is study that will allow 'salary, dignified and honest work, a profession' (sic). In such moments, the children show a possible identification with the adult through positive identification with the school.

Anyway, how is knowledge built in school? How do children refer to the teacher and talk about the knowledge produced in school? The best way to find out about this is to let the child answer it.

Adult 4:   What is a good class like?
Child: It's when the teacher asks me to write on the board the names of the people who are talking.
Adult: Write names on the board?
Child: It's like this: the teacher says to me 'Evandro, take a piece of chalk from the box and write the names of those who are talking and not paying attention. The people you write on the board will have to do verbs and be punished.'
Adult: And do you like that?

Child: Sure! I don't have to do anything, just write the names on the board. I get everyone into trouble. They just have to open their mouths and I write their names on the board.

Adult: What about you? Don't you ever talk?

Child: I used to talk a bit in second grade and in first grade. Then the teacher punished me by making me do the multiplication chart on the board, so never again.

...

Child: This is the first test I get a *D* in.

Adult: So, the first. Is it bad to get a bad mark in a test?

Child: Of course.

Adult: Why?

Child: Because your mother beats you.

...

Adult: What about the things you study in there, what are they like?

Child: It's pencil and notebook ... The classroom is good, isn't it?

...

Adult: Why do you study?

Child: To have a better future. To have a better life.

...

Child: School is good because you can improve in your job. School teaches.

The children's text shows us in an expressive way the fundamental paradox of school experience nowadays. The proof that the school, throughout its existence, has become the very place where the child risks losing, perhaps forever, the possibility of having a dignified and true relationship with knowledge and its endless possibilities of transforming the individual and the culture. Both the teacher and the student face an everyday relation with knowledge and school activities which is totally technical and instrumental, devoid of meaning, but which fills the tremendous emptiness into which school has been transformed. In scenes such as these, which are repeated in classrooms throughout the country, what other options can intervene in and vivify the meeting between the teacher and the student? In which way can the relation with school knowledge be changed? The dialogues between children and adults show us that the teacher no longer talks about the place of knowledge, but of the place where it has become impossible to make this knowledge come true. There is mutual disbelief. While the child does not believe in great changes in school, the teacher, on his part, expresses low expectation in what regards the student. The consequences of this perverse pact are disastrous for the formation of the child.

Paradoxically, what stands out from the interviews we have made is that, although school today generates a feeling of uneasiness, it also cradles the promise of a better future. The school cannot be seen only as a place to be valued, or the opposite. In between these two extremes there is a series of nuances which say much about the school experience in a society split in the distribution of its cultural assets, thus making a positive school experience a privilege enjoyed by only a small portion of the population. The exclusion strategies are defined, on the one hand, by the political and economical organisation which sustains our social context in a broader, more hegemonic way. On the other hand, they are constantly up-dated in the interactions between people in the most distinct contexts. The school is one of the privileged institutions where we can exercise the experience of reproducing or subverting the established order.

Childhood and Contemporaneity: New Challenges

Children no longer mingle with adults. They write their histories separately. In the past children were used to mingle with adults, and every gathering, whether for work or play, put children and adults together. However, nowadays, there is a growing tendency to separate the child's world from the adults', and this is one of the most radical consequences for modern childhood. The education of children, which used to happen in this natural environment of work and leisure, was substituted by schooling. Work required a more specialised knowledge, thereby starting a long process of 'confining' children, and adults also, which in our time goes from schooling up to more sophisticated and subtle ways of spatial confinement. Therefore, it is necessary to build the theoretical instruments that will allow us to think about the organisation of the time-space in which we live today, trying to explain the new forms of 'violence' engineered by electronic technology.

Within these questions is the issue of alterability, but from other parameters. Perhaps in the form of complicity, a whole generation that escapes the care of adults is no longer concerned about becoming adult, assuming the destiny of an endless and aimless adolescence. A generation that becomes self sufficient, without caring about the other, eventually violent with the 'other', against the adult no longer seen as the antecedent (Baudrillard 1995). Yes, children no longer recognise themselves as the continuation of their parents' history, they have become strangers in their own homes. Transformed by us, without piety or indignation, into merchandise of a time, the contemporary child's fate is to float eternally among adults who do not know what to do with the child anymore. As a consequence, children start to share with each other their most frequent experiences, which in most cases is limited to contact with the televised other, distant, virtual, mechanical (Jobim e Souza et al. 1997).

This distancing from the adult thrusts the child into a world of culture, mediated by identification with a virtual order. After all, who are the children and the adolescents of this new age, deprived of objective limits, but who float, however, in an electronic Eden, showing their intense and spontaneous affinity with the new technologies?

It is essential that this lack of dialogue be taken into consideration with respect to our acquisition of knowledge about childhood. If in modern times the child starts to be seen as an individual, gains a new status and is valued for his/her ability to build a dialogue, the absence of the adult interlocutor will condemn him/her to a monologue which will have as a consequence the creation of a 'childhood ghetto'. The rebuilding of this dialogue is the challenge proposed for the 'childhood experts'.

References:

Adorno, T., Horkheimer, M. (1986). *Dialética do esclarecimento*. Rio de Janeiro: Zahar.

Ariès, P. (1978). *História Social da Criança e da Família*. Rio de Janeiro: Guanabara.

Bakhtin, M. (1981). *Marxismo e filosofia da linguagem*. São Paulo: Hucitec.

Bakhtin, M. (1985). *Estética de la creación berbal*. Madrid: Siglo XXI editores.

Baudrillard, J. (1995). Le continent noir de l'enfance. *Journal Liberation*, 18/10/95.

Benjamin, W. (1987). *Infância em Berlim por volta de 1900*. In Walter Benjamin (ed.), *Obras Escolhidas*. Vol. II. São Paulo: Brasiliense.

Buck-Morss, S. (1987). Piaget, Adorno and dialectical operations. In J.M. Broughton (ed.), *Critical theories of psychological development*. New York and London: Plenum Express.

Gagnebin, J.M. (1997). *Linguagem, Memória e História*. Rio de Janeiro: Imago.

Geertz, C. (1989). *A interpretação das culturas*. Rio de Janeiro: LTC editora.

Jobim e Souza, S. (1996). Re-significando a psicologia do desenvolvimento: Uma contribuição crítica à pesquisa da infância. In S. Kramer & M.I. Leite (eds.), *Infância: Fios e Desafios da Pesquisa*. Campinas: Papirus.

Jobim e Souza, S. (1997). *Infância e Linguagem*. Campinas: Papirus.

Jobim e Souza, S., Castro, L.R. (1994/95). Desenvolvimento humano e questões para um final de século: tempo, história e memória. *Psicologia Clínica: Pós-graduação e Pesquisa: Vol. 6.* NAU, PUC-Rio.

Jobim e Souza, S., Garcia, C.A. & Castro, L.R. (1997). Mapeamentos para a compreensão da infância contemporânea. In S. Jobim e Souza, C.A. Garcia & L.R. Castro (eds.), *Infância, Cinema e Sociedade.* Rio de Janeiro: Ravil/Escola de Professores.

Lins, D. (1997). *Cultura e Subjetividade — Saberes nômades.* Campinas: Papirus.

Matos, O. (1989). *Os arcanos do inteiramente outro.* São Paulo: Brasiliense.

Nunes, M.F. & Pereira, R.M.R. (1996). Buscando o mito nas malhas da razão: uma conversa sobre educação e teoria crítica. In S. Jobim e Souza, S. Kramer (eds.), *Histórias de professores.* São Paulo: Ática.

Pasolini, P.P. (1990). *Os Jovens Infelizes. Antologia de Ensaios Corsários.* São Paulo: Brasiliense.

16 A Relational Approach to Understanding Classroom Practice

Carol Linehan and John McCarthy

Introduction

Our aim in this chapter is to describe aspects of participation in one primary school classroom with a view to specifying some patterns of organising in this particular community of practice. We use 'community of practice' as a generative metaphor for our analysis of participation in classroom activities and not as a designation of the pedagogical practices observed there. We will draw on approaches to 'community' particularly those of Greeno (1998), Rogoff, Matusov & White (1996) and Lave (Lave 1988; Chaiklin & Lave 1993; Lave & Wenger 1991) and on the basis of our empirical analyses of classroom interaction, nuance the community of practice metaphor. As the particular classroom environment we studied does not fit the stereotype for a communitarian pedagogical environment, it is an interesting test bed for the general value of the metaphor.

Participation in a Community of Practice

Putting the spotlight on any particular aspect of an activity can be either illuminating of the potential for change and development or inhibiting. By definition, it foregrounds some aspects in an analysis and backgrounds others and it is difficult to predict at the outset whether the choice of aspects to foreground will be illuminating or not. Shotter (1996) has pointed out that Wittgenstein's approach was to look for new ways of looking at things, to give 'prominence to distinctions which our ordinary forms of language easily make us overlook' (Wittgenstein 1953, no. 132). Our analysis is not aimed at hunting out new facts; rather it is about wanting to understand something that is already in plain view. Our aim is to point towards possibilities for participation by pointing to the practices of participation that are already in plain view.

Community of practice seems like a new way of seeing participation in school. It provides us with the option of developing syntheses of unhelpful polarities in psychology and education such as those represented by behavioural and cognitive approaches (Greeno 1998). Greeno argues that the situative perspective entailed in 'community of practice' supports a synthesis of aspects of knowledge and motivation by conceptualising both in terms of participation in social practices. Instead of dealing separately with cognitive and motivational aspects, we are presented with a complementarity in which communities of practitioners share standards of what would be considered worthwhile problems in which to engage, why they are worthwhile, and what would constitute a satisfactory solution:

People participate in communities in many different ways — some by adopting the mainstream standards and values, some by rejecting them, and most by a mixture of conformity to and alienation from different aspects of the prevailing standards. … individuals develop identities in which they relate to the prevailing standards in a complex variety of ways. (p. 10)

According to this analysis, whether students are motivated to perform well and whether they have the strategic knowledge to do so depends largely on issues of affiliation and identity in communities of practice.

Where Greeno proposes situative accounts of learning and educational practice as a conceptual and practical synthesis, Rogoff et al. offer an alternative view. Rogoff, Matusov and White (1996) explicitly argue that the community of learners model is not a balance or blend of adult-run and children-run models, rather it is 'a distinct instructional model based on a different philosophy' (p. 396). They suggest that viewing learning developmentally as a community process of transformation of participation points to possibilities for theory and practice that are hidden in one-sided perspectives that emphasise either the transmission or acquisition of language. As long as learning is seen as the transmission or acquisition of language or facts, the research and practice focus is on issues such as instructional design, presentation of materials, student's attention, abilities, motivation, and so on. Putting participation centre stage in consideration of school learning brings other issues to the fore. For example, Rogoff and colleagues point out that one-sided perspectives are not only one-sided with respect to treatment of information but also with respect to social practice. Either teachers are actively transmitting and students passively receiving or students are actively acquiring and teachers passively transmitting. In each case, viewing some of the participants as passive has an impoverishing effect on our understanding of responsibility and accountability for school learning. The community of learners model offers an alternative gloss in which all parties are active and they share responsibility for the learning that inevitably occurs in the classroom.

Both Rogoff and Greeno open up possibilities for new ways of seeing classroom learning, but what looks like a substantial opening from a distance becomes more modest up close. Both move too quickly to systematisation of their talk about community, participation and practice and, in so doing, close off the opening a little. Early systematisation, with Rogoff et al. (1996) in terms of an instructional model, and Greeno (1998) in terms of a theoretical synthesis, risks turning 'community of practice' into a formalised concept. The danger with that is that 'community of practice', 'community of learners', 'community' are likely to become abstractions which describe none of the vitality of the lived practices. They become absorbed into a consensual reality, ways of talking about learning to which all can readily give assent without changing anything. In short, the metaphor when abstracted from the contingencies of practice is no longer generative, conceptually or practically.

There is a strong sense with Rogoff and Greeno's use of 'community', of the metaphor taking on an aspirational rather than descriptive role. While both claim to be concerned with classroom practice their use of the 'community' metaphor tends toward describing what they feel 'should be' with regard to classroom learning rather than 'what is'. To be fair, both acknowledge that students' affiliations to other communities, such as families and peer groups, can be crucial in forming their identities and that these identities can be formed in ways that oppose or facilitate students' engagement in school practices. It is just that too much is hidden in a relatively stable conceptualisation of the relations between individuals and different groupings, and the relations between different communities in which the individual participates for this to be an analysis that creates options for 'new ways of seeing'. Motivation and knowledge is replaced by identity and engagement in an alternative systematisation which renders the dynamics of participation stable and the dialectics of practice pre-determined.

Therefore, it is important to reflect on what various uses of the 'community of practice' metaphor conceal. Does the benign connotation of 'community' hide all possibility of conflict and tension? Does it promote a one sided account of change and transformation in which all participants learn to conform to the demands of the reified community? The question is this: can 'community of practice' be employed as a metaphor to open up options for participation at all or is the use of any, even the most potentially fruitful metaphor, ultimately an act of abstraction from the dynamics, and dialogics, of practice.

From a psychological standpoint, there is a range of approaches to understanding students' participation in education. For example, Finn's (1989, 1992, 1993) programme of research focused on explaining the causal link between engagement in or withdrawal from school and student achievement. His model of student experience involves both a behavioural component, labelled participation and a psychological component labelled identification. Finn argues that if a student is an active participant in classroom activities then their 'engaged' behaviours are likely to become elaborated, and to be accompanied by a sense of belonging in school and 'valuing school related outcomes, that is, identification' (1993, v). On the other hand, lack of participatory behaviours place the student at risk of withdrawing from schooling. In his research, explanations of different 'levels' of participation in educational activities focus almost exclusively on the student, problems of participation being identified with psychological attributes of the individual student. Finn's work exemplifies an approach which conceptualises learning and participation individually and entitatively, the practical implication of which is to improve participation by 'fixing' the student. Thus, the student's experience is cast only within a reductionist, entitative framework of understanding. In treating participants in interactions as separate and separable 'entities' people's capacity for intersubjectivity is neglected, that is, our abilities to 'go on' with each other in lived practices. In contrast, there is a range of approaches which attempt to deal with student participation in a more holistic, systemic manner.

Lave's analysis (Lave 1988, 1993; Lave and Wenger 1991), though deeply concerned with the theory of practice, seems always connected to the local detail of practice, always ready to acknowledge dilemmas in formulation or representation. This leads her to a standpoint which though systematic and theoretical is not systematised and abstracted. Instead of trying to pin down and define difficult concepts, she is ready to admit that, in practice and in theory, it is sometimes better not to pin them down, e.g.: 'If context is viewed as a social world constituted in relation with persons acting, both context and activity seem inescapably flexible and changing.' (Lave 1993, 5). Not pinning them down allows the dialogue to continue. Lave's work is open to the kinds of dilemmas and contradictions that are the stuff of generative dialogue. For example, she describes:

a contradiction between the use and exchange values of the outcome of learning, which manifests itself in conflicts between learning to know and learning to display knowledge for evaluation. (Lave and Wenger 1991, 110)

Unlike Finn's entitative, individualistic treatment of participation or Rogoff's treatment of 'community of learners' as an instructional model, and perhaps even a prescription for learning, Lave's use of the metaphor is rich in messy stuff, in conflict and contradiction and dilemmas of participation that can only be resolved in situated local practice.

Echoing this perspective, Shotter (1996) points out that communities cannot be planned and engineered in a technical way. Rather they are emergent from primitive reactions and interactions. For Shotter, participation in a community of practice involves sharing with others a sense of 'judgement without reflection' and a set of practical responses to shared concrete circumstances. It is with this view of participation that we began our investigation of classroom practices. Shotter sees a deep circularity in a position which tries to accommodate the emergence of community, a form of life which strengthens solidarity, and the kind of commitment to rational persuasion which presupposes incipient forms of community. He sees us as

acting into our surroundings, in terms of 'its' callings and discouragements, its invitations and oppositions, the opportunities and impediments, the aids and hindrances that it offers us (Dewey 1896 in Shotter 1996, 3).

This viewpoint is consonant with Holzman's (1997) critique of the commoditisation of school learning, which she characterises as an attempt to produce 'knowers', and which posits as a radical alternative non-epistemological environments where children create themselves by being who they are not.

Setting participation against the 'community of practice' metaphor, as employed by Lave, Shotter, Holzman and others, opens a space for dialogue around a variety of issues:

— the commoditisation of knowledge and the entailed conflict between learning for knowledge and learning for evaluation

— ownership issues which point to potential dilemmas of accountability in the form of contradictions between responsibility and control
— the character of surroundings into which learners act
— a learner's positioning in the community of practice

For the remainder of this chapter, our aim is to engage in the dialogue around participation by engaging with some of these issues as they appear in the local practices in Class A. The main focus of this paper is to develop an account of classroom interaction which encapsulates the participative nature of experience. In carrying out our empirical analysis, we are strongly aware of Shotter's advice which in this case we interpret as a gesture towards context and connection, local talk, gut reactions in a socio-historical setting.

Describing the Research Process

Interpretations of Classroom Practice

Our aim in this section of the chapter is to draw on, and interpret, excerpts of classroom social practice and students' accounts of practices to generate a dialogue around aspects of participation in this community of practice. We will explore how interactions are jointly organised and what possible consequences these forms of organisation may have for participants' ways of being in this setting. Our interpretations foreground issues such as responsibility and control relations in the class, practices of evaluating and legitimating knowledge, and the students' accounts of their location in practices.

The Research Site

Our data was collected through ongoing visits to 'Class A' which extended over two years and involved numerous observations in the classroom and some interviews with both students and teachers outside the classroom setting. The school is a national school for girls and while it operates in a disadvantaged area, it was felt necessary by the Department of Education to have a mixed intake of pupils in terms of socio-economic background and ability levels. The first year, observations of classroom activity involved a fourth grade group in which there were 27 girls aged between 9 and 10 with the same class teacher for the whole year. This class was then divided between two classes in fifth grade and we decided to follow both groups during the second year of observation.

Data Collection and Interpreting Procedure

In the first strand of research, data was gathered through written observer notes and audiotapes of approximately twenty-five one and a half hour blocks of classroom activity. The observer notes were typed up following each visit and the audiotapes were transcribed up to two months following the visit. The decision of what to transcribe from tapes was based on events we had marked in the write up of field notes as being potentially of interest. At times, other visits were transcribed in full to examine if any interesting or possibly contradictory events would come to light. The process of data collection, early interpretation and refinement of the research approach occurred in an iterative loop, with a refined research question feeding back in to influence later collection and analysis.

The transcripts were typed up with the following convention. Each speaker was identified if possible and the utterance ascribed to him or her. Interruptions and overlaps of speech were noted. Potentially salient events were commented on in the transcripts, for example the use of objects, interpretations of speech tone and addressee, rising or falling noise levels. Initial analysis of the transcripts consisted of reading through a transcript a number of times, marking some interesting utterances, highlighted possible patterns in language use for example use of referents (I/We) etc. Simultaneously, memos were written up about the data, drawing out possible patterns, research questions and ideas etc.

The interpretative process then moved on to place whole sequences of interaction together if they seemed to have some feature in common, a sanction mentioned, revision activities etc. This worked as an aid to identifying common and contrasting features of interaction across larger sections of data. Such 'features' did not categorise an interaction in a singular manner; rather, different features could be picked out of the same interaction depending on the researcher's reading of the data. When we had gathered sequences of interaction under a common theme for example 'accounts of knowing', we then read through them, picking out interesting or recurring features in the discourse and wrote up memos about these patterns. The strategy of looking for patterns across many interactions gave us some insight into the kinds of general ground rules for organising joint activities in classroom social practice. Part of the difficulty with taking an interpretative approach is the need to balance an 'open' inductive contextualised account of the discourse with the often reductive process of trying to produce a coherent 'reading' of the data. Our approach to try to resolve such tensions is to move from a familiarity with patterns that occur across many interactions to examine particular interactions in depth. There is some reduction involved but at the level of extracting a segment of meaningful activity rather than reducing activity to decontextualised codes and categories. Thus in order to deepen the analysis we wrote detailed descriptions of single pieces of interaction to try to present a more subtle account of the ways in which participating was constructed in specific episodes. Examples of this process of describing interactions in detail will be presented in the following section of this chapter.

Responsibility and Control Relations in Practice

The interaction, on which our first analysis is based, is set in the context of 'Class A' being introduced to and working on fractions. The class were engaged in a question and answer routine with teacher (T). T uses this routine frequently to check on students' knowledge, and in a later section we will examine in more detail how this 'knowing' is constructed and how students are located in practices. T is located as the legitimate questioner, individual students are called on and T checks their knowledge.

T:	... another one half? Lisa Murphy three-quarters plus how much makes one unit? Ah, no, don't look at your chart (other students: that's easy). For these girls, these are too easy, aren't they?
Amanda:	Ya, she doesn't know where we are.
Lisa:	I do Amanda.
	(pause)
T:	Lisa Murphy, now that couldn't take you that long if you were following it at all, three-quarters plus how much more to make one whole unit; if you had, if you got three quarters of the apple how much more would you need to make a full apple or how much of it was missing, how many quarters are there in anything, Lisa (pause), better hurry up Lisa or you'll be on a third class maths book if you're not careful (pause). Would you look up at the chart please on the blackboard and

	tell me how many quarters are there in any one unit, how many quarters are there in one unit.
Lisa:	Four fourths (low voice).
T:	Pardon.
Lisa:	Four fourths.
T:	How many quarters are there?
Lisa:	Four (very low voice).
T:	I can't hear you Lisa.
Lisa:	Four.
T:	Four what?
Lisa:	Four quarters.
T:	Four quarters. Now, if you have three quarters of something how much are you short to make the full unit?
Lisa:	One.
T:	Pardon.
Lisa:	One fourth.
S:	One quarter.
T:	Would you ever say quarter like a good girl, so read out your sum for me now the way you'd write it down in your copybook.
Lisa:	Three fourths and one/
T:	/Lisa! would you ever say quarter for me please?
Lisa:	Three quarters and one quarter equals one.

[T: teacher, S: student, /: indicates an interruption]

Lisa is called on to answer T's question, presumably Lisa glances toward a fraction chart and T attempts to stop her checking with this available resource 'Ah, no don't look at your chart for these'. T's comment functions to locate Lisa as a resource independent knower, who should be able to answer the question without the aid of resources as the question is deemed to be easy. T's addition of 'For these girls, these are too easy aren't they' underlines her perception of the unproblematic nature of her question. Particularly by saying 'too easy' and by addressing the class as a whole group she sets up the assumption that there is some kind of common standard in the class or at least an agreement that the material should be easy for everyone. An expectation is thus created that Lisa is within range of this common standard and so she becomes responsible for answering the question without further assistance either from the teacher or from the available chart. Resource use is deemed unsuitable when T presents material as being easy, it is possible to suggest from this that their use would be appropriate given difficult or perhaps new material, a situation where students would not be located as knowers and so could draw on resources to aid them. It is interesting also to see students concur with T's assessment of the material as easy. Note that T's utterance about not using the available resource and the students' affirmation of the material as easy act to restrict Lisa's control over how she makes her response to the question. Alternatively, the fraction question could have been put to Lisa without the imposition of an assumed standard of knowledge, thus leaving the manner of arriving at a response to Lisa's discretion. So, through T's utterance, while the student has been positioned as responsible for producing the 'right' answer her control over her performance has been constrained.

Before Lisa has a chance to respond, another student (Amanda) accuses her of not 'knowing where we are'. This utterance is an example of a student performance which is often overlooked in 'teacher led' accounts of classroom practice. In this community of practice there are negative sanctions associated with not listening to the teacher, so a change in Lisa's location, from resource independent knower to problematic student, becomes a possibility through Amanda's utterance. It is a possibility Lisa seems aware of and she defends herself immediately by refuting Amanda's accusation. In a sense, Amanda adopts the teacher's voice and in doing so she exerts some control in shifting the character of the surroundings in which the T/Lisa exchange is situated. Lisa's subsequent pause is problematic, if this material is easy and she is assumed to be able to work independently of resources then her answer should be quicker. There are a number of occasions in the transcripts where T associates knowing something with the ability to give the right answer quickly. T's response to Lisa's pause highlights the problem 'Lisa Murphy, now that couldn't take you that long if you were following it at all', Lisa should know the answer and is accountable for not following the material if she doesn't know it. Lisa's accountability is underlined by T using the student's full name and by T framing her utterance as a statement which sounds quite accusatory. As the interaction develops, Lisa's position shifts more toward being accountable for not knowing and therefore being a problematic student, as this occurs T's location also changes from one of eliciting unproblematic knowledge to attributing responsibility to Lisa for her unsatisfactory performance. Alternatively, for example, T could simply have asked her if she were following the material.

Using a familiar repertoire in the question-answer routine T, having located the student herself as problematic, then goes on to offer a prompt 'three quarters plus how much more to make one whole unit; if you had, if you got three quarters of the apple how much more would you need to make a full apple or how much of it was missing, how many quarters are there in anything, Lisa'. T restates the original question and then goes on to reframe it in terms of something more concrete 'an apple', she then changes the question twice 'how much of it was missing' to 'how many quarters are there in anything'. This last question being more basic probably in T's view as this is something they have definitely covered. Note that T draws on an imagined concrete resource 'the apple' in an attempt to guide Lisa to the right answer. A pause follows and Lisa does not answer, again T responds to this by locating the problem with Lisa 'better hurry up Lisa or you'll be on a third class maths book if you're not careful'. T's reference to a 'third class maths book' is a commonly used threat of punishment for students. It is interesting that the resource can be used to locate students as backward in some way and also that they are attributed agency in this process by the teacher, 'if you're not careful', implying that if Lisa were careful she wouldn't be threatened with a third class book. Again, there is no immediate answer from Lisa and T refers back to the resource 'Would you look up at the chart please on the blackboard and tell me how many quarters are there in any one unit, how many quarters are there in one unit'. The resource which initially was not needed is now being drawn on but not until the student has been identified as a problem and threatened with a sanction. Lisa's hesitation in answering seems to shift T's position from that of eliciting unproblematic knowledge from a student to one of prodding the student toward the 'right' answer. An important point which follows from such an interpretation of practice is that while T may be recognised as the overt authority in the classroom, her location with regard to control and responsibility is only determined *through practice in relation to* students.

T directs Lisa to 'look up at the chart please on the blackboard and tell me how many quarters are there in any one unit', the model of student activity seems to be one of perception 'look', and reproduction 'tell', the chart offers unproblematic information which the student can easily reproduce in answer to T's questions. Lisa does give an answer but the interaction which follows her answer is quite disturbing. Even though Lisa has answered correctly, T's questions are quite abrupt and offer no praise or encouragement to the student. T insists on Lisa answering in a particular format 'How many quarters are there?' and 'Four what?'. T does not explain (or account for her preference) to Lisa why saying quarters might be more appropriate than fourths (if it is for some reason). In the final section of this interaction, T moves back to the original question 'if you have three quarters of something how much are you short to make the full unit'. Lisa replies with the correct quantity 'One' but she doesn't add the appropriate marker 'quarter', which T signals by saying 'Pardon' a prompt to Lisa to amend her answer. T asks Lisa to say 'quarter' rather than 'fourth' however again she does not offer any explanation to Lisa why this might be more appropriate. In finishing the sum, T asks Lisa to 'read out your sum for me now the way you'd write it down in your copybook'. This seems an odd request when doing maths orally, however it does stress the importance of resources to constrain the course of activity. Students can be directed by T to recall or respond in the manner that the available texts represent material.

Throughout this interaction, there are shifts, both in the meanings associated with resources and in participants' location relative to both each other and the available resources. At the start of the interaction, the teacher addresses Lisa as a resource independent store of the requisite information to a position where she directs her to use the available resources in order to arrive at a correct answer. Not only does the expressed relationship between the student and resource change but also that between T and student. T's repertoire changes from one of eliciting unproblematic information from a student to one of coercion, by which we mean she offers support to the student but only in the context of positioning the student herself as problematic. T's repertoires construct the activity as easy and the student as knower independent of resources. As the interaction goes on there are changes in the repertoires used, the location of the student and the way resources are drawn on. In all, what the student is participating in could be represented as a shifting network of control and responsibility relations which has consequences for her and implications for ways of being in the class.

This section has described in detail an interaction between T and student and shown that they are participating in a jointly organised interaction in which their positions can shift relative to one another, particularly with regard to responsibility and control relations. Thus far our dialogue around participation has pointed toward the shifting processes of meaning making in this classroom community. However, we have seen that relations in the classroom community of practice can be organised in a manner that seems to divide responsibility and control for activities in odd ways, ways which have *consequences* for those participating in the community. In the next section, we will examine, through accounts in and of practice, issues to do with knowledge evaluation and legitimation, and subsequently student location. We will explore how particular sense making activities to do with these issues have consequences in terms of developing ways of being in this classroom community.

Practices of Knowledge Evaluation and Legitimation

It seems to be a generally accepted position in the classroom community of practice that students should know more as they progress through lessons and through the school year. The importance attributed to knowing and knowledge in classroom social practice can be seen through the sanctions imposed on students who do not 'know', as in the previous section where a student (Lisa) was held accountable for not knowing certain material. It also seems to be accepted that students need to participate in class in order to reach the goal of knowing more. However what is not accepted or reflected upon in this community is that sense making activities associated with 'knowing' and 'learning', and which are created through practices, will have consequences for the ways of participating that are facilitated or constrained in the classroom setting. To examine what 'knowing' seems to mean in this setting we will give some examples of participants' accounts of 'knowing' both in and of practice. This depiction of knowing will not be exhaustive in terms of all possible meanings or even shifts in meanings associated with knowing that occur in joint activities. Rather we will explore some interesting patterns in accounts of knowing and their consequences in terms of how they relate to possible ways of being in the classroom setting. Finally, in discussing 'knowing' and 'knowledge' here we are not reifying or objectifying such concepts but rather using these labels as those which are closest to participants own accounts of particular ways of going on with each other.

T:	Right. Now Marie is now going to stand up and tell us what she remembers from Friday when we did it. What you know they, three things about ants that you know.
Marie:	Ahm.
T:	That was in our (…) book.
Marie:	Ahm (pause) how the queen went on (…) marriage flight she/
T:	/well that wasn't in our story. Give me some of the first things we could tell somebody about ants, the basic things. Right, Veronica.

This account in practice occurred as T examined students' knowledge about ants, based on information given at a lesson the previous Friday. On reading this excerpt there are a number of interesting features about the construction of knowing and knowledge that are worth highlighting. In a familiar routine it is T who requests a student to 'stand up and tell us' what she knows about ants. The student (Marie) must make a public display of 'what she remembers from Friday when we did it'. T's request seems to construct knowledge as something that is remembered by an individual, who can share this information publicly with others, and that this knowledge can be quantified 'three things' as perhaps so many facts or bytes of information. There is also a sense that T assumes Marie has the appropriate knowledge because 'we did it', implying that the group activity of reading about, and discussing ants translates into the individual having stored in memory the appropriate information. T's utterance seems to move from the public arena 'tell *us*' and '*we* did it' to the personal arena 'what *you* know', 'that *you* know'. This would seem to suggest that while knowledge here can be introduced and shared at a group level, knowing ultimately becomes the individual's responsibility.

Marie's subsequent pause is met by T's prompt of 'that was in our (…) book'. If we assume that T's statement was an attempt to help Marie remember some information about ants then it seems a bit odd that she chooses a textbook as a reminder rather than using what someone had said about ants or a personal experience. Marie begins to reproduce some information about ants, which sounds particularly vivid with the inclusion of 'queen' and 'marriage flight', however her response is interrupted by T on the grounds that 'that wasn't in our story'. Based on previous question and answer routines between T and students it is to be expected that Marie's response, her knowledge, will be assessed by T for its adequacy as happens in this excerpt. However, it seems strange that T would discount Marie's answer because it doesn't include 'first things', 'the basic things' about ants. The information about queen ants and marriage flights had actually been discussed during the previous lesson but it wasn't 'basic' information that was available 'in our (…) book'. T's evaluation of Marie's answer seems to suggest that in this setting the legitimacy of knowledge is determined by T. Her criteria for legitimate knowledge seem to include starting with the basic knowledge which is more important in some putative hierarchy of information on a topic (here ants) and the use of a resource such as their textbook to limit what information will be accepted as evidence of knowing.

What knowledge is deemed to be is inextricably linked to the position/location of those participating in classroom practice. Due to the position of T, she can question students' knowledge and assess the merit of their answers, the assumption being that she has the requisite knowledge store to enable her to make such judgements. The knowledge that is being transmitted appears to be viewed as a template which will not be altered as a result of student's or T's interaction with it. In fact, students are sometimes explicitly told to reproduce knowledge in the manner in which the template was given, by the teacher, book or chart etc. This places T and students in particular relation to one another and to 'knowledge'. That is, T exercises most control in directing activities (she determines what they do, for how long, in what manner etc.) while students have very little control over what is done. Such a description at first glance seems to fit the stereotype of teacher led activity and passive students. However, this contradiction of student having responsibility, without having control over, 'knowing' creates a dilemma for them which complicates the stereotype of student passivity. The dilemma of accountability is something with which they actively engage so as to avoid negative sanctions in this community of practice.

R:	Ya, and what would happen if you didn't know something then?
Louise:	I think she'd send you down to the office if you knew something you're after doing already, like how many halves are in anything.
R:	Ya.
R:	So its stuff you've done for quite a while that you should know?
Lisa:	Ya.
Tara:	If she examines it.

[R: researcher]

So, while students may not be actively engaged in learning subject material, they present a coherent account of their location in practice in terms of accountability for knowing. Students' location with respect to accountability for knowing is further underlined by Tara's addition of 'If she examines it'. The students' relationship to knowledge is presented in terms of the social practices of knowledge evaluation in the classroom.

Melissa:	Well, like, say she teaches us the exact (pause) thing …
Jennifer:	… words and can't get them wrong and a week later then we'd have to think of it … but you can't remember everything

R: So what do ye have to do, if that's good teaching, what do ye have to
           do to be good students?
Marie: Listen and …
S: Listen?
Jennifer: Listen and take it in.
Caroline: Take in what she says.

This extract highlights the students' account of their role in classroom social practice in relation to T. T is seen as 'educational' which in Melissa's and
Jennifer's account seems to involve her teaching them the 'exact thing'. Note
that it is T who is presented as active in this account, she is the person teaching and the students' learning is not directly mentioned. Jennifer's statement
then points to a student's location in this practice 'and can't get them wrong'
and 'we'd have to think of it … but you can't remember everything'. The
student's location in practice seems to be a reactive one in relation to T, they
must respond correctly to her questions. In fact, the language used by Jennifer seems to imply a prescribed responsibility for students, 'we can't' and
'we'd have to', in terms of their location in joint activities. The implications
for participating in classroom social practice were further underlined by
their response to being asked by the researcher 'what do ye have to do to be
good students'. Good students, from the girls' accounts, 'listen' and 'take it
in'. The image is predominantly one of students passively absorbing information from T and other available resources, with the complication that they
realise they are responsible for reproducing this information if requested by
T. Students' accounts of their apprenticeship in this community of practice
seem to place T in an active position of controlling joint activities while they
are placed in a position of responsibility for reproducing knowledge they are
assumed to have 'taken in'. Such control and responsibility relations have
implications for students' ways of participating in relation to the community
of practice metaphor.

Conclusions

Activities in the classroom seem to fit with the community of practice
metaphor for a number of reasons. Classroom activities are seen to have a
purpose by the wider community that is, one of educating children. Within
the metaphor, students could be seen as apprentices in the school setting and
there is a sense that their activities in the classroom are influenced by, and

part of, ongoing historical and cultural practices of schooling. However, due to the patterns of organising joint activities which have been observed in one particular classroom it is time to extend the metaphor or perhaps to see it in a different way. The community of practice metaphor has been used almost exclusively to inspire or describe engagement in an active learning process, but we find that in a classroom setting the apprentices are most directly engaged in control and responsibility relations which constrain their possible ways of being in that setting. Students are learning in this setting, however, in practices which construct knowledge as an unalterable template to be transmitted and reproduced on request, they are more actively engaged in negotiating their location in practice.

The interesting element in this community is that while terms such as child centred education and the importance of active participation in learning and sharing knowledge, have become common parlance, the implications of such concepts for actual practices have not been examined by teachers. In a sense, such terms have been transplanted into teachers' accounts of classroom practice to describe rather than question or change their practice. Such is the case also in academic accounts of learning and participation in which new labels such as community of practice have become positive abstractions which are not examined in the light of actual forms of life. Such abstractions result in discussions, among both academics and teachers, of whether children are participating or participating adequately in learning. However, what we seem to have missed is that participation is in one sense a given thing and what we need to examine are the forms of life which people co-create in their communities of practice. When we do this our questions change from 'are they participating' to 'what forms of participation are possible' given a community's practices? The dilemmas students face have less to do with grappling with subject material and more to do with protecting themselves from the consequences of 'not knowing'. We would argue that due to the manner in which joint activities are organised students become apprentices to, for example, control and responsibility relations rather than learning subject material. In the classroom, setting students are judged often and publicly on their efficacy at reproducing requested knowledge. These judgements have immediate outcomes for the students in terms of sanctions but they also have longer term and cumulative effects on their construction of self and their commitment to and level of participation in community practice. Given such practices it would be a mistake to reify the 'community of practice' metaphor as a wholly positive abstraction which should then be translated back into directives for practice. The usefulness of the metaphor lies in its close alliance to local practices, practices which may include scenes of conflict, shifting responsibility and control relations, and negative sanctions, which we have pointed toward in this chapter.

References

Finn, J. (1989). Withdrawing from school. *Review of Educational Research*, 59(2), 117-42.

Finn, J. (1993). *School engagement and students at risk*. Washington: National Centre for Education Statistics.

Finn, J. & Cox, D. (1992). Participation and withdrawal among fourth grade pupils. *American Educational Research Journal*, 29(1), 141-62.

Greeno, J.G. (1998). The situativity of knowing, learning, and research. *American Psychologist*, 53(1), 5-26.

Holzman, L. (1997). *Schools for growth: Radical alternatives to current educational models*. Mahwah N.J.: Lawrence Erlbaum Associates.

Lave, J. (1988). *Cognition in practice: Mind, mathematics, and culture in everyday life*. Cambridge: Cambridge University Press.

Lave, J. (1993). The practice of learning. In S. Chaiklin & J. Lave (eds.), *Understanding practice: Perspectives on activity and context*. Cambridge: Cambridge University Press.

Lave, J. & Wenger, E. (1991). *Situated learning: Legitimate peripheral participation*. Cambridge: Cambridge University Press.

Rogoff, B., Matusov, E. & White, C. (1996). Models of teaching and learning: Participation in a community of learners. In D. Olson & N. Torrance (eds.), *The handbook of education and human development: New models of learning, teaching, and schooling*. Cambridge: Blackwell Publishers.

Shotter, J. (1996) *Vico, Wittgenstein, and Bakhtin: 'Practical Trust' in dialogical communities*. Draft paper for the conference: Democracy and Trust, Georgetown University, Nov. 7-9 1996. http://www.massey.ac.nz/~ALock/virtual/js.htm

Wittgenstein, L. (1953). *Philosophical investigations*. Oxford: Basil Blackwell.

17 Teachers' Experience of School and Knowledge through Childhood Memories

Maria Teresa de A. Freitas

That which I reveal
and the rest which is still hidden
in vitreous trap-doors
is human news, simple being-in-the-world,
and plays on words,
a being-without-being,
the game and the confession
burning in such a way
that even I myself cannot distinguish
what was lived and what was invented.
Everything lived? — Nothing.
Nothing lived? — Everything.

Carlos Drumond de Andrade (1997, 63)

Introduction

How do present-day adults relate their childhood experience of knowledge and school? What role does memory play in the new meaning given to teachers' stories about reading and writing? To answer these questions we attempted to understand the childhood experiences of Brazilian basic-level teachers through their accounts of these experiences, trying to interpret them in the light of Vygotsky's socio-historical viewpoint.

For Vygotsky, knowledge is built from dialogue. First it is built on the relationship between people and is later internalised. This whole process can only be understood through the notion of mediation, which is central to this theory. The relationship of the subject with the world is not a one-way process, but is constantly mediated by instruments and signs which enable us to interpret the world, to understand our surroundings. This position places semiology at the very centre of the relationship between the psychological subject and reality. The world is an environment seen with meaning and the course of the subject's behaviour is traced by the meaning that this subject has of the world. According to Vygotsky, the basic systems of mediation for human mental functioning are cultural creations, products of social history, preserved in human activity.

Because we are concerned with a school which will create space for dialogue in which language is seen as the production and component of the subjects, we undertook some research to help us clarify and understand teachers' practices of reading and writing. In order to understand today the way the teachers speak, read and write, it is necessary to recover what was left from the past, i.e., to make past, present and future intersect. According to Chiara (1993), building future history will depend on our capacity to reconstruct our past history. Hence our interest in working with the recollections of teachers.

Research Participants

Participants in the project were teachers who work at public and private schools in Juiz de Fora, Brasil. As a criterion for their selection, it was opted to assemble a group of subjects of various ages and length of service, who had worked in different grades in primary and middle schools. This group comprised seven primary and middle school teachers, their ages ranging between 27 and 42 years old and whose working experience ranged from 5 to 22 years. The teachers were asked to participate in open interviews. Some of the interviews took place at schools and others at the teachers' homes.

Without attempting to analyse every single word of their stories, we tried to pick up, through their words, some 'human news' among the 'realities and inventions' that memory has retained and revealed. We shall speak of news that brings back a childhood where reading and writing mingle with family scenes, games, 'church services like schools' and the subversion of an adult world's impositions.

Travelling through the Realms of Memory

I arrive at the fields and vast places of the memory where there are the treasures of innumerable images brought by all kinds of perceptions. All that we think is hidden there too, sometimes increasing, sometimes decreasing or even changing in any manner at all the objects that the senses had perceived. In short, there lies all that was handed over and deposited with them, if forgetfulness has not yet absorbed and buried it. (Saint Augustine 1975, 42)

Aware of the value of memory as a constituent of collective history, of a culture, we attempted to recover the history of a particular social group (Brazilian basic-level teachers).

As listeners and interlocutors, we asked our teachers to go on a journey, to surrender themselves to reminiscence, to the memory of events they had lived, understanding that

lived events are finite, or at least enclosed within the sphere of things lived, whereas remembered events are limitless, because they are merely a key to all that came before and after. (Benjamin 1987, 37)

Once this key was in our possession, we asked them to open the doors … and we entered with them into the kingdom of recollection.

Remembering is an opportunity for self-knowledge. Memory searches in the depths of us for what is there, helping us to build knowledge about ourselves, and also about the world that surrounds us.

For Gusdorf, quoted by Freeman (1993), in the immediateness of the present the agitation of things around us prevents us from seeing them in their entirety. We live episodes, but we do not establish the connections to capture their meaning. It is memory which enables us to integrate events into a historical perspective, contextualising them in time and space.

It is not just a question of retelling the past, but seeking the sense of it, as in an interpretative act at the end of which our understanding of ourselves is broadened. In fact, autobiography is a creative process in an interpretative context, where a new relationship is also created between the past and the present so that the text of the ego can be rewritten. It is in this sense that the narrator gives a meaning to events that they did not have at the moment when they happened. He narrates events with present-day perception, so the meaning is a present one. It is a reading of the past in the light of the present. Bakhtin interprets the role of memory in the transformation and comprehension of the past in its inconclusive character in this way:

the objective philosophical aspect of the past cannot be changed; however, the aspect of meaning, the expressive and discursive aspect can be changed, because it is inconclusive and does not coincide with itself. (1985, 393)

This is also Benjamin's opinion when he says that

to articule the past historically does not mean knowing it as it really was. It means grasping a reminiscence, just as it sparkles in a moment of danger. (1987, 224)

In this way, we offered our teachers the opportunity to tell their stories so that their narrative of the past could also map out the course of how their egos are progressing.

A memory which not only deepens the understanding of the ego preserving the past, but situates it in relation to other people, to the world: this is the social constitution of individual memory.

Thus, our teachers began to search for hidden treasures in their memories. Recalling their own childhood they brought to light precious secrets: the loving mother who started her daughter in the rudiments of writing, giving her letter-forming exercises or teaching her to write her name, the father who was a walking encyclopaedia; the very religious grandmother from a little town in the provinces who made her granddaughter go to mass on Sundays; the bible reading; the stories told at night by a beloved aunt; the absence of a father which made it difficult to form the abstract mathematical concept of a pair.

My mother used to teach me at home. I used to do letter-forming exercises ... up and down goes Granny's ball of wool. (Luciana)

I remember clearly! she was ironing clothes and she said: 'Let's write letters!' Then she wrote a 'J', an 'I' and I copied them, and I wrote my name, before having any contact with school, and she said: — 'Look, that's great, you've written your name!' So for me, that was the greatest. (Janaína)

I would spell the words out, joining the syllables up, but if they asked me what I had read I didn't know. I think I used to do that because in fact I didn't have anything to do and my grandmother used to make me go to mass and follow the news-sheet … so I learned to read from church news-sheets. (Maria Lúcia)

My father, then, was extremely important. Because I had a father who was a walking encyclopaedia. Yes, when I had a research project from school I didn't go to the library, I would say: 'Dad, there's this topic', and he would sit with me and say the project for me … All out of his head, and afterwards he would even help me to illustrate it. So my research projects were always commented on by my teachers because it all came out of my father's head, so it was a sort of innovation, something different … that left a real mark on me. (Janaína)

But at home my mother helped a lot. She would sit with us and help us write the stories … (Luciana)

I remember I had an aunt, she was called Dindinha, she used to read to us at night … She had a big thick book […] the only story I remember is Pinocchio. She would read that scene when the whale swallows up Pinocchio's father … The only part of the story I remember, I would imagine the waves and the whale, that struggle, you know? (Hilda)

I had great difficulty understanding what a pair was. I didn't understand, it just didn't sink in at all … It was a struggle, a problem! I was almost beaten because of pairs. I didn't understand that it was two things. Then one day my mother came to O.F., sat down with me and explained to me, using the example of a married couple: father and mother. Then I understood. (Maria Lúcia)

Stories of mothers and fathers who struggle with financial difficulties, who work hard so that their children can have what they did not have: the chance to study. People with little learning, but who left their mark on their children's lives sharing their knowledge with them. Incomplete families … children brought up without a father. Mothers who are not there because they go out to work, to have an occupation, to earn money. A patchwork of life, little stories within a bigger story. Memory, the inspiration of narrative which gathers together a great number of scattered facts. Memory, which helps to reconstruct simple family homes where, in the warmth and comfort of family relationships, children enter into a world of letters. Letters full of religiousness: the bible, the church newsletter. Letters which mark people's identity, their ego. Letters from the book, in the voice of the aunt telling stories, which lead to the wonderful world of imagination with fantastic characters. Letters that come out of the girl's father's head for her school research project. Words which need someone else for their meaning to be recovered. Strange stories, but which reflect a little of all our stories.

And in these stories, we keep coming across the presence of other people, who, according to Vygotsky (1991), are the mediators of knowledge. Mother, father, aunt, grandmother, loving hands that help children enter a world of culture. Adult's words which children internalise. Knowledge which is built within a relationship. Other people always present, others who are more experienced and who serve as a model for children to imitate. Knowledge which is built first between people, to be internalised later, and become intrapersonal, as Vygotsky claims:

All the functions of a child's development appear twice: first, in social development, and then, at the individual level; first, between people (interpsychological) and later, within the child (intrapsychological). (Vygotsky 1991, 64)

In these scenes recovered by people's memory, we always observe an adult introducing the child to new knowledge with language as the mediator. It is through dialogue, or interaction, that children enter into the current of language, understanding the world around them, becoming subjects.

Childhood Games Re-Visited through Memory

We also discover in the accounts of a distant but ever-present childhood, the place of games, characters from children's books.

According to Vygotsky (1991), games are relevant in the development of children, since they satisfy the children's need to get to know, to experience, to create and to take part in the social world. Through games, children free their imagination, experiencing situations, playing the role of others, using objects and transforming them at will.

Through games children project themselves into the adult activities of their culture, rehearse their future roles and values. Thus games anticipate development, with them children begin to acquire the motivation, the skills and the attitudes necessary for their social participation, which can only be completely achieved with the assistance of their companions of the same age and older. (Vygotsky 1991, 146)

Games, imagination and fantasy are for Vygotsky (1991) activities which not only give pleasure, but mainly mean satisfying needs. Children in the pre-school phase do not act so much according to objects as in the previous phase, but rather according to their ideas.

So, it was that Maria Lúcia playing alone (living with her grandmother and an elderly aunt, she wasn't allowed to play at friends' or cousins' houses) invented new games, and substituted her friends with day-to-day objects. She subverted then, acting in the way Vygotsky indicates:

… in games, objects lose their determining force. The child sees an object, but acts differently in relation to what he sees. In this way, the child reaches the condition in which he begins to act independently of the things he sees. (Vygotsky 1991, 110)

So, I only used to play on my own … I played at being at mass or at the office. I didn't like playing with dolls very much. I hardly ever played with dolls. There was the local newspaper. My grandmother used to buy it, and I used to collect them and take them home to play being at mass and at offices. I used to like books, I used to like writing. That's why I used to play being in an office, because for me that was where people were always writing. (Maria Lúcia)

We didn't even have television. It used to be … playing house, and … tying a piece of wood, it was a doll. And I don't feel, I don't feel at all sad recalling that phase of my childhood because it gave me the chance to … let my imagination run wild. (Élida)

When they were old and had been thrown out, the piece of wood, the church newsletter, the local newspaper, were rubbish, but they had sparked the child's imagination. In the words of Jobim e Souza (1996), this is the game allowing the child's complicity with objects, saving the child from being consumed by conceit.

Hilda's statement is also provocative: 'There was very little fun … we really had to study.' There was no place for games. It was seriousness, study, commitment, religion. Things which have left a mark on her to this day. She does not allow herself pleasure, the pleasure of reading without commitment, buying a novel from the newsagent. She buys only books on education. Nor is there the pleasure of personal writing — only professional writing for school, plans, planning, prayers … The mark of religion where there is no room for pleasure is striking in her narrative:

At home there was that Bible reading, my mother was always very religious … […]
She used to read the Bible even if we didn't know how to, it was always open and
she would read.. My mother used to read lots of books about saints. […] At Christmas it was always Baby Jesus. Always reading. At night we would get toys as
presents, it was all that. Even our presents, we used to put them in the crib, you
know? They would stay there till the next day. Everything that was ours had to be
put there for Baby Jesus first. We could only take it out of the crib the next day […]
Every day we prayed a lot, everyone with their little prayer book in their hands.

But there was some escape. Some type of subversion. And Hilda would
make a little game out of the ritual; she would use laughter as an escape
from the imposition. This is laughter in the Bakhtinian sense, which unre-
presses and represents a position of opposition to the official world.

Those things left a mark. That part of the litany, almost learnt by heart. The Litany
of our Lady Aparecida,[1] then … I remember there was one part that went like this:
'Virgin Mother', *but my sisters used to say* 'vermin mother' … *when they said* 'vermin
mother', *stop now!* my mother said, who was always serious, you know? I kept trying to control myself so as not to laugh, you know?

And Hilda laughs now, she gives a good hearty laugh, searching for that
laugh that was kept in the past for so long, in her memory. At the time, it
couldn't be an explicit laugh, but it was a laugh inside her which she subverted, which turned the moment of prayer into a game which she looked
forward to.

You could mark the place; you knew which bit was going to be really good because
of the ending. These bits these stood out. (Hilda)

Games, however, are not remembered very much in the stories they told.
Why were they not pulled out of their memory's trunk? Is it because they
were never put there? Is it because they are in the realm of forgetfulness?
Why did this happen? Or did they really never exist? Have today's teachers,
involved in their daily routine at home and at school, lost the wonderful
memory of the world of enjoyment, of fantasy? How do they see their
pupils' games nowadays? What place is there for games in their classrooms?

---

1. Brazilian Saint, patron saint of Brazil.

In fact, very little. When the teachers tell about their lives at school, games do not make an appearance. Nor are they present to any noticeable extent in their classrooms today. Games which had so little meaning during childhood were erased from the memory. A school where laughter, enjoyment and games were not included were not worth a mention. Something was lost there ...

Remembering Reading in Childhood and Adolescence

But if games remain well hidden in the memory, at least fantasy is set free among the characters of books. We put books taken from the past on the bookshelves of the present. From the bottom of the trunk appear the most beautiful stories, the 'Ugly Duckling', 'Little Red Riding Hood', 'Cinderella', the 'Goat and the Jaguar', the 'Three Little Pigs', the 'Prancing Nanny-Goat', the 'Devil's Protegé', the 'Cheated Hunter', 'Snapper and Barker', the story of 'Paraffin', 'The musician who when he blew the sheets of music flew away and he couldn't play', 'The Firefly collection', 'The Lost Island', 'Tilly the Butterfly'. And we must not forget the comics: 'Little Lulu's Club', 'Tubby's Club', 'The Little Witch', 'The Story of Pimples'.[2]

Books which also peopled our imaginary worlds also formed part of our childhood. Through these characters, children enter into the world of fantasy — fantasy which is necessary to gain a better understanding of reality.

And I kept imagining other events in these stories, I often wrote words for the characters that weren't in the book. I invented ... It was funny at times what I did to change the course of the stories. (Maria Lúcia)

Just as she used to play offices, making the old newspapers her friends, Maria Lúcia used her imagination, her capacity to break away from reality through story books, living together with the characters, giving them life, inventing, changing the story, as she would perhaps like to change hers ...

2. Brazilian titles of fairy-tale books: 'O Patinho feio', 'O Chapeuzinho vermelho', 'Cinderela', 'O bode e a onça', 'Os três Porquinhos', 'A cabra Cabrioloa', 'O afilhado do diabo' 'O caçador logrado' 'Totolino e o Totolão', 'A história do Parafino', 'Coleção "Vagalume"', 'A ilha perdida', 'A borboleta Atíria'. Original titles of the comics are: 'Clube da Luluzinha', 'Do Bolinha', 'Bruxinha Meméia', 'História da Brotoeja'.

there she was learning, rehearsing new possibilities of acting, of intervening in reality.

All the fruit of one's imagination, starting off from reality, is busy in describing a complete circle and embodying itself once again in reality. (Vygotsky 1987a, 51)

Beside the children's books, there is a row of teenage ones: *Pollyana*, *Sidartha*, the *Prophet*.[3] Authors are plucked from the memories of the teachers: Marina Colassanti, Cecília Meireles, Carlos Drumond, Orígenes Lessa, Eça de Queiroz, Manoel Bandeira, Machado de Assis.

Our girls and teenagers invented ... imagined ... fantasised, created. For Vygotsky (1987a) creation exists whenever human beings imagine, blend, modify and create something new. For him imagination which is based on experience tends to embody life. Fantasy is composed of elements taken from reality which are re-worked in our imagination.

The greater our experience, the more material our imagination will have at its disposal. And our interviewees imagined, guided by their experiences, that they lived in relationships with other people, and with books. Many books were taken out of memory's trunk and they tell us of children and teenagers who used to read and have pleasure in reading. Their very words are quite eloquent:

I always liked reading a lot ... I started reading very early, I used to read two books a month on average ... (Élida)

I really used to read collections of books, I devoured books ... and I always wrote at the same time ... Writing for me was always a natural thing, it was never forced, and always closely linked to my activities. (Janaína)

I always used to read and write. (Maria Lúcia)

I loved reading stories ... and my mother also had many books, old ones from the 60's, but there were lots of good things. Sometimes I used to read these stories. Then after a few days I'd go back and read them again. I liked reading. (Luciana)

---

3. Eleonor H. Porter, *Pollyana*, Rio de Janeiro: Ediouro, s/d; Herman Hesse (1998), *Sidartha*, Rio de Janeiro, 38a. ed.; Khalil Gibran (1997), *Profeta*, Rio de Janeiro: Nova Alexandria.

The Lost Lines

And what happened to this enjoyment of reading and writing? Looking through the words of the teachers, looking at the present, we see that the situation today is not the same. Reading is not done as it used to be: it is occasional, casual, closed in on their professional area or limited to quick information gleaned from the newspaper or an informative magazine. Writing is kept to a minimum — only that which is necessary, always impersonal and burocratic.

What happened? Where was the pleasure of reading and writing lost? A number of reasons are indicated: no time, no money to buy books … On becoming adults, they repeat the musician Paraffin's story … The one who upon blowing his instrument made the sheets of music fly and he couldn't play any more … The letters and books have flown away like the sheets of music … and the teachers cannot read. What wind was so strong that it took them so far out of their reach? How can we collect them together and bring them back? Is it the school that is responsible for this flight? What has the school done to these readers and writers?

Perhaps the answer is in the words of Maria Lúcia, the girl who played at being at mass, and at offices. In the day-to-day of this lonely girl, two realities of her cultured world left a mark on her experience, penetrating into her imagination, into the kingdom of games: mass and school. 'And I thought that mass was like school …' is how Maria Lúcia expressed herself. A short sentence so full of truth. Church and school: the places of stereotyped rituals, with their unchanging routine. They are part of the impersonal procedures to which people are subjected, the general rules, the silence which has certain correct moments to be interrupted. Collective gestures: sitting in rows, the right time to sit down, to stand up. The ceremony presided over by the 'priest-teacher'. The passive listening, seriousness, no spontaneous or individual speaking, no enjoyment, no laughter. The chorus of voices reading out loud, reciting. Reading by heart, but not from the heart, mechanically, without meaning. There is no room for personal expression, only for artificiality, for distance from life. Church and school: a sad portrait. A photograph taken by a girl who managed to take it at an angle where the two overlay.

This is also the portrait of the school that was painted with the strokes found in the teachers' memories. A place where reading and writing are closed in on the objectives of the school itself, they do not go beyond its walls. Obligatory reading, from the school and for the school, where books are read to be catalogued, where words are written to be copied.

The pupil submits himself to this, but somehow manages to subvert the order to dribble the obligations. This becomes clear in the stories of Luciana and Hilda, reacting to obligatory reading and copying at school.

I didn't read the whole book because you used to find ways round it, 'cause in the books there were always those index card things. After I discovered the ways round it, I didn't read them. There was one time; I'll never forget it. I hadn't read the book ... She called me ... I started to tell the beginning of the book ... I'd only read a little bit. I started talking up at the front, telling lots of the detail just so that she would get tired and call someone else. We'd got it figured out. I started telling the details, but ever so slowly, you know? ... And then it happened ... just as planned. She said: ... someone else now. She called someone else. I didn't read. Around that time, I got me a book that left quite a mark on me, it was a book of poetry by Manoel Bandeira, 'My Favourite Poems'. It was at home too, I don't know where the book came from ... it was just there. But Manoel Bandeira's books, I read them all. Nearly every day. But that's because no-one asked us to at school. The only one like that which I read for pleasure. (Hilda)

There's one thing I remember about writing: spelling practice. I remember clearly: teacher used to write the word on the board, we used to read the word, then she'd rub it off and we'd have to write it. I'd wait for her to rub it off and then I'd look at the little marks that were left on the board. That's the only thing I remember. (Luciana)

In whose interest is it that this ritual should continue? How long are we going to sit passively watching this situation? How long is the school going to ignore 'crimes' like these, pretending not to see them? Why is it so difficult to allow other people to speak, pupils, teachers?

These are questions that the facts registered by the memories of the teachers we interviewed cause us to reflect upon. Memories which illuminate a reality which has remained hidden: the loss of the social and cultural meaning of school. A school where there is no place for aesthetic, which are substituted by knowledge without meaning, unconnected with life. In this research, we are also committing a type of transgression: we have not investigated content and technique which could contribute to effective teaching, but we have pulled the strings of the teachers' memories to allow the person to emerge from them and find in this the possibilities of a transformation.

It is necessary, therefore, to give new meaning to church and school. So that in this new meaning they can become similar again, trying to celebrate life, gestures full of meaning, the subject that speaks and is heard, personal words, and words which together build new worlds.

We must gather up Paraffin's music-sheets so that we can play again ... A difficult task, but not an impossible one. This is the proposal of this research. To hear more teachers, to fetch other stories from their memories, stories of people, towns, schools ... which will lead us to discover their reading and writing ... bring them together so that we will have a beautiful sound, an orchestra playing.

References

Agostinho, S. (1975). *Confissões*. Porto: Apostoladoda imprensa.

Bakhtin, M. (Volosinov, V.N.) (1980). *Le freudisme*. Paris: Lage D'homme.

Bakhtin, M. (1985). *Estética de la criacion verbal*. Buenos Aires: Siglo Veintiuno, Argentina Editores.

Bakhtin, M. (1988). *Marxismo e filosofia da linguagem*. São Paulo: Hucitec.

Benjamin, W. (1987). *Obras escolhidas. Magia e técnica, arte e política*. São Paulo: Brasiliense.

Chiara, A.C.R. (1994). Leitura e memória. *Caderno de Leitura*. PROLER, 1, 67-83.

Drumond de Andrade, Carlos (ed.) (1997). *Antologia poética*. Rio de Janeiro: Ed. Record.

Freeman, M. (1993). *Re-writing the self. History, memory, narrative*. London: Routledge.

Galeano, E. (1991/1993). *O livro dos abraços*. Porto Alegre: L & PM.

Jobim e Souza, S. (1996). Re-significando a psicologia do desenvolvimento: uma contribuição crítica à pesquisa da infância. In S. Kramer and M.I.F.P. Leite (eds.), *Infância: Fios e desafios da pesquisa*. Campinas: Papirus.

Kramer, S. (1995). *Alfabetização, leitura e escrita. Formação de professores em curso*. Rio de Janeiro: Escola de professores.

Vygotsky, L.S. (1987a). *La imaginacion y el arte en la infancia*. México: Hispanicas.

Vygotsky, L.S. (1987b). *Pensamento e linguagem*. São Paulo: Martins Fontes.

Vygotsky, L.S. (1987c). Memory and its development in childhood. In L.S. Vygotsky, *Problems of general psychology*. New York: Plenum Press.

Vygotsky, L.S. (1991). *A formação social da mente*. São Paulo: Martins Fontes.

18 Teacher's and Researcher's Interactions in Classroom Discourse: Different Ways of Organising Salient and Problematic Actions

Maria Cecília Camargo Magalhães

I have been working with teacher in-service training since 1988 (Magalhães 1990, 1994, 1994a, 1996, 1996a, 1999) in order to investigate how to develop procedures in language classes to collaboratively[1] handle those meanings, assumed as true, discuss and transform them. In other words, I became interested in making sense of my own discourse and how it might contribute to the deconstruction of expected or taken-for-granted meanings in classroom discursive practices, as well as contribute to the construction of new meanings. That is to say, I became interested in understanding how classroom research — aimed at creating contexts to rethink the relationship between theory and practice, as well as the contexts in which teachers and researcher collaborate to reflect on educational practices — could thereby assist the teacher in questioning:

— what was taught, how it was taught, and the theories, objectives and motives underlying the choices made during classroom practices;
— how students' were allowed to voice their opinions;
— which interests those discursive practices served; and
— how to reconstruct classroom practices as a result of collaboration and reflection.

This project has been based on theoretical support that emphasised the importance of reflective and collaborative processes in education that sup-

---

1. Collaboration is understood as co-construction of knowledge by all participants throughout the course of the project.

port worries about the 'utilitarian ends' of reflection (Goodman 1988, 18; Wong 1993).

The project aimed at analysing the process of interactions that took place between five teachers and myself, as researcher, during a shared (de)constructing of meaning in teaching and learning in language and writing classes in an elementary state school. During this process, I realised that the ways I organised my discourse to deal with problematic issues and conflict differed from that of the teachers' (Magalhães 1999). The aim of this paper is to discuss these different ways of discourse organisation, during an interaction in which I (R) and three of the five teachers (J, 2nd grade teacher; E, 2nd grade teacher; C, 1st grade teacher) discuss one of the teacher's (J) practices during the activity of writing a book with the children. The teachers and I are collaborators in the research process so that I am to be viewed as an external researcher.

First, the theories which this paper draws on will be discussed. The crucial importance of language and collaboration for critical reflection in the school context of continuing education, and the different ways of organising discourse to introduce controversy concerning the issues discussed will be stressed. Next, the contexts of data collection and data analysis will be described, and, finally, I will present reflections on teacher's and researcher's differing discourse practices in order to establish controversy and its relation to the construction of meaning by the teachers.

Language as the Locus of Intervention

This study is based on the understanding of human action as significant, that is, as socio-historically situated action whose structural and functional organisation is a product of socialisation. As discussed by Bronckart (1997) verbal actions are understood as language in their discursive dimension and seen as constitutive of human action, i.e., as forms of actions that show the agent's appropriation of social activities mediated by language. It is through this process of meaning and negotiation of values in specific social and historical-cultural contexts that new forms of action are constructed, as well as consciousness of our identities *are* developed. As pointed out by Bruner (1997, 34), our values are always shared and related to a cultural community.

Habermas (1990, 1982, 1987) discusses this negotiation process as *communicative action*, i.e., as a process through which we constitute the social contexts and ourselves as reflective agents. We fix the boundaries for choices of action by organising collective and social knowledge into three formal worlds: objective, social and subjective. During the discursive practices oriented towards mutual understanding, the agents define their plans of action collaboratively and through actions of language evaluate and question the intended validity of each other's understanding (representations) related to each of the worlds. During this evaluative process, the validity of the presupposition of the agent may be questioned by the participants in the interaction and may be transformed.

Therefore, the (de)construction of meaning in language classroom practices as well as the understanding of action motivated by an intention (proactive projections towards the represented worlds) and by a reason (retroactive projections towards the represented worlds) *are* central concepts to this study (Bronckart 1993, 1997, 1999). In other words, an investigation in which the further education of teachers emphasises specific contexts as the locus of theory (de)construction needs to focus on what teachers know about themselves as professionals in specific contexts, their understanding of their students cognition, interests, needs, (what students know, what they need to know) and how to handle this knowledge during classroom practices.

Collaboration and Reflection in the Context of the Further Education of Teachers

In this study, teachers' negotiations with the external researcher are understood as a locus of collaborative investigation into the conflicting ways the participants' evaluate and represent their own ways of acting, their intentions and motives, as well as those of the others within a specific school context. This makes it possible to understand how:

— classroom discursive practice is organised;
— classroom discursive practice is questioned;
— new forms of knowing and acting are constructed.

Furthermore, it facilitates both an understanding of and a confrontation with how discourses that aimed at questioning the relationship between teaching-learning theories and the ways classroom practices are organised.

I call this process of self-consciousness 'reflection' of verbal actions. *Reflection* is understood as the reorganisation or reconstruction of practices that may lead to a new understanding of the context of a specific action (Grimmett 1988 in Pérez Gómez 1992, 12) which is seen by a participant in an interaction as problematic. According to Grimmett, reflection is understood as a means to practice understanding and transformation and involves (a) rethinking the situation by asking questions which need clarification; (b) discussing aspects that had previously been ignored; (c) attributing new meanings to a situation already discussed.

Smyth (1992, 295), based on the work of Freire (1972), proposes four ways of acting in order for teachers to be engaged in reflection. These are related to different ways of self-questioning:

Describing	– What do I do?
Informing	– What does it mean?
Confronting	– How do I come to be like that?
Reconstructing	– How could I act differently?

These actions would allow the agents to reflect upon their classroom language actions; describing such actions, questioning them, looking at them with new eyes and in this way gaining knowledge themselves as a result of the questions and the new meanings introduced by other participants. It will be possible for these agents to confront their representations of themselves as professionals (what it means to be a teacher in that specific context, what kind of student they are forming, as well as the real interests that inform their action, are they working to maintain or transform the institutional context, discourses, and the values they are questioning). In fact, following Habermas (1987, 430), in order to question the meaning, it is necessary to establish a problem.

Therefore, by engaging in these four forms of actions related to their teaching, teachers will focus on those aspects that, for any reason, are a problem for them, or are questioned by another participant. Also, by addressing the problem with other participants' collaboration it may be easier for them to deal with conflicting meanings, to reflect on them, to uncover how they come to act that way, and to reconstruct theory and practice. So, these actions make it possible for agents to reflect upon and question their classroom actions, as well as their representation of the interests for which they are working (Habermas 1987). In the context of further education, it is crucial for transformation to investigate how the interacting participants organise their discourses to evaluate themselves and the others, to question the validity of their and the others' discursive practices and to introduce new ways to look at teaching and learning, as well as to themselves as teachers, based on local narratives (related to that specific context).

Contrasting Ways to Organise Controversy

Kress discusses that both, narrative and argument,

as cultural textual forms provide sharply contrasting means of dealing with the same — fundamental — social and cultural issue: how to accommodate difference, contestation, conflict around salient social and cultural values in any domain and provide integrative rather than fissive resolutions of such differences. (1989, 11)

In fact, as emphasised by the author, all cultures need both argument and narrative in order to deal with these contrasting needs. For him, the argument will provide textual organisation to address difference, which is a crucial issue if we intend to create contexts for questioning and discussion of values and representations related to education. The resolution of difference and closure in this textual organisation is usually given by an event external to the text or by the intervention of an authority.

On the other hand, the narrative will provide a means for dealing productively with difference, a means for the resolution of differences. As discussed by Kress (p. 14), 'the resolution in this case comes from within the text, so that resolution is neither overtly visible nor problematic'.

I have noticed in teacher/teacher and teacher/researcher interactions that other textual organisations work in the same direction, that is, they suppress the appearance of difference. For instance, scripts and/or description of actions may be used to reconcile competing explanations to specific problems. The use of one, the other, or both, to organise our discourse to deal with controversy, is a choice based on agents' objectives in a specific situation and culture, i.e., stressing difference and critique or resolution and closure. However, the choices will greatly affect the meaning produced as well as the possibility to reach the objective proposed: convincing the other to re-think his/her practice and the theories behind his/her choices.

As discussed by Kress, all cultures need ways of handling difference, since these are the motor of transformation of values and representations. In that direction, investigations conducted by Liberali (1999); Machado and Magalhães (1999) revealed the close relationship between critical reflection

and argumentative processes, as well as its crucial importance for the transformation of educational practices.

The Objective and Socio-Cultural Contexts for Data Collection

Data for this study was collected at a Brazilian public school in a poor
district of São Paulo, an industrial city in the southeast of Brazil, during a
discussion session between this researcher and three volunteer teachers (J, E
and C). The teachers and I had agreed on a contract to jointly reflect on our
actions during classroom activities, as well as during sessions we called 'reflective'. It was our declared objective to reflect on the reasons why students
in these classes had problems with reading and writing. Although, it was my
aim to focus on reading, in the discussion we focused mainly on writing,
since this was the teachers' main interest.

The school is near a slum area (favela), and most of the students come
from low literacy homes (most parents were illiterate).

During a two-year period, I observed and videotaped the teachers' work
once a week, while participating in the classroom practices as a collaborator
(that was how I was introduced to the students). Once a week we worked together during that period officially designated to class planning and discussion. This was the session I call 'Reflective Session' as it was organised so
that all the project participants could interact and reflect on the classroom
practices of one particular teacher.

It is worth stressing that before the session, the participants had individually already watched the videotape of the session to be discussed. This was
a choice I made for two reasons: a) to provide teachers with some time to
think about their actions, without being placed in a stressing situation, and
b) to give more time to spend together in school. In fact, inviting me or other
colleagues to watch the classroom videotape was a decision that was taken
in the second year of conducting the project. However, the conditions for doing this in school were not good, and also the time available to us was not
enough.

Other decisions about conducting the project changed over time. At the
beginning of the study, the reflective session was conducted individually
with each teacher by the external researcher. However, as it had been agreed
from the beginning of the study that any of the participants could propose
changes in the direction of the research, the teachers decided that the session
should include the entire assembled group. From then on, this session aimed

Participants	Interventions	Initiations
Researcher: R	112	11
Teacher: J	74	13
Teacher: E	34	2
Teacher: C	23	2

Table 18.1. Summary of Discursive Events (27 exchanges).

at constructing in the school a context for discussion in which all the teachers and the researcher could mutually consider each other as a professional. They interacted in studying and discussing the theoretical bases of their discursive practices, as well as constructing new ones, and reflected on teaching-learning objectives for that specific context, students needs, and how to work with them in order to reach the proposed aims. In other words, a context in which the practice was seen as a locus for the (de)construction of meaning.

Data Analysis

It was my purpose to understand how the 'communicative action' of the participants worked while interacting in a specific situation with regard to teaching-learning in language classes. I wanted to question each participant's representation related to the three worlds — the objective, the social and the subjective — discussed by Habermas (i.e., the forms and types of verbal interactions and the concrete conditions of their realisation). I also looked for decisions on the forms of organising content based on motives and intentions in prototypical sequences (Adam 1992; Bronckart 1999) that could reveal how each participant, as a response to the constructed interactional context, had organised her action in order to deal with contestation, conflict and tension, as well as with the knowledge that resulted from them.

The session was organised mainly as an interactive dialogical discourse, and, as expected, most of the interventions (Roulet 1991) were between me (R as external researcher) and J (whose class was the focus of discussion) who was responsible for most of initiations as shown in Table 18.1.

Teachers' and Researcher's Discourse Practices

This section discusses how teachers and researcher organised their discourse to negotiate meaning in the classroom writing practices of J in her second-grade class with students from homes with a low literacy level, while reflecting also on concrete instances of her practice concerning text production (for a book). In the first part, I will discuss how I, as researcher, organised my discourse to negotiate new ways of understanding and reconstructing action.

Pressing J to describe her classroom practices. As it was my aim to create contexts for meta-processes, I (R) based on Smyth (1992) organised my discourse in order to ask J to *describe* her classroom action and the objectives that supported her choices. Description would engage J in rethinking her actions, during text production in her second-year class, based on theories that supported the representations of working with reading and writing in that context. It would be possible for the participants (including herself) not only to evaluate J's actions, but also their own actions. In fact, asking J to describe her practice, as well as establishing a controversy, aimed at creating a context for other kinds of meta-actions that compose reflection: informing, confronting, reconstruction.

I initiated the interaction by asking J to describe her pedagogical practice with writing:

R1: There is something I would like to ask. It is this: when you worked with the little books ... ah ... those right there (points to the books with J). It was their first draft ... why, how did you do that? *I would like you to tell me a little bit about this process to do these books.*

J1: When?

R2: On that day I was there, you told the story and ... and then?

J2: ... Yeah ... I returned the little books to them [the children] and then we tried a little bit together, I kind of tried to retell the story with them, right? And they were supposed to do it like this, they were supposed to try to read and try to see what they thought was written, what was necessary ... what it needed ... If they understood what they had written.

The negotiation process: establishing controversy. Several linguistic choices I made, following J's description, reveal my representations of her classroom action on:

— my role as an external researcher in that specific context;
— teaching-learning as related to both situations, classroom and reflective session;
— the writing process, based on that specific context.

The fragment below shows how I organised my discourse in order to provide a new context for looking at J's work, and the students' problems while learning how to write:

R3:   But did you discuss with them how they were supposed to read, how they were supposed to ask questions, what they were supposed to check?

J3:   You mean … like getting a text, for instance?

R4:   Yeah, didn't you discuss with them before, write on the board, discuss it with everybody, didn't you offer a model?

J4:   No, no, I didn't.

R5:   Because, in fact, you see, J …

J5:   Yeah, I think it is still missing something, because on that day they couldn't finish it. Many of them didn't finish it on that day. On another day, I repeated it, like in an attempt for them to finish their own writing, the rewriting of the story. Now, for instance, for us to work this correction together, I didn't do this.

R6:   In fact, this book should be the final process. They should have already written, rewritten, corrected … and then done the book. Final process, right? Because, what is writing? Isn't it a process?

J6:   Well …, in this case they were writing somewhere else.

I initiated my discourse with the argumentative operator 'but' (R3) in order to establish a controversy and to stress the difference that I wanted to bring in. However, to clarify my questions and also to provide a resolution of difference, I organised my discourse with a description of the actions that, from my point of view, should have been enacted (R4). This organisation had the purpose of bringing up the theory of reading and writing which we had already discussed and to justify my conclusion in (R6) 'this book should be the final process … what is writing? Isn't it a process?'

J's answer (J5) reveals that she took my questioning into consideration (it is important to remember my role in that context, in terms of knowledge, I was in a position of power as a researcher). She initiates her answer by justifying her action — the work is not complete yet — but recognises she had not developed collaborative work with the students during the process (J5) and asks for clarification (J6). It is interesting to realise that J initiates her enunciation with the mark 'well' (J6) which has a fatic function, but also introduces a presupposition of the suspension of disbelief, i.e., the idea that I might be right — let's suppose you are right, then ...

All through the session, one can see the organisation of my discourse with argumentative sequences to deal with issues I considered problematic and wanted to discuss, or issues with which I disagreed, with regard to reading and writing in that specific context. I clearly presented my controversy, and my conclusions (restated throughout the session) were supported by arguments that had the purpose of orienting towards the theoretical reasons of acting in another way.

However, my discourse was also organised into instructional sequences in order to clearly establish the relationship between theory and practice, as well as to demonstrate how to act in that new theoretical paradigm. By constantly emphasising the same conclusion — reading and writing are processes that have to be taught to students in that specific context — I was arguing in favour of a new organisation of the work in the process of writing. Thus, arguing based on theoretical knowledge, as well as describing procedural actions, was aimed at demonstrating how the pedagogical practice could be structured, in order to provide the teacher's context for reflection (informing, confronting, relating new concepts to practice and reconstructing). The linguistic characteristics of my enunciation such as: 'you start by', 'the process of writing is', 'the students have to think beforehand', 'you have to' also revealed my representations on my role as teacher-developer.

The fragment below exemplifies such an organisation:

R: On the very first day of the first year of school you start a process you will always use, right? Then, what is the writing process? It is thinking of what you are going to write, and always telling them why it is important to act like this. S/he can write, s/he can tell his/her neighbour about what s/he intends to write, about the kind of text s/he is supposed to do, right? But s/he has to think beforehand. Why? Because this planning is an important part of the writing process. You have to organise your thoughts first, then write. Have a global view of what you are going to develop, right? Then, all right, then you see 'We are going to tell the story again. Then we are going to write on the board what is more important in the story, then we are going to write the story again'. What helps you in this story is the narrative. If you rewrite a text that is narrative, the structure of the story helps you ... But an interesting idea is always to go back to the structure of the story. 'What have you got in a story? Which are the parts of a story?'

Also, to show the importance of understanding the specific context in which teaching and learning has taken place, I worked to establish a controversy (based on their discourse) concerning the representations they had of their students, their needs and the teaching-learning in that context, as seen in the example below:

R: But, you see, if you don't work with this (how to structure thought in the reading and production of narratives) they will never learn, J, you can see that, we are always saying 'they can't'

J: I ... this way ... it is difficult. I haven't been working it more because it is difficult.

R: They don't have these structures; they don't know how to organise their thoughts this way. It is difficult, now, if you don't do anything because it is difficult, because they are not able, then, it doesn't work either. Then, in fact, what you are supposed to do is ... all the time ... you can show how you think (...)

Until now I have examined the ways I organised my discourse during the negotiation process in order to involve J in describing her classroom action, informing and confronting them. Next, I will discuss how this discursive pattern made it possible for J to reflect and develop a discourse about her own teaching, uncovering the representations that are guiding her classroom action, asking questions that problematise her teaching and acting on the world in order to change it.

J's reflective processes. Although, J's interventions bring about some questions to justify her actions, they, at the same time, reveal the assumptions they are based on, such as, 'our students can't read'; 'I haven't been working with it more because it is difficult' and 'I think it is already much better, for instance, if they are already able to write this here'. They also ask for confirmation of the new information being introduced by me, as in:

J: Then, in this case the text was given, we read the text and then, next I'm supposed to tell them to write, or not? ... Tell me, go back a little bit to the part you were saying. Previously ...

Still, some fragments reveal moments in which J thinks her action over, informs herself and reflects aloud on how to reconstruct classroom practices. For instance, in the excerpt below she proposes a reformulation of the oral practices to teach her students to organise their oral production, based on what was being discussed about the organisation of written language in reading and writing practices:

J: I was thinking of doing it like this ... when they come to class, they want to tell something, right? They arrive telling things ... many things going on, right? 'then, Pluf, right?' Then I do ... 'I can't understand anything of what you are saying'. Then I am thinking about doing it orally, you know? I think it is so difficult ... in my mind I would like to use this you are saying when they want to tell their things, you know ...

Also, the same happens when she herself sums up the evaluations of her work with writing:

J: Then, in my class, you think like the process was not enough, ... it is mainly the matter of, like ... text structure that I think it was like ...

Teachers' changing language dealing with controversial actions. The ways J, E and C organised their discourse in order to state a problem (a controversy) concerning a colleague's classroom practice, or concerning my discourse, differ from the ways I had organised mine (previously described). Their discourse to deal with difference had an argumentative function (Kress 1998), i.e., aimed at showing disagreement, sharing opinion or representation, in order to convince the participant, it was not structured in an argumentative sequence. The controversy is referred to, but it is not emphasised through an argumentative structure that would bring into discussion the difference supported by arguments and would provide context for reflection and new meaning construction. Teachers usually organise their verbal action into scripts/ descriptions of actions that describe their way of dealing with that problematic situation, ways of resolving difference, i.e., the text is organised towards the resolution of difference. For instance, in the intervention below E reports her different understanding of her students' behavior during classroom action. This was evaluated by the researcher as 'too messy'. E begins by reporting what she had observed in one of the videotapes of her classroom:

E: When they were there, on that day, I think we were kind of excited, you and I, we were excited, because I saw it on the tape, the students were great. They participated. Now, we were the ones who were anxious. Ciça (the researcher) couldn't take any talk. She (referring to me) went like this: 'We will have to work this', and it came out a fine job, they participated, and that second part, Ciça, with our complementing it [the teacher and children's work] on the board, you should see how much they participated.

E: I thought it was interesting. And, by that time, we were not happy. I was … the great majority was working. And silently.

R: OK. I saw on the tape, the problem was the outside noise, but some of the students are too talkative. Well, maybe we could reorganise the classroom some way. Because some … you know … maybe observe who sits near who … reorganise the classroom, because there are some students at the back, they play all the time. The problem, I think, started because I was near them, at the back and I became irritated with them playing all the time. It seems we have got a problem, there, E, because some of them are good students, but others do not work at all. Well …

In this fragment, E shows her disagreement concerning my judgement of her classroom management (creating a learning environment, maintaining student involvement) by reporting her understanding of the students' great involvement and blaming my anxiety. The possibility of discussion is created by the researcher's answer that stresses difference and supports her conclusion on concrete data — some students were playing all the time, and there is a need for classroom reorganisation because some are not working. In fact, E was not reflecting on the problem I had pointed out, but only presenting her different opinion concerning my understanding of her classroom.

Another example of this type of discourse to handle conflict is provided by J, who talks about the tables in the classroom organised in a 'U' form. An organisation I had suggested:

J: I ... I decided to organise the classroom as a U. You can't believe what happened. By half of the time, the room ... well ... do you know when you spread out the desks in the middle of the classroom? Nothing was organised. Everything was spread out. Well ... you know it, when you spread out desks through all classroom. I said: 'Guys, I want all of you to stand up, and to look at what happened with the classroom'. They did that and five minutes later, everything was in rows again. They were all in rows.

R: In rows, because this is the way they are used to.

J: Yes, but I thought that was a crazy situation. Do you know when you mix lots of things? Everything was mixed.

R: When you tried that time, do you remember E? You had the same problem. They have to learn to do that in an organised way.

J: We organised in a U, and during break the desks were mixed again.

R: They are not used to.

J: I do not know. I did not see how it had happened. When I saw, I thought: 'My Goodness, if someone else came into this room, he/she is going to ...'. It was when I asked them to look at that mess.

C: Hum ...

J: I think we have to experience it many times. It is too different from what they are used to ...

C: Last Wednesday we had a number of activities, so I asked them (the students) before going into the room: 'Listen, guys, today we have this, this, and that. What do you think about leaving the desks as they are, or rearranging them again?' 'Oh, no, teacher, this way I don't want it' 'me either'. They don't want to be in rows anymore.

This fragment shows how J stresses that she disagrees with the researcher who was suggesting that they organise the tables in the room in the form of a U. She structures her discourse with the report of her classroom experience (description of action) to justify her controversy. Similarly, C structures her controversy towards J and her agreement concerning my suggestion, by describing her students' reaction towards organising the chairs in rows.

The reports of classroom experiences, as it was used in the fragments above, reveals that the teacher's discursive choices, focused on describing the action to deal with controversy, and she did not provide a context to stress the importance of a different organisation of teaching-learning. Therefore, they did not create a context for critical reflection, since the focus is on discussion of utility (it works, it does not work). In other words, the focus is on the resolution of differences.

Reflections on Teachers' and Researcher's Different Discourse to Deal with Controversy

Hence, the analysis of the ways that I (as researcher) and the teachers organised verbal actions to focus on issues considered problematic, and posed for discussion, either by me or by a teacher, reveals that scripts and reports of classroom events are the teachers's most used form to question the practice of others and to provide a solution for a controversy. Descriptions of action have the purpose of questioning, of revealing the teachers' ideas on the issue discussed and of providing a resolution to difference. That is, reporting experiences works to argue in favour of or against a given issue without bringing difference into discussion. Therefore, it provides the means to discuss the difference, the meaning that underlies each choice, or the interest each is serving: maintaining or transforming discursive practices in the classrooms, and therefore changing actions in that particular context. But, the change in textual organisation does not clearly problematise the object of discussion, which is that it is important to point out that to collaborate in the process of negotiating and reflecting upon a problem does not only mean to agree or to disagree, but to justify a position based on reasons supported by theories about teaching-learning and by the students' needs and language capacities. It is necessary to provide a context for self-understanding and reconstruction that involves actions that inform and confront the teacher with these theories, as well as students' needs and language capacities.

However, it seems that the teachers' choices were not based on their desire to avoid conflict, since they emphasised disagreement, but they were based on an organisation of verbal action toward the immediate solution of problems, as discussed by Goodman (1984) and Wong (1993), as common in school contexts.

By observing the teachers' and the researcher's discourses to establish controversy, and the teachers' thinking processes that result from both, it seems that the organisation of argumentative sequences favours reflection

(Smyth 1992) about theories that underlie different actions, and about results reached in choosing to act one way, instead of another. The organisation in reporting experiences with argumentative value seems to favour a utilitarian end (Goodman 1984). That is, verbal action is organised to present a solution for a situation considered problematic.

I have observed, in other discussions during this project (Magalhães 1994, 1994a), that a teacher may really modify her action based on another teacher's description and suggestion of alternative action. However, since the reason *why* to act in a specific way in a particular situation is not always focused on, teachers may just substitute the problematic action with the one suggested. It seems, though, that this choice is not due to reflection upon the action based on the needs of the actual situation, or on teaching-learning theories, but it is due to the description being appropriated as a *receipt* (utilitarian end).

So, considering the importance for self-understanding and transformation that emphasising conflict brings about, whether in the discursive practices in the classroom, in the case of this paper, referring to teachers-teachers and teacher-researcher relationships, or in the discursive practices in the classroom between students-students and student-teacher, it seems crucial that differences are clearly brought to light. That is, it is important that the reasons for them are presented, as well as the arguments that support them. It seems also crucial that the different organisation of discourse is pointed out and worked through with teachers, not only to gain a better understanding of their own action, but also to gain a better understanding of what a different organisation of their discourse means.

References

Adam, J.M. (1992). *Les textes: Receit, description, argumentation et dialogue.* Paris: Nathan.

Bronckart, J.P. (1993). Action theory and the analysis of action in education. Paper presented at the 5th European Association for Research on Learning and Instruction.

Bronckart, J.P. (1997). Teorias de la acción, lenguaje, lenguas y discurso. In J. Wertsch, P. del Rio, A. Álvarez (eds.), *La mente sociocultural: aproximaciones teóricas y aplicadas.* Madrid: Fundación Infancia y Aprendizaje.

Bronckart, J.P. (1999). *Actividade de linguagem, textos et discursos: Por un interacionismo sócio-discursivo* (Anna Rachel Machado, trans.). São Paulo: EDUC.

Bruner, Jerome (1997). *Atos de significação*. São Paulo: Artes Médicas.

Freire, P. (1972). *Pedagogy of the oppressed*. Harmondsworth: Penguin.

Goodman, J. (1984). Reflection and teacher education: A case study and theoretical analysis. *Interchange*, 15(3), 9-26.

Habermas, J. (1982). On systematically distorted communication. In E. Bredo and W. Feinberg (eds.), *Knowledge and values in social and educational research*. Philadelphia: Temple University Press.

Habermas, J. (1987). *Teoría de la acción comunicativa*. Vol. I & II. Madrid: Taurus.

Habermas, J. (1990). *Pensamento pós metafísico: Jürgen Habermas*. Rio de Janeiro: Tempo Brasileiro, 90.

Kress, G. (1989). Texture and Meaning. In R. Andrews (ed.), *Narrative and argument*. Milton Keynes: Open University Press.

Liberali, F. (1999). Developing argumentative processes for critical reflection. Paper presented at the Fourth Conference on Reflective Teaching, Leuven, Belgium.

Machado, A.R, Magalhães, M.C.C. (1999). Projeto Integrado de Pesquisa A Linguagem e a apropriação de competências discursivas na universidade. Projeto com Formação de Professores em desenvolvimento em universidade brasileira.

Magalhães, M.C.C. (1990). *A Study of teacher-researcher collaboration on reading instruction for Chapter One students*. Doctoral Dissertation, Virginia Polytechnic Institute and State University, Va., USA.

Magalhães, M.C.C. (1994). An understanding of classroom interactions for literacy development. In N. Mercer & C. Coll (eds.), *Teaching, learning and interaction*. Madrid: Infancia y Aprendizaje.

Magalhães, M.C.C. (1994a). Teacher and researcher dialogical interactions: learning and promoting literacy development. In A. Alvarez & P. del Rio (eds.), *Education as social construction*. Madrid: Infancia y Aprendizaje.

Magalhães, M.C.C. (1996). Contribuições da pesquisa sócio-histórica para a compreensão dos contextos interacionais da sala de aula de línguas: Foco na formação de professores. *The ESPecialist*, 17(1), 1-12.

Magalhães, M.C.C. (1996a). Pesquisa em formação de educadores: A pragmática como negociação de sentidos. *Cadernos de Lingüística Aplicada*, 30, 57-70.

Magalhães, M.C.C. (1999). Formation continue de professeurs: Séance de réflexion comme espace de négociation entre professeurs. *Cahiers De La Section Des Sciences De L'Éducation*, 91, 191-214.

Pérez Gómez, A.P. (1992). Formar professores como profissionais reflexivos. In A. Nóvoa (ed.), *Os professores e sua formação*. Lisboa: Publicações Dom Quixote.

Roulet, E. (1991). Vers une approche modulaire de l'analyse du discours. *Cahiers de linguistique Française: analyse du discours et de l'interaction — modèle théoriques, études et ouvertures*, 12, 53-81.

Schön, D. (1987). *Educating the reflective practicioner.* San Francisco: Jossey Bass Publishers.

Smyth, J. (1992). Teacher's work and the politics of reflection. *American Educational Research Journal*, 29(2), 267-300.

Vygotsky, L.S. (1978). In M. Cole et al. (eds.), *Mind in society.* Cambridge: Harvard University Press. (Original work published 1930)

Wertsch, J. (1997). La necesidad de la acción en la investigación sociocultural. In J. Wertsch; P. del Rio; A. Álvarez (eds.), *La mente sociocultural: aproximaciones teóricas y aplicadas.* Madrid: Fundación Infancia y Aprendizaje.

Wong, K. (1993). Governance structure, resource allocation and equity policy. *Review of Research in Education*, 20, 257-89.

Index